MW01090138

The DEATH PENALTY and INTELLECTUAL DISABILITY

Edward A. Polloway, Editor

aaidd

American Association
on Intellectual and
Developmental Disabilities

Published by
American Association on Intellectual and Developmental Disabilities
501 3rd Street, NW, Suite 200
Washington, D.C. 20001
www.aaidd.org

To order
AAIDD Order Fulfillment
501 3rd Street, NW, Suite 200
Washington, D.C. 20001
phone: 202-387-1968 x 216
email: books@aaidd.org
online: http://aaidd.org/publications/bookstore-home

Product No. 4134

Printed in the United States of America

The DEATH PENALTY
and INTELLECTUAL DISABILITY

Edward A. Polloway, Editor

American Association on Intellectual and Developmental Disabilities

Washington, D.C.

Items:

Qty	Title	Locator	Condition	ISBN
1	The Death Penalty and Intellectual Disability	042D	Good	1937604136

Subtotal:
Shipping:
Total:

3860 La Reunion Pkwy.
Dallas, TX 75212
serviceca@hpb.com

Marketplace: AmazonMarketplaceUS
Order Number: 1626918
Ship Method: Standard
Customer Name: Robert Walker
Order Date: 6/22/2017 8:12:44 AM
Marketplace Order #: 112-3078953-1886653
Email: p5czz1wpk6d79zw@marketplace.amazon.com

Thanks for your Order!

If you have any questions or concerns regarding this order, please contact us at serviceca@hpb.com

Table of Contents

List of Tables and Figures

Tables

Figures

Preface

Following the Supreme Court decision in *Atkins v. Virginia* (2002), which prohibited the execution of individuals with intellectual disability, significant attention has been given to questions concerning the determination of intellectual disability for individuals who have been accused of capital crimes, have been convicted of such crimes, or are under post-conviction review and who are thought to have this condition. While 18 states (as of the publication of this manual) no longer include capital punishment as an option for persons convicted of capital crimes, for the remaining states, the US government, and the U.S. military services, the death penalty is an option considered in those cases. Individuals who may be identified as having an intellectual disability will likely be a very small but nevertheless important minority of the individuals who may be involved in such cases.

Significant controversy about the application of diagnostic information concerning intellectual disability within death penalty cases has existed since the *Atkins* decision and continues to this day. Further, the issues concerning the determination of intellectual disability also apply to non-capital criminal justice cases as well as considerations beyond the criminal justice system (e.g., high-stakes assessment related to eligibility for services and supports for persons with intellectual disability).

To respond to the important concerns related to intellectual disability determination, this book was developed to provide an authoritative, unbiased source for use by a range of professionals who are involved in the determination process for intellectual disability. All chapter authors have committed to bringing the best science to their discussions of intellectual disability and assessment considerations. As a consequence, we collectively trust that the information provided in this book will be of great assistance in making appropriate determinations in such critical situations.

The process of preparing this book for publication has been challenging and one that has required significant professional contributions from many persons who provided their expertise, time, and effort with no compensation. A robust thank you is due to all of the individuals who are designated within the book as authors or co-authors of one or more of the chapters. Their commitment to professionalism in the preparation of this book has been extraordinary. In addition to developing individual chapters, virtually all of the chapter authors also have been involved in the peer review process providing important feedback to colleagues, as they completed their respective chapters.

In addition, I also want to acknowledge the important assistance provided by a number of individuals who were not directly involved in the writing of the chapters but who offered their services in reviewing one or more of the chapters and/or in providing research support in some of the chapters: Rachel deLacy, Tom Smith, Glenn Buck, Gena Barnhill, Deanna Cash, John Hoover, and Marce Dresbaugh. In particular, I acknowledge the great work done by Jenevie Bailey, Antonia Charles, and Jacqueline Lubin in coordinating the editorial process for the book and working with our authors, as they moved the manual toward completion.

EDWARD A. POLLOWAY
Editor

Foreword

In 2002, in *Atkins v. Virginia,* the U.S. Supreme Court banned the execution of persons who are mentally retarded, a population now referred to as individuals with intellectual disability. Although the Court cited to the AAMR and DSM-IV definitions of mental retardation, it did not mandate that the states (and the federal government itself) must follow any particular definition. To the contrary, the Court proclaimed, "we leave to the States the task of developing appropriate ways to enforce the constitutional restriction." The result has been something of a fiasco.

In general, the states have enacted definitions of intellectual disability through statutes or court decisions that contain three prongs: significantly subaverage intellectual functioning, significant deficits in adaptive functioning, and onset of the condition in the developmental period. The problem with many of the "*Atkins* cases" lies less in the general definition of the diagnosis, and more in the details—whether commonly accepted scientific principles should be applied, or ignored; what evidence is relevant; how much weight should be afforded to different pieces of evidence; whether so-called malingering tests are appropriate and should be employed; what psychological instruments for assessing intellectual and adaptive function are appropriate and should be used; and what to do with all the different tests scores that a person may have amassed over a lifetime.

The expert chapter authors of *The Death Penalty and Intellectual Disability* have plunged headlong into the morass and provided the reader with a carefully written and comprehensive analysis, which represents the best practices to be followed in diagnosing intellectual disability.

Diagnosing intellectual disability is not simply a matter of administering an IQ test battery. The process of deriving a scientifically sound diagnosis is complicated. The experts, and ultimately the judge or jury, must consider multiple sources of data, some of which may confirm a diagnosis, other parts which may conflict with the presumed diagnosis. Judges who assign equal probative weight to group-administered or short form IQ test scores as they do to full form, well-validated IQ test battery scores[1] are doing a disservice. Moreover, determining a person's level of intellectual functioning requires more than simply averaging the test scores obtained over that person's lifetime. Yet some courts have done just that.[2]

IQ scores are often given too much emphasis by judges and juries. The two other prongs—deficits in adaptive functioning and onset in the developmental period are equally important. Many of the *Atkins* progeny were woefully inadequate in their approaches to these other elements of the diagnosis. From the ill-conceived *Briseño* factors of the Texas Court of Criminal Appeals (and later adopted by other some other states' courts) to the inappropriate emphasis of a few adaptive strengths in the face of considerable evidence of adaptive deficits, folklore has sometimes triumphed over science. Similarly, as discussed by Professors Blume and Salekin in Chapter 4, as well as by some of the other authors, judges and juries often operate using inaccurate stereotypes of intellectual disability that wrongly influence their adjudication of the claim. This book provides a greater insight into the nature of intellectual disability, helping to correct many of the inaccurate stereotypes and unscientific conclusions seen in many of the *Atkins* cases.

Not every person who presses an *Atkins* claim has intellectual disability. But each deserves a decision befitting the punishment which hangs in the balance. After all, as the Supreme Court made clear in the landmark 1972 case of *Furman v. Georgia*, death is different. Courts should pay heed to the advice given in the following pages—this book offers a valuable guide for prehearing orders governing expert testimony, jury instructions, and the final decision itself.

Honorable Kevin F. Foley*
U.S. Administrative Law Judge

1. See, i.e., *Henderson v. Director,* No. 1:06-CV-507 (E.D. Tex., Sept. 6, 2013) and *Myers v. Workman,* 2010 U.S. Dist. LEXIS 51434, Case No. 02-CV-140 (N.D. Okla. May 25, 2010), *writ of habeas corpus denied,* 2011 U.S. Dist. LEXIS 112774 (N.D. Okla. Sept. 30, 2011).

2. See, i.e., *Moore v. Quarterman,* 342 Fed. Appx. 65, 83 (5th Cir. 2009), *cert. denied,* 130 S. Ct. 1736 (2010) and *Tarver v. Thomas,* No. 07-294 (S.D. Ala., Sept. 24, 2012).

*The views expressed in this foreword, do not represent the views of the Social Security Administration or the United States Government. They are solely the views of Judge Foley in his personal capacity. He is not acting as an agent or representative of the Social Security Administration or the United States Government. There is no expressed or implied endorsement of views or activities by either the Social Security Administration or the United States.

About the Authors

John H. Blume, JD, is a professor of law at Cornell University and director of the Clinical, Advocacy and Skills Programs and the Cornell Death Penalty Project. Professor Blume clerked for the Hon. Thomas A. Clark of the U.S. Court of Appeals for the Eleventh Circuit after graduating from Yale Law School. He joined the Cornell Law School faculty in 1993, and, in conjunction with Cornell Professors Sherri Lynn Johnson and Stephen Garvey, formed the Cornell Death Penalty Project. Professor Blume has argued eight capital cases before the United States Supreme Court and been co-counsel or amicus curiae counsel in numerous other Supreme Court cases. He is the co-author of two books, *A Modern Approach to Evidence* and *Death Penalty Stories*, and he has authored numerous articles in the areas of capital punishment, criminal procedure, and evidence. One of his primary areas of academic interest is capital punishment for persons with mental disabilities. Professor Blume teaches Criminal Procedure, Evidence, and the Death Penalty in America and supervises the Capital Punishment Clinic.

Melissa Collins is a PhD candidate in Applied Developmental and Educational Psychology at Boston College. Her research focuses on understanding sources of individual differences in learning from a mix of cognitive, sociocultural, and bioecological perspectives. She has worked on multiple projects related to the social inclusion of students with intellectual and developmental disabilities as a research consultant at the Center for Social Development and Education.

Mark D. Cunningham, PhD, ABPP, is a clinical and forensic psychologist, whose practice in capital sentencing determinations and *Atkins* evaluations is national in scope. A Fellow of the American Psychological Association, Dr. Cunningham's research, scholarship, and practice contributions have been recognized by the *2012 National Register of Health Service Psychologists A. M. Wellner, Ph.D. Distinguished Career Award,* the *2006 American Psychological Association Award for Distinguished Contributions to Research in Public Policy*, and the *2005 Texas Psychological Association Award for Outstanding Contribution to Science.*

Timothy J. Derning, PhD, MSEd, is a clinical and forensic psychologist who has testified nationally as an expert since 1987 in State and Federal courts concerning the effects of intellectual limitations on psychological test interpretation, legal competencies, criminal involvement, psychosocial development, and suggestibility. Dr. Derning has frequently written, lectured, and taught about individuals with cognitive impairments in the criminal justice system. He has an independent practice in the San Francisco Bay Area and is a member of AAIDD and other professional associations.

Caroline Everington, PhD, FAAIDD, is an Associate Dean and professor of special education at Winthrop University. She holds a doctorate in special education with an emphasis on intellectual disability from the University of New Mexico and BS and MS degrees in special education with emphasis on intellectual disability from Vanderbilt University. She has worked on assessment issues of individuals with ID in the criminal justice issues for over twenty-five years, authoring an assessment of competence to stand trial (CAST-MR), as well as numerous referred publications and has testified as an expert in intellectual disability in capital cases since 1991.

David Freedman, PhD, is a Senior Research Scientist at the CUNY Institute for State and Local Governance, where he provides technical assistance, research, and policy reform measurement consultation to governmental and nongovernmental organizations on criminal justice and mental health policy. David obtained his PhD in Epidemiology at Columbia University's Mailman School of Public Health, having been awarded an NIMH fellowship in psychiatric epidemiology. Since 1991, he has worked as a mental health and mitigation consultant in death penalty cases.

Stephen Greenspan, PhD, is emeritus professor of educational psychology at the University of Connecticut and clinical professor of psychiatry at the University of Colorado. He received his doctorate in psychology from the University of Rochester and was a postdoctoral Fellow in intellectual disability at the UCLA Neuropsychiatric Institute and a research Fellow at the Boys Town Center for the Study of Youth Development. He is widely known for his research on social processes, especially gullibility, in adaptive functioning of people with intellectual and developmental disorders and was co-editor of the AAIDD book *What is Mental Retardation?* He resides in Colorado, and has served as a consultant in many *Atkins* cases.

Denis W. Keyes, PhD, is a Professor of Special Education in the Teacher Education Department of the College of Charleston, in South Carolina. Having Masters degrees in special education and school psychology from Miami University (Ohio), he was awarded a PhD in special education from the University of New Mexico in 1992. He served on the Board of Directors of AAIDD from 2009 to 2012. A nationally known expert in the assessment of adaptive skills, Dr. Keyes has testified in numerous capital cases involving people with intellectual disability. His research has been cited in several cases, including *Atkins v. Virginia*.

Gilbert S. Macvaugh III, PsyD, is a clinical and forensic psychologist in independent practice in Mississippi. Dr. Macvaugh specializes in forensic mental health evaluations of competence to stand trial, criminal responsibility, competence to waive *Miranda* rights, competence to be executed, and intellectual disability in death penalty cases. He has published articles and book chapters on various topics related to forensic psychology. Dr. Macvaugh has testified as an expert in numerous pre-trial and post-conviction *Atkins* cases for state and federal courts.

Kevin S. McGrew, PhD, is the director and owner of the Institute for Applied Psychometrics (IAP). He is a visiting professor in educational psychology at the University of Minnesota. He was a practicing school psychologist for 12 years and a professor of applied psychology at St. Cloud State University for 10 years. He conducts research in the areas of human intelligence, intelligence testing, adaptive behavior, and applied psychometrics. He is a coauthor of the Woodcock-Johnson IV assessment battery.

J. Gregory Olley, PhD, is a psychologist at the Carolina Institute for Developmental Disabilities and clinical professor in the Department of Allied Health Sciences at the University of North Carolina at Chapel Hill. He is a Fellow of AAIDD and a Fellow and past president of the Division on Intellectual and Developmental Disabilities of the American Psychological Association.

James R. Patton, EdD, is an adjunct associate professor of special education at the University of Texas at Austin. He has taught students with disabilities at the elementary, secondary, and postsecondary levels of schooling. He is a past president of the Division on Autism and Developmental Disabilities of the Council for Exceptional Children. His main professional interests relate to assessment of adaptive functioning, transition assessment, and issues related to individuals with intellectual disability.

Edward A. Polloway, EdD, FAAIDD, is the Rosel H. Schewel Chair of Education at Lynchburg College, where he has taught since 1976. He serves as VP for Community Advancement and Dean of Graduate Studies. He received his graduate degrees from the University of Virginia. He served twice as president of the Division on Developmental Disabilities of the Council for Exceptional Children. He also served on the committee that developed the 1992 AAIDD definition of intellectual disability (mental retardation). He is the author of 22 books and over 100 articles in the field of special education.

Richard Ruth, PhD, is associate professor of clinical psychology and director of clinical training at the PsyD program at George Washington University and on the faculty and steering committee of the Child and Adolescent Psychotherapy Program at the Washington School of Psychiatry. His research, teaching, and clinical work have involved issues at the intersection of disability, psychological assessment, and cross-cultural psychology. For more than a decade, he chaired the Study Group on Disability of the American Orthopsychiatric Association.

Karen L. Salekin, PhD, is an associate professor at the University of Alabama in the law-psychology concentration. She graduated with a Ph.D. in clinical psychology in 1997 and completed the University of Massachusetts Medical Center Fellowship in forensic psychiatry in 1998. Her specialty area is forensic assessment with a primary focus on intellectual disability and the legal system. She has served as an expert for both the defense and prosecution in *Atkins* cases and serves as a member of the *Ad Hoc* Committee on Intellectual Disability and the Death Penalty of the American Psychological Association.

Gary Siperstein, PhD, is the Director of the Center for Social Development and Education and emeritus professor at the University of Massachusetts Boston. He is a Fellow of the American Psychological Association and past president of the Division of Research of the Council for Exceptional Children. He has served as Associate Editor of AJMR and Editor of AAIDD's Monograph series. His research for 45 years has focused on the social aspects of intellectual disability, particularly the social inclusion of persons with intellectual disability in society. He wrote for and personally testified in the *Atkins v. Virginia* case.

J. David Smith, EdD, FAAIDD, is professor emeritus at the University of North Carolina at Greensboro. He earned both baccalaureate and MS degrees from Virginia Commonwealth University. He was awarded a second master's degree and his doctorate from Columbia University. His professional experience includes work as a special education teacher, school counselor, professor, department chair, dean and provost. He has made numerous invited presentations to national and international audiences. He regularly contributes to scholarly and professional journals, and he is the author of fourteen books. One of the integrating themes of his research and writing has been a concern for the rights and dignity of people with disabilities.

Harvey N. Switzky, PhD, is emeritus professor of educational psychology at Northern Illinois University. He received his doctorate in psychology from Brown University and was a postdoctoral Fellow in intellectual disability at the John F. Kennedy Center at Vanderbilt University and director of psychological services at the Northern Wisconsin Colony and Training School. He is widely known for his research on motivational and personality processes in children and adults with intellectual and developmental disorders and was co-editor of the AAIDD book *What is Mental Retardation?* He resides in southern Alabama and is clinically licensed there and in neighboring states, and has served as a consultant in several *Atkins* cases.

Marc J. Tassé, PhD, is the Director of the Ohio State University Nisonger Center, a University Center for Excellence in Developmental Disabilities, and professor in the Departments of Psychology and Psychiatry. He is a Fellow of the American Association on Intellectual and Developmental Disabilities (AAIDD), American Psychological Association (APA), and International Association for the Scientific Study of Intellectual and Developmental Disabilities (IASSIDD). Tassé is also a past president of the American Association on Intellectual and Developmental Disabilities.

Dale Watson, PhD, is a clinical and forensic neuropsychologist practicing in the San Francisco Bay Area. He is an adjunct professor at the Wright Institute in Berkeley, where he teaches cognitive and psychological assessment. He also consults regarding the neuropsychological functioning of patients recovering from brain injuries. He has extensive experience in the evaluation of traumatic brain injuries and intellectual disability. He is a frequent consultant to attorneys regarding the interface between neurocognitive dysfunction and criminal law, testifying in state and federal courts. He has made numerous national presentations on neuropsychology and the evaluation of intellectual disability.

Keith F. Widaman, PhD, is a distinguished professor in the Graduate School of Education at the University of California at Riverside. He received his doctorate from the Ohio State University, with a major in developmental psychology and minor in quantitative psychology. He is a Fellow of the American Psychological Association (APA; Divisions 5, 7, and 33) and of the Association for Psychological Science and past president of the Society of Multivariate Experimental Psychology and of Division 5 of APA. He has published work on the structure of adaptive behavior, family influences on development, and issues related to diagnosis of intellectual disability, and also publishes work on longitudinal modeling and statistical techniques. He resides in Southern California and has served as consultant on several *Atkins* cases.

George W. Woods, MD, is adjunct professor of psychiatry, Morehouse School of Medicine and lecturer at the University of California-Berkeley's Boalt Hall School of Law. He received a medical degree from the University of Utah, and did his psychiatric training at the Pacific Medical Center. He is Board Certified in psychiatry, and has an active clinical and forensic neuropsychiatric practice in San Francisco, focusing on brain-based disorders. His publications deal with neuropsychiatric assessment and cultural factors in neurodevelopmental disorders. He has consulted in numerous criminal proceedings, including those involving *Atkins* determinations. He is president-elect of the International Academy of Law and Mental Health, and is newsletter editor for the Challenging Behaviors and Mental Health Special Interest Group of the International Association for the Scientific Study of Intellectual and Developmental Disabilities.

PART I

Foundational Considerations

1 | The Death Penalty and Intellectual Disability: An Introduction

Edward A. Polloway
James R. Patton
J. David Smith

The decision of the U.S. Supreme Court in *Atkins v. Virginia* (2002) increased the attention given individuals with intellectual disability (ID) who have been accused, and possibly convicted, of capital offenses in states where the death penalty is still imposed. In the aftermath of the *Atkins* decision, the attention given to capital punishment and persons with ID has accelerated significantly, as professionals in the criminal justice system seek to use assessment data to determine the validity of the diagnosis of ID. Given the fact that the resolution of that question can result in a court decision with a life or death consequence, the importance of careful attention to this is more than obvious.

As a result of these concerns, the American Association on Intellectual and Developmental Disabilities (AAIDD) established a task force to study important considerations and provide guidance to professionals involved in legal proceedings (e.g., judges, prosecutors, defense attorneys, forensic psychologists, clinical psychologists, mitigation specialists, and, ultimately, juries), as well as others who have, or may have, roles in making appropriate decisions related to the diagnosis of intellectual disability in capital cases on the best available scientific information. It is significant to note that the term "intellectual disability" has now been almost universally adopted as the preferred alternative to the use of "mental retardation." The latter term had been used extensively, particularly in the United States, for over 60 years. However, in recent years and consistent with international trends (Brown & Percy, 2007), the United States federal government, professional organizations, and state legislatures have increasingly modified their terminology to use the term intellectual disability (e.g., Schalock et al., 2007; Schalock et al., 2010). Of particular note is the federal legislation, "Rosa's Law" (2010), which made the change in terminology from mental retardation to intellectual disability official in

U.S. legislation. Therefore, ID is the term used in this book. It is nevertheless acknowledged that capital cases considerations were based previously on the use of the term mental retardation and, in some instances, it is still used.

Persons With Intellectual Disability in the Criminal Justice System

The professional literature in the field of ID is replete with references to an overrepresentation of persons with this disability within the criminal justice system (e.g., Davis, 2006; Hassan & Gordon, 2003; Newman, Wagner, Cameto, & Knokey, 2009; Petersilia, 2000a, 2000b; Polloway, Patton, Smith, Beyer, & Bailey, 2011; Smith, Polloway, Patton, & Beyer, 2008). In the National Longitudinal Transition Study-2, Newman et al. (2009) noted a relatively large percentage of individuals with ID who had been detained by police for reasons other than traffic violations (31.0%). This included those arrested (18.4%), spent a night in jail (10.3%), and/or placed on probation or parole (9.5%) at some point in their lives. While such reports obviously do not suggest a causative relationship between ID and the likelihood of engaging in crime, they, nevertheless, underscore the need for careful attention to the nature of this relationship.

Of particular concern is whether individuals with ID face special challenges in the criminal justice system because of certain deficits that they may have related to reasoning, thinking, learning, and social interactions. Polloway and colleagues (2011) highlighted potential challenges that individuals with ID encounter at various stages of interaction with the criminal justice system, including initial contact/arrest and intake, interrogation, judicial proceedings, sentencing, potential incarceration, and release/parole.

While general considerations within the criminal justice system related to persons who have ID include many issues, the primary focus of this text relates to the specific situation in which individuals are accused of, or are convicted of, capital offenses. The initial case that received significant national attention was *Penry v. Lynaugh* (1989). Johnny Paul Penry was convicted of a capital offense and sentenced to execution by the state of Texas. His case extended over almost two decades through ongoing review by federal courts with recommendations back to Texas in terms of the necessary consideration of "mental retardation" as a mitigating circumstance in the crime and, thus, in sentencing. While the case did not disallow the use of capital punishment for individuals with ID, the scrutiny of the process ultimately led to Penry being sentenced to life imprisonment rather than being executed. Of greatest significance, however, was *Atkins v. Virginia*, which was decided by the U.S. Supreme Court in 2002. The consequence of the *Atkins* decision was that no person diagnosed as having ID could be executed within the United States (Patton & Keyes, 2006; Greenspan, 2011).

Hall v. Florida

This book was in production when a momentous event occurred that will have significant implications for the way in which *Atkins* hearings are conducted and decided, especially in states with so-called "bright line" interpretations of ID. The event we are referring to is the announcement in May, 2014, of the U.S. Supreme Court's decision in *Hall v. Florida* (2014).

The *Hall* ruling, a 5-4 decision written by Justice Anthony Kennedy, was prompted by a *habeas* appeal made by Freddie Lee Hall, a condemned prisoner in Florida. As in many *Atkins* cases, Mr. Hall had a number of intelligence quotient (IQ) assessments over the years, most of them under the strict 70 IQ ceiling used in Florida, but some above it. His *Atkins* petition was rejected by the Florida courts because of this fact, while the other (e.g., adaptive behavior) evidence supporting his claim was a less significant consideration in this case. The *habeas* petition made by Mr. Hall's attorneys focused mainly on the statistical issue of standard error and the lack of scientific support for the state's use of IQ as an absolute number not subject to broader interpretation. In its opinion, the Supreme Court rejected the use of the 70 bright line cutoff, and actually went beyond the defendant's narrow psychometric position in taking a broader view of what states can or cannot do when considering ID petitions in capital cases.

While acknowledging that states still have the right to establish their own rules for handling *Atkins* cases, the court stated that they were not free to ignore scientific and medical consensus regarding intelligence and the nature and diagnosis of ID. As Justice Kennedy stated, "intellectual disability is a condition, not a number" (*Hall v. Florida*, 2014). Asserting that the "dignity" of death penalty petitioners requires that they have a chance to make a full case for their claim to have ID, Kennedy said that all evidence (including adaptive behavior evidence) pertinent to an *Atkins* claim should be considered, and that it is patently unfair to automatically refuse to consider such evidence just because one or more IQ scores are above an arbitrary number.

The *Hall* decision will have broader implications for the handling of *Atkins* claims than just the narrow (but important) issue of rigid IQ cutoff scores. For example, the interpretation of adaptive behavior is also something about which there is some scientific consensus, and such consensus cannot be ignored when states or courts make up their own interpretations that fail to take such consensus into account.

The chapters in this book reflect the scientific and clinical/medical consensus to which the Supreme Court was addressing in its decision in *Hall*. We trust that this book will be of assistance not only to practitioners, but also to courts as they move forward in exploring the ramifications of this landmark decision.

Purpose

Subsequent to the Supreme Court decision in *Atkins*, individuals identified as having ID were no longer subject to being executed under state-based death penalty laws. Rather, these individuals were instead subject to prison terms, including life in prison with or without parole, but not to the death penalty. Substantial attention since this decision has been centered on the diagnostic procedures that are critical to an accurate determination of ID and that have literally become a matter of "life-and-death" in numerous court cases.

Cognizant of these concerns, AAIDD convened a task force in January, 2010, to focus on capital cases. The genesis for this book began with a discussion of the challenging issues concerning this matter. The specific focus of the task force was to be on the implications of the *Atkins* decision for individuals with key roles in the legal arena, as well as those who have significant interests in persons with ID in general.

The purpose of the book is straightforward: to present accurate, nonbiased information that reflects the most current views of the science of diagnostics for ID as related to the criminal justice system in general, but for capital cases in particular. The expressed purpose also is to ensure that the text does not take the form of, or be presented as, advocacy concerning the identification of persons with ID within the criminal justice system. The challenges that have been identified within the system warrant nothing less than accurate and scientifically validated guidance to enable persons in the legal system to make appropriate judgments about individuals with these disabilities and the realities of their lives.

American Association on Intellectual and Developmental Disabilities

The American Association on Intellectual and Developmental Disabilities (AAIDD) has a long history of serving as the primary professional organization for individuals working in this field. It was founded originally in Philadelphia in 1876 as the Association of Medical Officers of American Institutions for Idiots and Feeble-Minded Persons. Subsequently, the name was changed in 1906 to the American Association for the Study of the Feebleminded, and again in 1933 to the American Association on Mental Deficiency (Kanner, 1964). As terminology and focus in the field made a shift, the organization then modified its name to the American Association on Mental Retardation in 1987. In 2009 it was renamed the American Association on Intellectual and Developmental Disabilities (AAIDD) in light of the most recent changes in terminology (see Schalock et al., 2007; Schalock et al., 2010).

The AAIDD has been the primary professional organization for individuals working in the field of ID across a wide variety of disciplines including psychology, special education, medicine, administration, communication disorders, community services, direct support, gerontology, legal processes, religion, and social work. The mission of the organization is to "promote progressive policies, sound research, effective practices, and universal human rights for people with intellectual and developmental disabilities" (AAIDD, 2011, p. 1). A core focus of AAIDD historically has been to serve as a scientifically focused organization promoting research related to understanding, diagnosing, and serving and supporting persons with ID.

Throughout its history, AAIDD has focused in particular on definitions, terminology, and classification systems. In 1961, it published its first widely cited formal definition

(Heber, 1961) and its subsequent series of manuals (in 1973, 1977, 1983, 1992, 2002, and 2010; see Greenspan & Switzky, 2006) provided updates on definition, recommended modifications in terminology, and offered a series of classification schemes. The most recent manual, *Intellectual Disability: Definition, Classification, and Systems of Supports* (Schalock et al., 2010), presented a contemporary definition of intellectual disability that is the next iteration of the definition that was cited in the *Atkins* decision in 2002 (see Chapter 2).

Capital Punishment Task Force

In 2009, AAIDD established a number of task forces to investigate key issues and concerns within the field of ID. One of the task forces was created in order to study the death penalty, particularly in light of the broad implications of *Atkins v. Virginia*. The task force was conceptualized as being multidisciplinary in nature in order to include participation and input from individuals representing clinical psychology, developmental psychology, forensic psychology, law, and special education. While it was a task force established by AAIDD, the group maintained its independence as it moved forward with the development of this book. A core consideration has been ensuring that the task force includes individuals who have served in professional roles on behalf of the prosecution and the defense, as well as others who have made significant contributions to the literature in the field but have not been directly involved to a significant extent in specific capital cases. Further, representatives on the task force have professional relationships with other key organizations (e.g., Division 33 of the American Psychological Association and the Division on Autism and Developmental Disabilities of the Council for Exceptional Children).

Organization of the Book

The book has been conceptualized around the critical considerations that relate directly to death penalty cases involving persons with ID. It builds on other important works in the field that have provided definitions and diagnostic procedures, but it extends that information by providing this information within the context of its application in capital cases.

In the first section, the chapter authors address foundational considerations. Chapter 2 focuses on current definitions of ID as promulgated by professional organizations and individual states. The third chapter then addresses considerations of ID with a focus on those historically identified with higher intellectual functioning within the ID population. The purpose of the chapter is to highlight common, group characteristics as well as misconceptions that may be associated with this population. Chapter 4 provides an analysis of cases subsequent to the *Atkins* decision, providing a discussion of the evolution of legal attention in this area followed by an analysis of the decisions made throughout the country on a subsequent series of so-called "*Atkins*" cases.

The second section focuses on assessment and diagnostic considerations. First, topics of general importance are addressed, including concepts of measurement and special considerations related to the developmental period and age of onset for disability. Next, relevant issues within the two primary prongs or dimensions of intellectual disability are discussed. First, considerations related to intellectual functioning are addressed, including conceptual and assessment issues, the question of the variability of IQ scores over time, and the implications of the Flynn effect. Second, within the adaptive behavior prong, attention is given to conceptual and assessment issues, specific challenges related to adaptive behavior assessments in capital cases, and special age considerations.

The third section addresses related issues of importance to the field that also have implications within the criminal justice system. These topics include the following: the importance and influence of cultural factors; the question of competence to stand trial and competence to confess; considerations of retrospective assessment and malingering; the challenges of differential diagnosis and comorbidity; the use of historical records; the relevance and non-relevance of other assessments; and questions of professional practice as related to training, qualifications within the legal arena, and ethical considerations.

The authors of the following chapters of this book collectively represent a group of individuals who have made significant contributions to the literature in the field of ID and who have been actively involved in criminal justice considerations related to defendants with ID.

Concluding Notes

The chapter authors hope that this text will prove to be an important resource for those individuals who are charged with the most serious task of considering diagnostic information for individuals who have been accused and/or convicted of a capital crime and who may, or may not, have ID. Further, the content provided here should prove helpful in the broader sense by promoting a further understanding of people with ID and procedures for assessing these individuals..

We offer our sincere thanks and appreciation to those individuals who have contributed the chapters to this text, as well as the numerous individuals who have served as peer reviewers for individual chapters and for the book in general.

References

American Association on Intellectual and Developmental Disabilities. (2011). *Mission statement*. Retrieved from www.AAIDD.org/content_443.cfm? navID=129

Atkins v. Virginia, 536 U. S. 304, 318 (2002)

Brown, I. & Percy, M. (2007). *A comprehensive guide to intellectual & developmental disabilities.* Baltimore, MD: Paul H. Brookes.

Davis, L. A. (2006). *The Arc's justice advocacy guide: An advocate's guide on assisting victims and suspects/defendants with intellectual disabilities.* Silver Spring, MD: The Arc of the United States.

Greenspan, S. (2011). Homicide defendants with intellectual disabilities: Issues in diagnosis in capital cases. *Exceptionality, 19*(4), 219–237. http://dx.doi.org/10.1080/09362835.2011.611086

Greenspan, S. & Switzky, H. N. (2006). Forty-four years of AAMR manuals. In H. N. Switzky & S. Greenspan (Eds.), *What is mental retardation? Ideas for an evolving disability in the 21st century* (pp. 3-28). Washington, DC: American Association on Mental Retardation.

Hall v. Florida, 572 U.S. 12-10882 (2014)

Hassan, S. & Gordon, R. (2003). *Developmental disability, crime, and criminal justice: A literature review.* (Criminology Research Centre Occasional Paper #2003-01). Burnaby, CA: Simon Fraser University, Criminology Research Centre.

Heber, R. (1961). *A manual on terminology and classification in mental retardation* (2nd ed.). [Monograph supplement]. *American Journal of Mental Deficiency, 64.*

Kanner, L. (1964). *A history of the care and study of the mentally retarded.* Springfield, IL: Charles C. Thomas.

Newman, L., Wagner, M., Cameto, R., & Knokey, A. (2009). *The post-high school outcomes of youth with disabilities up to 4 years after high school. A report from the National Longitudinal Transition Study-2 (NLTS2)* (NCSER 2009-3017). Washington, DC: U. S. Government Printing Office.

Patton, J. R., & Keyes, D. (2006). Death penalty issues following Atkins. *Exceptionality, 14*(4), 237–255. http://dx.doi.org/10.1207/s15327035ex1404_5

Penry v. Lynaugh, 492 U. S. 302, 335 (1989)

Petersilia, J. (2000a). *Doing justice? Criminal offenders with developmental disabilities.* Irvine, CA: California Research Center, University of California, Irvine.

Petersilia, J. (2000b). *Doing justice: The criminal justice system and offenders with developmental disabilities.* Irvine, CA: Mental Retardation/Developmental Disabilities Research Center, University of California, Irvine.

Polloway, E. A., Patton, J. R., Smith, T., Beyer, J., & Bailey, J. W. (2011). Special challenges for persons with intellectual disabilities within the criminal justice system: An introduction to the special series. *Exceptionality, 19*(4), 211–218.

Rosa's Law, Pub. L. 111-256 (2010)

Schalock, R., Luckasson, R. A., Shogren, K. A., Borthwick-Duffy, S., Bradley, V., Buntinx, W. H. E., ... Yeager, M. H. (2007). The renaming of mental retardation: Understanding the change to the term intellectual disability. *Intellectual and Developmental Disabilities, 45,* 116–124.

Schalock, R. L., Borthwick-Duffy, S. A., Bradley, V. J., Buntinx, W. H. E., Coulter, D. L., Craig, E. M., Gomez, S. C., Lachapelle, Y., Luckasson, R., Reeve, A., Shogren, K. A., Snell, M. E., Spreat, S., Tasse, M. J., Thompson, J. R., Verdugo-Alonso, M. A., Wehmeyer, M. L., & Yeager, M. H. (2010). *Intellectual disability: Definition, classification, and systems of supports* (11th ed.). Washington, DC: AAIDD.

Smith, T., Polloway, E. A., Patton, J. R., & Beyer, J. F. (2008). Individuals with intellectual and developmental disabilities in the criminal justice system and implications for transition planning. *Education and Training in Developmental Disabilities, 43,* 421–430.

2 | Intellectual Disability: A Review of Its Definition and Diagnostic Criteria

Marc J. Tassé

There are essentially two nationally recognized authoritative sources that provide the definition and diagnostic criteria for intellectual disability (ID) in the United States. These references are (1) *Intellectual Disability: Definition, Classification, and Systems of Supports, 11th Edition,* published by the American Association on Intellectual and Developmental Disabilities (AAIDD) (Schalock et al., 2010) and (2) the *Diagnostic and Statistical Manual of Mental Disorders* (DSM) published by the American Psychiatric Association (APA; currently in its 5th edition and referred to as DSM-5); (American Psychiatric Association, 2013). There are also secondary resources that discuss ID and present recommendations for eligibility criteria (e.g., U.S. Social Security Administration; Reschly, Myers, & Hartel, 2002), alternate diagnostic criteria that have little legitimacy of enforcement (e.g., American Psychological Association Division 33; Barclay et al., 1996), and a larger international classification system that has little reach in the United States regarding its diagnostic criteria for ID (e.g., *International Classification of Diseases–10th Edition* published by the World Health Organization, 1992). Further, it should be noted that a number of individual states in the United States have developed their own definitions or use earlier versions of organizational definitions for either educational or forensic purposes (e.g., Polloway, Patton, Smith, Antoine, & Lubin, 2009).

The majority of this chapter is devoted to a more detailed presentation and discussion of the AAIDD manual (Schalock et al., 2010) and DSM-5 (APA, 2013) definition and diagnostic criteria, and only briefly presents the three secondary resources regarding ID. It should be noted that, in its 2002 opinion of *Atkins v. Virginia* barring the execution of persons with ID, the U.S. Supreme Court referenced the AAIDD and DSM as the nationally recognized authoritative treatises defining and establishing the diagnostic criteria for ID. Although *Atkins v. Virginia* used "mental retardation," the terminology in use at the time, it is widely accepted that "mental retardation" has been replaced by the less pejoratively tainted "intellectual disability." Persons diagnosed with ID represent the same individuals known previously as having mental retardation (Schalock et al., 2007).

American Association on Intellectual and Developmental Disabilities

AAIDD was founded in 1876 as an interdisciplinary professional society and has since been the leader in establishing the definition and diagnostic criteria for ID for more than a century. AAIDD has revised its definition of ID a total of 10 times in its history to reflect the changes in research and understanding of the condition. Schalock and his colleagues were charged with developing the 11th and most recent edition of *Intellectual Disability: Definition, Classification, and Systems of Supports* (Schalock et al., 2010), which defined ID as "characterized by significant limitations both in intellectual functioning and in adaptive behavior as expressed in conceptual, social, and practical adaptive skills. This disability originates before age 18" (p. 1). The AAIDD operationally defined "significant limitations" to be at least two standard deviations or more below the population mean (i.e., typically a standard score of approximately 70 when the mean = 100 and the standard deviation = 15). The adaptive behavior prong of the AAIDD definition is met if the individual presents with significant limitations in (1) conceptual, practical, or social skills or (2) the overall composite (e.g., full-scale) score of adaptive behavior. The three adaptive skills domains are defined as follows:

- **Conceptual Skills:** Defined by communication skills, functional academics, and self-direction.
- **Social Skills:** Defined by such abilities as interpersonal skills, social responsibility, following rules, and self-esteem. Higher-order social skills have also been identified to include such elements as gullibility, naiveté, and avoiding victimization.
- **Practical Skills:** Basic personal care skills such as hygiene, domestic skills, health, and safety, as well as work skills.

AAIDD specified:

> for the purpose of making a diagnosis or ruling out ID, a comprehensive standardized measure of adaptive behavior should be used in making the determination of the individual's current adaptive behavior functioning in relation to the general population, The selected measure should provide robust standard scores across the three domains of adaptive behavior: conceptual, social, and practical adaptive behavior. (Schalock et al., 2010, p. 49)

Furthermore, AAIDD guides clinicians to avoid certain instruments that might be appropriate for intervention planning but are not appropriate for diagnostic purposes: "The potential user must employ adaptive behavior assessment instruments that are normed within the community environments on individuals who are of the same age grouping as the individual being evaluated" (Schalock et al., 2010, p. 51). Hence, assessing an individual's adaptive behavior in an institutional context is not relevant for the purpose of making a determination of ID. Assessing if someone is well adapted to an institutional setting (e.g., prison or developmental center) might be useful for determining if additional structure is needed or for planning interventions to facilitate integration, but has no relevance in determining how an individual's adaptive functioning compares to the general population for the purpose of ruling in/out a diagnosis of ID. There are five essential assumptions that accompany the AAIDD definition:

1. Limitations in present functioning must be considered within the context of community environments typical of the individual's age peers and culture.
2. Valid assessment considers cultural and linguistic diversity as well as differences in communication, sensory, motor, and behavioral factors.
3. Within an individual, limitations often coexist with strengths.
4. An important purpose of describing limitations is to develop a profile of needed supports.
5. With appropriate personalized supports over a sustained period, the life functioning of the person with mental retardation generally will improve (Schalock et al., 2010, p. 1).

The AAIDD definition of ID has been adopted historically by federal and state governments as well as the APA's DSM in defining ID.

American Psychiatric Association

The DSM-5 (American Psychiatric Association, 2013) is consistent with AAIDD and defined ID as follows: "Intellectual disability (intellectual developmental disorder) is a disorder with onset during the developmental period that includes both intellectual and adaptive functioning deficits in conceptual, practical, and social domains" (p. 33). In an effort to harmonize the DSM-5 with the World Health Organization's eventual publication of the 11th edition of the *International Classification of Diseases* (ICD-11), the American Psychiatric Association included the parenthetical "intellectual developmental disorder" with ID. As discussed later in this chapter, this effort at harmonization may have been premature, since it appears that the ICD-11 will not be retaining the term "intellectual developmental disorder." The DSM-5 specified its three-prong diagnostic criteria as follows:

• Significant deficits in intellectual functioning, such as reasoning, problem solving, planning, abstract thinking, judgment, academic learning, and learning from experience. Deficits in intellectual functioning should be assessed using both clinical assessment and standardized testing. When using appropriate individually administered standardized measures of intellectual functioning, a significant deficit is defined as a standard score that is approximately two standard deviations or more below the population mean.

- Deficits in adaptive functioning involve impairments in conceptual, practical, and social domains. Adaptive functioning involves both clinical assessment and individually administered standardized measures of adaptive behavior. Similarly to the AAIDD definition, the second prong of the DSM-5 is met when the individual presents with significant deficits in one or more of the three adaptive domains (conceptual, social, and practical). Unlike with the first prong, the DSM-5 did not operationally define "deficits in adaptive functioning."
- Onset of these deficits occurs during the developmental period. Again, the DSM-5 chose NOT to operationally define the "developmental period," thus, leaving it up to the clinician's judgment to make that determination.

The DSM-5 and AAIDD are in agreement on many aspects of their respective definition and diagnostic criteria for ID. AAIDD and the DSM-5 agree that the process of diagnosing of ID is based on both a clinical assessment and standardized testing of the individual's intellectual functioning and adaptive behavior. Regarding the assessment of intellectual functioning, both AAIDD and DSM-5 stipulated that testing must be done using a valid and reliable individually administered comprehensive standardized test of intelligence. The results obtained from group-administered tests of intelligence or abbreviated measures (i.e., short form) of intellectual functioning lack sufficient reliability and psychometric robustness to be used for the purpose of making a diagnosis of ID. These instruments serve a screening purpose but should not be relied upon when making or refuting a diagnosis of ID.

Another important area of agreement between these two treatises for ID relates to the assessment of adaptive behavior. AAIDD and the DSM-5 agree that the most knowledgeable informants regarding adaptive behavior are parents, family members, teachers, care providers, and others who know the individual well. Also, adaptive behavior is the product of the interaction between the individual and the community. In an issue that matters particularly to capital cases, the DSM-5 clearly stated "adaptive functioning may be difficult to assess in a controlled setting (e.g., prisons, detention centers); if possible, corroborative information reflecting functioning outside those settings should be obtained" (p. 38). AAIDD's manual, *Intellectual Disability: Definition, Classification, and Systems of Supports* (Schalock et al., 2010), and its subsequent *User's Guide to Intellectual Disability: Definition, Classification, and Systems of Supports* (Schalock et al., 2012) discuss at length retrospective assessment of adaptive behavior.

AAIDD and the DSM-5 both stipulate that an individual may have ID and antisocial personality disorder, ID and learning disability, or ID and any other mental disorder found in the DSM-5. For an in-depth discussion of psychiatric issues in ID, the reader is referred to Chapter 19 of this book.

The DSM-5 has abandoned the classification of the severity of ID that was previously based solely on the individual's IQ score. This is a major shift from previous editions of the DSM. The DSM-5 stated ". . . because it is adaptive functioning that determines the level of supports required," as the rationale for moving away from an IQ-based severity level in favor of a severity classification of ID (Mild, Moderate, Severe, and Profound) that is based on the individual's level of adaptive behavior. The proposed severity levels are heavily predicated on clinical judgment. The clinical validity and utility of these severity levels remain to be empirically assessed.

AAIDD and the DSM-5 agree on the importance of taking into consideration all factors that may contribute errors to the obtained IQ test results when interpreting someone's intellectual functioning for the purpose of making a diagnosis of ID. AAIDD stated the following: ". . . it is the position of AAIDD that intellectual functioning (as defined at the beginning of this chapter) is best conceptualized and captured by a general factor of intelligence (*g*)" (Schalock et al., 2010, p. 34). Furthermore, according to the DSM-5 (American Psychiatric Association, 2013), the IQ prong of intellectual disability is met if an individual's full-scale IQ score falls below 70–75 (roughly accounting for a 95% confidence interval resulting from standard error of measurement [SEM] on most IQ tests) or lower. In addition to the *SEM*, sources of error surrounding the obtained IQ score may include error that is attributable to aging norms of the test used, practice effect, administration errors, etc. and, thus, the interpretation of the results should take account of these factors (see APA, 2013; Schalock et al., 2010). Chapters 7 and 8 provide an in-depth discussion of intellectual assessment.

Other Systems and Diagnostic Criteria

Social Security Administration

The U.S. Social Security Administration (SSA) convened a panel of experts to review the existing literature and propose recommendations to the SSA regarding criteria to identify individuals as having ID (see Reschly et al., 2002). Although not meant as a diagnostic system but, rather, as recommendations to develop the eligibility criteria for SSA benefits under the classification of ID (it should be noted that the Social Security Administration announced in 2013 that it was replacing the term "mental retardation" with "intellectual disability"; Social Security Administration, 2013), Reschly and his colleagues proposed a definition that included the same three prongs (intellectual functioning, adaptive behavior, and age of onset). Much like AAIDD, the SSA taskforce made a strong recommendation that intellectual and adaptive functioning assessment be conducted using comprehensive standardized measures. Significant deficits in intellectual functioning were defined as a composite IQ test scores two or more standard deviations below the mean. An upper boundary full-scale IQ test score of 75 is set by SSA and an individual can meet this prong if they have a full-scale IQ test score between 71–75 if one scale score (e.g., Verbal IQ, Performance IQ, Perceptual Reasoning, Verbal Comprehension) is two standard deviations or more below the mean (Reschly et al., 2002, p. 139–140).

The biggest difference with the SSA determination criteria relates to the age of onset. The upper limit of SSA age of onset is set at age 22 years. This age of onset is more in line with the federal definition of developmental disability, which also has an age of onset of 22 years. Developmental disability is defined as "a severe, chronic disability of an individual that is attributable to a mental or physical impairment or combination of mental and physical impairments, is manifested before the individual attains age 22; is likely to continue indefinitely and results in substantial functional limitations in three or more of the following areas of major life activity: (1) self-care, (2) receptive and expressive language, (3) learning, (4) mobility, (5) self-direction, (6) capacity for independent living, and (7) economic self-sufficiency; and reflects the individual's need for a combination and sequence of special, interdisciplinary, or generic services, individualized supports, or other forms of assistance that are of life-long or extended duration and are individually planned and coordinated" (Developmental Disabilities Assistance and Bill of Rights Act, 2000). Individuals with a diagnosis of ID may or may not also qualify for services under developmental disabilities. Conversely, some individuals with a determination of developmental disabilities may not have ID.

APA Division 33

The APA's Division 33 is a group of psychologists interested in issues related to intellectual and developmental disabilities. In 1996, APA's Division 33 formed a panel to develop a definition of ID. This definition was published in the opening chapter of a handbook on ID published by the APA (see Jacobson & Mulick, 1996). The APA Division 33 definition has never been widely cited. This definition established the following same three criteria as defining ID: (1) significant limitations in intellectual functioning as expressed by a full-scale IQ test score that is two or more standard deviations below the mean; (2) significant limitations in adaptive functioning as determined from a comprehensive standardized measure that situates the overall adaptive score to be two standard deviations or more below the mean; and (3) these significant limitations originate before the age of 22 years. This definition was innovative because, at the time of its publication, it was the first formal definition recommending the use of a standardized measure and a criterion based on standard deviations below the population mean for the adaptive behavior criterion. This operational definition of prong 2 was later adopted by AAIDD in the tenth edition of *Mental Retardation: Definition, Classification, and Systems of Supports* (Luckasson et al., 2002).

ICD-10

The World Health Organization (WHO) publishes the *International Classification of Diseases*, currently in its 10th edition (ICD-10; WHO, 1992). The ICD-10 is used by physicians around the world to diagnose all forms of disease and is also used for the coding of diseases for epidemiological, reporting, and billing purposes. Intellectual disability is found in the "Mental and Behavioral Disorders" section of the ICD-10. It is less frequently used in the United States for diagnosing mental and behavioral disorders, with the DSM being preferred over the ICD. The ICD-10 defines ID as follows:

> Mental retardation is a condition of arrested or incomplete development of the mind, which is especially characterized by impairment of skills manifested during the developmental period, which contribute to the overall level of intelligence, i.e., cognitive, language, motor, and social abilities. Retardation can occur with or without any other mental or physical disorder. However, mentally retarded individuals can experience the full range of mental disorders, and the prevalence of other mental disorders is at least three to four times greater in this population than in the general population. In addition, mentally retarded individuals are at greater risk of exploitation and physical/sexual abuse. Adaptive behavior is always impaired, but in protected social environments where support is available this impairment may not be at all obvious in subjects with mild mental retardation. (WHO, 2010, p. 176)

The ICD-10 IQ cutoff for ID is a full-scale IQ test score of 69 or less. The ICD-10 states that "for a definite diagnosis, there should be a reduced level of intellectual functioning resulting in diminished ability to adapt to the daily demands of the normal social environment" (WHO, 2010, p. 177). They also strongly recommended using individualized standardized measures to document deficits in intellectual and adaptive functioning, but do not operationally define these deficits as clearly as they define deficits in intellectual functioning. The ICD-10 also has an age of onset criterion mentioned as the "developmental period." However, most likely out of a concern for international applicability and potential for cultural bias, ICD-10 does not specify a cutoff in chronological age for the end of the developmental period. Hence, the developmental period could vary from country to country.

It should be noted that WHO, at the time of the publication of this book, is working on the 11th edition of the ICD. It would appear that the ICD-11 will likely adopt the term "disorders of intellectual development" as its term for the condition known by most as ID and its definition will be closely aligned with the current AAIDD definition (Reed, 2013).

Summary

In essence, the consensus is that ID is defined by the presence of significant deficits in intellectual functioning and adaptive behavior and these deficits originate during the developmental period. The AAIDD and DSM-5 systems provide the most rigorous and complete description of how to operationally and clinically define and implement these criteria. *Intellectual Disability: Definition, Classification, and Systems of Supports* (Schalock et al., 2010) and its companion *User's Guide* (Schalock et al., 2012) are the most comprehensive and thorough. Using these resources should guide clinicians, educators, lawyers, and policy makers towards a better understanding of the condition, its diagnostic criteria, and the inherent uncertainty surrounding our standardized measures that assist us in making these clinical determinations.

References

American Psychiatric Association. (2013). *Diagnostic and statistical manual of mental disorders* (5th ed.). Washington, DC: Author.

Barclay, A. G., Drotar, D. D., Favell, J., Foxx, R. M., Gardner, W. I., Iwata, B. A., . . . Thompson, T. (1996). Definition of mental retardation. In J. W. Jacobson & J. A. Mulick (Eds.), *Manual of diagnosis and professional practice in mental retardation* (pp. 13–47). Washington, DC: American Psychological Association.

Developmental Disabilities Assistance and Bill of Rights Act (2000). Public Law 106–402. 106th US Congress, 2000.

Hall v. Florida, 572 U.S. 12-10882 (2014)

Jacobson, J. N., & Mulick , J. A.(1996). *Manual of diagnosis and professional practice in mental retardation*. Washington, DC: American Psychological Association.

Luckasson R., Borthwick-Duffy S., Buntinx W. H. E., Coulter D. L., Craig, E. M., Reeve, A., Schalock, R. L., Snell, M. E., Spitalnik, D. M., Spreat, S., & Tassé, M. J. (2002). *Mental retardation: Definition, classification, and systems of supports* (10th ed.). Washington, DC: American Association on Mental Retardation.

Polloway, E. A., Patton, J. R., Smith, J. D., Antoine, K., & Lubin, J. (2009). State guidelines for intellectual and developmental disabilities and intellectual disabilities: A re-visitation of previous analyses in light of changes in the field. *Education and Training in Developmental Disabilities, 44,* 14–24.

Reed, G. M. (2013). *Intellectual disability and the revision of ICD-10 mental and behavioural disorders.* Webinar on May 19, 2013. Retrieved from aaidd.org/media/3192013.pdf

Reschly, D. J., Myers, T. G., & Hartel, C. R. (Eds.). (2002). *Mental retardation: Determining eligibility for social security benefits.* Washington, DC: National Academy Press.

Schalock, R. L., Buntinx, W. H. E., Borthwick-Duffy, S., Bradley, V., Craig, E. M., Coulter, D. L., Gomez, S. C., Lachapelle, Y., Luckasson, R. A., Reeve, A., Shogren, K. A., Snell, M. E., Spreat, S., Tassé, M. J., Thompson, J. R., Verdugo, M. A., Wehmeyer, M. L., & Yeager, M. H. (2010). *Intellectual disability: Definition, classification, and system of supports* (11th ed.). Washington, DC: American Association on Intellectual and Developmental Disabilities.

Schalock, R. L., Luckasson, R., Bradley, V., Buntinx, W. H. E., Lachapelle, Y., Shogren, K. A., Snell, M. E., Thompson, J. R., Tassé, M. J., Verdugo-Alonso, M. A., and Wehmeyer, M. L. (2012). *Users guide to intellectual disability: Definition, classification, and systems of supports.* Washington, DC: American Association on Intellectual and Developmental Disabilities.

Schalock, R. L., Shogren, K. A., Luckasson, R., Borthwick-Duffy, S., Buntinx, W. H. E., Coulter, D., . . . Yeager, M. (2007). The renaming of mental retardation: Understanding the change to the term intellectual disability. *Intellectual and Developmental Disabilities, 45,* 116–124.

Social Security Administration. (2013). Changes in terminology: Mental retardation to intellectual disability. *Federal Register, 78*(18), 5755–5757.

World Health Organization. (1992).*The international classification of diseases* (10th rev.). Geneva, Switzerland: Author.

World Health Organization. (2010). *The ICD-10 classification of mental and behavioural disorders clinical descriptions and diagnostic guidelines.* Geneva, Switzerland: Author.

3 | Intellectual Disability

Gary N. Siperstein
Melissa A. Collins

Within the diagnosis of intellectual disability (ID), there is immense variation in both cognitive functioning and adaptive behaviors, with the majority of individuals with ID functioning at the upper end of the disability range. In 1992, the American Association on Mental Retardation (AAMR) estimated that 89% of people with ID fell within the mild category (Petersilia, 2000; more recent estimates are not available due to the elimination of the severity categories in official American Association on Intellectual and Developmental Disabilities (AAIDD) definitions and the extreme difficulty in estimating prevalence.). It is these individuals—at the upper end of the ID spectrum—who are the focus of this chapter, because in a categorical sense they are the most difficult to diagnose and the least immediately recognizable as having ID. As MacMillan, Siperstein, and Leffert (2006) put it, in contrast with others with more significant disabilities, "individuals with mild intellectual disability represent 100% of the cases in which the answer to the question 'Does this individual have an intellectual disability?' is actually in doubt," and, consequently, "professionals must depend upon a definition and classification system for help in resolving uncertainty" (p. 197). The history of this group of persons is complex and controversial. Due to issues related to classification, increased vulnerability to negative outcomes, and inaccurate public perceptions, this group requires careful attention, particularly within the context of the American judicial system.

History of Categorization Within ID

It is important to note that the differentiation of intellectual disability into discrete categories has a long history. In fact, the subcategorization of ID based on functional level has been an issue of contention for hundreds of years, and the classification of the group of persons with mild ID specifically has long been a source of debate. Interestingly, one of the first attempts to classify ID began with the differentiation of ID from mental illness, a distinction first made in the sixteenth and seventeenth centuries by philosophers, including Fitzherbert in 1534 and John Locke in 1690 (Braddock & Parish, 2002; MacMillan & Reschly, 1997). Long after that initial and important distinction was made, practitioners recognized that there was a need for further classification, with subcategorization within ID beginning in the mid-nineteenth century (MacMillan & Reschly, 1997). Because it is a disability characterized by impairments in cognitive functioning, it is not surprising that ID was first differentiated by degree of impairment. For example, though offensive terms by today's standards, "idiot" and "imbecile" were used to distinguish individuals by perceived level of functioning as early as the 1830s, as was "moron" in the early 20th century. However, although level of impairment was one of the earliest categorization dimensions, other factors such as etiology were also considered along the way.

Beginning in the late nineteenth century, individuals were often grouped together based on the believed sources of their disability. For example, William Ireland based his 1877 10-category classification system largely on etiology (e.g., "genetous idiocy," "inflammatory idiocy") and included "idiocy by deprivation" for those without evident physical causes (Scheerenberger, 1983). Etiology continued to be used as a major factor in classification through the mid-twentieth century, with Heber's categories including ID due to disease or infection in 1959 and cerebral palsy and convulsive disorders in 1961. Though classification by etiology eventually fell out of practice, some continued to argue even as late as the 1980s that behavioral differences existed for individuals with ID of different etiologies (e.g., Burack, Hodapp, & Zigler, 1988).

Another framework for classification emerged in the mid-twentieth century when service providers began to classify individuals with intellectual disability based on their prognosis and malleability. In this period, perceived educability became the main dimension of classification, and individuals were diagnosed as "educable" or "trainable." Individuals considered educable were believed to be higher functioning and capable of learning some academic subjects, while those considered trainable were believed to be incapable of academic learning but to be capable of learning certain life skills if given appropriate support (Weber, 1962). Thus, by the 1960s, classification had shifted from focusing on the etiology of disability to focusing on the potential to learn if given appropriate supports.

Irrespective of these different classification factors, arguably no factor has been more integral to the history of classification of intellectual disability than the intelligence quotient (IQ). With the emergence of IQ testing in 1905, the identification of individuals with intellectual disability was standardized for the first time (Cardona, 1994). The former subjective categories of "idiot" and "imbecile" that had been used since the 1830s were standardized such that individuals with an IQ test score in the range of 50–75 were considered morons, those with IQ test scores between 25–50 were imbeciles, and those with IQ scores less than 25 were idiots. Over time, the terminology for different categories shifted away from these pejorative terms, but the categories of intellectual disability continued to be based largely on IQ (MacMillan & Reschly, 1997).

Although IQ did allow for more standardized diagnosis within ID, it has not been without criticism and debate. The underlying theme of this controversy is directly relevant to the group of persons with mild levels of ID, and it relates to how inclusive or exclusive the diagnosis and subcategories of ID should be. First, there was significant debate within the field regarding where to set the upper IQ score cutoff. This boundary determines who has a disability and who does not, and, consequently, determines who is eligible to receive services and supports. The most common cutoff has typically been two standard deviations below the mean (100), or an IQ test score of 70–75, but there was a period in the 1960s where the cutoff was recommended to be as high as one standard deviation (-1 SD) below the mean, or an IQ test score of 85 (Heber, 1961). This change led to an instantaneous potential increase in prevalence of ID from 2% to 16% of the population (Zigler, Balla, & Hodapp, 1984). Until Grossman's 1973 definition, those individuals who were between one and two standard deviations below the mean (IQ 85–70) were labeled "borderline MR," a distinct category within ID that was subsequently eliminated when a new definition was released that year. Some have argued that the elimination of this category had negative impacts for those in the borderline group, as it left them without any means for government support (Zetlin & Murtaugh, 1990). At the same time, however, the positive outcome from this change was to avoid association of people with higher functioning with people classified as having intellectual disability.

The other source of debate over IQ relates to the level of flexibility allowed and/or needed in interpreting test results. While some argue for flexibility in interpreting IQ test scores based on the standard errors of the tests (Baroff, 2006), others have countered that too much flexibility can lead to subjective evaluation and, consequentially, perceptions of unfairness in diagnosis (MacMillan, Siperstein, & Leffert, 2006; MacMillan & Siperstein, 2002). Again, this debate is especially relevant to the group of persons with mild levels of ID. Clearly, whether the cutoff is rigid or flexible is most consequential for people with ID at the upper end of the spectrum or on the borderline, as too rigid a cutoff may lead to false negatives and denial of services for those who, for all intents and purposes, actually have ID, while too flexible a cutoff may lead to ambiguity and indecision.

Notwithstanding these debates, IQ did more than provide much-needed standardization in the diagnosis of ID. The emergence of IQ also presented a means of estimating expected distributions of intelligence within the population. IQ is a standardized measurement of intelligence that is calibrated to be normally distributed (i.e., essentially a model to reflect the fact that most individuals have IQs that are within one standard deviation above or below the mean and relatively few have IQs that are further above or below) around the population mean of 100. However, it was discovered early on that there are many more in the low range than expected based on the normal distribution (i.e., Gaussian curve). This statistical aberration led to the hypothesis that there are two groups that have been labeled in a number of different ways over time. In 1933, Lewis made one of the earliest attempts to differentiate these groups by dividing ID into subcultural, or "extreme variety of normal variations of cognitive capacities," and pathological, or "mental defectiveness . . . associated with and in most cases a result of recognized organic insult" (as cited in Burack, 1990, p. 31). Other labels have included "physiological" and "pathological" (Dingman & Tarjan, 1960) and "organic" and "non-organic" or "cultural-familial" (Burack, 1990, pp. 30-31).

Regardless of the specific wording applied, these terms reflect a two-group approach, which is "based on the theoretical premise that the majority of [individuals with intellectual disability] do not differ qualitatively from the normal [sic] population" (Burack, 1990, pp. 30–31). According to this model, there are individuals "who deviate *statistically* from the norms for average functioning even though they may not differ *qualitatively*" (pp. 30–31). In other words, only a fraction of individuals with ID are qualitatively different from the normal population in that their impaired cognitive functioning is due to biological factors such as chromosomal irregularities and physical trauma. Conversely, the majority of individuals with ID reflect expected variability in intelligence based on the Gaussian curve and statistical chance, even in the absence of physical causes. For some time, these individuals were considered to have familial intellectual disability, which has no known etiology, is more common in groups in lower socioeconomic positions, and typically have IQ test scores in the upper range of ID.

In sum, ever since the advent of compulsory education in the United States brought their existence to light and no matter the particular label applied to the group (e.g., cultural-familial, familial, educable mentally retarded, intergenerational), individuals with levels of ID at the upper end of the spectrum have long been recognized as possessing different abilities and needs than those with more significant impairments (MacMillan et al., 2006). Moreover, there has been a clear trend over the last few centuries of confusion and disagreement regarding those near the higher end of the spectrum who have less severe levels of impairment. Indeed, throughout the many fluctuations in terminology and classification across the history of intellectual disability, those individuals who are near the top of the spectrum and whose impairments are less extreme and often are context-specific have consistently presented the greatest challenge for classification.

Current Status of Categorization of Intellectual Disability

Given the history of classification within the field of ID, it is perhaps not surprising that some disagreement remains regarding how to most appropriately classify individuals with these disabilities. AAMR removed subcategories from its 1992 definition of mental retardation in order to focus less on deficits and more on supports needed (Luckasson et al., 1992). Rather than having classifications of mild, moderate, severe, and profound, the 1992 definition divided individuals based on a continuum of supports needed and included the designations of intermittent, limited, extensive, and pervasive levels of supports (Greenspan & Switzky, 2006; Luckasson et al., 1992). The 2002 AAMR (Luckasson et al., 2002) and 2010 AAIDD (Schalock et al., 2010) definitions continue the practice from the 1992 manual with regard to the elimination of severity levels and the omission of any reference to the former subcategories. Following the recommendations of these manuals, the use of the term "mild intellectual disability" is no longer affirmed, although clearly there is a substantial number of individuals characterized as having ID whose level of functioning is at the higher end of the IQ test score range for the ID spectrum. As noted earlier, it is this population of individuals that is the focus of consideration in *Atkins* cases.

Ultimately, perspectives on the most appropriate way to differentiate groups within the ID spectrum depends on the individual's or group's goals of classification. An effective classification system allows for a systematic way to allocate resources and distribute services. However, the purpose behind classification can determine how specific or inclusive categories should be. As MacMillan and Reschly (1997) contended, "persons with different perspectives (legislators who must appropriate funds vs. advocates who wish to serve all deserving persons) often attempt to promote less or more inclusive interpretations of existing diagnostic constructs" (p. 48). For the purposes of the courts, having clearly defined classification levels could facilitate diagnosis of individuals on the borderline and could increase awareness of the different functioning levels of individuals with ID. Furthermore, classification levels also could clarify expectations for abilities and challenges for individuals of different functioning levels. In this way, classification levels are more than just diagnostic terminology, but rather provide information for people interacting with, providing services to, or making decisions about persons with ID. Therefore, since the dissolution of "mild ID'" as an official category in the AAIDD definition, some have advocated for a return to severity level classification (e.g., MacMillan et al., 2006), and many continue to use the category designation in research and practice (e.g., Larkin, Jahoda, & MacMahon, 2012). Nevertheless, it is important for individuals in the court system to examine the diagnosis of ID within the context of scientific shifts and to ensure that treatment of intellectual disability in the court system reflects the current standards of the field.

What Is the Upper End of the Intellectual Disability Spectrum Today?

Individuals at the upper level of the ID spectrum differ in the presentation of their disability when compared to those with more significant levels of impairment. MacMillan and colleagues (2006) contended that individuals at the upper end of the ID spectrum have "distinctive characteristics" that distinguish them from those with more severe levels of impairment, and that the differences among severity levels are "qualitative rather than merely a matter of degree" (p. 198). To be sure, many of the impairments or difficulties shown in moderate or severe levels of impairment are not present in those at the higher end of the ID spectrum. For individuals at the middle and lower levels of ID, in addition to academic and cognitive difficulties, daily living skills are impaired, independent living is often not possible, and it is generally easy to detect that a disability is present. They may have difficulty in basic adaptive behaviors, such as toileting and dressing, and struggle with even low-level cognitive skills, such as memorizing their phone numbers (MacMillan et al., 2006).

Comparatively, the limitations in individuals with ID at the upper end of the spectrum are more subtle, more difficult to detect, and often context-specific. Most individuals with ID at the upper end of the spectrum do not experience problems in the practical skills measured by adaptive behavior scales, such as dressing oneself or using the telephone. However, they typically display significant deficits in adaptive skills in the social and conceptual domains. Family members, employers, friends, and others who interact closely with an individual with ID at the upper end of the spectrum typically observe qualitative differences in their behavior in comparison to others in the environment. While they generally do not recognize the problem as ID, they frequently describe the individual as displaying characteristics of ID such as being "slow," having difficulties with memory and directions, or understanding social pragmatics.

Indeed, rather than displaying significant general dysfunction, individuals with ID at the upper end of the spectrum struggle more with abstract thinking (MacMillan, Siperstein, & Gresham, 1996), and they generally show deficits in planning, problem solving, and decision making. They may also have difficulty in social perception, understanding, and judgment (Leffert & Siperstein, 2002; Leffert, Siperstein, & Widaman, 2010; MacMillan et al., 2006). Additionally, some individuals with ID at the upper end of the spectrum are vulnerable to experiencing comorbidity, such as attention deficit hyperactivity disorder (Rose, Bramham, Young, Paliokostas, & Xenitidis, 2008), autism (Matson & Shoemaker, 2009), communication disorders (Pinborough-Zimmerman, Satterfield, & Miller, 2007), and psychiatric conditions, such as schizophrenia (Lehotkay, Varisco, Deriaz, Douibi, & Carminati, 2009). Overall, compared to the typically developing population, they are more likely to live in poverty (Emerson, 2007); be socially isolated (Hemphill & Siperstein, 1990; Lippold & Burns, 2009); and be more suggestible, gullible, and credulous (Baroff, 2006), putting them at risk for engaging in criminal or antisocial behaviors. Considering the cumulative impact of these challenges, the group of persons with ID at the upper end of the spectrum seems at times to be at risk for unsuccessful integration into society.

Despite these risk factors, if given the opportunity, individuals with ID at the upper end of the spectrum can participate in their communities in ways that far exceed public expectations. After graduating high school, some individuals with ID at the upper end of the spectrum take advantage of the limited but increasing opportunities to attend postsecondary education, such as vocational programs at community colleges (Papay & Bambara, 2011) and, more recently, participating in 4-year colleges. Furthermore, although limitations in reading and similar academic skills may hinder their chances of successful employment in certain areas (Baroff, 2006), people with ID at the upper end of the spectrum can sustain gainful employment in appropriate settings (e.g., Jahoda et al., 2009). Indeed, the abilities of people with ID at the upper end of the spectrum are evident throughout their daily activities. People with mild levels of ID can participate in a variety of community and leisure activities (Dusseljee, Rijken, Cardol, Curfs, & Groenewegen, 2011), such as competing in sporting events (Harada, Siperstein, Parker, & Lenox, 2011), attending religious services (Shogren & Rye, 2005), volunteering in the community (Trembath, Balandin, Stancliffe, & Togher, 2010), driving cars (Dixon & Reddacliff, 2001), and having long-term relationships (Siebelink, de Jong, Taal, & Roelvink, 2006). Additionally, research has demonstrated their ability to master independent living skills, such as using ATMs (Davies, Stock, & Wehmeyer, 2003), cooking (Taber-Doughty et al., 2011), and making financial decisions (Suto, Clare, Holland, & Watson, 2005). Many can use computers, the Internet, and other technologies (Wehmeyer et al., 2006), and navigate urban settings (Wright & Wolery, 2011) or ride public transportation (Davies, Stock, Holloway, & Wehmeyer, 2010). This range of abilities and activities corresponds with the fact that many are able to live independently, with varying levels of support (Bond & Hurst, 2009).

The range of abilities and activities of people at the upper end of the ID spectrum and the varying presentation of their disabilities make identification a challenge. In other words, individuals functioning in this range can be difficult to identify as a result of their higher levels of adaptive behaviors. Consequently, many may go undiagnosed or misdiagnosed because they do not demonstrate obvious impairments in these skills and behaviors.

In fact, whether or not an individual functioning in this range is actually diagnosed is largely a factor of context and definition. Both the 2002 AAMR (Luckasson et al., 2002) and 2010 AAIDD (Schalock et al., 2010) definitions of ID included requirements that "limitations in present functioning must be considered within the context of community environments typical of the individual's age peers and culture" (Luckasson et al., 2002). Any consideration of context in diagnosing ID highlights the important role of current societal demands. As Connolly and Bruner (1974) stated, "in any given society there are sets of skills which are essential for coping with existing realities," and the extent to which any individual functions in society depends on the acquisition and application of these skills (p. 4). Therefore, Leland (1969) contended that

> we must remember that as society becomes more complex and as the intellectual requirements placed on the individual become more demanding, many behaviors which in a previous period were acceptable as representing an average level, no longer may be considered to do so. (p. 534).

Taking a historical perspective shows us that higher-functioning individuals, who we now know constitute the majority of those with mild levels of ID, were not even diagnosed for hundreds of years. Most people in the general population were illiterate and manual jobs were not cognitively demanding; consequently, intellectual disability was not manifested (Mesibov, 1974).

Thus, given that context is such a critical factor in diagnosis, ID "can be understood only in terms of the transaction between the individual's cognitive inefficiencies and the environmental demands for problem-solving" (MacMillan, Siperstein, & Gresham, 1996, p. 356). Consequently, the same individual could potentially be seen as competent in one environment and incompetent in another. Indeed, deficits associated with the upper end of ID generally present themselves only within specific contexts, such as schools (MacMillan et al., 2006). The importance of context for diagnosis is reflected by the fact that it is much more common in low SES, minority families (Browman, Nichols, Shaughnessy, & Kennedy, 1987) and may be related to geographic locale (Reschly & Jipson, 1976). Therefore, researchers have advocated for sensitivity to differences in language and culture when evaluating cognitive abilities in our more diversified society (Greenspan & Switzky, 2006).

Public Perceptions and Misconceptions

The conundrum, both for the courts and for society at large, is that the public may not *perceive* these individuals to have disabilities. Indeed, even considering their impaired cognitive and social functioning, the greatest challenge that individuals with mild levels of ID face is their own invisibility. Individuals with mild levels of ID are in a precarious position—they possess a number of abilities that distinguish them from others with greater levels of impairment, yet they are still vulnerable to a host of challenges as compared to the typically developing population. The influential role of context creates much ambiguity in the diagnosis of ID, and the manifestations of mild levels of ID do not align with societal expectations. Notwithstanding the conceptual and definitional approach to categorizing ID and defining and understanding mild levels of ID, what is the societal understanding of the disability?

Research overall has shown vast misconceptions regarding ID in the general public, and even among professionals. For example, although pediatricians have been shown to recognize different abilities for children with ID at the upper end of the spectrum, as compared with those at the middle and lower ranges of the ID spectrum (Wolraich, Siperstein, & O'Keefe, 1987), disagreement exists among professionals from medicine, education, and social work regarding the abilities and disabilities of persons across the spectrum of the disability (Wolraich & Siperstein, 1986). While professionals may disagree about the extent of variability in functioning within ID, the public does not even recognize that such variability exists. According to public opinion, the average person with ID is believed to have a significant impairment (Siperstein, Norins, Corbin, & Shriver, 2003).

For example, a national study of youth attitudes found that students tend to perceive peers with ID as being moderately, rather than mildly, impaired (Siperstein, Parker,

Norins Bardon, & Widaman, 2007). Earlier research showed that, when asked to imagine a person with ID, the public tended to picture a person with Down syndrome (Gottlieb & Siperstein, 1976; Siperstein & Gottlieb, 1977). The public also tends to view ID as due to physical causes, permanent in nature (Goodman, 1989; Gottlieb, 1975; Jones et al., 1984), and physically evident (Gottlieb, 1975), which are all common indicators of more significant levels of impairment. These perceptions are evident as young as third grade (Goodman, 1989) and lead to public reactions of hopelessness and rejection (Jones et al., 1984). In addition, multinational research has found that these misperceptions are present to varying degrees all over the world (Siperstein et al., 2003).

Despite the wide spectrum within ID, individuals with more significant levels of impairment have become the default prototype for ID in the public's eye. Consequently, the public tends to underestimate the abilities of many people with ID. When asked about the perceived abilities of an individual with ID, 83% reported that someone with ID could wash and dress themselves, but only half thought they could prepare their own food or handle money (Siperstein et al., 2003). These misconceptions have serious consequences. Despite the importance of early intervention, there is often reluctance to diagnose a child with ID, as parents do not perceive their child's impairment to be significant enough to warrant diagnosis. Considering a hypothetical 4-year-old child, just 51% of parents responded that they would refer the child for special education services if he or she demonstrated a mild level of impairment, compared with 91% for moderately impaired children (Goodman, 1987). When one considers the fact that the large majority of individuals with ID actually function at the upper end of the spectrum, the disconnect between what the public believes and what in reality is true is stark. Consequently, those with ID at the upper end of the spectrum are most likely to be misdiagnosed or not diagnosed at all because others don't *perceive* them as having a disability or because of the stigma historically associated with the label "mental retardation." As a result, these individuals may be frequently not served or underserved—particularly within the context of public education—placing them at risk for a number of negative outcomes in adulthood (Zetlin & Murtaugh, 1990).

Challenges in the American Judicial System

For all of the challenges in classification and diagnosis, widespread misconceptions of capabilities, and general low understanding of functioning variability within ID, those individuals at the upper end of the ID spectrum are the most challenging for the courts. As Baroff (2006) stated, "for judges who must follow state legal statutes that set IQ [at] 70, or 69, as the boundary for (intellectual disability previously known as) mental retardation, the distinction, in capital cases, may truly be one of life or death" (p. 34). In general, individuals with ID are viewed as having a lesser level of culpability than persons without ID (Baroff, 2006). In fact, multinational research has shown that the majority of the public believes that individuals with ID should receive special dispensation in a court of law (Siperstein et al., 2003). However, this can be a difficult issue when one considers the discrepancy between what the public perceives ID to be and the actual characteristics of a person with ID at the upper end of the spectrum. How might public opinion change in the face of a person who does not fit the perceived schema for ID?

The gravity of the situation is aggravated by the prevalence of offenders with ID. In accordance with the traditional idea of a "six-hour retarded child" (The President's Committee on Mental Retardation, 1969), adults who formerly received special education services frequently "disappear into society in their adult years" (Larson et al., 2001, p. 232). However, the same cognitive impairments remain and, because these individuals may no longer be part of a system of supports, these impairments may resurface through criminal behavior. Subsequently, when suspects with ID are arrested, they are uniquely vulnerable while navigating the court system because they may lack understanding of their own legal rights and the judicial process (e.g., Applebaum 1994); may have difficulty processing instructions, commands, and questions; or may have difficulty remembering the details or sequences of events of a case (Davis, 2009). Thus, identification and proper procedures in the court system are not only extremely complex, due to the ambiguity in borderline cases, but also extremely consequential.

In conclusion, it is quite clear that people with ID represent a diverse group, with those individuals who are at the borderline of being diagnosed or not diagnosed being the most prevalent and being both quantitatively and qualitatively different from those with more significant levels of impairment. History underscores this and points to factors such as etiology and context as driving who is diagnosed as having ID and who is not—not to mention who is misdiagnosed. All of this is compounded by the fact that the public (e.g., employees, service professionals, and even jurors, who represent a cross-section of the public) understand ID to be singular. This "schema" for a person with ID is far from a representation of a person who, albeit has difficulty in abstract thinking and complex problem solving, is capable of being employed, living independently (with supports), and engaging in the community. The public's image on the contrary can be found in an eleventh-grade boy's characterization of a person with ID:

> [People with ID] are not able to comprehend what life really is. They are unable to function as normal (*sic*) people because of brain disease or damage. I know this from viewing them doing their menial tasks and from books I have read. They got that way because of a lack of air during birth, thus their brain damage, or because of freak mutations like too many chromosomes—just one extra will do it. They are outwardly obvious, that is, they have cloudy haircuts, outdated clothes, and cheap eyeglasses. They feel nothing. They haven't the capabilities to understand what they are. (as quoted in Siperstein & Bak, 1980, p. 207)

Beyond empirical support for this overall lack of understanding of the capabilities of people with ID, this perception is pervasive throughout television and film. Judges and jurors potentially, without an understanding and appreciation of the wide spectrum of challenges and capabilities of individuals with ID, may find it difficult to juxtapose and reconcile their beliefs and perceptions with the reality of an individual with ID at the upper end of the spectrum. *Atkins v. Virginia* (2002) put the history of subgrouping individuals with ID and the conceptual and practical/programmatic issues of defining and identifying individuals with ID squarely in the courtroom. The other chapters in this book address the identification process of ID, such as measurement and assessment considerations and issues related to intellectual functioning and adaptive behavior. While considering all these matters, however, it is critical that the population of individuals at the upper end of the ID spectrum not be viewed as a special or unusual circumstance; rather, it must be remembered that they make up the majority of the population with ID, and, yet, at the same time, are uniquely different from people in the middle and lower ranges of the ID spectrum and from public expectations.

References

American Association on Intellectual and Developmental Disabilities. (2010). FAQ on the AAIDD definition on intellectual disability. Retrieved from http://www.aaidd.org/IntellectualDisabilityBook/content_7473.cfm?navID=366

Applebaum, K. L. (1994). Assessment of criminal-justice-related competences in defendants with mental retardation. *The Journal of Psychiatry and Law, 22*(3), 311–327.

Atkins v. Virginia, 536 U.S. 304, 310 (2002).

Baroff, G. S. (2006). On the 2002 AAMR definition of mental retardation. In H. N. Switzky & S. Greenspan (Eds.), *What is mental retardation? Ideas for an evolving disability in the 21st century* (pp. 29–38). Washington, DC: American Association on Intellectual and Developmental Disabilities.

Bond, R. J., & Hurst, J. (2009). How adults with learning disabilities view living independently. *British Journal of Learning Disabilities, 38*(4), 286–292. doi: 10.1111/j.1468-3156.2009.00604.x

Braddock, D., & Parish, S. L. (2002). An institutional history of disability. In Albrecht, G. L., Seelman, K. D., & Bury, M. (Eds.), *Handbook of disability studies* (pp. 11–68). Washington, DC: American Association on Mental Retardation.

Browman, S., Nichols, P. L., Shaughnessy, P., & Kennedy, W. (1987). *Retardation in young children: A developmental study of cognitive deficit.* Hillsdale, NJ: Erlbaum.

Burack, J. A. (1990). Differentiating mental retardation: The two-group approach and beyond. In R. M. Hodapp, J. A. Burack, & E. Zigler (Eds.), *Issues in the developmental approach to mental retardation* (pp. 27–48). New York, NY: Cambridge University Press.

Burack, J. A., Hodapp, R. M., & Zigler, E. (1988). Issues in the classification of mental retardation: Differentiating among organic etiologies. *Journal of Child Psychology and Psychiatry, 29*(6), 765–779.

Cardona, F. A. (1994). Milestones in the history of mental retardation. *The Journal of the South Carolina Medical Association, 90*(6), 285–288.

Connolly, K. J., & Bruner, J. S. (1974). Competence: Its nature and nurture. In K. J. Connolly & J. S. Bruner (Eds.), *The growth of competence* (pp. 3–7). London, England: Academic Press.

Davis, L. A. (2009). People with intellectual disabilities in the criminal justice system: Victims and suspects. *The Arc Q & A.* Retrieved from http://www.thearc.org/page.aspx?pid=2458

Davies, D. K., Stock, S. E., Holloway, S., & Wehmeyer, M. L. (2010). Evaluating a GPS-based transportation device to support independent bus travel by people with intellectual disability. *Intellectual and Developmental Disabilities, 48*(6), 454–463. doi: http://dx.doi.org/10.1352/1934-9556-48.6.454

Davies, D. K., Stock, S. E., & Wehmeyer, M. L. (2003). Application of computer simulation to teach ATM access to individuals with intellectual disabilities. *Education and Training in Developmental Disabilities, 38*(4), 451–456.

Dingman, H. F., & Tarjan, G. (1960). Mental retardation and the normal distribution curve. *American Journal of Mental Deficiency, 64*, 991–994.

Dixon, R. M., & Reddacliff, C. A. (2001). Family contribution to the vocational lives of vocationally competent young adults with intellectual disabilities. *International Journal of Disability, Development, and Education, 48*(2), 193–206. doi: http://dx.doi.org/10.1080/10349120120053667

Dusseljee, J., Rijken, P., Cardol, M., Curfs, L., & Groenewegen, P. (2011). Participation in daytime activities among people with mild or moderate intellectual disability. *Journal of Intellectual Disability Research, 55*(1), 4–18. doi: 10.1111/j.1365-2788.2010.01342.x

Emerson, E. (2007). Poverty and people with intellectual disabilities. *Mental Retardation & Developmental Disabilities Research Reviews, 13*(2), 107–113. doi: 0.1002/mrdd.20144

Goodman, J. F. (1987). Reluctance to refer the mildly retarded child: Implications for labeling. *Early Child Development and Care, 29*, 331–341. doi: 10.1002/mrdd.20144

Goodman, J. F. (1989). Does retardation mean dumb? Children's perceptions of the nature, cause, and course of mental retardation. *Journal of Special Education, 23*(3), 313–329.

Gottlieb, J. (1975). Public, peer, and professional attitudes toward mentally retarded persons. In M. J. Begab & S. A. Richardson (Eds.), *The mentally retarded and society: A social science perspective* (pp. 99–125). Baltimore: University Park Press.

Gottlieb, J., & Siperstein, G. (1976). Attitudes toward mentally retarded persons: Effects of attitude referent specificity. *American Journal of Mental Deficiency, 80*, 376–381.

Greenspan, S., & Granfield, J. M. (1992). Reconsidering the construct of mental retardation: Implications of a model of social competence. *American Journal of Mental Retardation, 96*(4), 442–453.

Greenspan, S., & Switzky, H. N. (2006). Forty-four years of AAMR manuals. In H. N. Switzky & S. Greenspan (Eds.), *What is mental retardation? Ideas for an evolving disability in the 21st century* (pp. 3–28). Washington, DC: American Association on Intellectual and Developmental Disabilities.

Grossman, H. J. (Ed.). (1973). *Manual on terminology in mental retardation* (rev. ed.). Washington, DC: American Association on Mental Deficiency.

Harada, C. M., Siperstein, G. N., Parker, R. C., & Lenox, D. (2011). Promoting social inclusion for people with intellectual disabilities through sport: Special Olympics International, global sport initiatives and strategies. *Sport in Society, 14*(9), 1131–1138. doi: 10.1080/17430437.2011.614770

Heber, R. (1959). A manual on terminology & classification in mental retardation [Monograph Supplement]. *American Journal of Mental Deficiency, 64*(2).

Heber, R. (1961). Modifications in the manual on terminology and classification in mental retardation. *American Journal of Mental Deficiency, 65*(4), 499–500.

Hemphill, L., & Siperstein, G. (1990). Conversational competence and peer response to mildly retarded children. *Journal of Educational Psychology, 82*(1), 128–134. doi: 10.1037/0022-0663.82.1.128

Jahoda, A., Banks, P., Dagnan, D., Kemp, J., Kerr, W., & Williams, V. (2009). Starting a new job: The social and emotional experience of people with intellectual disabilities. *Journal of Applied Research in Intellectual Disabilities, 22*(5), 421–425. doi: 10.1111/j.1468-3148.2009.00497.x

Jones, E. E., Farina, A., Hastorf., A., Marjus, H., Miller, O., & Scott, R. (1984). *Social stigma: The psychology of marked relationships.* New York, NY: W. H. Freeman.

Larkin, P., Jahoda, A., & MacMahon, K. (2012). Interpersonal sources of conflict in young people with and without mild to moderate intellectual disabilities at transition from adolescence to adulthood. *Journal of Applied Research in Intellectual Disabilities, 25*(1), 29–38. doi: 10.1111/j.1468-3148.2011.00652.x

Larson, S. A., Lakini, K. C., Anderson, L., Kwak, N., Lee, J. H., & Anderson, D. (2001). Prevalence of mental retardation and developmental disabilities: Estimates from the 1994/1995 National Health Interview Survey Disability Supplements. *American Journal on Mental Retardation, 106*, 231–252.

Leffert, J. S. & Siperstein, G. N. (2002). Social cognition: A key to understanding adaptive behavior in individuals with mental retardation. In L. M. Glidden (Vol. Ed.), *International review of research in mental retardation* (vol. 25, pp. 135–181). San Diego, CA: Academic Press.

Leffert, J. S., Siperstein, G. N., & Widaman, K. F. (2010). Social perception in children with intellectual disabilities: The interpretation of benign and hostile intentions. *Journal of Intellectual Disability Research, 54*(2), 168–180. doi:10.1111/j.1365-2788.2009.01240.x

Lehotkay, R., Varisco, S., Deriaz, N., Douibi, A., & Carminati, G. G. (2009). Intellectual disability and psychiatric disorder: More than a dual diagnosis. *Schweizer Archiv für Neurologie und Psychiatrie, 160*(3), 105–115.

Leland, H. (1969). The relationship between "intelligence" and mental retardation. *American Journal of Mental Deficiency, 73,* 533–535.

Lippold, T., & Burns, J. (2009). Social support and intellectual disabilities: A comparison between social networks of adults with intellectual disability and those with physical disability. *Journal of Intellectual Disability Research, 53*(5), 463–473. doi: 10.1111/j.1365-2788.2009.01170.x

Luckasson, R., Borthwick-Duffy, S., Buntinx, W. H. E., Coulter, D. L., Craig, E. M., Reeve, A., Schalock, R. L., Snell, M. E., Spitalnik, D. M., Spreat, S., & Tassé, M. J. (2002). *Mental retardation: Definition, classification, and systems of supports* (10th ed.). Washington, DC: American Association on Mental Retardation.

Luckasson, R., Coulter, D. L., Polloway, E. A., Reiss, S., Schalock, R. L., Snell, M. E., . . . Stark, J. A. (1992). Mental retardation: Definition, classification, and systems of supports (9th ed.). Washington, DC: American Association on Mental Retardation.

MacMillan, D. L., Gresham, F. M., & Siperstein, G. S. (1993). Conceptual and psychometric concerns about the 1992 AAMR definition of mental retardation. *American Journal on Mental Retardation, 98,* 325–355.

MacMillan, D. L., Gresham, F. M., Siperstein, G. N., & Bocian, K. M. (1996). The labyrinth of IDEA: School decisions on referred students with subaverage general intelligence. *American Journal on Mental Retardation, 101,* 161–174.

MacMillan, D. L., & Reschly, D. J. (1997). Issues of definition and classification. In W. E. MacLean, Jr. (Ed.), *Ellis' handbook of mental deficiency, psychological theory, and research* (3rd ed., pp. 47–74). Mahwah, NJ: Erlbaum.

MacMillan, D. L., & Siperstein, G. N. (2002). Learning disabilities as operationally defined by schools. In R. Bradley, L. Danielson & D. Hallahan (Eds.), *Identification of learning disabilities: Research to practice.* Mahwah, NJ: Lawrence Erlbaum Assoc.

MacMillan, D. L., Siperstein, G. N., & Gresham, F. M. (1996). A challenge to the viability of mild mental retardation as a diagnostic category. *Exceptional Children, 62,* 356–371.

MacMillan, D. L., Siperstein, G. N., & Leffert, J. S. (2006). Children with mild mental retardation: A challenge for classification practices–revised. In H. N. Switzky & S. Greenspan (Eds.), *What is mental retardation? Ideas for an evolving disability in the 21st century.* (pp. 197–220). Washington, DC: American Association on Mental Retardation.

Matson, J. L., & Shoemaker, M. (2009). Intellectual disability and its relationship to autism spectrum disorders. *Research in Developmental Disabilities: A Multidisciplinary Journal, 30*(6), 1107–1114. doi: 10.1016/j.ridd.2009.06.003

Mesibov, G. B. (1974). *Attributions of responsibility: A cognitive interpretation.* Brandeis University, Waltham: MA.

Papay, C. K., & Bambara, L. M. (2011). Postsecondary education for transition-age students with intellectual and other developmental disabilities: A national survey. *Education and Training in Autism and Developmental Disabilities, 46*(1), 78–93.

Petersilia, J. (2000). *Doing justice? Criminal offenders with developmental disabilities.* Berkeley, CA: California Policy Resource Center, University of California Berkeley.

Pinborough-Zimmerman, J., Satterfield, R., & Miller, J. (2007). Communication disorders: Prevalence and comorbid intellectual disability, autism, and emotional/behavioral disorders. *American Journal of Speech-Language Pathology, 16*(4), 359–367. doi:10.1044/1058-0360(2007/039)

President's Committee on Mental Retardation. (1969). *The black six-hour retarded child: A report on a conference on problems of education of children in the inner city (Warrenton, Virginia, August 10–12, 1969).* Washington, DC: Author.

Reschly, D. J., & Jipson, F. J. (1976). Ethnicity, geographic locale, age, sex, and urban-rural residence as variables in mild retardation. *American Journal of Mental Deficiency*, *81*(2), 154–161.

Rose, E., Bramham, J., Young, S., Paliokostas, E., & Xenitidis, K. (2008). Neuropsychological characteristics of adults with comorbid ADHD and borderline/mild intellectual disability. *Research in Developmental Disabilities*, *30*(3), 496–502. doi: 10.1016/j.ridd.2008.07.009

Schalock, R. L., Borthwick-Duffy, S. A., Bradley, V. J., Buntinx, W. H. E., Coulter, D. L., Craig, E. M., Gomez, S. C., Lachapelle, Y., Luckasson, R., Reeve, A., Shogren, K. A., Snell, M. E., Spreat, S., Tassé, M. J., Thompson, J. R., Verdugo-Alonso, M. A., Wehmeyer, M. L., & Yeager, M. H. (2010). *Intellectual disability: Definition, classification, and systems of supports (11th ed.)*. Washington, DC: American Association on Intellectual and Developmental Disabilities.

Scheerenberger, R. C. (1983). *A history of mental retardation*. Baltimore, MD: Brookes.

Shogren, K. A., & Rye, M. S. (2005). Religion and individuals with intellectual disabilities: An exploratory study of self-reported perspectives. *Journal of Religion, Disability, & Health*, *9*(1), 29–53. doi:10.1300/J095v09n01_03

Siebelink, E. M., de Jong, M. D. T., Taal, E., & Roelvink, L. (2006). Sexuality and people with intellectual disabilities: Assessment of knowledge, attitudes, experiences, and needs. *Mental Retardation*, *44*(4), 283–294. doi: 10.1352/0047-6765(2006)44[283:SAPWID]2.0.CO;2

Siperstein, G., & Bak, J. J. (1980). Students' and teachers' perceptions of the mentally retarded child. In J. Gottlieb (Ed.), *Educating mentally retarded persons in the mainstream* (pp. 207–230). Baltimore, MD: University Park.

Siperstein, G., & Gottlieb, J. (1977). Physical stigma and academic performance as factors affecting children's first impressions of handicapped peers. *American Journal of Mental Deficiency*, *81*, 455–462.

Siperstein, G. S., Norins, J., Corbin, S. B., & Shriver, T. (2003). *Multinational study of attitudes toward individuals with intellectual disabilities* [Special report]. Washington, DC: Special Olympics.

Siperstein, G., Parker, R., Norins Bardon, J., & Widaman, K. (2007). A national study of youth attitudes toward the inclusion of students with intellectual disabilities. *Exceptional Children*, *73*(4), 435–455. doi: 10.1177/001440290707300403

Suto, W., Clare, I., Holland, A., & Watson, P. (2005). Capacity to make financial decisions among people with mild intellectual disabilities. *Journal of Intellectual Disability Research*, *49*(3), 199–209. doi: 10.1111/j.1365-2788.2005.00635.x

Taber-Doughty, T., Bouck, E. C., Tom, K., Jasper, A. D., Flanagan, S. M., & Bassette, L. (2011). Video modeling and prompting: A comparison of two strategies for teaching cooking skills to students with mild intellectual disabilities. *Education and Training in Autism and Developmental Disabilities*, *46*(4), 499–513.

Trembath, D., Balandin, S., Stancliffe, R. J., & Togher, L. (2010). Employment and volunteering for adults with intellectual disability. *Journal of Policy and Practice in Intellectual Disabilities*, *7*(4), 235–238. doi: 10.1111/j.1741-1130.2010.00271.x

Weber, E. W. (1962). *Educable and trainable mentally retarded children*. Springfield, IL: Thomas.

Wehmeyer, M. L., Palmer S. B., Smith, S. J., Parent, W., Davies, D. K., & Stock, S. (2006). Technology use by people with intellectual and developmental disabilities to support employment activities: A single-subject design meta-analysis. *Journal of Vocational Rehabilitation*, *24*, 81–86.

Wolraich, M. L., & Siperstein, G. N. (1986). Physicians' and other professionals' expectations and prognoses for mentally retarded individuals. *American Journal of Mental Deficiency*, *91*(3), 244–249.

Wolraich, M. L., Siperstein, G. N., & O'Keefe, P. (1987). Pediatricians' perceptions of mentally retarded individuals. *Pediatrics, 80*(5), 643–649.

Wright, T., & Wolery, M. (2011). The effects of instructional interventions related to street crossing and individuals with disabilities. *Research in Developmental Disabilities, 32*(5), 1455–1463.

Zetlin, A., & Murtaugh, M. (1990). Whatever happened to those with borderline IQs? *American Journal of Mental Retardation, 94*(5), 463–469.

Zigler, E., Balla, D., & Hodapp, R. (1984). On the definition and classification of mental retardation. *American Journal of Mental Deficiency, 89*(3), 215–230.

4 | Analysis of *Atkins* Cases

John H. Blume
Karen L. Salekin

Daryl Atkins and William Jones were charged in a Virginia court in 1996 with kidnapping, robbery, and murder. Following their arrest, both defendants acknowledged being involved in the crime, but each claimed the other was the "trigger-man." Due to inconsistencies in Atkins's statements, the prosecution offered Jones a plea bargain in exchange for his testimony against Atkins. Atkins was convicted and sentenced to death.

Both at trial and on appeal to the Virginia Supreme Court, Atkins maintained that he could not be sentenced to death because he was "mentally retarded" (now referred to as having intellectual disability). There was, however, one significant obstacle to Atkins's legal argument—the United States Supreme Court's decision in *Penry v. Lynaugh* (1989). In *Penry*, a majority of the Court found that a national consensus barring the death penalty for a person with intellectual disability had not yet been established, and, consequently, protections were not put in place. Since the Court's decision in *Penry*, however, there had been a "dramatic shift in the state legislative landscape" (*Atkins v. Virginia*, 2002, p. 310). Thus, the Supreme Court granted Atkins's petition for a writ of certiorari (the Supreme Court's decision to listen to an appeal from a lower court). Several months earlier, the Court granted certiorari in *McCarver v. North Carolina* (2001) and then replaced *McCarver* with *Atkins v. Virginia*, after North Carolina passed a statute barring the execution of persons with intellectual disability, thus making *McCarver* moot. The issue at hand was whether the execution of persons with intellectual disability was cruel and unusual punishment under the Eighth Amendment. With a 6-3 majority, in an opinion authored by Justice Stevens, the Court ultimately concluded that it did. The Court began by establishing that a fundamental "precept of justice [is] that punishment for crime should be graduated and proportioned to [the] offense" (*Atkins v. Virginia*, 2002, p. 311). This proportionality concept is—and was even before

Atkins—an integral part of any Eighth Amendment analysis. The Court also made clear that making the determination as to whether a punishment is constitutionally excessive or cruel and unusual is judged by current standards, not by those which existed at the time the Eighth Amendment was ratified. The core Eighth Amendment concept is the "dignity of man" and, thus, its constitutional content must be informed by "the evolving standards of decency that mark the progress of a maturing society." (*Atkins v. Virginia,* 2002, pp. 311–312). Because "evolving standard[s], . . . should be informed by objective factors to the maximum possible extent" (*Atkins v. Virginia,* 2002, p. 312), the Court reaffirmed that the most reliable evidence of this standard is found in state legislative enactments and jury verdicts. However, the Court was also adamant that "in the end [its] own judgment [would] be brought to bear on the question of the acceptability of the death penalty under the Eighth Amendment [for people with intellectual disability]" (*Atkins v. Virginia,* 2002, p. 312).

Its course set, the Court first reviewed the lay of the legislative land. The Court was impressed with the fact that, at the time of its decision in *Penry* (1989), only two death penalty states and the federal government prohibited the death penalty for offenders with intellectual disability; however, since that time, an additional 16 states had taken death off the punishment table for people with intellectual disability (*Atkins v. Virginia,* 2002). Moreover, the Court noted, "i[t] is not so much the number of these States that is significant, but the consistency of the direction of change" (*Atkins v. Virginia,* 2002, p. 315). The Court viewed these enactments, especially "[g]iven the well-known . . . [popularity of] anticrime legislation," as "powerful evidence that today our society views mentally retarded offenders as categorically less culpable than the average criminal" (p. 315–316). The Court also looked to the opinions of social and professional organizations with "germane expertise," the opposition to the practice by "widely diverse religious communities," international practice, and polling data (p. 317). These factors gave further support to the Court's opinion that there was a consensus opposing the practice "among those who have addressed the issue" (*Atkins v. Virginia,* 2002, p. 317). Finally, the Court also noted that, even in those states that retained the death penalty for persons with intellectual disability, only five had actually carried out the execution of these individuals since *Penry.* Since "[t]he practice . . . has become truly unusual, . . . it is fair to say, that a national consensus has developed against it" (p. 316).

The Court then examined the underlying merits of the consensus, beginning with the observation that it reflected a "judgment about the relative culpability of mentally retarded offenders, and the relationship between intellectual disability and the penological purposes served by the death penalty" (*Atkins v. Virginia,* 2002, p. 317). The Court noted that, due to their impairments, they "have diminished capacities to understand and process information, to communicate, to abstract from mistakes and learn from experience, to engage in logical reasoning, to control impulses, and to understand the reactions of others" (p. 318). These deficiencies, while not justifying an exemption from criminal liability, did, in the Court's view, diminish the personal culpability to the extent that neither of the justifications advanced by states in support of the death penalty—retribution and deterrence—would be served by permitting their execution.

As noted by the Court, retribution (i.e., "just deserts") "depends on the culpability of the offender," and as such, determined that the death penalty was excessive due to the "lesser culpability of the mentally retarded offender" (*Atkins v. Virginia*, 2002, p. 319). The Court also concluded that deterrence interests are not served by the execution of offenders with intellectual disability because "capital punishment can [only] serve as a deterrent when [a crime] is the result of premeditation and deliberation," that is, when the threat of death "will inhibit criminal actors from carrying out murderous conduct," but that this type "of calculus is at the opposite end of the spectrum from [the] behavior of [the] mentally retarded" due to their cognitive and behavioral impairments (*Atkins v. Virginia,* 2002, pp. 319–320).

In addition to concluding that retaining the death penalty for people with intellectual disability would not further legitimate interests in retribution or deterrence, the Court also found that "[t]he reduced capacity of mentally retarded offenders provides a second justification for a categorical rule making such offenders ineligible for the death penalty" (*Atkins v. Virginia*, 2002, p. 320). Due to their impairments, there were a host of reasons, including the increased risk of false confessions, the likelihood of difficulties in communicating with counsel, and a lesser ability (due to limited communication skill) to effectively testify on their own behalf, that, "in the aggregate," rendered offenders with intellectual disability subject to an unacceptable "risk of wrongful execution" (*Atkins v. Virginia,* 2002, pp. 320–321). The Court also noted the particular danger that their "demeanor may create an unwarranted impression of lack of remorse for their crimes," which could enhance the likelihood that the jury will impose the death penalty due to a belief that they pose a future danger (*Atkins v. Virginia,* 2002, p. 321).

Thus, the Court concluded that its "independent evaluation of the issue reveals no reason to disagree with the judgment of the legislatures that have . . . concluded that death is not a suitable punishment for a mentally retarded criminal," and therefore, the Constitution "places a substantive restriction on the State's power to take the life' of a mentally retarded offender" (*Atkins v. Virginia*, 2002, p. 321).

An Overview of Post-*Atkins* Decisions

In his dissenting opinion, Justice Scalia predicted that virtually all death row inmates would claim they had intellectual disability and would do so in an attempt to cheat the executioner (*Atkins v. Virginia*, 2002, p. 353). In his opinion, he stated that "this newest intervention promises to be more effective than any of the others in turning the process of capital trial into a game." His prediction was wrong. Only approximately 7% of death sentenced inmates have raised *Atkins* claims (i.e., claims alleging that they are persons with intellectual disability and thus ineligible for execution; Blume, Johnson & Seeds, 2009a). Furthermore, the claimant has prevailed (i.e., has been determined to in fact be a person with intellectual disability) in approximately 40% of the cases where an *Atkins* claim was asserted (Blume et al., 2009a). These two data points combined establish that few "frivolous" contentions of intellectual disability are filed, especially when one takes into account that the actual number of successful cases is higher than reported here because a significant number of cases have been "settled" in unreported negotiated dispositions due to the strength of the merits of the *Atkins* claim.

It is important to note that success rates of *Atkins* claims vary significantly from state to state. In some states (e.g., North Carolina, South Carolina), the overall rate at which claimants prevail has been greater than 80% (Blume et al., 2009a). In others (e.g., Alabama, Texas), only about 10% of those who have claimed to be a person with intellectual disability were ultimately successful (Blume et al., 2009a). In the majority of the unsuccessful cases (56%; Blume et al., 2009a), the claimant was found to have failed to demonstrate both significantly sub-average intellectual functioning and deficits in adaptive functioning. The remaining losses were divided almost equally between cases that failed on either intellectual functioning or adaptive behavior. A small handful of cases, less than 2%, were found wanting on onset during the developmental period.

In the successful prong 1 (i.e., significant limitations in intellectual functioning) cases, most of the claimants (60%) did not have an IQ test score over 70. However, in approximately 15% of the cases, the average of the claimant's IQ scores exceeded 70 and in a few cases, the claimant had never earned a score below 70. As for the unsuccessful prong 1 cases, 35% of the claimants' average IQ test scores exceeded 70; surprisingly, 21% did not have a single score above 70. In 18% of these same cases, the claimant had IQ test scores that fell both above and below 70; in the end the triers-of-fact determined that the higher scores were more reliable and often discounted or refused to consider the standard error of measurement, the Flynn effect, and/or the practice effect (Blume at al., 2009a).

In looking at the cases that prevail on prong 2 (i.e., significant limitations in adaptive functioning), the most commonly established deficits were functional academics (57%), social skills (33%), communication skills (37%), and work skills (19%). An examination of the unsuccessful prong 2 cases revealed several recurring nonclinical considerations that the court determined precluded a determination of significant deficits in adaptive functioning. Examples include the "sophistication" of the crime, some aspect of the individual's prison behavior (e.g., the individual has successfully "adapted to prison life"), and the claimant's in-court behavior (e.g., defendant talked to his attorney in court) (Blume at al., 2009a).

Prong 3 (i.e., age of onset) has been, by and large, a minor consideration in post-*Atkins* litigation. In the few cases where age of onset has been a concern, the case has generally failed because the individual failed to present proof of a pre-18 standardized IQ test score below 70 (Blume at al., 2009a).

At present, it is impossible to explain with precision exactly why the rates of success vary so widely, but it appears to be a combination of the availability of funding for investigative and expert services to "prove" an *Atkins* claim, and the particular jurisdiction's definition of intellectual disability. North Carolina and South Carolina both have reasonable indigent defense funding systems, whereas Alabama and Texas do not. From the outset, North Carolina and South Carolina adhered to the clinical definition of mental retardation and have taken into account the standard error of measurement and, if appropriate, the "Flynn effect," which refers to the widely recognized phenomenon that scores on standardized intelligence tests go up over time (this phenomenon is discussed in detail in chapter 10). In contrast to North and South Carolina, up until 2014, Alabama was one of a few states that employed a strict 70 IQ test score cutoff (also known as the "bright line standard) and Texas had identified seven "evidentiary factors," or "Briseño factors," (see Chapter 15) that triers-of-fact can consider when making their determination in *Atkins* cases. These factors include, for example, whether the defendant can formulate and carry out plans, can effectively lie or hide facts to protect the person's self-interest, and can respond appropriately and coherently. Though the decision as to how much weight to give to each factor is left to the trier-of-fact, it appears that Texas courts permit the death penalty if just one Briseño factor is met. Clearly, when Courts have gone outside of the bounds of the standards of practice, they have done so in a manner that makes it more difficult for claimants to succeed (Blume, Johnson, & Seeds, 2009b).

Another consideration to briefly mention is the state's choice of procedures (Blume, Johnson, & Seeds, 2012). There are two important ones: the first is the burden of proof and the second is whether the ultimate determination is made by a judge or a jury. With regard to burden of proof, most states require that the claimant prove ineligibility for the death penalty by a preponderance of the evidence. However, a few states have imposed higher burdens. One example is Georgia, where the defendant bears the burden of proving mental retardation beyond a reasonable doubt. Factors present in many *Atkins* cases (e.g., I.Q. test scores are not precise, the possibility of malingering, retrospective assessment) make it relatively easy for prosecutors to inject "reasonable doubt" into an *Atkins* proceeding. Imposing such a high burden of proof on defendants alleging that they have intellectual disability has made it virtually impossible for defendants to prevail (Blume et al., 2012).

The choice of a judge or a jury as the decision maker has been shown to have an impact on the outcome of *Atkins* proceedings. In jurisdictions where the fact-finder is the jury (e.g., Georgia, North Carolina, Texas), the success rate is low. As of 2012, not a single Texas jury had found a capital defendant to be a person with intellectual disability (Blume et al., 2012). As previously noted, in cases where judges are decision makers, the success rate is 40%. We cannot say exactly why juries are seemingly less receptive to assertions of ID than judges, but the empirical evidence suggests that jurors have more stereotypical views or misperceptions of the abilities of a person with ID, especially those at the upper end of the ID spectrum (see Chapter 3). It appears that jurors believe that a person who can read at all, work in any capacity, drive a car, or parent a child cannot have ID (Blume et al., 2012). Additionally, jurors appear to be more impacted by the facts of the crime than are judges (Boccaccini, Clark, Kan, Caillouet & Noland, 2010).

Assessment of Intellectual Disability in Capital Cases

Evaluations for the purpose of *Atkins* hearings must be exceedingly thorough, carefully documented, and conducted in a manner consistent with existing professional standards (as discussed throughout this book). The data gathered and reviewed must be expansive and contact with collateral sources mandatory rather than optional, with the number of contacts higher rather than lower. It is not acceptable to limit contacts to a few people or to just one domain of functioning; there must be breadth to the investigation. Contact with many people familiar with the claimant across settings (e.g., a teacher who was also a coach) or within one specific setting (e.g., an employer) must be attempted. Though not exhaustive, a list of potential collateral contacts includes family members (immediate and extended), friends, prior employers, coworkers, teachers, neighbors, and medical personnel. In many cases, these individuals will not have the level of contact necessary to complete a measure of adaptive behavior; however, their information remains very important. Qualitative information from sources such as these gives depth to the evaluation and allows for an intimate look into the day-to-day functioning of the claimant. Similar information can be gleaned from a broad and comprehensive review of records.

In all cases, two time points are of primary interest to the Court: (1) pre-18, which is necessary to qualify for the diagnosis, and (2) at the time of the crime. While not all courts require a current finding of ID, in virtually all cases, testimony regarding a claimant's functional abilities within the department of corrections will be presented. Despite concerns regarding bias, lack of knowledge regarding ID, and observations made solely within a restricted environment (i.e., behavior exhibited in a correctional facility), evaluators must not ignore this domain. Useful information can come from fellow inmates, correctional officers, medical staff, and clergymen, among others, so they should be interviewed and asked about their experiences with, and observations of, the claimant. What should not occur is the administration of an adaptive behavior measure within a correctional facility. These measures were designed to evaluate functioning in a community setting and are to be completed by people who have an intimate knowledge of the day-to-day functioning of the individual in that setting. Even in a community setting, few people meet the stringent criteria set forth in the manuals; in a setting as structured as that of a prison or jail, it is clear that an appropriate respondent does not exist.

The evaluation of ID in the context of an *Atkins* hearing requires a level of investigation that is far more in-depth than those conducted in a community setting. There must be a complete awareness on the part of the evaluator that the results of the investigation will be used in an adversarial setting and that their methods and interpretation of data will be scrutinized at a microscopic level. With the recognition that the perfect evaluation does not exist and each case is different, when the outcome is life or death, evaluators must be certain that they have provided data sufficient for the Court to make a fully informed decision. More importantly, evaluators must be able to explain their findings and do so in a clear and concise manner and be able to educate the Court about ID— what it is, what it is not, and how to assess the disorder in a manner that comports with research and standards of practice.

Stereotypes

Clinicians know that individuals who have ID show great diversity in abilities, interests, aptitudes, and personality, making them as unique as any individual without a disability. However, a review of reported cases and our own experience has demonstrated often that judges and jurors do not share this understanding. This is supported by social science research that has established that the public holds many inaccurate and generally negative stereotypes of individuals with ID (see also Chapter 3). Five decades ago, Guskin (1963) demonstrated that terms such as quiet, timid, unintelligent, abnormal, strange, helpless, and clumsy were adjectives representative of this population; these negative attitudes and attributions continue many years later (see for example, Antonak, Fiedler, & Mulick, 1989; Siperstein, Norins, Corbin, & Shriver, 2003; Siperstein, Parker, Bardon, & Widaman, 2007). In short, many people believe that persons with ID have no desirable characteristics or abilities, and a review of the cases decided suggests that evidence of adaptive strengths, even if quite limited, can, in the fact-finder's eyes, overwhelm evidence of adaptive deficits. Thus, a clinician conducting an *Atkins* evaluation must be aware of the presence of inaccurate, stereotypic beliefs and be prepared to inform the trier-of-fact of the nature of intellectual disability.

Another issue evaluators must be aware of is the strongly held, but false, belief that people with ID can be easily identified by external appearance (Antonak et al., 1989). In reality, the majority of individuals with ID cannot be identified by physical features and, in fact, are often described as "slow, but not mentally retarded." Descriptions such as this should be anticipated and evaluated for what they are: just one piece of information that cannot be considered dispositive one way or the other. Of note, individuals with little understanding of ID and who have had limited to no contact with individuals who have ID are often those that make such statements (e.g., correctional officers, employers, neighbors). Furthermore, our society has perpetuated the negative stereotype by producing movies that characterize people who have ID as predominately dependent (rather than independent) and easy to identify by speech (rate, tone and content), physical characteristics, and mannerisms (e.g., the main characters in the movies *Dominick and Eugene* and *Forrest Gump*). While these beliefs may be ameliorated by contact, the assumption can safely be made that the majority of people, including triers-of-fact, will have had limited contact with people who have ID.

A final stereotype should also be briefly discussed. In many cases, a death row inmate's positive adjustment to prison has been interpreted as evidence that he is not a person with ID. While clinicians understand that, for many reasons, that is not an accurate window into an individual's adaptive deficits, it is an issue that frequently arises and that evaluators must be prepared to address.

Standards of Practice

Regardless of the venue, the assessment of ID must be the same: there are three prongs to be assessed and, for two of the prongs (intelligence and adaptive behavior), tools are available. However, there is very little that has been standard in *Atkins* cases, and review of case law brings forth the realization that the bar has been raised. No longer is it acceptable for an evaluation to consist solely of the administration of an IQ test, the completion of adaptive behavior measures, and review of school records; the evaluation must extend beyond people who are invested in the well-being of the individual and must delve deep into the details of day-to-day functioning across multiple contexts. In addition, a prior finding of ID, whether it be in a legal proceeding (e.g., an evaluation for competence to stand trial) or in the community, is not sufficient to establish ID in the context of a capital proceeding.

Review of judicial opinions can provide insight into the way the judiciary views the methods of assessment in *Atkins* cases. Case law can inform clinicians about many issues that are novel to and/or confusing to the Court. Included among many are the presence of strengths and deficits for individuals with ID, proper and improper interpretation of tests (e.g., the application of the standard error of measurement; see Chapter 5), and the variability of skills exhibited by individuals who have intellectual disability. Adherence to standards of practice, within the confines of a retrospective assessment, is critical, as is interpretation of data and communication with the judiciary.

The Evaluator: Methods, Interpretation, and Communication Under the Microscope

First, consider a recent case in which the Court compared the validity of methodology employed by prosecution and defense experts. The following quotations were excerpted from *U.S. v. Smith* (2011; references to page numbers referencing testimony omitted). *Smith* was chosen as an example based on the level of detail provided in the opinion and had no relation to the outcome of this case (other cases in which analyses were also similarly complex are available and the interested reader is referred to the following cases: *Brumfield v. Cain,* 2012; *State v. Goodwin,* 2006; *United States v. Hardy,* 2010; *Holladay v. Campbell,* 2006; *Johnson v. State,* 2011; *State v. Lawson,* 2008).

Analysis

1. *Factor One: Significantly Sub-average Intellectual Functioning*

   a. Defense experts 1 & 2 administered the WAIS-III (defense expert 3 did not evaluate Smith, but instead testified to other issues, including the methods of assessment and the interpretation of data); expert 1 obtained a Full Scale IQ (FSIQ) = 67 and expert 2 an FSIQ= 67 (the former in 2004 and the latter in 2006). The Court noted that the consistency between these two scores supported the reliability of results, but still chose to conduct a more detailed investigation. The Court looked at verbal and performance IQ scores (which were nearly identical across the two administrations) and proceeded to conduct a fine-grained analysis of both raw scores and standard scores. The consistency was noted to be remarkable, and all three experts for the defense stated that this degree of consistency indicated good effort on the part of Smith and supported the validity and reliability of the results. The Court agreed with the opinion of the three experts.

   b. Prosecution expert 1 chose not to administer an IQ test, but instead "drew her conclusions as to Smith's intellectual functioning from his school, Job Corps, military, and prison records" (p. 34). The Court noted that this information is relevant to the assessment of adaptive behavior, but did not find it a substitute for a properly administered test of intelligence. Prosecution expert 1 cited ethical concerns regarding the videotaping of the administration of the IQ test; she stated that the concern related to public dissemination of the test questions which would render the test unusable. The Court did not believe that her concern was disingenuous, but that her choice not to follow the official position of the National Academy of Neuropsychology which identifies protective arrangements or protective orders from the court as possible solutions was in error.

   c. Prosecution expert 1 did interpret the WAIS-III data obtained by defense experts 1 and 2 and came up with vastly different conclusions. As noted in the judicial opinion, prosecution expert 1 "found several aspects of the comparative IQ testing to criticize which she asserted undermined their reliability" (p. 18). Prosecution expert 1 focused on perceived inconsistencies in response patterns between two different subtests (i.e., Digit Span and Letter-Number Sequencing), which the Court noted to be problematic: "As a threshold, the Court questions the appropriateness of comparing the results of one subtest with a different subtest and then arguing they are somehow inconsistent. It is akin to the proverbial comparing of apples and oranges" (p. 19). Similar sentiments were expressed by defense expert 3, who was noted to have "testified persuasively that it is not accepted practice in the professional community to compare answers to even the same question from one administration to another since natural variations occur within the same person from test to test." (p. 19). In the end, the Court found that the level of consistency found between the same subtests across evaluations supported the reliability of testing.

d. Prosecution expert 1 chose to focus on discrepancies in responses within the following three subtests: (1) vocabulary, (2) similarities, and (3) information. The Court deemed that not only was prosecution expert 1 in error for focusing on a few individual examples across test administrations, but noted that one of these interpretations was inaccurate to the degree that her qualifications and credibility were called into question.

e. Prosecution expert 1 interviewed Smith and during the interviews asked questions akin to those asked on the WAIS-III. Defense Expert 3 stated that the "idiosyncratic use of the WAIS items, without the standard instructions and with impermissible prompts, was unacceptable in the scientific community" (p. 21).

f. Prosecution expert 1 applied the Barona formula to the results of the intelligence tests administered by defense experts 1 and 2. The Barona formula is a demographically based index of premorbid intelligence for the WAIS-R, which, when applied to Smith's scores, resulted in a full scale IQ score in the average range. Defense expert 3 testified that the application of this formula is unacceptable and not in line with prevailing standards of practice. In fact, defense expert 3 informed the Court that "the lowest possible score a 59 year old black man could receive—"even if he's been hospitalized and is in a coma his whole life"—was a 73.9" (p. 36). Prosecution expert 1 was chided for her resistance to concede that the formula results in meaningless findings and was reminded that the Court had rejected this imputation in *Hardy*.

g. Prosecution expert 1 extrapolated Smith's IQ test score based on data from an unscored Wechsler Memory Scale. She testified that it is appropriate practice to extrapolate from IQ scores to predict WMS scores and, because of this, thought that it was equally appropriate to do the reverse. When asked if this was standard practice for psychologists, prosecution expert 1 stated that "she thought that many would but she did not know in fact if any actually did." (p. 37). Defense expert 3 explained to the Court that the reverse extrapolation was unacceptable in the professional and scientific community, and the Court agreed.

2. *Factor Two: Significant Limitations in Adaptive Functioning*

The Court directly stated that, unlike IQ testing, the assessment of adaptive behavior was inherently subjective and because of this, there is a heavy reliance on clinical judgment. She noted that "as the degree to which a matter is left to an individual clinician's judgment increases, so does the degree to which the Court must rely on its assessment of the relative competence and credibility of the individual experts to resolve disputes between them" (p. 47). In this case, the assessment of the credibility and competence of the experts was based in part on her current experience with each of them and in part on her past experiences with them in *Hardy*. As was the case in *Hardy*, the experts came to diametrically opposed positions with regard to deficits in adaptive behavior. Defense expert 1 found that Smith had substantial limitations in six areas with onset prior to the age of 18, while the prosecution expert found no significant adaptive functioning deficits once illicit substance use was taken out of the equation.

a. Defense expert 1 did the following: (1) reviewed records; (2) interviewed Smith; (3) interviewed family members; (4) administered adaptive behavior measures to three raters who were deemed to be appropriate; (5) required raters to complete adaptive behavior measures with regard to their memories of Smith's abilities when he was 17 years of age; (6) conducted non-standardized testing to evaluate Smith's ability to carry out some actions and how long they would take him; (7) administered the abbreviated version of the Kaufman Test of Educational Achievement–II to assess reading, spelling, and mathematical skills.

b. Prosecution expert 1: (1) reviewed records; (2) interviewed Smith; (3) criticized the results of the adaptive behavior measures, based on inconsistencies found on individual questions; (4) provided four reasons that supported the position that defense expert 1 had not scored the adaptive behavior measures according to the correct norms; (5) criticized the decision to use family members as the raters of adaptive behavior and cited bias as the reason; (6) did not speak to family members (she stated that she was told it was not possible), prior employers or friends of Mr. Smith; (7) tried to locate school personnel, but was unsuccessful; (8) had correctional officers fill out a measure of adaptive behavior

c. The Court: (1) undertook independent review of the responses to one of the adaptive behavior measures and found that 72% of the questions were identical for all three raters and where a discrepancy occurred, in the majority of the cases it was no more than one ranking and most often two of the three raters provided identical ratings. The same review was conducted on the other adaptive behavior measures and a similar level of consistency was found; (2) found that the reasons to believe that the adaptive behavior measures were incorrectly scored were "largely speculative and non-expert in nature" (p. 62); (3) used the consistency between raters to support the lack of bias, because if one or more of the raters deliberately downplayed Smith's level of functioning, it would have shown as an outlier; (4) reviewed the videotaped interviews and evaluated the interviewing skills/style/possible bias with regard to interpretations made by the experts; (5) evaluated the value of the data compiled by each expert to determine how much weight to give that information; (6) evaluated whether actions carried out by Smith were those that a person with mild intellectual disability could or could not do; and (7) reviewed records and/or evaluated the interpretations of the information as testified to during the hearing.

The discussion above, summarized from *U.S. v. Smith* (2011) illustrates the complexity of the review of diagnostic data. It is certainly typical for a court to conduct an analysis of methodology and to make a determination based on the breadth of the evaluation and the use of data. As made evident in *Smith,* expert methods, opinions and/or data are given different weight by the trier-of-fact and, in some cases, completely discarded. However, scrutiny goes beyond the trier-of-fact and extends to other members of the judiciary, as well as other mental health experts who participate in clinical or clinical-forensic assessment. As illustrated by the example of Dr. George Denkowski (see the following paragraph), experts can be sanctioned for using nonscientific approaches to assessment in *Atkins* cases.

In 2008, a model for evaluating the adaptive behavior of *Atkins* claimants was proposed by Denkowski and Denkowski. Based on opinion and conjecture, the Denkowskis created a model of assessment that purported to produce adaptive behavior scores that reflected "only *bona fide* disability" (p. 46). The model required that clinicians look at each skill rated less than 3 (the highest value) and decide if the skill was not used because it was "never taught (though could be learned), and/or for which there existed little performance incentive" (p. 46) and, in these cases, the rating should be adjusted upward. According to Denkowski and Denkowski, the need for correction was based on "socioculturally based suppression" secondary to an impoverished upbringing and the impact of lifestyle choices on the development of customary adaptive skills They also stated that scores should be adjusted for "adaptive skills that were demonstrated during the commission of crimes" (p. 55) and noted that they typically load on scales tapping the constructs of communication, self-direction (i.e., planning), and community use.

The Denkowski and Denkowski (2008) method has been criticized in the research community and regarded by the courts to be unreliable. George Denkowski acted as an expert in at least 25 *Atkins* cases, the majority for the state, and at least 14 people that he testified against were on death row at the time of his sanction in 2011. Following review of complaints to the Texas Board of Examiners in Psychology, the board chose to fine him and to ban him from conducting assessments of intellectual disability in *Atkins* cases. Though courts do not have to revisit the claims in the cases in which he acted as an expert, it is likely that many will. A statement by Senator Rodney Ellis (Connelly, 2011) captures the essence of the need to do so:

We must make sure that every case where Mr. Denkowski served as an expert is reviewed by the courts. We cannot simply shrug our shoulders and sit by and watch while the state uses legal technicalities to execute these people with intellectual [disability], especially on the word of someone who is no longer permitted to make these kinds of determinations.

A competent examiner conducts a comprehensive evaluation and demonstrates to the court that they have: (a) collected all available data (or attempted to); (b) considered all the data, the validity of the data, and the weight with which to give it; and (c) ruled out alternative diagnoses. Testimony and written reports provide avenues for communication with the Court and, because of this, fact-finders look to these documents to assess the credibility of the expert and their opinions. In *Thomas v. Allen* (2009), the Court directly stated that this type of analysis was conducted while, at the same time, highlighting the importance of comprehensive coverage of information in all documents provided for consideration:

> While the deficiencies of Dr. _____'s written report are painfully obvious, this court still must examine and consider his testimony at the evidentiary hearing to determine whether the paucity of substantive information contained in his written report simply reflects poor reporting practices, or whether it is indicative of an abbreviated, cursory evaluation (p. 67).

In this case, the issue noted above related to the lack of detail provided in the report. While there are no rules stipulating length of reports or even the content therein, guidelines for forensic practice exist and are readily available (see *Specialty Guidelines for Forensic Psychology, Committee on Ethical Guidelines for Forensic Psychologists,* Committee on Ethical Guidelines for Forensic Psychologists, 1991, 2013; Melton, Petrilla, Poythress, & Slobogin, 1997, 2007). The most recent version of the Specialty Guidelines Committee (American Psychological Association, 2013) is far more detailed than that of the original. The guidelines specifically address the issue of accuracy and completeness of written and oral communication within section 11.04:

> Consistent with relevant law and rules of evidence, when providing professional reports and other sworn statements or testimony, forensic practitioners strive to offer a complete statement of all relevant opinions that they formed within the scope of their work on the case, the basis and reasoning underlying the opinions, the salient data or other information that was considered in forming the opinions, and an indication of any additional evidence that may be used in support of the opinions to be offered. (p. 11)

Consistent with the above recommendations, all communications with the Court should be comprehensive and detailed. The trier-of-fact must be armed with enough information to competently evaluate the methods used by all experts and to understand how each came to their determinations.

Malingering

In any forensic case, especially one where life and death is literally at stake, questions of malingering (see Chapter 18) will frequently arise. Even when there is no hint of the process having arisen, prosecutors may argue that the claimant or collateral source (e.g., mother, employer, friend) has exaggerated or fabricated characteristics consistent with the diagnosis of ID. Thus, a clinician should always be prepared to address the issue and must show that they have critically evaluated the possibility and have done so in ways that comport with the methods appropriate for this population.

In *U.S. v. Smith* (2011), the Court cast light on the complexity of the assessment of malingering in cases in which ID is a possibility. Judge Berrigan made it clear that she looked at the totality of information when making her decision on the veracity of the final opinion as to malingering. For example, she looked at the consistency of data between tests, the results of two malingering tests completed during an ancillary assessment, and Smith's scores on the Digit Span subtest of the WAIS-III. Judge Berrigan also referenced the vast experience of two of the three examiners and noted that she trusted their clinical judgment over the results of testing. Of note is the judge's explicit recognition that the assessment of malingering for individuals suspected of having ID is in its infancy and that mistakes can be made:

> *Lastly*, the Court is not persuaded that malingering tests are particularly effective in populations suspected of possible intellectual disability. The reason should be obvious. If a person is genuinely mentally retarded, his responses may be similar to a person of normal intelligence who is trying to feign intellectual disability. Dr. _____ testified that formal effort assessments have not been standardized against a mentally retarded population, and Dr. _____ testified that formal malingering tests are not very reliable with persons in the lower cognitive functioning range. Therefore, using those formal assessments to determine malingering prior to first determining whether Smith is mentally retarded in the first place in effect puts the cart before the horse.

Salekin and Doane (2009) noted that available research demonstrated that assessment instruments used to assess cognitive malingering were ineffective for individuals with intellectual disability and that the errors in classification were in a dangerous direction. Misclassifications are those of *bona fide* cases being identified as malingered, a mistake that can result in the execution of an individual with ID. Data published since 2009 have continued to demonstrate errors in this direction (see, for example, Shandera et al., 2010).

An *Atkins* hearing is not a place to test new theories or base decisions on assumptions; it is a venue for clinicians who are ready to look at the construct of intellectual disability at its most microscopic level and move forward with an opinion based on science and the ethical and objective standards of practice.

References

Antonak, R. F., Fiedler, C. R., & Mulick, J. A. (1989). Misconceptions relating to mental retardation. *Mental Retardation, 27*, 91–97.

American Psychological Association (2013). Specialty guidelines for forensic psychology. *American Psychologist, 68*, 7–19.

Atkins v. Virginia, 536 U.S. 304, 310 (2002)

Blume, J. H., Johnson, S. L., & Seeds, C. C. (2009a). An empirical look at Atkins v. Virginia and its application in capital cases. *Tennessee Law Review, 76*(3), 627–640.

Blume, S. L., Johnson, S. L., & Seeds, C. C. (2009b). Of Atkins and men: Deviations from the clinical definition of mental retardation, *Cornell Journal of Law and Public Policy, 18*(3).

Blume, J. H., Johnson, S. L., & Seeds, C. C. (2014). Atkins: State procedural choices and their effect on outcome in capital cases. Unpublished manuscript, Cornell University.

Boccaccini, M. T., Clark, J. W., Kan, L., Caillouet, B., & Noland, R. M. (2010). Jury pool members' beliefs about the relation between potential impairments in functioning and mental retardation: implications for *Atkins*-type cases. *Law & Psychology Review, 34*, 1–24.

Brumfield v. Cain, No. 04–787–JJB–CN, 2012 WL 602163, at *18 (M.D. La. Feb. 23, 2012)

Committee on Ethical Guidelines for Forensic Psychologists. (1991). Specialty Guidelines for Forensic Psychologists. *Law and Human Behavior, 15*, 655–665.

Committee on Ethical Guidelines for Forensic Psychologists. (2013). Specialty Guidelines for Forensic Psychologists. *American Psychologist*. Retrieved from http://www.apa.org/practice/guidelines/forensic-psychology.pdf.

Connelly, R. (2011, April 15) Retrieved from http://blogs.houstonpress.com/news/2011/04/george_c_denkowski_dr_death_pe.php).

Denkowski, G. C., & Denkowski, K. M. (2008). Adaptive behavior assessment of criminal defendants with a mental retardation claim. *American Journal of Forensic Psychology, 26*, 43–61.

Ford v. Wainwright, 477 U.S. 399, 405(1986)

Guskin, S. L. (1963). Measuring the strength of the stereotype of the mental defective. *American Journal of Mental Deficiency, 67*, 569–575.

Holladay v. Campbell, 463 F.Supp.2d 1324 (N.D. Ala. 2006)

Johnson v. State, 59 So.3d 194 (Fla. 4th DCA 2011)

Koon v. Cain, (2008) No. 01-cv-327-JJB (M.D. La. Feb. 1, 2007) Doc. 111 at **13, 26 (slip op.) (unreported), *aff'd*, 277 Fed.Appx. 381 (5th Cir. 2008)

Melton, G., Petrila, J., Poythress, N., & Slobogin, C. (1997). *Psychological evaluations for the courts: A handbook for mental health professionals and lawyers* (2nd ed.). New York, NY: Guilford.

Melton, G., Petrila, J., Poythress, N., Slobogin, C., Lyons, P., & Otto, R. K. (2007). *Psychological evaluations for the courts: A handbook for mental health professionals and lawyers* (3rd ed). New York, NY: Guilford.

McCarver v. North Carolina, 533 U.S. 975 (2001).

Penry v. Lynaugh, 492 U.S 302 (1989).

Salekin, K. M., & Doane, M. (2009). Malingering intellectual disability: The value of available measures and methods. *Applied Neuropsychology, 16*(2), 105–113.

Shandera, A. L., Berry, D. T. R., Clark, J. A., Schipper, L. J., Graue, L. O., & Harp, J. P. (2010). Detection of malingered mental retardation. *Psychological Assessment, 22*, 50–56.

Siperstein, G. N., Norins, J., Corbin, S., & Shriver, T. (2003). *Multinational study of attitudes toward individuals with intellectual disabilities: General findings and call to action.* Washington, DC: Special Olympics.

Siperstein, G. N., Parker, R. C., Bardon, J. N., & Widaman, K. F. (2007). A national study of youth attitudes toward the inclusion of students with intellectual disabilities. *Exceptional Children, 73*, 435–455. doi: 10.1177/001440290707300403

State v. Williams, 2002831 So.2d 835, 859 (La. 2002)

State v. Goodwin, SC 86278., May 02, 2006—(MO Supreme Ct. 2006) S. L. (1963)

State v. Lawson, 12th Dist. Clermont No. CA2007-12-116, 2008-Ohio-6066 (*Lawson IV*)

Thomas v. Allen, 614 F. Supp.2d 1257 (N.D. Ala. 2009)

United States v. Hardy, 762 F. Supp. 2d 849, 866–68 (E.D. La. 2010)

United States v. Smith, 790 F.Supp.2d 482 (2011)

PART II
Assessment Considerations

A. General Topics

5 | Concepts of Measurement

Keith F. Widaman

Measurement and the accurate assessment of psychological characteristics are foundational problems for psychological science in general and for the diagnosis of intellectual disability (ID) in particular. But, psychology is not alone in the need for accurate measurement. All scientific work in any field rests on the qualities of the measurements obtained. If measurements are poor, scientific understanding and analyses of data will be compromised. Conversely, if high-quality measurements are available, firmer conclusions can be drawn in research settings and in applied decision making.

This chapter will discuss basic concepts of measurement. First, measurement will be defined and examples of measurements will be discussed. Next, levels of measurement will be distinguished, appropriate transformations of scores will be identified, and implications of these matters for applied work will be outlined. Third, the two major measurement theories—classical test theory and item response theory—will be briefly characterized. Then, the concept of reliability will be discussed, highlighting the central role of reliability in the concept of the standard error of measurement and its calculation. Fifth, the concept of validity will be introduced, with the six-pronged notion of construct validity that has become well established. The chapter will close with a series of implications for practice, based on problems with accurate measurement that arise in the evaluation of persons for having ID.

Measurement

Measurement is basic to work in any scientific field. However, careful consideration of the core aspects of measurement is often overlooked or taken for granted. Researchers and practitioners should be wary of neglecting any component of measurement, because precise understanding of the qualities of scores on intelligence tests and measures of adaptive behavior is predicated on a clear appreciation of all aspects of measurement. In this section, a standard definition of measurement will be discussed, followed by a discussion about the accuracy of measurements of manifest and latent variables.

Measurement Defined

Measurement may be defined as the *application of standard rules or procedures for assigning numbers to observations (or persons) to indicate the presence or absence or the magnitude of a characteristic*. The key components of this definition will be discussed in turn.

The first component of the definition of measurement is the need for standard rules or procedures of measurement of a characteristic. Rules and procedures involve multiple considerations. For example, when administering an intelligence test to a person, the setting in which the test is administered should be engaging and nonthreatening. The test administrator is advised to take time to develop rapport with the person to be assessed. But these are only the initial forms of rules and procedures. When giving a test, the test administrator must adhere to a wide range of rules. Included among these are rules regarding an appropriate starting point on each subtest, whether prompts can be given if an initial response to an item does not garner full credit and the form of prompts that are appropriate, the proper criterion for stopping the administration of items on each subtest, and then the manner in which item responses are combined into raw and standardized scores. Only if all standard rules and procedures are followed will test scores be interpretable.

The second aspect of the definition concerns the assigning of numbers. School children, members of the general public, and scientific researchers are all so well acquainted with the assigning of numbers to represent performance, such as school achievement, that little detail here is needed regarding the use of numbers to represent characteristics. But, as discussed in a later section, the numbers assigned for a particular characteristic will fall on one of several scales or levels of measurement. These different scales serve different purposes, have different properties, and are subject to different constraints with regard to transformation of numeric values. Therefore, the seemingly simple process of assigning numbers to observations may be more complex, or at least have more involved implications, than may be perceived initially.

The third component of the definition of measurement involves the observations to which the numbers are assigned. The term "observations" can seem stilted, because the observations in *Atkins* capital cases are of persons who are to be evaluated with regard to having ID. But, use of the term observations can be justified on several grounds, two of which are highlighted here. First, the generic term observations can apply to many fields of study, in many of which the observations are not persons. Ranging across fields of study, observations may be animals, minerals, plants, or even trials in a nuclear accelerator when trying to split an atom. Second, and germane to *Atkins* case dispositions, we make observations on observations. That is, we make observations (i.e., measurements) on observations (i.e., persons). The key observations of our measurement are persons, about whom a diagnosis of ID is of concern. But, we also must keep in mind that we only have the opportunity to observe the person in certain situations on certain occasions. These various observations—each with numbers applied to indicate characteristics—must then be combined in the process of clinical judgment to arrive at a diagnostic decision.

The fourth and final aspect of the definition concerns the characteristic to be assessed. Some characteristics are either present or absent, such as presence of cerebral palsy. In these situations, the numbers assigned serve a naming function, indicating that the person falls in one class or another. Other attributes are assumed to fall on a continuum, so numbers are used to indicate individual differences in magnitude of the characteristic. The two key domains (or prongs) used in diagnosing intellectual disability are intelligence and adaptive behavior. Both of these are personal competence attributes and they fall on two different continuums. Regardless of whether the characteristic reflects a classification or a continuum, the characteristic being assessed is perhaps the most important object of measurement—that is, the construct used to characterize the person.

Measurement Exemplified

With a definition of measurement outlined, examples of how measurements are obtained are useful. Here, we will distinguish between measurement of manifest characteristics and of latent characteristics. Examples with manifest characteristics allow concrete examples of how to measure accurately. These ideas will be generalized to the assessment or measurement of latent, less apparent characteristics.

Manifest characteristics. Certain attributes or characteristics are important in their manifest or directly observable form. Two examples are height and weight. Height and weight of a newborn are carefully measured because of their importance in prognosis of the path of early development. Then, throughout childhood and into adolescence, doctors continue to monitor growth in height and weight to ensure that optimal patterns of growth are occurring.

Consider measurement operations designed to assess height most accurately in children or adolescents. Measurements of height could be made in a fairly direct simple fashion, asking the target person to stand next to a wall, placing a mark on the wall corresponding to the top of the person could be made in a fairly direct fashion, asking the target person to stand next to a wall, placing a mark on the wall corresponding to the top of the person's head, and then using a tape measure to find the distance from the floor to the mark on the wall. But, certain refinements will help ensure that the measurement of height is more accurately determined. For example, the target person should remove his or her shoes, so that the thickness of the soles of shoes is not included in the height measurement. Then, the person should be told to stand up as straight as possible, and the use of an apparatus that can be raised or lowered so that it just touches the top of the person's head will provide for greater accuracy in determining standing height.

Even with all diligence in measuring height accurately, multiple measurements of the height of the same target person—by different examiners, perhaps at multiple points of an assessment session—may not agree perfectly. If this should occur, the mean (arithmetic average) of the multiple measurements will probably be the optimal estimate of the person's height. Importantly for the present discussion, the standard deviation of the multiple measurements is an index of the precision with which height is measured. The larger the standard deviation, the less accurately height was measured; conversely, the smaller the standard deviation, the greater the accuracy in height measurements. This standard deviation is the standard error of measurement of height, and the concept of a standard error of measurement will attain crucial importance when we attempt to measure or assess intelligence or adaptive behavior (see later in the chapter).

Latent characteristics. Concrete, manifest characteristics provide a useful introduction to the assessment of attributes. But, many of the characteristics of most interest to researchers of ID are latent variables or characteristics, characteristics that cannot be assessed directly. Indeed, the two central constructs used in diagnosis of ID—intelligence and adaptive behavior—are latent characteristics or constructs. One cannot directly measure either intelligence or adaptive behavior. Instead, professionals must rely on scores derived from administration of batteries of measures to the person being evaluated and/or to individuals who know the person well. When an intelligence test is administered to a person, we use the responses by the person to the items on the test to infer that the person has a particular level of intelligence. This issue should always be borne in mind—that we cannot measure intelligence directly, only indirectly. Moreover, combining item responses to yield a particular intelligence test score provides a basis for inference, involving clinical judgment, of the level of the target person's intelligence.

Ideas about the accuracy of measures of latent characteristics are similar, but not identical, to those developed for manifest characteristics. The similarities include the notion of a standard error of measurement, which will be of great importance when evaluating scores on tests of intelligence and batteries of adaptive behavior. But, assessment of latent characteristics (e.g., general intelligence) provides notable contrasts when compared to measurement of manifest characteristics (e.g., a full-scale IQ score). Chief among the differences between assessments of the two types of characteristics is this: whereas one could conceive of using the same instrument (e.g., a tape measure) an infinite number of times to measure the height of an individual, using the same instrument an infinite number of times to measure the intelligence of an individual would not be advised. Using the same tape measure a large number of times would not be likely to lead to any systematic bias over time when assessing height. But, when assessing intelligence, using the same measuring instrument or test on numerous occasions might well lead to memory (or practice) effects that might, for example, enhance scores over time or lead to a fatigue effect that would serve to lower scores over time. Suffice it to say that measurement of latent characteristics is substantially more difficult and involved than assessment of manifest attributes, and the need for clinical judgment to combine all information to arrive at important diagnostic decisions is always a component of this assessment task.

Scales of Measurement

The numbers assigned to observations are just numbers. But, the numbers used to assess one characteristic may have very different properties than the numbers used to assess a different characteristic. These differential properties of numbers used to measure characteristics are usually discussed under the rubric of different levels or scales of measurement.

The delineation of four levels or scales of measurement has been a customary way to discuss differences among types of measurements. These four levels are the nominal, ordinal, interval, and ratio levels of measurement. The notion that all measurements fall at one or another of these four levels is an oversimplification, as additional levels of measurement could be identified. These four levels of measurement, however, enable discussion of key distinctions among different types of scales and are sufficient for present purposes.

Nominal Scale

The first and most basic level of measurement is the nominal scale. Befitting its title, a nominal scale uses numbers as names, to indicate that a person falls in one class or another. Nominal variables are common in the behavioral sciences. Some nominal scales describe two classes, such as the variable of sex, with males (= 0) and females (= 1) constituting the two classes. Work on test bias seeks to investigate whether items or tests demonstrate bias or, in other words, function differently across ethnic groups. In work of this sort, an ethnicity variable might have 4 or 5 or more categories, such as European American (= 1), African American (= 2), Hispanic (= 3), Asian American (= 4), and Other (= 5).

The numeric values on a nominal scale can be easily transformed or changed in any way and still retain the information provided by the numbers. The ordering of values on a nominal variable has no implication for "more or less" of an attribute, so changing the numeric values assigned to classes has no fundamental importance. For example, the variable of sex could employ values of 0 for male and 1 for female, 1 for male and 2 for female, or 9 for male and 20 for female. Use of any of these sets of numeric values is arbitrary and performs the same function of differentiating males and females. Certain values may be more useful when used in particular statistical models. In this regard, the use of (0, 1) coding has benefits when estimating coefficients in regression models. However, aside from this consideration, numeric values on a nominal scale can be transformed in any fashion with no loss of information.

Ordinal Scale

The ordinal scale is the next level of measurement and provides basic information about the magnitude of a characteristic. Numeric values can range from one value that represents the lowest level of the attribute, another value that represents the highest level of the attribute, and values between these two that reflect ordered levels of the attribute. Perhaps the most common exemplar of an ordinal scale is the Mohs mineral hardness scale, which ranges from talc (= 1) to diamond (= 10). Numeric values on the hardness scale reflect the ability of one mineral to scratch another. All other minerals can scratch talc and talc cannot scratch any other mineral, so talc has the lowest value on the scale (= 1); diamond can scratch all other minerals and no minerals can scratch diamond, so diamond has the highest value on the scale (= 10). The so-called Likert rating scales frequently used in psychology and many other disciplines, which may range from 1–5 or 1–7, are essentially ordinal scales of measurement.

As noted above, numeric values on an ordinal scale range from a lowest value to a highest value, and the values indicate relative position on the underlying continuum. However, the distance between particular scale values is not invariant across the scale. That is, the difference between values of 1 and 2 may not represent the same difference on the underlying attribute as the difference between values of 4 and 5. When assessing adaptive behavior, for example, ratings on items are often collected on a scale such as 0 = cannot perform the behavior, 1 = can perform but only with substantial support, 2 = can perform with minimal support, and 3 = can perform without support. Values on this 0–3 scale clearly reflect different levels of facility in performing the behavior. However, it would be difficult to say whether the movement from 0 to 1 on this rating scale is a smaller, equal, or larger change than that represented by movement from 2 to 3. Thus, the ordinal scale has numeric values that reflect relative standing on an attribute, but the numeric values have intervals of unknown or undefined value or magnitude.

Acceptable transformations of ordinal scale values must retain the relative standing of observations, but a numeric transformation is acceptable. For example, on the Mohs mineral hardness scale, one could retain the numeric values for minerals between 1 and 5, and then add 10 to all values above 5, so diamond would now have a hardness scale value of 15. Such a rescaling might make little sense for empirical application, but does retain the relative standing of observations, so it is acceptable. Standard forms of parametric statistics (parametric statistics refer to statistical analyses based on assumptions about the parameters of a distribution, as noted with these two examples), such as correlation and linear regression, are technically difficult to justify when applied to ordinal variables, given the wide range of transformations of numeric values that are acceptable with such variables. If a nonlinear transformation of values on an ordinal scale were made, the resulting variable would likely have a very different correlation with external variables than would the original ordinal variable. Nonparametric statistics (nonparametric statistics refer to statistical analyses in which such assumptions about the parameters distribution cannot be met, as is typically the case with ordinal data) for testing differences between means and estimating correlations between variables have been developed as an alternative for statistical analysis; these nonparametric statistics yield invariant values under transformations and, therefore, can be used with ordinal variables. Thus, care must be taken to select proper statistical techniques when analyzing ordinal variables.

Interval Scale

An interval scale adds to the ordinal scale the stipulation that differences between scale values are identical across the scale. Consider the Fahrenheit temperature scale (°F), with values of 32 °F and 212 °F for the freezing and boiling points, respectively, of water at sea level. On this scale, the one-unit difference between 34 °F and 35 °F represents exactly the same change in thermodynamic activity as the one-unit difference between 134 °F and 135 °F, and this holds for all one-unit differences on the scale. The zero point on an interval scale is often arbitrary, as is true of the Fahrenheit scale. But, the equal intervals at all points on the interval scale make the use of standard parametric statistics analyses appropriate. The subtest, part, and global composite adaptive behavior and intelligence test scaled or standard scores for all major intelligence tests used in the diagnosis of ID (also see Chapter 7) are interval scale metrics.

Linear transformations of numeric values on an interval scale are acceptable (a linear transformation has the form $Y' = a + bY$, where Y' represents values on the transformed scale, a is an additive constant, b is a multiplicative constant, and Y represents values on the original interval scale. The only stipulation in the linear transformation is that b must be a positive value, so must be greater than zero). For example, the Celsius temperature scale (°C), which is used in most countries of the world, is a linear transformation of the Fahrenheit scale. The Celsius scale has 0 °C and 100 °C for the freezing and boiling points, respectively, of water at sea level. Thus, values on the Celsius scale can be obtained from the Fahrenheit scale using the following linear transformation: °C = (°F – 32) × (5/9). A reverse transformation can be used to obtain °F from °C, using °F = (°C × 1.8) + 32. The transformation of temperature readings from °F from °C or vice versa leaves all information about temperature and differences between temperatures intact. Linear transformations are used frequently in research in psychology and the behavioral sciences One of the most common is the transformation of values on a variable Y into z-score form. The z-score transformation is $[z_y = (Y - \bar{Y})/s_y]$, where z_y is the z transform of Y, $\bar{Y}$ is the mean of Y, and s_y is the standard deviation of Y scores. Once a variable is in z-score form, scores on the variable can be rescaled into any metric desired. For example, multiplying the z scores by 15 and then adding 100 rescales the scores into an IQ metric, with a mean of 100 and a standard deviation of 15. Employing a linear transformation leaves all information, including the correlation with external variables, unchanged.

Ratio Scale

The fourth scale of measurement is the ratio scale, which has equal intervals but also has an absolute, or non-arbitrary, zero point. Continuing the example of temperature, degrees on the Kelvin scale (K) fall on an absolute scale. The lowest temperature on the K scale is approximately –273.15 on the Celsius scale. Thus, 0 K is the lowest point on the Kelvin scale, and this temperature represents the absence of thermodynamic activity. Given the differences between the Kelvin and Celsius scales, 0 K is the absolute zero of the Kelvin scale, 273.15 K is the freezing point of water, and 373.15 K is the boiling point of water at sea level.

In the behavioral sciences, certain variables used in research deserve the denotation of a ratio scale. One example is reaction time to a stimulus. Reaction time is usually measured from the point at which a stimulus is given, and reaction time is the time from stimulus presentation to a button press that registers response. Some physiological signals also conform to the definition of a ratio scale, provided that the zero point on the scale has a non-arbitrary designation. Only on a ratio scale are conclusions regarding multiplicative relations among values justified. That is, it is accurate to say that a reaction time of 1200 ms is twice as long as a reaction time of 600 ms.

Transformations permissible for a ratio scale are primarily multiplicative. Multiplication by a positive constant (not equal to zero) preserves the location of the zero point and equality of intervals. For example, if reaction times are recorded in milliseconds, then 1000 ms corresponds to 1 sec. If reporting time in seconds, rather than milliseconds, is easier to discuss, then dividing values in milliseconds yields times in seconds. The scores derived from adaptive behavior and intelligence tests used in the diagnosis of ID do not fall on ratio scales.

Normative Samples and Normalizing Transformations

Constructs such as intelligence and adaptive behavior are typically measured using scales that consist of large numbers of items. Many items on intelligence tests are scored in dichotomous fashion (0 = incorrect, 1 = correct) or ternary form (0 = incorrect, 1 = partial credit, 2 = full credit). Other items may be scored based on time taken to complete a set of operations, so they might lead to a transformation of time, with longer times to solve receiving lower scores. On adaptive behavior batteries, items are usually rated on scales, such as 0 (= cannot perform behavior) to 3 (= can perform without support).

All of the preceding item types correspond, generally, to ordinal scales. Thus, at the item level, the measurement properties of each item do not convey equal interval information. Further, the ways to combine ordinal variables into total scores present difficulties when attempting to ensure that a total score across a number of items retains the same ordering of individuals, even if the items are separately transformed. Technically, if a variable is ordinal in nature, an ordinal statistical approach should be taken to analyze the scores from the variable. The advantage of ordinal statistical approaches is that statistical test results will be invariant under the nonlinear transformations that are permissible for ordinal variables.

Normative Samples

When large numbers of items are summed into total scores, the total scores, while still technically only ordinal in nature, begin to function much like interval scales. Because of this, it is reasonable, frequently, to compute means and standard deviations on total scores and to correlate total scores with other variables. Standard parametric statistics—such as t-tests, analysis of variance, and correlation/regression analysis—assume, at least implicitly, that the scores being analyzed fall on an interval scale. As noted, once a large number of items are summed to form a total score, the resulting total score tends to behave consistently when subjected to various kinds of parametric analysis, so the total scores are treated as if they conveyed interval information. The subtest, part, and global composite scores from adaptive behavior scales and intelligence tests are examples of scores that are based on the sum of items that can then be treated as interval scale scores.

The use of normative samples aids in the movement from ordinal item information to more metric total score information. All well-standardized measuring instruments have been administered to large, representative samples from across the country, samples called norming samples. A norming sample is typically selected to be representative of the population of a country with regard to region of residence, socioeconomic status, ethnicity, and other relevant demographic variables. The norming samples of adaptive behavior and intelligence tests serve as representative "snap shots" of the complete population or country. If a measure, such as an intelligence test or inventory of adaptive behavior, assesses constructs presumed to vary as a function of chronological age, then norming samples for each age level must be obtained.

Normalizing Transformations

Many human characteristics follow an approximate normal distribution, and researchers often assume that intelligence and adaptive behavior scores also are normally distributed. Based on this assumption, data from performance by a norming sample can be used to transform raw scores (derived from the summing of sets of individual items) into an approximate normal distribution of standardized scores. Such a transformation is called a normalizing transformation, because it transforms raw scores, which may be quite skewed positively or negatively, into standardized scores that are as normally distributed as allowed by the data. Once a normalizing transformation is applied, norm tables allow one to derive a standard score for an individual that represents his or her performance in relation to the population of persons of the same age. The standard scores, again technically only ordinal in nature, are commonly subjected to parametric statistical procedures that presume the presence of interval data, and results tend to generalize well across samples, justifying the practice.

Approaches to Test Development and Norming

One final issue that may have great importance for diagnosis of ID is the approach taken for norming an instrument. This refers to the differing approaches taken in formulating a single instrument for a wide age span versus the development of a number of different, coordinated forms for more restricted age spans. For example, the Stanford-Binet Intelligence Test (SB5; Roid, 2003) consists of a single instrument with a very large number of items that range in difficulty from items appropriate for young children all the way to items appropriate for persons in middle and older adulthood. The Woodcock-Johnson III (WJ III) tests (Woodcock, McGrew, & Mather, 2001; Woodcock, McGrew, Schrank, & Mather, 2007) and the new Woodcock-Johnson IV (WJ IV) (Schrank, McGrew, Mather, & Woodcock, 2014) also have this form and can be administered to persons between the ages of 2 and 89 years. For the SB5 and WJ III tests, the norming sample was one very large sample with large numbers of participants within key age ranges, spanning the entire age span from preschool through late adulthood.

The Wechsler tests were developed with a very different approach. The Wechsler Adult Intelligence Scale (WAIS; current version is WAIS-IV; Wechsler, 2008) is appropriate for persons ages 16 and older. Then, a downward extension was developed, the Wechsler Intelligence Scale for Children (WISC; current version is WISC-IV; Wechsler, 2003), which can be administered to persons between the ages of 6 and 16 years. Finally, yet another downward extension, the Wechsler Preschool and Primary Scale of Intelligence (WPPSI; current version is WPPSI-III; Wechsler, 2002) can be administered to children between the ages of 2.5 and 7 years. The norming samples for the WAIS-IV consisted of persons aged 16 to 90, with determination to sample extensively in the lower levels of this age range and then less extensively at older age ranges. Not surprisingly, the WISC-IV normative samples included only children and adolescents between the ages of 6 and 16 years, and the WPPSI-IV normative samples included children only between the ages of 2.5 and 7 years. As a result, performance on a given Wechsler test that falls outside normative performance for the particular test will not be accurately estimated.

Because scores on the SB5 and Wechsler tests tend to correlate at approximately .82 to .90, researchers and experts have long presumed that the two tests had very similar qualities. However, Silverman and colleagues (2010) uncovered striking differences in scores on earlier versions of the two tests. In their study, Silverman et al. examined data from a sample of 74 individuals with ID (primarily adults with Down syndrome) who had been administered the then-current version of both the Stanford-Binet and WAIS during the period 1949–2005. The sample had not been administered the SB5 or the WAIS-IV. Nevertheless, for cases that rely on retrospective diagnosis (e.g., *Atkins* cases), it is important to be aware that earlier versions of the Stanford-Binet may have yielded systematically lower scores than the Wechsler scales. In the Silverman et al. (2010) study, the WAIS yielded scores for this population that were an average of 16.7 points higher than the Stanford-Binet, although the two tests yielded scores that were correlated .82.

Although the SB5 and WAIS-IV do not appear to yield systematically different scores as earlier versions of these tests did, it is useful to note that they used different approaches to test development and norming. Because the SB5 (Roid, 2003) is a simple test for a wide age range, it can offer more accurate estimates of mental functioning and the associated IQ score in the lower tail of the distribution. In contrast, because the WAIS-IV (Wechsler, 2008) was formulated for assessing persons ages 16 and older, its normative samples do not allow for as accurate a determination IQ scores in the lower tail of the distribution.

Implications for Practice

Psychological measures of intelligence and adaptive behavior consist of large numbers of items, each of which falls on an ordinal scale. Although individual items are ordinal, the total scores based on large numbers of items represent sufficiently stable scores that can be assumed to have the characteristics and benefits of interval scaled scores. The numerical difference between an IQ score of 80 and one of 90 is 10 points and is the same numerical difference as the difference between IQ scores of 100 and 110. In addition, the expert should inspect the approach to the norming of a test, to determine whether the test has sufficient accuracy or precision in assessing intelligence or adaptive behavior in the range relevant for diagnosis.

Measurement Theories

In the early years of the 20th century, basic theoretical ideas concerning measurements and the attendant errors that perturb measurements were formulated. These ideas were formalized and became known as classical test theory. Then, in midcentury, a new measurement theory was developed, termed item response theory (IRT) or modern test theory. These two test theories are discussed briefly in the appendix to this chapter to highlight the unique features of each.

Reliability

The central notion of reliability involves the accuracy or precision with which an attribute is measured. In effect, the central question of reliability is the reproducibility of scores using the measuring instrument. Reliability thus answers the question about how accurately an instrument measures whatever it is that is being measured. The higher the reliability, the greater the precision with which observed scores on a measure represent an individual's true score on the dimension assessed. Whether an instrument measures what it is designed to measure is a topic covered under the heading of validity, to be discussed in a later section.

Types of Reliability

Reliability of a test score can be assessed in a number of ways. Several of the most important means for doing so are discussed in this section. Most of these forms of reliability are based on classical test theory approaches, but item response theory offers some new insights on reliability.

Parallel forms. Alternate forms of a test are considered parallel forms if, within limits of empirical precision, the forms tend to correlate highly and to have the same mean, same standard deviation, and same correlation with external variables. Parallel forms should be carefully designed to have different, but similar, content, so the two forms clearly assess the same domain of content. If parallel forms of a measure are available, one can administer the two parallel forms to a single sample at a single time of measurement. The correlation between scores on the parallel forms can be designated as r_{yy}, the reliability of each parallel form. That is, r_{yy} is the reliability of Form 1 using Form 2 as its parallel form, and the same value is the reliability of Form 2 using Form 1 as its parallel form. Parallel forms reliability has been termed a coefficient of equivalence, because it is an index of the similarity or equivalence of scores across the two forms. One notable example of parallel forms for assessing intelligence was the revised version of the Stanford-Binet intelligence test (Terman & Merrill, 1937), which had Forms L and M that were carefully constructed to be parallel in content.

Parallel forms reliability can lead to an underestimate of test reliability under certain circumstances. For example, if the forms are long, the participants may become fatigued, and may obtain lower scores on questions answered later in the sequence than they would have otherwise obtained. But, one advantage of parallel forms reliability is that, being administered at a single time of measurement, there is low likelihood that the characteristic being assessed has changed in any major way. Thus, information from parallel forms reliability must be integrated with other information to arrive at a clear understanding of reliability.

Test-retest. Parallel forms are expensive and difficult to develop, so test authors often prepare a single form of a test. If only a single form of a test is available, other forms of reliability must be calculated. One of the most common forms of reliability is test-retest reliability. Here, one administers a single test to a single group on two separate occasions, with a lag between measurements of 1 month, 2 months, or more. Test-retest reliability has been termed a coefficient of stability, because it indexes the degree of rank-order stability of scores across the two occasions.

Test-retest reliability can underestimate reliability of a measure for several reasons, including growth or change in the underlying dimension across time. However, for a relatively slowly changing characteristic, such as intelligence or adaptive behavior, a lag of 1 or 2 months between assessments should not be associated with substantial growth or change. Test-retest can also overestimate reliability due to memory or practice effects (that is, if the test administrations are done too closely in time; see also Chapters 7–9). Once again, test-retest reliability is just one approach to reliability and should be integrated with other information.

Internal consistency or homogeneity. A third form of reliability is based on administration of a single test to a single group at a single time of measurement. The first way of estimating reliability under these circumstances is termed split-half reliability. For example, one could derive one score from odd-numbered items, a second score from even-numbered items, and then correlate these two scores.

There are a large number of ways to divide a set of test items into split halves. Therefore, results were sought that would estimate a summary across all possible split halves. These coefficients are discussed under the rubric of internal consistency or homogeneity coefficients. For dichotomous items, Kuder and Richardson (1937) derived a number of important special cases, the most generally useful being the KR-20 formula, so named because it was the 20th formula in their article. The KR-20 formula provides the average of all possible split-half reliabilities for a test composed of dichotomous items. Later, Cronbach (1951) generalized this coefficient to items with more than two response categories (e.g., to items answered on 1–5 rating scales), and the resulting coefficient became known as coefficient alpha, the most widely used measure of reliability in psychology.

Later work by McDonald (1999), among others, led to various coefficients of reliability, including, most importantly, coefficient omega. Both coefficient alpha and coefficient omega require the assumption that a single dimension is being assessed by a set of items. More formally, if a factor analysis of correlations among items is performed, only a single factor will be present. An implicit assumption of the use of coefficient alpha is that all items have identical factor loadings in a raw score, or covariance, metric, which is a restrictive assumption. Coefficient omega is a more accurate estimate of reliability if a set of items has differing loadings on the single factor, which is usually a more reasonable expectation. Coefficient omega is greater than or equal to coefficient alpha, being equal to alpha when factor loadings are equal.

Homogeneity coefficients can be accurate estimates of reliability under most conditions. But, certain kinds of split-half reliability will be misleading if certain circumstances hold. For example, items on many intelligence tests and measures of adaptive behavior are ordered by difficulty, with easier items asked first and more difficult items asked later. Also, rules are often invoked to stop the administration of items, such as testing is discontinued after 3, 4, 5, or 6 consecutive items are failed (a ceiling rule). At the other end of the test continuum, examinees are often started at different initial points (based on age or grade), and the test directions require a minimum number of correct answers in a row, below which the easier items are not administered—assumed to be correct (a basal rule). Under such testing conditions, odd-even split-half reliability could lead to a serious positive bias in estimate of reliability, so should not be used. (In practice, this issue is often overcome by assuming that, for all subjects who took the set of items for a subtest in the norming sample, all items below a basal are correct and all items above the ceiling are incorrect. This results in a complete set of scores for all items, and thus split-half reliabilities can be calculated. These reliabilities are often considered reasonable approximations of the reliability of a test, although they likely reflect inflated estimates of the true reliability of the test.)

Other forms of reliability. Many other forms of reliability could be considered. For example, for tests in which some interpretation of responses is required, inter-scorer reliability might be an issue. Or, on adaptive behavior measures, a professional often interviews an informant who knows the target person well, and multiple informants might be available to report on the target person's behavior. In such situations, inter-informant reliability might be very important, with greater agreement across informants providing stronger presumptions that adaptive behavior scores accurately represent the target person. All of these forms of reliability should be considered when drawing conclusions about the accuracy and precision of scores from any psychological or behavioral test.

Marginal reliability. Marginal reliability is derived from the use of item response theory (IRT) methods (see the Appendix) and represents, in essence, the average reliability across the entire measurement scale. For example, intelligence test scores vary, largely, between about 60 and 140 in the population, with a few scores falling outside this range. The marginal reliability of an intelligence test would be the average reliability across the range from 60 to 140, acknowledging that reliability might be higher in some score ranges and lower in other score ranges.

Standard Error of Measurement

The standard error of measurement is a characteristic of a theoretical distribution, representing the standard deviation of scores on a given dimension for an individual across an infinite number of times of testing. That is, assuming that one could assess an individual an infinite number of times on, for example, a test of intelligence, one would not assume that the person would obtain precisely the same score on each administration. Instead, one would expect a distribution of scores, presumably a normal distribution, centered on the person's true score for intelligence. The mean of this theoretical distribution would be the best estimate of the person's true score, and the standard deviation of the distribution would be the standard error of measurement. Thus, the standard error of measurement indicates the standard deviation of errors when manifest IQ scores stand for true IQ scores.

Under classical test theory, the standard error of measurement is a function of reliability, with higher reliability associated with a smaller standard error of measurement. (The standard error of measurement, or σ_e, is computed as: $\sigma_e = \sigma_Y\sqrt{1 - r_{yy}}$ where all terms were defined above. For example, if IQ scores have a mean of 100 and standard deviation of 15 and the reliability of the scores were determined to be $r_{yy} = .96$, the standard error of measurement of these scores would be $\sigma_e = 15\sqrt{1-.96} = 15\sqrt{.04} = 15(.2)$

= 3 points.) With a standard error of 3 points, for example, a 95% confidence interval (high level of confidence in the score accuracy) estimate of a person's IQ score would be computed as the point estimate of IQ ± (i.e., plus or minus) 1.96 (3) points, or IQ ± 6 points. Some major intelligence tests report reliabilities in excess of .97, leading to a standard error of measurement around 2.5 points. A standard error of measurement of 2.5 leads to a 95% confidence interval that is the person's observed score ± 5 points. For this reason, the American Association on Intellectual and Developmental Disabilities (AAIDD) and other professional organizations (e.g., Schalock et al., 2010) often state that an IQ score in the range from 71–75 can be used to diagnose ID, because an observed IQ score in the 71–75 range is consistent with a true IQ score of 70, given the standard error of measurement.

Applied researchers and experts should beware of the use of potential positive bias in reliability estimates. All reliability estimates for a measure should be scrutinized in an effort to arrive at an informed sense of the accuracy of measures. The homogeneity coefficient, or split-half reliability, of a measure might be .96 or .97, but this might be a positively biased estimate. If the test-retest reliability is lower, say around .90, a substantial increase in the standard error of measurement would occur. For example, if r_{yy} = .91, then the standard error of measurement would be $\sigma_e = 15\sqrt{1 - .91} = 15\sqrt{.03} = 15(.3)$ = 4.5 points, and the 95% confidence interval around a person's observed score would their IQ ± 9 points, a much wider range of uncertainty with regard to the location of the person's true score. Under this scenario, an IQ score in the range from 71–79 or even 71–80 might be considered adequate for diagnosis of ID, based on the standard error of measurement.

One final topic regarding the standard error of measurement involves the use of IRT models to evaluate measurement instruments. Under IRT, the standard error of measurement is not assumed to be constant across the ability scale, as occurs under classical test theory. Instead, properties of items allow the calculation of the standard error of measurement for various score ranges. For many instruments, the resulting standard error of measurement may be relatively small in the middle of the score range (e.g., between about 80 and 120 on the IQ scale), but may be larger in the tails of the distribution. Because the lower tail of the distribution contains the typical cut-score for diagnosis of ID, a relatively large standard error of measurement in the lower tail would mean that scores in that part of the distribution are measured less accurately or precisely. If this should occur, the expert might use clinical judgment to argue for a wider uncertainty range (e.g., 71–80 might be sufficient to support a diagnosis of ID). As IRT becomes more widely used for test development, this concern will attain greater importance and become the focus of more discussion.

Implications for Practice

Experts who testify in *Atkins* hearings should pay particular attention to the estimates of reliability and standard error of measurement for any measure they use or interpret.

These estimates appear in the technical manuals for published tests and should be scru-tinized carefully. For instance, if the test-retest reliability of a measure is substantially lower than the split-half reliability, a case might be made that the test-retest reliability is a more reasonable basis for estimating the standard error of measurement. Further-more, for measures of adaptive behavior, it is common to have substantially lower lev-els of inter-respondent reliability than reported for the spilt-half reliability for a single respondent. Experts should identify the inter-respondent reliability for measures of adaptive behavior, which often falls in the range from .85 to .90. Having a firm grasp on the various kinds of reliability of a measure is critical to the development of an adequate portrayal of accuracy of scores.

The accuracy of scores in the lower tail of the distribution of intelligence and adap-tive behavior is of paramount importance in diagnostic situations. Experts should con-sult the technical manual for the tests that they use in order to be aware of different ways that reliability (and hence the standard error of measurement or standard error of estimate) might be calculated. Experts should also pay attention to estimates of stan-dard error of measurement that might vary across the ability scale, because a finding that standard error of measurement is larger (yielding less accurate scores) in the lower tail of the distribution would not be surprising.

Validity

Validity Defined

The core notion of validity is whether scores on a test assess the construct the test was designed to measure. Furthermore, a test might be designed to assess a particu-lar construct, but be used to predict many different criteria. As a result, validity of a test is usually described as the validity or accuracy of the inference a person wishes to make on the basis of the test score. For example, intelligence tests were initially developed to be an objective basis for understanding poor school performance, with low scores attributed to slowed mental development, hence mental retardation. It is not surprising that an IQ score is a good predictor of how a student will perform in school, so such a score supports an inference of this sort. In contrast, a good deal of research has found an approximate $r = .20$ correlation of IQ scores with standing height. An IQ score would obviously be a poor predictor of height, so it does not sup-port this inference.

For at least half a century, experts often portrayed validity citing the 3 Cs: content, criterion-related, and construct validity. Then, about two decades ago, Messick (1995) argued that all research involved construct validity, so construct validity was an over-arching term. He outlined six subtypes of construct validity that form, at least in part, a redefinition or reconstrual of the 3 Cs of validity, but add several key ideas. These six subtypes of construct validity are discussed below.

Forms of Validity

Content. The content validity concerns the relevance of the content included in the measurement device. The content in an instrument should be relevant to the underlying dimension to be assessed and should be representative of the content from the relevant domain. The manner in which content is sampled for the measure should be justified. Finally, the technical qualities of the measure—including psychometric properties, such as reliability—should be high, so the measure can be judged to be technically sound.

The standard measures of intelligence (see Chapters 7 and 8) and adaptive behavior (see Chapter 12) that are commonly used to support diagnoses of ID tend to meet standards for content validity. Clearly, the most basic form of evaluation of content validity is judgment by experts that the content of the measure is appropriate to assess the latent content of interest.

Substantive. The substantive validity concerns a topic formerly considered under the construct validity heading of the 3 Cs of validity. Here, the topic of concern is the theory driving the construction of the instrument and the underlying processes tapped by the test. General intelligence is a fairly nebulous construct, but experts agree that a multitest, multidimensional battery of tests should be used to assess intelligence, because intelligence is presumed to represent "intelligence in general" across multiple types of problems assessing mental ability (see also Chapter 7). As with content validity, commonly used measures of intelligence and adaptive behavior appear, generally, to satisfy the substantive prong of validity.

Structural. Structural validity has two key aspects. First, the hypothesized dimensional structure of the instrument should conform to the theoretical notions underlying its development. Second, the way in which the measure is scored should match the empirically derived dimensions for the instrument. For example, an intelligence battery might yield three or four primary factors when its subscores are analyzed, and this might be considered inconsistent with the concept of general intelligence. However, if these three or four factors are positively correlated, then a general factor derived from the correlations among the primary factors would represent general intelligence and justify developing a total IQ score.

Whether adaptive behavior measures satisfy the structural prong of validity is more open to question, at least for certain batteries. For example, Wei, Oakland, and Algina (2008) reported that a single-factor solution appeared adequate to represent the correlations among the 10 adaptive behavior scales from the Adaptive Behavior Assessment System-II (ABAS-II; Harrison & Oakland, 2003) parent form scales. Now, the ABAS-II has a scoring system to derive standard scores for conceptual, social, and practical adaptive behaviors, consistent with the AAIDD manual (Schalock et al., 2010). But, if a single, general factor is sufficient to represent relations among the 10 scales, the empirical dimensionality of the ABAS-II (one factor) appears to be inconsistent with the scoring structure of the instrument (three separable scores). The extent to which this is a problem with other standard instruments of adaptive behavior is unclear.

Generalizability. The generalizability aspect of validity involves questions regarding whether scores on a measure are affected by properties of the settings in which test administration is given or the persons to whom it is administered. One way to evaluate generalizability is to administer multiple test batteries designed to assess the same construct and then see if comparable scores are obtained. Thus, one might administer the SB5 and the proper (age-related) Wechsler test to an individual to determine if similar IQ scores are obtained. If this did occur, the results would demonstrate generalizability across the different tasks contained on the two test batteries.

This issue of generalizability attains greater import in the assessment of adaptive behavior. An expert might seek out various respondents to report on the adaptive behavior of a target individual. In doing so, a parent as respondent might report, primarily, on the target person's behaviors at home and in the neighborhood; a teacher as respondent might report on behavior in school; and a peer as respondent might report only on behavior by the target person in social groups in the neighborhood. The greater the comparability of scores across respondents or settings, for example, the greater the generalizability of the scores and the greater the confidence that an accurate account of the person's adaptive functioning has been obtained.

External. External validity is the form of validity formerly identified as criterion-related validity. The key feature of external validity is evidence of correlations of a measure with external measures, primarily if these correlations are consistent with the theory underlying the development of the instrument. The external validity criterion can also involve assessment of convergent and discriminant validity. Convergent validity is the finding of strong correlations with criteria that were predicted to occur, and discriminant validity refers to a finding of relatively low correlations with certain criteria when these were predicted. This issue of convergent and discriminant validity is of particular concern for the three domains: conceptual, social, and practical adaptive behavior. For example, conceptual adaptive functioning might relate most strongly to school and job performance, social functioning to making and keeping friends in the community, and practical functioning to successful adaptation in an independent living setting. To the extent that scores on these three dimensions demonstrate notable differential, unique levels of correlation with external criteria, the patterns of correlation would demonstrate discriminant validity.

Consequential. The sixth aspect of construct validity is consequential validity. Messick (1995) discussed this form of validity primarily with regard to education tests. Consequential validity involves the use and implications of test scores, the consequences of use of test scores, and the possibility of test invalidity due to test bias or lack of fairness. This aspect of validity has clear application when considering *Atkins* cases. A diagnosis of ID can be a "life or death" determination, so the consequences of this determination are most serious. Tests should be used in a fashion that is fairest to the person being assessed. For example, if a person has poor understanding of English and a version of a test is available in the person's native language, this latter test would clearly be preferred and expected to give a more accurate reading of the person's level of performance.

Implications for Practice

The review of the literature on measurement presented within this chapter has a number of implications for appropriate practice in assessment, and has particular relevance for assessments within *Atkins* cases. Scores that are obtained from assessments are manifest, or observed, scores. They should be interpreted as representative of an individual's relative placement on an underlying theoretical dimension (e.g., intellectual functioning or adaptive behavior). But, these scores do not represent latent variable scores with complete accuracy. As a consequence, clinical judgment is needed to integrate all available data.

The majority of measures used in the assessment of intellectual functioning, in particular, are ordinal in nature. Nevertheless, the large number of scale points on many tests in psychology yield information that approaches the interval level of measurement. Consequently, scores that are obtained from comprehensive and psychometrically sound assessments can be seen as having the characteristics of interval scales. As a consequence, for example, a 10-point differential in IQ would have essentially the same meaning along a full range of possible IQ scores.

The scores obtained from psychological tests are only as good as the normative sample from which they are derived. Consequently, consideration of such scores requires examiners to carefully consider all information concerning the representativeness and adequacy of the norming samples. Further, both the norming strategy used and the test construction itself may impact the quality of the scores. This concern is particularly important when considering the tails of a particular distribution of abilities being assessed (such as intelligence) and, consequently, caution must be taken in using information from certain tests to assess certain individuals, including potentially those with ID, because of insufficient accuracy in certain score intervals.

An important concern is the reliability of an instrument, which refers to the repeatability of test scores. Higher reliability is associated with higher repeatability and, consequently, the precision of scores. All forms of reliability for a given instrument should be studied to ensure that adequate attention has been given to the reliability of the assessment instrument. The standard error of measurement should be calculated with the most accurate estimate of reliability that is available.

Assessment instruments must be evaluated for all forms of validity, as discussed within this chapter. Substantive and structural validity should be shown before the use of multiple scores is allowed. In addition, scores on an individual instrument should have adequate generalizability in order to ensure a valid interpretation of test scores. Appropriate steps should be taken in order to ensure that standard forms of invalidity, such as test bias, have not affected scores for the individual being assessed.

References

Bruininks, R. H., Woodcock, R. W., Weatherman, R. F., & Hill, B. K. (1996). *Scales of Independent Behavior-Revised: Comprehensive manual.* Chicago, IL: Riverside.

Cronbach, L. J. (1951). Coefficient alpha and the internal structure of tests. *Psychometrika, 16,* 297–334. doi: 10.1007/BF02310555

Harrison, P. L., & Oakland, T. (2003). *Adaptive behavior assessment system.* San Antonio, TX: The Psychological Corporation.

Kuder, G. F., & Richardson, M. W. (1937). The theory of estimation of test reliability. *Psychometrika, 2,* 151–160. doi: 10.1007/BF02288391

McDonald, R. P. (1999). *Test theory: A unified treatment.* Mahwah, NJ: Erlbaum.

Messick, S. (1995). Validity of psychological assessment: Validation of inferences from persons' responses and performances as scientific inquiry into score meaning. *American Psychologist, 50,* 741–749. doi: 10.1037/0003-066X.50.9.741

Roid, G. H. (2003). *Stanford–Binet Intelligence Scales* (5th ed.). Itasca, IL: Riverside Publishing.

Schalock, R. L., Buntinx, W. H. E., Borthwick-Duffy, S., Bradley, V., Craig, E. M., Coulter, D. L., Gomez, S. C., Lachapelle, Y., Luckasson, R. A., Reeve, A., Shogren, K. A., Snell, M. E., Spreat, S., Tassé, M. J., Thompson, J. R., Verdugo, M. A., Wehmeyer, M. L., & Yeager, M. H. (2010). *Intellectual disability: Definition, classification, and system of supports* (11th ed.). Washington, DC: American Association on Intellectual and Developmental Disabilities.

Schrank, F.A., McGrew, K.S., Mather, N., & Woodcock, R.W. (2014). *Woodcock-Johnson IV.* Rolling Meadows, IL: Riverside Publishing.

Silverman, W., Miezejeski, C., Ryan, R., Zigman, W., Krinsky-McHale, S., & Urv, T. (2010). Stanford-Binet and WAIS IQ differences and their implications for adults with intellectual disability (aka mental retardation). *Intelligence, 38,* 242–248. doi: 10.1016/j.intell.2009.12.005

Tassé, M. J., Schalock, R. L., Balboni, G., Bersani, H., Borthwick-Duffy, S. A., Spreat, S., Thissen, D. M., Widaman, K. F., & Zang, D. (in press). *Diagnostic Adaptive Behavior Scale.* Washington, DC: American Association on Intellectual and Developmental Disabilities.

Terman, L. M., & Merrill, M. A. (1937). *Measuring intelligence: A guide to the administration of the new revised Stanford-Binet tests of intelligence.* New York: Houghton Mifflin.

Wei, Y., Oakland, T., & Algina, J. (2008). Multigroup confirmatory factor analysis for the Adaptive Behavior Assessment System-II parent form, ages 5–21. *American Journal on Mental Retardation, 113,* 178–186. doi: 10.1177/0734282909350209

Wechsler, D. (2002). *Wechsler Preschool and Primary Scale of Intelligence-Third edition.* San Antonio, TX: Psychological Corporation

Wechsler, D. (2003). *Wechsler Intelligence Scale for Children - Fourth edition: Manual.* San Antonio, TX: Psychological Corporation.

Wechsler, D. (2008). *Wechsler Adult Intelligence Scale - Fourth edition.* San Antonio, TX: Pearson.

Woodcock, R. W., McGrew, K. S., & Mather, N. (2001). *Woodcock-Johnson III Tests of Cognitive Abilities.* Itasca, IL: Riverside Pub.

Woodcock, R. W., McGrew, K. S., Schrank, F. A., & Mather, N. (2007). *Woodcock-Johnson III normative update.* Rolling Meadows, IL: Riverside Pub.

Appendix 5-1

Classical Test Theory

Classical test theory is the measurement theory with which most practicing scientists are acquainted. Classical test theory starts with a set of simple assumptions, the first of which is that the score on any manifest variable Y is an additive function of a true score T and an error score E, such that

$$Y_i = T_i + E_i$$

where the i subscript ($i = 1, \ldots, N$) stands for a random individual, N is the size of the total sample of persons, and other terms were described above. Then, assumptions are made about the true and error scores. The most important of these are that the error scores have a mean of zero, have nonzero variance, and are uncorrelated with true scores.

Based on these assumptions, it is possible to derive a number of important results with regard to precision of measurement. Perhaps the most important of these concerns reliability and the associated standard error of measurement. Here, we note two important outcomes. First, the variance of a measure, σ_Y^2, is the additive sum of true score variance, σ_T^2, and error variance, σ_E^2, or

$$\sigma_Y^2 = \sigma_T^2 + \sigma_E^2$$

where all terms were defined above. Second, reliability of a test score, r_{yy}, is defined as *the ratio of true score variance in a measure over total score variance*, or

$$r_{yy} = \frac{\sigma_T^2}{\sigma_Y^2} = \frac{\sigma_T^2}{\sigma_T^2 + \sigma_E^2}$$

where again all terms were defined above. Therefore, the reliability of a test represents the proportion of variance in the test that is true score variance. Now, the only scores we have are the Y scores, which are scores on the manifest variable Y; the true and error scores are theoretical entities, so we cannot estimate variances of these scores directly. However, certain correlations between scores from a test can be interpreted directly as the reliability of the test.

Classical test theory is a theory about total scores, not item scores, at least with regard to the derivation of the central notions of reliability of a measure. Items are, of course, very important, because they serve as the basis for the calculation of a total score. But, reliability under classical test theory is a theory about the total score derived from a test, and different approaches to estimating reliability are based on different ways of obtaining a total score from a set of item scores.

Item Response Theory

In the middle of the 20th century, a new measurement theory was proposed—item response theory (IRT), or modern test theory. Details of IRT will not be given here for two major reasons. First, the mathematical formulations representing item responses are technical, and this level of technical detail is not needed for present purposes. Second, although IRT has been widely used in the development of academic achievement tests, it has been relatively little used in the development of intelligence tests and measures of adaptive behavior. The latter is changing, as IRT was used in the standardization of the Woodcock-Johnson Tests of Cognitive Abilities (Woodcock, McGrew, & Mather, 2001), the Scales of Independent Behavior–Revised (Bruininks, Woodcock, Weatherman, & Hill, (1996) and in the forthcoming Diagnostic Adaptive Behavior Scales (Tassé et al., in press). Still, given the relatively rare use of IRT for intelligence and adaptive behavior measures, only limited information need be given here.

There are several reasons for mentioning IRT. The use of IRT is continuing to grow, so its existence should be acknowledged. In the future, practicing scientists and experts who diagnose ID will need to know the basics of IRT to interpret test statistics accurately. In addition, several key concepts—such as test bias and differential item functioning across groups—have ready implementation and interpretation in IRT.

Perhaps the most important reason to mention IRT here is that the basic concepts of reliability and precision have altered meaning in IRT models. Under IRT models, it is possible to derive an average reliability for a test. But IRT models allow the calculation of the amount of information generated by items at all levels of the total score range. At score ranges with higher amounts of information, the standard error of test scores is smaller, and, therefore, the confidence interval around observed scores is smaller. As a result, precision of measurement is not constant at all levels of the total score continuum, as is true under classical test theory. Consequently, the expert must engage in more detailed inspection of test data to determine the precision with which the score on the test has been determined.

6 | Age of Onset and the Developmental Period Criterion

Stephen Greenspan
George W. Woods
Harvey N. Switzky

Intellectual disability (ID) is part of a group of "developmental" disorders. Prong 3 of the 3-part definition of ID is typically termed "age of onset" and is the criterion that is intended to tap into the developmental aspect of the disorder. The typical operational definition used for prong 3 is evidence that the disability first manifested during the "developmental" (i.e., childhood or adolescence) period. In this chapter, we discuss how the developmental criterion is approached and explore what is meant by the term "manifesting."

The Developmental Criterion

The concept of the developmental criterion has a long history of being seen as a basic consideration in the definition and diagnosis of ID. One of the pioneers in the field of ID, Edgar Doll, formulated what was then a widely cited definition that incorporated age of onset into considerations of ID. Doll (1941, p. 215) defined ID (at the time "mental deficiency") as "social incompetence, due to mental subnormality, which has been developmentally arrested, which obtains at maturity, [and] is of constitutional origin ..." The concept of early onset is reflected in "constitutional origin," which implies early manifestation. Further, "developmentally arrested" and "obtains at maturity" also speak to the developmental criterion.

In the first modern clinical manual (Heber, 1961), the American Association of Mental Deficiency (AAMD; later the American Association on Mental Retardation [AAMR] and now the American Association on Intellectual and Developmental Disabilities [AAIDD]) terminology and classification committee established the third definitional prong as onset before age 16. Twelve years later (Grossman, 1983), it was changed to 18 (see Greenspan & Switzky, 2006, for a historical overview of the evolving AAIDD definitions). In terms of criminal statutes or precedents defining ID in *Atkins* proceedings, most states use the pre-18 cutoff, but some jurisdictions (e.g., Indiana, Maryland, Utah), perhaps inspired by federal developmental disability legislation, set the age cutoff at 22. However, there are some states (notably Nebraska and New Mexico, predating its recent abolition of the death penalty) that do not require evidence of pre-18 onset because of a specific recognition that, in terms of the underlying purpose of death penalty exemption (cognitively mediated inability to reflect on the criminal nature of one's conduct), age of onset should make no difference. This point is made in a recent legal article by Mulroy (2012), who argued that the "childhood onset" criterion is arbitrary and unjustifiable from a legal equity standpoint. Although the fifth edition of the *Diagnostic and Statistical Manual of Mental Disorders* (DSM-5; American Psychiatric Association, 2013) does not provide any justification, its dropping of any specific age-of-onset operational definition of prong 3 likely reflects a view that brain development (and, therefore, possibility for onset of ID) does not necessarily end at age 18.

What Does "Manifested" Mean?

The wording of legal definitions of ID vary from jurisdiction to jurisdiction, but the two most common alternate approaches to the wording for prong 3 are: (a) that the disorder first manifested before age 18 (or 22) or (b) that significant deficits in prong 1 (intellectual functioning) and prong 2 (adaptive behavior) first manifested before the indicated age. Experts and courts differ somewhat on the evidence that must be gathered before they consider that the "manifestation" threshold has been met, with the two poles in this debate ranging from specific evidence (such as having been labeled ID, or having below-70 IQ test scores from childhood) to more general evidence (such as being held back one or more grades or having concerns raised, such as in referral for special education services).

The latter, more general, approach is more clinically accurate, for a host of reasons, including: (a) many schools are reluctant to assign the ID label, especially to poor minority children, both because of legal concerns about over-labeling, and also because of "cultural overshadowing" (i.e., the tendency to attribute all incompetence in minority individuals to environment and to deny the role of even obvious biological risk factors; Woods, Greenspan & Agharkar, 2011); (b) differences among parents in their ability or willingness to advocate for services for their child or to understand the reality of their child's limitations; and (c) significant geographic variability in the availability or competence of developmental or educational professionals and services, including the administration and interpretation of intelligence or other psycho-educational tests. This recommended flexible approach to establishing prong 3 in *Atkins* proceedings is, in fact, the way ID diagnosis is already approached for nonforensic purposes, such as eligibility for human services.

The most useful and valid approach to establishing whether ID manifested during the developmental period is to see if there is evidence of what has been termed a "continuity of concern" (Greenspan, 2011). This means that various people, both professionals (such as educators) and nonprofessionals (such as family members or neighbors), described the defendant from a relatively early age as "slow" and as needing help (formal or informal) in mastering or carrying out various life tasks that individuals of the same age and cultural background are expected to master or carry out without assistance. The key thing here is not whether the person was seen as having ID (although one may find that peers or family members called him "retard" or used similar pejoratives) but, rather, whether there were clear signs that the person's post-18 impairment did not emerge suddenly (perhaps because of an illness or injury) in adulthood and without earlier signs of, and related concerns about, a failure to develop in an age-expected manner. It should be noted, however, that establishing such a continuity of concern can be difficult, given that schools or families often fail to recognize or understand the seriousness of the developmental limitations of students who may later end up in serious difficulty.

Use of Retrospective Methods in Establishing Prong 3

One method that can be used to establish pre-18 onset is the use of retrospective adaptive behavior ratings, in which a rater is asked to describe the defendant not as he is today but as he was at some point in time during childhood or adolescence. Such data can be important in establishing whether prong 3 is met, given that: (a) in some jurisdictions (e.g., California) impairment before age 18 is all that the court really considers; and (b) for any number of reasons (e.g., school district policy, lost or discarded records), contemporaneous evidence, such as test data, may not be available.

In doing a retrospective assessment of adaptive behavior, the informant is asked to respond to each of the items on an adaptive behavior rating scale, such as the ABAS-II (Harrison & Oakland, 2003) or the Vineland-2 (Sparrow, Chichetti, & Balla, 2005) not as the person he or she is today but as he or she was at a point in the past (such as before his or her 18th birthday). The target age picked is one that the informant attests was during a period when he or she lived with or interacted with the defendant on a very frequent (i.e., daily or weekly) basis. The informant is reminded frequently of the target age, as it is easy to slip into a later time frame without such reminders.

Use of retrospective ratings has been endorsed, especially for high-stakes purposes such as *Atkins* assessments, by the AAIDD (Schalock & Luckasson, 2007). Nevertheless, such a use is sometimes questioned on two grounds: (a) that the instruments were not normed for retrospective use; and (b) that retrospective assessments are inherently unreliable, because of the demands they make on memory. The response to the first argument is that nonstandard uses are acceptable under special circumstances. The response to the second argument is that response protocols are only used when informants are able to answer authoritatively without excessive guessing, Multiple raters should be used to ensure consensual validity, and ratings should align with social history and other evidence to ensure congruent validity. The main indicator of valid retrospective assessment is the use of multiple informants and the attainment of an adequate degree of agreement (on summary scores, not necessarily individual items) across raters. Such agreement, of course, is also a check against the possibility of biased responding in informants who might have motivation to lie. The importance of a solid social history in an *Atkins* assessment cannot be overemphasized, especially as a mechanism for validating the results of retrospective adaptive behavior ratings. Further discussion of retrospective assessment is provided in Chapter 18.

Role of Physical Etiology

Although there are hundreds of known biological causes of ID, in many cases of mild levels of ID, a cause is unknown or can only be speculated about. Thus, ID can be described as a "functional" disability, in that unlike most medical disorders, evidence of a specific etiology is not needed to establish the diagnosis. However, where there is evidence of a biological etiology that is associated with ID, then prong 3 (age of onset) may be virtually automatically established. One example involves a pretrial hearing in which a home delivery that caused significant perinatal anoxia, followed by a pattern of grand mal seizures, was cited by an expert (and the judge, in his subsequent *Atkins* ruling) as explaining the defendant's adaptive incompetence when compared to his siblings who were equally disadvantaged and who, nevertheless, all developed into competent adults. As enhanced diagnostic procedures (such as improved brain scan techniques) are developed for detecting high frequency biological causes of mild levels of ID—such as with fetal alcohol spectrum disorders (FASD)—the role of organic factors will likely come to play a more important role in establishing both prong 3 and the appropriateness of an ID diagnosis. It should be noted, however, that identification of brain pathology, typically from neuropsychological test results, is not in itself sufficient to establish a diagnosis of ID; the same can be said of a medical diagnosis, such as FASD.

Conclusion

The third prong of the definition of ID focuses on the developmental criterion. To confirm that an individual is appropriately labeled as having ID, there must be verification of origin during the developmental period. Specifically, information must be confirmed that the disability was manifested prior to the age of 18, although this refers to establishing early noted problems, and not the existence of early IQ test scores or ID diagnoses, the absence of which should not be used to argue that prong 3 is not met.

References

American Psychiatric Association. (2013). *Diagnostic and statistical manual of mental disorders* (5th ed.). Washington, DC: Author.

Doll, E. A. (1941). The essentials of an inclusive concept of mental deficiency. *American Journal of Mental Deficiency, 46,* 214–229.

Greenspan, S. (2011). Homicide defendants with intellectual disabilities: Issues in diagnosis in capital cases. *Exceptionality, 19,* 219–237. doi: 10.1080/09362835.2011.611086

Greenspan, S., & Switzky, H. N. (2006). Forty-four years of AAMR manuals. In H. N. Switzky & S.Greenspan (Eds*.), What is mental retardation?: Ideas for an evolving disability in the 21st century.* (pp. 3–28). Washington, DC: AAMR.

Grossman, H. J. (1983). *Classification in mental retardation.* Washington, DC: American Association on Mental Deficiency.

Harrison, P.L,& Oakland, T. (2003). *Adaptive behavior assessment system—second edition.* San Antono, TX: Pearson Assessment.

Heber, R. F. (1961). *A manual on terminology and classification in mental retardation.* Washington, DC: American Association on Mental Deficiency.

Schalock, R. L., Buntinx, W. H. E., Borthwick-Duffy, S. A., Luckasson, R., Snell, M. E., Tasse, M. J., & Wehmeyer, M. (2007). *User's guide: Mental retardation: Definition, classification and systems of support* (10th ed.). Washington, DC: American Association on Intellectual and Developmental Disabilities.

Sparrow, S. S., Chichetti, D. V., & Balla, D. A. (2005). *Vineland Adaptive Behavior Scales* (2nd Ed.) (Vineland-II). San Antonio, TX: Pearson.

Woods, G. W., Greenspan, S., & Agharkar, B. S. (2011). Ethnic and cultural factors in identifying fetal alcohol spectrum disorders. *Journal of Psychiatry and Law, 39* (1), 1–9.

PART II
Assessment Considerations

B. Intellectual Functioning

7 | Intellectual Functioning

Kevin S. McGrew

This chapter focuses on intellectual functioning, the first prong of the definition of intellectual disability (ID). The initial focus is on a review of the literature on intelligence and the assessment of intellectual functioning. Attention is given to psychometric theories of intelligence, contemporary research, an overview of intelligence test batteries, related measurement concepts, relationships between intelligence test scores, and the relationship between measures of intelligence and adaptive behavior scores. The chapter then provides implications for the implementation of this research in practice.

Summary of Related Research

Psychometric Theories of Intelligence

The *psychometric* approach is the most well-established approach to studying intelligence, dating to Galton's attempt in the late 1800s to measure intelligence with psychophysical measures (Sternberg & Kaufman, 1998). Psychometric theories of intelligence are "based on or tested by scores on conventional tests of intelligence . . . these theories are often, but not always, based on FACTOR ANALYSIS, that is, they specify a set of factors alleged to underlie human intelligence" (capitalization in the original; Vanden-Bos, 2007, p. 754). Psychometric theories have been the most influential approach to measuring and studying intelligence, have generated the most systematic research and, more importantly, have facilitated the development of the reliable, valid, and practical individually administered intelligence test batteries (Neisser et al., 1996) used in the identification of individuals with ID. Space does not allow for a detailed treatment of the lengthy history of research on psychometric-based theories of intelligence in this book. For those interested, more thorough historical accounts can be found in Brody (2000), Carroll (1993), Cudek and MacCallum (2007), Horn and Noll (1997), Schneider and McGrew (2012), and Wasserman (2012).

Psychometric theories of intelligence have their roots in the work of Charles Spearman. Spearman (1904, 1927) initially reported the phenomena of *positive manifold,* or the tendency for all tests of mental ability to be positively correlated. Spearman's g-theory posits that all mental tests are positively correlated due to the influence of a common cause, g (Jensen, 1998). Although Spearman's g-theory is most often described as single factor theory, this characterization is not entirely accurate (Carroll, 1993; Schneider & McGrew, 2012). Scores from individual mental tests were viewed as being due to the influence of g and by specific (s) abilities unique to each individual test.

From the 1940s to 1960s, psychometric intelligence research focused on the identification of multiple primary abilities. Thurstone's Primary Mental Abilities (PMAs; Thurstone, 1938, 1947; Thurstone & Thurstone, 1941) theory was most prominent and identified between seven and nine PMAs. Thurstone (1947) was willing to accept the possible existence of g above the PMAs, but believed it was less important than the PMAs (Carroll, 1993; Schneider & McGrew, 2012). Summaries of this period of intense factor analysis research suggested over 60 possible separate PMAs (Carroll, 1993; Ekstrom, French, & Harman, 1979; French, 1951; French, Ekstrom, & Price, 1963; Guilford, 1967; Hakstian & Cattell, 1974; Horn, 1976).

The next significant phase in the development of psychometric theories of intelligence was driven largely by the research of Raymond Cattell. Based on an extensive program of factor analysis research, Cattell concluded that Spearman's g was best explained by splitting it into general fluid (g_f) and general crystallized (g_c) intelligence (Cattell, 1941, 1943). Horn, Cattell, and many others published systematic programs of factor-analytic research (from 1965 to the late 1990s) that confirmed the original Cattell Gf – Gc model and added new factors. Horn extended the Gf – Gc theory to eventually include 9–10 broad abilities (Horn, 1989). In 1993, Carroll published his seminal work, *Human Cognitive Abilities: A Survey of Factor-Analytic Studies,* that summarized his re-factor analysis of more than 460 different datasets since the time of Spearman. The result was Carroll's three-stratum hierarchical model of intelligence that included general (g) intelligence at the apex, which subsumed eight *broad* intellectual abilities that, in turn, subsumed over 70 *narrow* PMAs. Most other psychometric scholars concur that Carroll's work presented the first validated hierarchical taxonomy of human intelligence (Ackerman & Lohman, 2006; Burns, 1994; Jensen, 2004; Kaufman, 2009; Keith & Reynolds, 2010; McGrew, 2005, 2009; Schneider & McGrew, 2012).

The remarkable similarities between the Carroll and Cattell–Horn models resulted in their integration as the Cattell-Horn-Carroll (CHC) theory of intelligence (Daniel, 1997, 2000; Kaufman, 2009; McGrew, 1997, 2005, 2009; Schneider & McGrew, 2012; Snow, 1998). Eight to nine broad ability domains (fluid intelligence or reasoning, *Gf;* crystallized intelligence or comprehension-knowledge, *Gc;* long-term storage and retrieval, *Glr;* short-term and working memory, *Gsm;* visual-spatial processing, *Gv;*

auditory processing, *Ga;* intellectual processing speed, *Gs;* quantitative knowledge, *Gq*) are generally accepted as the primary foundation of CHC theory (see McGrew, 2005, 2009, and Schneider & McGrew, 2012, for detailed definitions). These five to eight CHC broad ability domains are represented by one or more subtests on some, but not all, intelligence batteries.

Contemporary Neurocognitive, Neuropsychological, and Developmental Research

The content of contemporary intelligence batteries has also been influenced by current theories and research in cognitive neuroscience, neuropsychology, and developmental psychology (Drozdick, Wahlstrom, Zhu & Weiss, 2012; Naglieri, Das & Goldstein, 2012). In particular, recognition of the importance of the constructs of planning, working memory, and intellectual processing speed have resulted in the inclusion of more tests of these abilities in intelligence batteries. The neuropsychological theory of Luria (see Naglieri et al., 2012) has also influenced the revisions of some intelligence batteries. Briefly, Luria's theory defines intelligence as being based on four functional aspects related to brain structures. These four functional components are best articulated in the contemporary Planning, Attention-Arousal, Simultaneous, and Successive (PASS) theory of intelligence, which proposed that cognition consists of the functional brain processes of planning, attention, and simultaneous and successive processing (Naglieri et al., 2012; Singer, Licthenberger, Kaufman, Kaufman, & Kaufman, 2012). Developmental intelligence research, particularly that reporting developmental changes in intellectual processing speed and the dynamic interaction of working memory and processing speed in adulthood, has informed the revision of adult intelligence batteries (Drozdick et al., 2012; Wechsler, 2008).

Available Intelligence Test Batteries

Table 7.1 presents a summary of the comprehensive, nationally normed, individually administered contemporary intelligence batteries that possess satisfactory psychometric characteristics (i.e., national norm samples, adequate reliability and validity for the full-scale IQ score) for use in the diagnosis of ID. Only three of the intelligence batteries (i.e., Stanford-Binet Intelligence Scales, fifth edition [SB5, Roid, 2003], Wechsler Adult Intelligence Scale, fourth edition [WAIS-IV], and Woodcock-Johnson Tests of Cognitive Abilities, third edition [WJ III]) have adult norms suitable for testing adults. However, the files of many adults often contain scores or reports from intelligence testing during the individual's childhood and adolescence. The most commonly administered contemporary childhood and adolescent intelligence batteries are also listed in Table 7.1.

The "full-scale IQ score" column in Table 7.1 lists the full-scale general intelligence score provided by each intelligence battery. This score is the best estimate of a person's general intellectual ability for the purposes of diagnosing ID from each respective battery. All full-scale IQ scores listed in Table 7.1 meet Jensen's (1998) psychometric sampling error criteria for measuring general intelligence (*g*). As recommended by Jensen

TABLE 7.1. Individually Administered Comprehensive Intelligence Batteries

Intelligence Battery	Publication Date	Age Range (years)	Composite g-score	Name	Scales g loadings[b]	h[2c]
CAS	1997	5–17	Full Scale (FS)	Simultaneous	0.77	0.59
				Planning	0.75	0.56
				Attention	0.75	0.56
				Successive	0.66	0.44
DAS-II	2007	2–17	General Conceptual Ability (GCA)	Nonverbal Ability	0.81	0.66
				Spatial Ability	0.80	0.64
				Verbal Ability	0.78	0.61
				Working Memory	0.69	0.48
				Processing Speed	0.54	0.29
KABC-II	2004	3–18	Mental Processing Index (MPI) Fluid-Crystallized Index (FCI)	Gf/Planning	0.81	0.66
				Gc/Knowledge	0.81	0.66
				Gv/Simultaneous	0.77	0.59
				Glr/Learning	0.75	0.56
				Gsm/Sequential	0.67	0.45
SB5	2003	2–85+	Full Scale IQ (FS IQ)	Quantitative Reasoning	0.89	0.79
				Knowledge	0.86	0.74
				Visual-Spatial Processing	0.88	0.77
				Fluid Reasoning	0.86	0.74
				Working Memory	0.85	0.72
WAIS-IV	2008	16–90+	Full Scale IQ (FS IQ)	Working Memory Index	0.85	0.72
				Perceptual Reasoning Index	0.85	0.72
				Verbal Comprehension Index	0.83	0.69
				Processing Speed Index	0.74	0.55
WISC-IV	2004	6–16	Full Scale IQ (FS IQ)	Perceptual Reasoning Index	0.84	0.71
				Verbal Comprehension Index	0.83	0.69
				Working Memory Index	0.78	0.61
				Processing Speed Index	0.72	0.52
WJ III /NU	2001, 2007[a]	2–90+	General Intellectual Ability (GIA-Standard; GIA-Extended)	Comprehension-Knowledge	0.74	0.55
				Long-term Storage & Retrieval	0.74	0.55
				Fluid Reasoning	0.70	0.49
				Auditory Processing	0.62	0.38
				Short-term Memory	0.62	0.38
				Visual Processing	0.55	0.30
				Processing Speed	0.52	0.27

Note: CAS = Cognitive Assessment System (Naglieri & Das, 1997); DAS-II = Differential Ability Scales—Second Edition (Elliott, 2007); KABC-II = Kaufman Assessment Battery for Children—Second Edition (Kaufman & Kaufman, 2004); SB5 = Stanford Intelligence Scales—Fifth Edition (Roid, 2003); WAIS-IV = Wechsler Adult Intelligence Scale—Fourth Edition (Wechsler, 2008); WISC-V = Wechsler Intelligence Scale for Children—Fourth Edition (Wechsler, 2004); WJ III / NU = Woodcock-Johnson Battery—Third Edition and Normative Udate (Woodcock, McGrew, Schrank, & Mather, 2001, 2007).

a = WJ III was first published in 2001 and then the norms were "freshened" with a normative update in 2007.

b = Within each battery principal component analysis was used to extract a single g-component from correlation matrices reported in the respective technical manuals. Tables A.10 and A.11 were used from the CAS manual, Tables 8.2 and 8.3 from the DAS-II manual; Tables 8.10 to 8.13 from the KABC-II manual, Table A.6 from the SB5 manual, and Tables 5.1 from the WAIS-IV and WISC-IV manuals. For the WJ III the principal axes g-loadings reported by Floyd, McGrew, Barry, Rafael & Rogers (2009) were used. When more than one correlation matrix was analyzed, the median value was calculated and is reported in this column. These values were used to order the respective component part scales from the highest to the lowest within-battery values. It is important to note that these are within-battery estimates and comparisons across the different batteries is not appropriate.

c = communality or percent of variance shared with principal g-factor.

(1998), "the particular collection of tests used to estimate g should come as close as possible, with some limited number of tests, to being a representative sample of all types of mental tests, and the various kinds of test should be represented as equally as possible" (p. 85). At a minimum, a measure of general intelligence (i.e., full-scale IQ) should be based on a variety of different tests that vary on information content, skills, and mental operations, and sample from at least three primary intelligence domains (e.g., at least three of the broad CHC intelligence domains) (Jensen, 1998). All IQ test batteries included in Table 7.1 meet these criteria.

Also included in Table 7.1 are the part-scale scores (e.g., WAIS-IV Verbal Comprehension Index, Perceptual Reasoning Index, Working Memory Index, and Processing Speed Index) provided by each battery, followed by their respective within-battery g-loadings. This part-score information is included in Table 7.1 as it is relevant to the use of IQ part scores, in place of the full-scale IQ scores, for the diagnosis of ID in certain situations (see the "Use of General Intelligence Full Scale and Composite Part Scores" section for explanation and definition of terms). Space does not permit a detailed discussion and comparison of the strengths and limitations of each of the batteries listed in Table 7.1. Overviews of each of the major intelligence test batteries can be found in Flanagan and Harrison (2012).

Comparability of IQ Scores

"Not all scores obtained on intelligence tests given to the same person will be identical" (Schalock et al., 2010, p. 38). For example, Schalock et al. (2010) reported that, although Wechsler Intelligence Scale for Children, third edition (WISC-III) and Stanford-Binet Intelligence Scales, fourth edition (SB-IV) IQ test scores were significantly correlated in one sample of students with ID at the upper end of the range; on the average, the WISC-III scores were eight IQ points lower. Although the lay public often assumes that IQ scores from different tests should be similar, and for the majority of individuals they are reasonably comparable when using technically sound comprehensive measures of general intelligence, 1-to-1 IQ test score correspondence for all individuals is not supported by the available research. That is, one cannot assume that for all individuals the IQ scores from different IQ tests will be similar—and often they can be markedly different.

Full-scale IQ test scores from different tests are frequently similar or are reasonably close (when measurement error is taken into consideration). In other instances, IQ test scores will be markedly different (Floyd, Clark & Shadish, 2008; Macvaugh & Cunningham, 2009)—a finding that often produces consternation for examiners and recipients of psychological reports. The fundamental issue underlying discussions of IQ-IQ score comparisons in cases is that of IQ battery score exchangeability. "[E]xchangeability refers to the assumption that the IQ a person receives will be reasonably constant no matter which intelligence test battery is used" (italics in original; Floyd et al., 2008, p. 415). The obvious differences in the test stimuli, task requirements, and test content among different intelligence test batteries would lead most to the conclusion that not all intelligence scores will be exchangeable:

Exchangeability is thought to be plausible because of the principle of aggregation ... [t]hat is, influences associated with individual tests in a battery are averaged out when multiple test scores are aggregated into an IQ. As a result, only a single ability, general intelligence, is thought to remain as the systematic source of variance. (Jensen, 1998; Spearman, 1927; Floyd et al., 2008)

In one of the better investigations of IQ score exchangeability to date, Floyd et al. (2008) evaluated IQ-IQ exchangeability across 10 different IQ battery full-scale IQ scores (comprising 6 to 14 individual tests) across approximately 1,000 subjects from six different IQ test validity study samples. Comparisons included most major individually administered IQ test batteries, such as the Differential Ability Scale (DAS; Elliott, 2007), the Kaufman Assessment Battery For Children—Second Edition (KABC-II, Kaufman & Kaufman, 2004), the Kaufman Adult Intelligence Test (KAIT; Kaufman & Kaufman, 1993), the Wechsler Intelligence Scale For Children—Third Edition and Fourth Editon (WISC-III/IV; Wechsler, 1991, 2003) the Wechsler Adult Intelligence Scale—Third Edition (WAIS-III; Wechsler, 1997), and the Woodcock-Johnson Tests of Cognitive Abilities (WJ III; Woodcock, McGrew, & Mather, 2001), in various combinations. Five of the six samples included subjects without disabilities from ages 8 to 16. The sixth sample was a mixed sample of university students with and without learning disabilities. Floyd et al. (2008) reported that different intelligence test batteries produce less similar IQs than expected from the apparent high degree of correlations (r range = .69 to .93; median r = .76). These authors concluded that "psychologists can anticipate that 1 in 4 individuals taking an intelligence test battery will receive an IQ more than *10 points higher or lower* [emphasis added] when taking another battery" (Floyd et al., 2008, p. 414).

Similar variability in IQ test scores has been demonstrated in samples of individuals with low general intelligence. Whitaker (2008) conducted a meta-analysis of 18 studies (total n = 2,006 individuals) that investigated the stability of IQ scores for individuals with IQ test scores less than 80. Across the various editions of the Wechsler scales (i.e., Wechsler Intelligence Scale for Children—WISC; Wechsler Intelligence Scale for Children—Revised, WISC-R; WISC-III; Wechsler Adult Intelligence Scale, WAIS; Wechsler Adult Intelligence Scale—Revised,WAIS-R) and the 1960 and 1972 Stanford-Binet, the average stability coefficient (mean assessment interval of 33.5 months) for the total IQ test score was .82. In the eleven studies with adequate information, 57 % of the IQ test scores changed by less than six IQ test score points. However, 14 % of the individuals had IQ test scores that changed by 10 points or more. Given the bright line emphasis in many *Atkins* cases, a shift of one IQ test score point (e.g., from 70 to 71) can often result in a different decision by the courts. A change of 10 IQ test score points could move an IQ test score that is clearly within the ID score range (e.g., 68) to a score (e.g., 78) that is beyond the bright line cutoff score of 70 and even beyond the upper bound score (e.g., 75) that accounts for the standard error of measurement (± 5 IQ test score points).

IQ-IQ Score Differences: Basic Measurement Concepts

Understanding why different full-scale IQ scores may be reported for an individual on different occasions or from different intelligence batteries requires an understanding of a number of basic measurement concepts. This discussion builds on the topics addressed in Chapter 5, which provides a detailed discussion of basic measurement concepts.

Intelligence score correlations. Comparing different IQ scores requires an understanding of the statistical concept of correlation. The *APA Dictionary of Psychology* (VandenBos, 2007) defines the related statistical concepts of *correlation, correlation coefficient*, and the *coefficient of determination* as:

> *Correlation:* "The degree of relationship (usually linear) between two attributes." (p. 234)

> *Correlation coefficient (r):* "A numerical index reflecting the degree of relationship (usually linear) between two attributes scaled so that the value of +1 indicates a perfect positive relationship, −1 a perfect negative relationship, and 0 no relationship." (p. 234)

> *Coefficient of determination (r^2).* "A numerical index that reflects the degree to which variation in the dependent variable is accounted for by one independent variable. Also called **determination coefficient.**" (bold emphasis in original; p. 186)

Correlations reported between full-scale IQ scores from the major individually administered intelligence batteries usually range from the .60s to .80s, with the highest correlations reported in the .70 to .80 range. Although these are statistically significant high correlations, it is important to recognize that correlations estimate the relations of two IQs across individuals (i.e., in the research sample group) and can lead to a false sense of expected IQ-IQ correspondence for a specific individual.

The *coefficient of determination* (r^2) is most informative in understanding expected score similarities or differences as it quantifies the amount of shared or common test score variance between the two tests (Neisser et al., 1996; Sattler, 2001). This index is obtained by squaring a reported correlation (e.g., $.70 \times .70 = .49$) and multiplying the result by 100. For example, if $r = .70$, the result is 49.0%. What does this statistic mean? In this example, the .70 correlation indicates that the global IQ scores from two different test batteries have approximately 50% common or shared test score variance. The remaining 50% of unshared variance is due to (a) different abilities being measured by the two different intelligence test batteries; and (b) to a lesser extent, measurement error due to less than perfect reliability for each test score. Knowing that two intelligence test batteries may have approximately 50% shared (common) and unshared (uncommon) IQ test score variance should lead the reader to the conclusion that not all individuals will receive the same IQ test score (or nearly similar scores) on two different intelligence tests that correlate at .70.

An example is provided to illustrate this important point. In the third edition of WAIS's (WAIS-III) technical manual (Wechsler, 1997) a correlation of .88 (statistically significant and high) is reported between the WAIS-III Full Scale IQ and the Stanford-Binet Intelligence Scale–Fourth Edition (SB4) global score (n = 26 adult subjects). A correlation of .65 is also reported between the WAIS-III IQ and the special purpose Raven's Standard Progressive Matrices (SPM; Raven, 1976) in the same sample. Correlations of this magnitude, when converted to coefficients of determination, indicate that the WAIS-III has approximately 77% and 42% common or shared variance with the SB4 and SPM, respectively. The WAIS-III/SB4 77% value is high and impressive. Yet, again, it is important to recognize that this group study suggests that the WAIS-III and SB4 still have 23% (approximately 1/4) of their respective test score variance that they do *not* share in common. The WAIS-III and SPM have more they do not share (58%) than they do measure in common (42%).

The only time one can expect two different intelligence tests to provide approximately the same IQ test scores for all individuals is if the tests are nearly perfectly correlated (correlation approaches +1.0). This is not the reality reflected by decades of IQ test comparison research. Although the typical correlations reported between major intelligence tests (.60s to .80s) may sound impressive to nonpsychometricians, correlations of this magnitude suggest that different intelligence tests measure approximately 40% to 60% common abilities and, thus, different IQs are to be expected with regularity (Floyd et al., 2008).

Before interpreting differences between two IQ test scores, one must first determine if the IQ-IQ difference score is a statistically significant and reliable difference. That is, one must determine if the IQ-IQ score difference is not simply due to chance. Understanding a number of statistical concepts is necessary to make this evaluation—*reliability* and the *standard error of the difference score* are briefly defined below (see Chapter 5 for a more thorough discussion).

> *Reliability:* "The degree to which test scores for a group of test takers are consistent over repeated applications of a measurement procedure and hence are inferred to be dependable, and repeatable for an individual test taker; the degree to which scores are free of errors of measurement for a given group." (American Educational Research Association, American Psychological Association, & National Council on Measurement in Education [AERA, APA, & NCME], 1999, p. 180) Reliability "refers to the consistency of measurements." (Sattler, 2001, p. 102)
>
> *Reliability coefficient (r_{11}):* "Expresses the degree of consistency in the measurement of test scores. The symbol is the letter r with two identical subscripts (r_{xx} or r_{tt}). Reliability coefficients range from 1.00 (indicating perfect reliability) to .00 (indicating the absence of reliability." (Sattler, 2001, p. 102)
>
> *Standard error of difference score (SE_{diff}):* "This statistic provides an estimate for the standard deviation of the sampling distribution of the difference between the

two obtained index scores. Multiplying the SE_{diff} by an appropriate z value yields the amount of difference required for statistical significance at any given level of confidence." (italics in original; Wechsler, 2008, p. 53)

It is important to note that the reliability of the difference between two IQ test scores (IQ-IQ = IQ difference score) will be smaller than the reliability of the two individual scores. The *standard error of difference score* (SE_{diff}; Anastasi & Urbina, 1997) reflects this statistical fact by incorporating the reliability of the two compared scores in the calculation of the SE_{diff}, which is then used to evaluate the statistical significance of an IQ-IQ difference score. It is important to note that the SE_{diff} for a difference between two scores will be larger than the standard error of measurement (*SEM*) of the individual scores. Reliabilities for composite IQ scores should be available in each test's technical manual. When the tests are on the same standard scale ($M = 100$; $SD = 15$) the formula for calculating the SE_{diff} using the respective reliability coefficients for each IQ score (r_{11} and r_{22}), is:

$$SE_{diff} = 15 \times \sqrt{[2 - r_{11} - r_{22}]}$$

Given two IQ tests with full-scale IQ score reliabilities of .95 and .93, $SE_{diff} = 15 \times \sqrt{[2 - .95 - .93]}$, or $SE_{diff} = 5.2$. To determine how large a score difference could be obtained by chance (.05 level of probability), SE_{diff} (5.2 in example) is multiplied by 1.96 with a result of approximately 10.2 (rounded to 10 for discussion purposes). In this example, before interpreting the differences between two IQ test scores as significant ($p < .05$), an IQ-IQ difference would need to be at least ± 10 points.

It is important to note that the above example is based on internal consistency derived reliability for each of the two test batteries and does not incorporate the lower test-test reliability (stability) present when comparing IQ test scores across time. For example, in the previously mentioned Whitaker (2008) meta-analysis of the stability of IQ test scores for individuals with low general intelligence, the 95% IQ-IQ test score difference confidence interval may be as large as approximately ± 12.5 IQ points for two IQ test scores separated, on average, by approximately three years. (See Chapter 5 for further discussion of stability of IQ scores across time.)

Possible Explanations for IQ-IQ Score Differences

Factors contributing to significant IQ score differences are many and may include: (a) procedural or test administration errors (e.g., scoring errors, improper nonstandardized test administration, malingering, age vs. grade norms, practice effects); (b) test norm or standardization differences (e.g., norm obsolescence or the Flynn effect); (c) content differences across different test batteries or between different editions of the same battery; or (d) variations in a person's performance on different occasions (Floyd et al., 2008; McGrew, 1994; Schalock et al., 2010). Due to space limitations, only parts of (a) and (c) will be addressed here, as Chapters 5 and 10 address issues involved in topics (b) and (d).

Test procedural and administration errors. Ramos, Alfonso, and Schermerhorn (2009) summarized the extant research on examiner errors and reported sufficient average examiner error to produce significant changes in IQ test scores for many individuals. The most frequent types of errors reported included a failure to record responses, use of incorrect basal and ceiling rules, reporting an incorrect global IQ test score, incorrect adding of subtest scores, incorrect assignment of points for specific items, and incorrect calculation of the individual's age. On Wechsler-related studies, Ramos et al. (2009) found that studies have reported average error rates from 7.8 to 25.8 errors per test record, almost 90% of examiners making one error, and, in one study, two thirds of the reviewed test records resulted in a change in the full-scale IQ. Examiner errors do not appear to be instrument-specific, as Ramos et al.'s study reported an average error rate of 4.6 errors per test record on the WJ III.

The importance of verifying accurate administration and scoring is evident in the finding that, across both experienced psychologists and students in graduate training, differences between original obtained IQ scores and correctly scored IQ scores were as high as 25, 22, and 22 points for the WAIS-III Verbal, Performance, and Full Scale IQ test scores, respectively (Ryan & Schnakenberg-Ott, 2003). Despite examiners reporting confidence in their scoring accuracy, Ryan and Schnakenberg-Ott reported average levels of agreement with the standard (accurate) test record of only 26.3% (Verbal IQ), 36.8% (Performance IQ), and 42.1% (Full Scale IQ). This level of examiner error is alarming, particularly in the context of IQ test score-based life-and-death decisions such as in *Atkins* cases.

Content differences between IQ test batteries and within different editions of the same IQ test battery. As is often the case in *Atkins* cases, individuals have frequently been tested multiple times and often with different editions of a battery (e.g., WAIS-R, WAIS-III, and WAIS-IV). Psychologists who compare and interpret the consistency or variability of these scores must be aware of significant content changes across editions that may explain differences in the full-scale IQ scores. This point is illustrated with the adult Wechsler battery in Table 7.2. The points made also pertain to changes in different versions of other intelligence batteries and are not specific to the adult Wechsler series.

First, it is important to know that the adult Wechsler scales are based on 10 or more subtests that are added together to provide part scores (e.g., Verbal IQ, Performance IQ), as well as the full-scale IQ test score. The original Wechsler Adult Intelligence Scale (WAIS) and its second, revised, version (WAIS-R) were both comprised of six verbal tests that produced a Verbal IQ and five nonverbal tests that produced the Performance IQ score. The eleven tests together comprised the WAIS and WAIS-R Full Scale IQ. This is illustrated by the first two columns in Table 7.2. The gray shading indicates that the same eleven subtests were the basis of the WAIS and WAIS-R Full Scale IQ scores.

TABLE 7.2. Changes in Subtests Contributing to Adult Wechsler Full Scale IQ Scores Across Four Editions

Subtests	WAIS (1955)	WAIS-R (1981)	WAIS-III (1997)	WAIS-IV (2008)
Information	X	X	X	X
Comprehension	X	X	X	0
Arithmetic	X	X	X	X
Similarities	X	X	X	X
Vocabulary	X	X	X	X
Digit Span	X	X	X	X
Letter-Number Seq.			0	0
Picture Completion	X	X	X	0
Picture Arrangement	X	X	X	
Block Design	X	X	X	X
Object Assembly	X	X	0	
Digit Sym/Coding	X	X	X	X
Symbol Search			0	X
Matrix Reasoning			X	X
Visual Puzzles				X
Figure Weights				0
Cancellation				0

Note. X = subtests included in the calculation of the FS IQ for each edition of the WAIS.
0 = Supplemental tests. Shading demonstrates continuity of comosition of FS IQ scores.

As can be seen in Table 7.2, the WAIS-III started a process of revision to the adult Wechsler's wherein which all original 11 subtests were retained, but new subtests were added. More important is the fact that those WAIS-III subtests, designated by gray shading, no longer match the exact set of 11 subtests as in the WAIS and WAIS-R. Thus, the WAIS-III Full Scale IQ test score is based on a different mixture of subtests and abilities than the earlier WAIS and WAIS-R. When the WAIS-IV was published, it contained 15 subtests. More importantly, those subtests that contributed to the Full Scale IQ are not 100% comparable to the same set as in the WAIS-III or the WAIS and WAIS-R. The important conclusion from Table 7.2 is that, as the adult Wechsler battery evolved, the specific combination of tests that comprise the Full Scale IQ (i.e., the score used to aid in the diagnosis of ID) changed in composition. The result is that the full-scale IQ scores from the later WAIS-III and WAIS-IV are not 100% comparable in subtest (and abilities measured) to the earlier WAIS and WAIS-R, nor are the latest editions 100% comparable.

The differences in the ability domains measured by different intelligence batteries can produce significant and valid IQ score differences. Furthermore, when a specific line of intelligence test batteries is revised (e.g., Wechsler-Bellevue Intelligence Scale, WAIS, WAIS-R, WAIS-III, WAIS-IV; see Table 7.2), changes are often made to item content and old subtests are eliminated, demoted to supplemental status, or are

FIGURE 7.1. Changes in Proportional CHC Abilities Represented in Adult Wechsler Full Scale IQ Score Across Editions

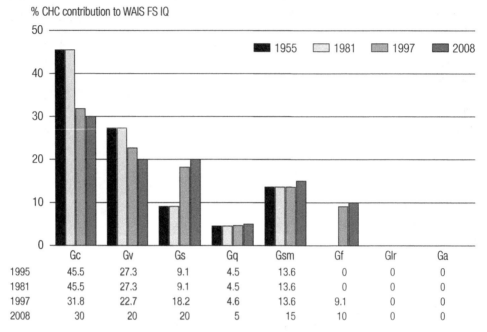

% CHC contribution to WAIS FS IQ

	Gc	Gv	Gs	Gq	Gsm	Gf	Glr	Ga
1995	45.5	27.3	9.1	4.5	13.6	0	0	0
1981	45.5	27.3	9.1	4.5	13.6	0	0	0
1997	31.8	22.7	18.2	4.6	13.6	9.1	0	0
2008	30	20	20	5	15	10	0	0

Source: McGrew, K. (2010). *Applied psychometrics 101 brief #6: Understanding Wechsler IQ score differences—the CHC evolution of the Wechsler FS IQ score.* Retrieved from http://www.iqscorner.com/2010/02/ap101-brief-6-understanding-wechsler-iq.html
Gc = Comprehension-knowledge; Gv = Visual-spatial processing; Gs = intellectual processing speed; Gq = quantitative knowledge; Gsm = short-term and working memory; Gf = Fluid intelligence or reasoning; Glr = long-term storage and retrieval; Ga = auditory processing.

replaced with completely new subtests. These changes can result in different editions of the similarly named intelligence battery (e.g., WAIS-R, WAIS-III, WAIS-IV) providing full-scale IQ test scores with enough substantive content differences to change the composition or flavor of the total IQ test scores that are compared.

Figure 7.1 demonstrates the changes in the abilities represented by the full-scale IQ test scores from the different editions of the adult Wechsler battery when results from CHC-based within- and cross-battery factor analysis studies have been completed (see Flanagan, Ortiz, & Alfonso, 2007; Keith & Reynolds, 2010; McGrew, 1997; McGrew & Flanagan, 1998, for summaries of this research). It is clear that the full-scale IQ scores from the 1955 WAIS and 1981 WAIS-R were measuring similar abilities. However, the advent of the 1997 WAIS-III resulted in a shift in abilities measured—less *Gc* (verbal) and *Gv* (visual-spatial), more *Gs* (processing speed), but similar proportions of *Gq* (quantitative knowledge) and *Gsm* (short-term and working memory). The decreasing importance of *Gc* and *Gv* continued in the 2008 WAIS-IV concurrently with a slight increase in *Gs* and *Gsm*. *Gq* and *Gf* were approximately the same in proportional contribution to the WAIS-IV Full Scale IQ as was in the WAIS-III. It should be obvious from this review that different IQ scores may result from individuals who have taken different versions of the adult Wechsler batteries. An understanding of the abilities comprising the composite IQ test score in intelligence batteries is required when attempting to understand and interpret possible IQ-IQ score differences within and across different series of intelligence tests.

It is clear from the above discussion that understanding a range of technical issues may be required when dealing with *Atkins* cases where significant IQ-IQ test score variability is present. If the professionals who administer or interpret the scores from IQ tests do not possess the necessary expertise regarding these technical issues and literature, then consultation with specialists who possess such expertise should be considered.

Use of General Intelligence Full Scale and Composite Part Scores

Examiners are typically faced with IQ battery subtest or part-score profiles that display some degree of variability between the part scores (e.g., the four WAIS-IV index scores) or between the individual subtest scores. The extant research suggests that a certain degree of within-profile variability is normal and not diagnostically significant. However, there are situations when the observed score variability is so large that the validity of the total full-scale IQ should be questioned. More importantly, there are situations where select IQ battery component part scores may be better estimates of an individual's general intelligence than the full-scale IQ. As summarized by Reschly, Meyers, & Hartel,

> whenever the validity of one or more part scores (subtests, scales) is questioned, examiners must also question whether the test's total score is appropriate for guiding diagnostic decision making. The total test score is usually considered the best estimate of a client's overall intellectual functioning. However, there are instances in which, and individuals for whom, the total test score may not be the best representation of overall cognitive functioning. (2002, p. 106–107).

In the Reschly et al. (2002) National Academy of Sciences report, "Committee member Keith Widaman dissents from this part of the recommendation. Dr. Widaman believes that IQ part scores representing crystallized intelligence (*Gc*, similar to Verbal IQ) and fluid intelligence (*Gf*, related to performance IQ) have clear discriminant validity and represent broad, general domains of intellectual functioning" (Reschly et al., 2002, p. 3, footnote 1).

A number of issues must first be considered before using component part scores to estimate an individual's level of general intelligence—statistical significance, meaningful differences, and appropriate intellectual abilities (Reschly et al., 2002). First, preference for part scores (instead of the full-scale IQ) should occur only if there are statistically significant differences between the intelligence battery part scores that contribute to the full-scale IQ. The technical manual and/or computer-generated score interpretation report for each intelligence battery typically includes the necessary information to determine if the part scores are statistically different. If not, "the total score is unequivocally the best indicator of overall cognitive functioning and should be used for decision making" (Reschly et al., 2002). Second, the presence of statistically significant part score differences is a necessary, but not sufficient, condition for not interpreting the full-scale IQ score. The differences must also be meaningful differences—relatively rare or unusual in the general population. This is often referred to as base rate, which is defined as "the unconditional, naturally occurring rate of a phenomenon in a population" (VandenBos, 2007, p. 103). Statistically significant part-score differences that occur less frequently than approximately 25% of the general population have been recommended as an appropriate base rate for considering IQ part scores in the determination of general intelligence (Reschly et al., 2002). Collectively, these first two points indicate that part-score differences should be *both* statistically significant and relatively unusual in the population before an examiner determines that the total full-scale score is not the best indicator of an individual's general level of intellectual functioning. If these two conditions are met, then one or more of the part scores might be used to estimate the individual's general intelligence. However, the examiner cannot just use any part score(s) for ID determination. Only the most appropriate part-score measures should be used to diagnose ID. The use of part scores is not the generally accepted method for diagnosing ID and should only be used in unusual cases where the validity of the full-scale IQ score is clearly in doubt. The use of part scores in idiosyncratic "junk science" interpretations is not appropriate.. The joint test standards established by AERA, APA, & NCME (1999), in particular, should be adhered to in these unusual cases and would include, at a minimum, (a) providing evidence to support the use of particular part scores as the best proxies for estimating general intelligence for the specific case (Standard 1.4); (b) minimizing potential misinterpretations and unintended consequences in the use of part scores (Standard 11.5); (c) the articulation of a scientific-based logical analysis of relevant reliability and validity evidence to support inferences and interpretations (Standard 12.13); and (d) use of multiple sources of convergent and collateral data to support the unique case-specific interpretation (Standards 12.18 and 12.19). The use of part scores should not be used as a justification for abbreviated evaluations, a means to not sufficiently explore diagnostic questions, or to solve sociopolitical problems. Formalized clinical judgment, as articulated by Schalock and Luckasson (2005), must be followed. Such clinical judgment is characterized as "being systematic (i.e., organized, sequential, and logical), formal (i.e., explicit and reasoned), and transparent (i.e., apparent and communicated clearly)" (p. 1).

The issue of appropriate intellectual abilities deals with which part scores within an intelligence battery are most associated with general intelligence (*g*). The part scores that are more associated with general intelligence are often referred to as the high *g*-loading scores. The research- and theory-based consensus is that measures of *Gc* and *Gf* are the highest *g*-loading measures and constructs and are the most likely candidates for elevated status in diagnosing ID (Reschly et al., 2002). However, examination of the *g*-ness of composite scores from existing batteries (last three columns in

Table 7.1) suggests this traditional assumption may *not* hold across all intelligence batteries. (The h^2 values are the values that should be used to compare the relative amount of *g*-variance present in the component part scores within each intelligence battery.)

In the case of the SB5, all five composite part scores are very similar in *g*-loadings (h^2 = .72 to .79). No single SB5 composite part score appears more superior to the other scores when attempting to diagnose ID on the basis of these scores (and not the full-scale IQ score). At the other extreme is the WJ III, where the Fluid Reasoning, Comprehension-Knowledge, and Long-Term Storage and Retrieval clusters scores are the best *g*-proxies for part-score based interpretation. The WJ III Visual Processing and Processing Speed clusters are not composite part scores that should form the primary basis for an argument of ID due to their relatively low *g*-loadings. Across all batteries that include a processing speed component part score (i.e., Differential Ability Scales–Second edition [DAS-II], WAIS-IV, WISC-IV, WJ III), the processing speed scale is always the weakest proxy for general intelligence and, thus, would not be viewed as a good standalone estimate of general intelligence.

It is also clear that one cannot assume that composites with similar sounding names of measured abilities will have similar relative *g*-ness status within different batteries. For example, the *Gv* (visual-spatial or visual processing) clusters in the DAS-II (Spatial Ability) and SB5 (Visual-Spatial Processing) are relatively strong *g*-measures within their respective battery, but the same cannot be said for the WJ III Visual Processing cluster. Even more interesting are the differences in the WAIS-IV and WISC-IV relative *g*-loadings for similarly sounding index scores.

For example, the Working Memory Index is the highest *g*-loading component part score (tied with Perceptual Reasoning Index) in the WAIS-IV, but is only third (out of four) in the WISC-IV. The Working Memory Index comprises the Digit Span and Arithmetic subtests in the WAIS-IV and the Digit Span and the Letter-Number Sequencing subtests in the WISC-IV. The Arithmetic subtest has been reported to be a factorially complex test that may tap fluid intelligence (quantitative reasoning), quantitative knowledge, working memory, and possibly processing speed (Keith & Reynolds, 2010; Phelps, McGrew, Knopik & Ford, 2005). The factorially complex characteristics of the Arithmetic subtest (which, in essence, makes it function like a mini-*g* proxy) would explain why the WAIS-IV Working Memory Index is a good proxy for *g* in the WAIS-IV, but not the WISC-IV.

The above within and across intelligence battery examples of relative part score *g*-ness illustrate that those who pursue a diagnosis of ID based on such scores must be aware of the composition and psychometric *g*-ness of the component scores of the intelligence battery scores interpreted. This is not a new problem in the context of naming factors in factor analysis and, by extension, factor-based intelligence test composite scores. Cliff (1983) described this nominalistic fallacy in simple language—"if we name something, this does not mean we understand it" (p. 120). Not all component part scores in different intelligence batteries are created equal (with regard to *g*-ness).

Finally, before one or more part scores are used to estimate a person's general level of intellectual functioning (in place of the full-scale IQ score), the part score(s) should be evaluated to determine that it is representing a unitary ability. In the context of the WAIS-IV, but relevant to all part scores within all intelligence batteries, Lichtenberger and Kaufman (2009) explained that

> a unitary ability is an ability (such as Crystallized Intelligence or Processing Speed) that is represented by a cohesive set of scale scores, each reflecting slightly different or unique aspects of the ability. Thus, when the variability among the subtest scale scores that compose a WAIS-IV Index is not unusually large, the ability presumed to underlie the index is considered unitary and may be interpreted. (p. 167)

The technical manuals and/or scoring interpretative software for intelligence batteries typically provide the necessary information that allows examiners to ascertain if the variability between the subtests that comprise a part score is relatively consistent and, thus, indicating that a part score can be interpreted as a measure of a valid intellectual ability. If significant and meaningful differences are present among the subtest scores for a part score, then the part score may not be interpretable (Lichtenberger & Kaufman, 2009).

Relation Between Intelligence and Adaptive Behavior Scores

Given the pivotal role intelligence tests and scales of adaptive behavior (AB) play in the diagnosis of ID, it is important to know the typical relation (correlation) between their respective scores. Numerous AB/IQ correlations studies were published in the late 1970s and 1980s between a wide variety of adaptive behavior scales and intelligence tests. Probably the best synthesis of this research was provided by Harrison (1987), which included a table of over 40+ AB/IQ correlations. Harrison (1987) concluded that "the majority of correlations fall in the moderate range" (p. 39). When the correlations with maladaptive measures are excluded from Harrison's table, the correlations range from .03 to .91. Harrison could not identify a specific explanation for the variability or range of the correlations.

The Committee on Disability Determination for Mental Retardation published a National Research Council report (*Mental Retardation: Determining Eligibility for Social Security Benefits*; Reschly et al., 2002) that also addressed the AB/IQ relationship. The report concluded that AB/IQ studies report correlations

> ranging from 0 (indicating no relationship) to almost +1 (indicating a perfect relationship). Data also suggest that the relationship between IQ and adaptive behavior varies significantly by age and levels of retardation, being strongest in the severe and moderate ranges and weakest in the mild range. There is a dearth

of data on the relationship of IQ and adaptive behavior functioning at the mild level of retardation. (p. 8)

Factors identified as moderating the AB/IQ correlation were scale content, measurement of competences versus perceptions, sample variability, ceiling and floor problems of the scales, and level ofintellectual disability .

Recently, McGrew (2012) combined the 40+ AB/IQ correlations from Harrison (1987) with those reported in the technical manuals of the three most frequently used contemporary adaptive behavior scales (i.e., Vineland Adaptive Behavior Scale, Sparrow, Cicchetti & Balla, 2005; Adaptive Behavior Scales—II, Harrison & Oakland, 2008; Scales of Independent Behavior-Revised, Bruininks, Woodcock, Weatherman & Hill, 1996). Also, the latent AB/IQ correlations (as estimated from confirmatory factor analysis models) reported by Ittenbach, Spiegel, McGrew, and Bruininks (1992); Keith, Fehrmann, Harrison, and Pottebaum (1987); and McGrew and Bruininks (1990) were included. This resulted in the addition of 17 AB/IQ correlations to the 43 from Harrison, for a total of 60 correlations. Focus was only on the composite IQ and AB correlations and not the part scores from the respective measurement instruments.

The 60 AB/IQ correlations ranged from .12 to .90 with a mean of .51, a median of .48, and a standard deviation of .20. McGrew (2012) concluded that an estimate of the typical AB/IQ correlation is approximately .50, with most correlations ranging from approximately .40 to .65. This finding is consistent with Harrison's (1987) conclusion of a moderate correlation. In practical terms, this means that, for any individual, standard scores from AB and IQ scales will frequently diverge and will not always be consistent.

Harrison (1987) provides a succinct explanation for the primary reasons for the moderate correlation between AB and IQ:

Although intelligence and adaptive behavior scales have many similarities in purposes and uses, several basic differences in the two types of scales warrant this type investigation. According to Meyers et al. (1979), the measurement of intelligence and adaptive behavior differs in several respects, including the following: (1) intelligence scales emphasize thought processes while adaptive behavior scales emphasize everyday behavior, (2) intelligence scales measure maximum performance or potential while adaptive behavior scales measure typical performance, and (3) intelligence scales presume a stability in scores while adaptive behavior scales presume modifiability of performance. (p. 39)

Implications for Practice

The following implications for practice are based on the integration of the content of the current chapter and recommendations from Schalock et al. (2010), the Committee on Disability Determination for Mental Retardation (Reschly et al., 2002), and the *Standards for Educational and Psychological Testing* (AERA, APA, & NCME, 1999). In addition, selected ethical and professional practice guideline publications were also considered in identifying implications (Gold et al., 2008; Macvaugh & Cunningham, 2009).

Intelligence test battery selection. The diagnosis of ID should be based on an individually administered, comprehensive, nationally, and recently normed intelligence battery that yields a full-scale score of general intellectual functioning (*g*-composite score). Intelligence batteries used in the diagnosis of ID must meet the appropriate professionally accepted psychometric standards of reliability, validity, representative norm sample, and test fairness for diagnostic purposes as per the joint test standards (AERA, APA, & NCME, 1999; see Reschly et al., 2002). The intelligence batteries listed in Table 7.1 meet this definition and standards and represent the most likely comprehensive, individually administered intelligence test batteries found in the records of *Atkins* cases. (The listing of the intelligence batteries in Table 7.1 indicates they meet the primary psychometric criteria for providing a valid measure of general intelligence in a representative sample. However, the publication dates of each battery should be inspected, as some of the batteries may have significant norm obsolescence (i.e., Flynn effect) issues.) Furthermore, often in *Atkins* cases, the individual has a file that may contain historical reports of prior intelligence test scores. In general, a majority of the earlier predecessors of the batteries listed in Table 7.1 meet most psychometric criteria for aiding in ID determination. There are too many exceptions to this statement to be covered in this chapter. For example, as described earlier with regard to the evolution of the WAIS to the WAIS-IV, the newer versions (WAIS-III and WAIS-IV) have benefited from decades of research on intelligence and are better measures of general intelligence (more aligned with contemporary research and theory) than the earlier WAIS and WAIS-R. The same applies to the other series of intelligence batteries listed in Table 7.1. Short-form, group, or computer-administered tests are inappropriate for determining an individual's level of general intellectual functioning for diagnostic purposes. Less comprehensive special purpose intelligence measures (e.g., measures that use nonverbal test administration procedures) should only play a role in estimating general intelligence when individual-specific characteristics (e.g., test fairness issues due to cultural, social, ethnic, or language factors) clearly suggest that the comprehensive individual intelligence batteries are inappropriate for this purpose. Several qualifying considerations are also discussed as follows:

Comprehensive intelligence battery defined. A measure of general intelligence (i.e., full-scale IQ) should be based on a variety of different tests that vary on information content, skills, and mental operations, and sample from at least three primary intelligence domains (e.g., at least three of the broad CHC intelligence domains; Jensen, 1998). These criteria ensure that the general intelligence estimate for an individual is based on a multidimensional (versus a unidimensional) estimate of intelligence. All intelligence batteries listed in Table 7.1 meet these criteria. Given the assumptions of exchangeability, the full-scale IQ scores from these batteries can be thought of as largely interchangeable, although there will be specific situations and unique characteristics of examinees for which the assumption will be untenable (see "Comparability/Exchange-ability of IQ Recommendation" section).

Credentials of the individual who is undertaking the assessment. The diagnosis of ID is a serious task, particularly in the context of *Atkins* cases. *Atkins*-related intellectual assessments should be completed and interpreted only by examiners who: (a) have experience with individuals who have ID, (b) are qualified in terms of professional and state regulations and licensing laws, (c) have met the test publisher's guidelines for using a specific battery, (c) are familiar with the strengths and limitations of the intelligence batteries from which they interpret full-scale IQ test scores, (d) are familiar with the assumptions and recommendations of the current AAIDD manual and relevant professional guidelines and principles of practice , and (e) are familiar with all the joint test standards relevant to the use of psychological tests for diagnostic and classification purposes (see also Chapter 22).

Measurement error and cut-scores. Intelligence tests are fallible instruments that result in the obtained full-scale IQ test score potentially being influenced by a number of sources of unreliability or measurement error (e.g., examinee characteristics, examiner influences, environmental conditions, psychometric issues; see Reschly et al., 2002 for discussion). The full-scale IQ test score must be reported with a 95% confidence interval based on the test's standard error of measurement (*SEM*), which for almost all intelligence batteries is approximately ±5 IQ test score points (see Chapter 5). The use of the *SEM* ensures that a specific IQ test score is interpreted as existing within a range of scores reflecting the known measurement error of the intelligence battery. The obtained score is only an estimate of an individual's "true" score. Examiners who provide reports, depositions, or expert testimony have an ethical and professional responsibility to educate the recipient(s) of their interpretations that the diagnosis of ID should not hinge on a single "bright line" specific cut-score. Rigid point-specific IQ cut-scores are arbitrary and fail to reflect the complexities of proper diagnosis of ID, especially a mild level of ID. Specific obtained scores must be interpreted within the context of the 95% confidence interval based on the *SEM*.

Test administration and scoring errors. The frequency and magnitude of test administration and scoring errors reported in intelligence testing research warrants special comment and recommendation. Before attempting to interpret any IQ test scores in *Atkins* cases, or trying to reconcile IQ-IQ test score differences between tests, the first step should be to seek an independent review of the examinee's test records. Any obvious errors should be corrected and new scores recalculated if necessary. Only then should professionals proceed to draw conclusions about scores. If possible, any intelligence test results used in an *Atkins* hearing should be subject to independent review of the original test protocol to ensure against administration or scoring errors that might result in significant differences in the reported IQ test score. Several professional training and monitoring recommendations have empirically demonstrated improvement in reducing such errors (see Erodi, Richard, & Hopwood, 2009; Hopwood

& Richard, 2005; Kuentzel, Hetterscheidt, & Barnett, 2011; Ramos et al., 2009; Ryan & Schnakenberg-Ott, 2003).

The Flynn effect. The Flynn effect (FE) relates to norm obsolescence, which must be recognized and incorporated in the interpretation of IQ test scores when scores from older editions of intelligence batteries are reported. In cases where a test with out-of-date norms was used, a correction for the age of the norms is warranted (Schalock et al., 2010; Schalock et al., 2012). See Chapter 10 for a thorough discussion of norm obsolescence.

Comparability and exchangeability of IQ scores. Succinctly stated, "not all scores obtained on intelligence tests given to the same person will be identical" (Schalock et al., 2010, p. 38). Professionals reporting multiple current or historical IQ scores must be aware of and make appropriate interpretations that recognize the various factors that may contribute to significant IQ test score differences. Assessment professionals should:

a. *Recognize the changing content of contemporary IQ test batteries.* The fact that contemporary intelligence test batteries have become more multidimensional as per contemporary intelligence research and theory warrants special comment and recommendations. Intelligence test battery content differences may be one of the more salient explanations of significant IQ-IQ test score differences. Assessment professionals interpreting IQ-IQ test score differences must integrate knowledge of the changing nature of the full-scale IQ test scores between different contemporary intelligence test batteries (e.g., WAIS-IV vs. SB5; see Flanagan & Harrison, 2012; Flanagan et al., 2007; and Keith & Reynolds, 2010), as well as content differences between older and newer versions of the same battery (e.g., WAIS-R vs. WAIS-III; WAIS-R vs. WAIS-IV), to appropriately interpret the score differences and to render an appropriate professional opinion regarding an individual's general level of intellectual functioning. If an assessment professional integrates the results of historical intelligence testing, it is the professional's responsibility to be familiar with the psychometric characteristics of these tests and possible content changes between instruments so that current and historical testing can be integrated in a scientifically based, professional, and ethical manner in the context of accepted clinical judgment procedures (Schalock & Luckasson, 2005). The *Mental Measurement Yearbook* online service (http://buros.unl.edu/buros/jsp/search.jsp) is accessible to assessment professionals when historical test information is needed.

b. *Prior to interpreting IQ-IQ test score differences, the SE$_{diff}$ statistic should be used to determine if IQ-IQ test score differences are significant.* It is recommended that the discussion and interpretation of discrepancies between IQ test scores incorporate the SE$_{diff}$ statistic to evaluate whether a difference is statistically significant.

c. *Interpretation of multiple and discrepant IQ scores.* When reports contain multiple IQ test scores, either given concurrently or over the lifespan of an individual, examiners should ascertain (to the best of their abilities given the psychological reports available) whether the respective full-scale scores that are compared were judged to be reliable and valid estimates at the original time of testing. When multiple reliable and valid IQ test scores are available, the goal is not to identify which single score is the "best" estimate of an individual's general intelligence. Assessment professionals should integrate the multiple scores and provide a scientific and professionally accepted estimate, using reliable and valid principles and methods, of the person's general level of intellectual functioning. When the multiple scores are reasonably consistent (i.e., a convergence of indicators) and any significant differences are explainable, assessment professionals can have greater confidence in their diagnostic conclusion. Conversely, when major score differences are present in a collection of IQ test scores, interpretations require assessment professionals to educate the recipients of their findings regarding the potential reasons for the IQ test score variability. For example, assessment professionals should address issues such as practice effects, stability of intelligence over time, content differences between different batteries, the Flynn effect, and other issues that affect the comparability of IQ scores included in their written reports or statements.

Use of composite part scores. The total full-scale IQ score is usually the best estimate of a client's overall intellectual functioning for diagnostic purposes. However, there are instances in which, and individuals for whom, the total test score may not be the best representation of overall intellectual functioning. These situations occur when statistically significant and meaningful differences are observed between the part scores that comprise the full-scale IQ score. In such situations, appropriate part scores that have high g-loadings (e.g., WAIS-IV Verbal Comprehension; WJ III Fluid Reasoning and Comprehension-Knowledge) may be used when the validity of the full-scale IQ score is in doubt. There are certain additional, related considerations:

a. *Appropriate part or component scores as g-proxies.* The use of part scores to diagnose ID must be done cautiously and be based on sound scientific evidence and be consistent with accepted professional standards. The use of part scores may increase the potential for more accurate diagnosis for individual cases, but also raises the possibility of misuse via selective "cherry picking" of part scores to either support or refute an ID diagnosis. For example, as reflected in Table 7.1 and the associated discussion in this chapter, processing speed (*Gs*) scores are the weakest proxies for general intelligence. An argument that a person's low processing speed scores support a diagnosis of ID, in the context of higher g-loading scores (e.g., fluid and crystallized intelligence) that are above the ID range, is not supported by, and would be contrary to, the scientific evidence regarding g-ness of part or component scores. The presence of a high and significantly discrepant

WAIS-IV Processing Speed Index score that raises the WAIS-IV Full Scale IQ just above the ID cutoff score, when combined with WAIS-IV Perceptual Reasoning, Verbal Comprehension, and Working Memory Index scores within the ID range, would be consistent with the possibility of a diagnosis of ID despite the full-scale IQ score. Alternatively, a low WJ III General Intellectual Ability (GIA) score just within the ID range might mask a proper ID diagnosis if the individual had relative weaknesses (significant and meaningfully different) on the low-g WJ III Visual Processing and Processing Speed clusters, but strengths noticeably above the ID cutoff score on high-g Fluid Reasoning, Comprehension-Knowledge, and Long-Term Storage and Retrieval clusters. These two examples could be repeated with all the intelligence batteries listed in Table 7.1.

The part-score g-loadings presented in Table 7.1 provide initial guidance to assist assessment professionals in evaluating which part scores may be the best proxies for general intelligence within each respective intelligence battery. Examiners should seek out and use additional scientific evidence from each intelligence battery's technical manual and independent published research to support interpretations based on the g-ness of part scores in individual cases. Assessment professionals should be familiar with the g-loading scientific literature regarding those instruments when they use the pattern of part scores to support or refute a diagnosis of ID. An ID diagnosis based on part scores should be supported by the presentation of relevant research, as discussed earlier in the chapter, in written reports and statements.

b. *Significant and meaningful differences and patterns.* When part scores are used to formulate a diagnosis of ID, professionals must offer psychometric evidence that the full-scale IQ score is likely an invalid estimate of a person's general intelligence. Differential interpretation of part scores must only occur when the assessment professional provides evidence that the differences between part scores are *statistically significant* and *meaningfully different*. Part scores may be statistically significant, but the base rate in the population may not suggest that such a difference is meaningful (see Reschly et al., 2002, for detailed discussion). When the differences between part scores are not statistically significant or meaningful, or when the pattern of intellectual strengths and weakness does not display an internally consistent high and low g-loading part score pattern, then the full-scale IQ score should remain as the primary IQ score for estimating an individual's general intellectual functioning, as per the AAIDD definition.

Clinical judgment is often required and necessary in the interpretation of intelligence test results. Professional clinical judgment is often required and necessary when interpreting scores from intelligence batteries, particularly when an *Atkins* client has a file that contains multiple IQ test scores that span many years or when part scores are used (in place of the full-scale IQ score) as the basis of a diagnosis of ID.

Clinical judgment is a process based on solid scientific knowledge and is characterized as being "systematic (i.e., organized, sequential, and logical), formal (i.e., explicit and reasoned), and transparent (i.e., apparent and communicated clearly)" (Schalock & Luckasson, 2005, p.1). The misuse of clinical judgment in the interpretation of scores from intelligence test batteries should not be used as the basis for "gut instinct" or "seat-of-the-pants" impressions and conclusions of the assessment professional (Macvaugh & Cunningham, 2009), or justification for shortened evaluations, a means to convey stereotypes or prejudices, a substitute for insufficiently explored questions, or an excuse for incomplete testing and missing data (Schalock & Luckasson, 2005). Idiosyncratic methods and intuitive conclusions are not scientifically based and have unknown reliability and validity. If interpretations and opinions regarding an individual's level of general intelligence are based on novel or emerging research-based principles, the assessment professional must document the bases for these new interpretations as well as the limitations of these principles and methods.

Comparison of adaptive behavior and IQ scores. Intelligence test information must be interpreted within the context of relevant collateral information. Adaptive behavior is one major source of collateral information. Adaptive behavior total composite and intelligence full-scale IQ scores correlate at a moderate level. Thus, assessment professionals should not always expect adaptive behavior and IQ scores to be consistent. These two scores represent distinctly different measures of different domains of personal competence. Users can expect that, 68% of the time, an adaptive behavior composite score can range from as much as 15 points lower to 15 points higher than the measured full-scale IQ test score. At the 95% confidence level, the adaptive behavior composite scores may range from up to ±30 points different from any specific IQ score. When significant and meaningful adaptive behavior and intelligence test score differences are present for individuals, professionals must provide scientific and professionally accepted interpretation for differences that may include, but are not limited to:

a. adaptive behavior scales are measuring typical performance, while intelligence test batteries are measuring maximal performance;

b. adaptive behavior scales focus on everyday behavior, while intelligence tests emphasis mental thought processes;

c. adaptive behavior measures competencies that are more malleable and subject to change due to either positive or negative changes in a person's environment(s), while intelligence test batteries measure a more stable set of abilities; and

d. third-party informants typically provide the raw material of adaptive behavior in contrast to the individuals themselves providing direct information via their responses in a structured and standardized 1-1 testing situation.

See Chapters 11–13 for more detailed discussion of issues surrounding the administration and interpretation of adaptive behavior scales.

References

Ackerman, P. L., & Lohman, D. F. (2006). Individual differences in cognitive functions. In P. A. Alexander & P. Winne (Eds.), *Handbook of educational psychology*—(2nd ed.) (pp. 139–161). Mahwah, NJ: Erlbaum.

American Educational Research Association, American Psychological Association, & National Council on Measurement in Education. (1999). *Standards for educational and psychological testing.* Washington, DC: American Educational Research Association.

Anastasi, A., & Urbina, A. (1997). *Psychological testing* (7th ed.). Upper Saddle River, NJ: Prentice Hall.

Brody, N. (2000). History of theories and measurements of intelligence. In R. J. Sternberg (Ed.), *Handbook of intelligence* (pp. 16–33). New York, NY: Cambridge University Press.

Bruininks, R. H., Woodcock, R. W., Weatherman, R. F., & Hill, B. K. (1996). *SIB-R: Scales of Independent Behavior—Revised.* Chicago, IL: Riverside.

Burns, R. B. (1994). Surveying the cognitive terrain. *Educational Researcher, 23*(2), 35–37.

Carroll, J. B. (1993). *Human cognitive abilities: A survey of factor analytic studies.* New York, NY: Cambridge University Press.

Cattell, R. B. (1941). Some theoretical issues in adult intelligence testing. *Psychological Bulletin, 38,* 592.

Cattell, R. B. (1943). The measurement of adult intelligence. *Psychological Bulletin, 40,* 153–193.

Cliff, N. (1983). Some cautions concerning the application of causal modeling methods. *Multivariate Behavioral Research, 18,* 115–126.

Cudek, R., & MacCallum, R. C. (2007). *Factor analysis at 100: Historical developments and future directions.* Mahwah, NJ: Erlbaum.

Daniel, M. H. (1997). Intelligence testing: Status and trends. *American Psychologist, 52,* 1038–1045.

Daniel, M. H. (2000). Interpretation of intelligence test scores. In R. Sternberg (Ed.), *Handbook of intelligence* (pp. 477–491). New York, NY: Cambridge University Press.

Drozdick, L. W., Wahlstrom, D., Zhu, J., & Weiss, L. G. (2012). The Wechsler Adult Intelligence Scale—(4th ed.) and the Wechsler Memory Scale—(4th ed.). In D. Flanagan, & P. L. Harrison (Eds.), *Contemporary intellectual assessment: Theories, tests, and issues* (3rd ed., pp. 197–223). New York, NY: Guilford.

Ekstrom, R. B., French, J. W., & Harman, H. H. (1979). Cognitive factors: Their identification and replication. *Multivariate Behavioral Research Monographs, 79*(2), 3–84.

Elliott, C. D. (2007). *Differential Ability Scales* (2nd ed.). San Antonio, TX: Pearson.

Erodi, L. A., Richard, D. C. S., & Hopwood, C. (2009). The importance of relying on the manual: Scoring error variance in the WISC-IV Vocabulary test. *Journal of Psychoeducational Assessment, 27*(5), 374–385. doi: 10.1177/0734282909332913

Flanagan, D. P., & Harrison, P. L. (Eds.). (2012). *Contemporary intellectual assessment* (3rd ed.). New York, NY: Guilford Press.

Flanagan, D. P., Ortiz, S. O., & Alfonso, V. (2007). *Essentials of cross-battery assessment* (2nd ed.). Hoboken, NJ: Wiley.

Floyd, R. G., Clark, M. H., & Shadish, W. R. (2008). The exchangeability of IQs: Implications for professional psychology. *Professional Psychology: Research and Practice, 39,* 414–423. doi: 10.1037/0735-7028.39.4.414

French, J. W. (1951). *The description of aptitude and achievement tests in terms of rotated factors* (Psychometric Monographs No. 5). Chicago, IL: University of Chicago Press.

French, J. W., Ekstrom, R. B., & Price, L. A. (1963). *Manual and kit of reference tests for cognitive factors.* Princeton, NJ: Educational Testing Service.

Gold, L. H., Anfang, S. A., Drukteinis, A. M., Metzner, J. L., Price, M., Wall, B. W., . . . & Zonana, H. V. (2008). AAPL practice guidelines for the forensic evaluation of psychiatric disability. *Journal of the American Academy of Psychiatry and the Law—Supplement, 36*(4), S3–S50. doi: 36/Supplement_4/S3

Guilford, J. P. (1967). *The nature of human intelligence*. New York, NY: McGraw-Hill.

Hakstian, A. R., & Cattell, R. B. (1974). The checking of primary ability structure on a basis of twenty primary abilities. *British Journal of Educational Psychology, 44*, 140–154.

Harrison, P. L. (1987). Research with adaptive behavior scales. *Journal of Special Education, 21*, 37–68.

Harrison, P. L., & Oaklan, T. (2003). Adaptive Behavior Assessment System manual (2nd ed.). Los Angeles: Western Psychological Services.

Hopwood, C. J., & Richard, D. C. S. (2005). WAIS-III scoring accuracy is a function of scale IC and complexity of examiner tasks. *Assessment, 12*, 445–454.

Horn, J. L. (1976). Human abilities: A review of research and theory in the early 1970s. *Annual Review of Psychology, 27*, 437–485.

Horn, J. L. (1989). Measurement of intellectual capabilities: A review of theory. In K. S. McGrew, J. K. Werder, & R. W. Woodcock (Eds.), *WJ-R technical manual* (pp. 197–245). Chicago, IL: Riverside.

Horn, J. L., & Noll, J. (1997). Human cognitive capabilities: Gf-Gc theory. In D. P. Flanagan, J. L. Genshaft, & P. L. Harrison (Eds.), *Contemporary intellectual assessment: Theories, tests and issues* (pp. 53–91). New York, NY: Guilford.

Ittenbach, R., Spiegel, A., McGrew, K. S., & Bruininks, R. (1992). A confirmatory factor analysis of early childhood ability measures within a model of personal competence. *Journal of School Psychology, 30*, 307–323.

Jensen, A. R. (1998). *The g factor: The science of mental ability*. Westport, CT: Praeger.

Jensen, A. R. (2004). Obituary—John Bissell Carroll. *Intelligence, 32*, 1–5. doi: 10.1016/j.intell.2003.10.001

Kaufman, A. S. (2009). *IQ testing 101*. New York, NY: Springer.

Kaufman, A. S., & Kaufman, N. L. (1993). Kaufman Adolescent and Adult Intelligence Test. Circle Pines, MN: American Guidance Service.

Kaufman, A. S., & Kaufman, N. L. (2004). *Kaufman Assessment Battery for Children* (2nd ed.). San Antonio, TX: Pearson.

Keith, T., Fehrmann, P., Harrison, P., & Pottebaum, S. (1987). The relation between adaptive behavior and intelligence. Testing alternative explanations. *Journal of School Psychology, 25*, 31–43.

Keith, T. Z., & Reynolds, M. R. (2010). Cattell–Horn–Carroll abilities and cognitive tests: What we've learned from 20 years of research. *Psychology in the Schools, 47*, 635–650. doi: 10.1002/pits.20496

Kuentzel, J. G., Hetterscheidt, L. A., & Barnett, D. (2011). Testing intelligently includes double-checking Wechsler IQ scores. *Journal of Psychoeducational Assessment, 29*, 39–46. doi: 10.1177/0734282910362048

Lichtenberger, E. O., & Kaufman, A. S. (2009). *Essentials of WAIS-IV assessment*. Hoboken, NJ: Wiley.

Macvaugh, G. S., & Cunningham, M. D. (2009). *Atkins v. Virginia*: Implications and recommendations for forensic practice. *Journal of Psychiatry and Law, 37*, 131–187.

Meyers, C. E., Nihira, K., & Zetlin, A. (1979). The measurement of adaptive behavior. In N R. Ellis (Ed.), Handbook *of mental deficiency: Psychological theory and research* (2nd ed., pp. 215–253). Hillsdale, NJ: Erlbaum.

McGrew, K. S. (1994). *Clinical interpretation of the Woodcock-Johnson Tests of Cognitive Ability Revised*. Boston, MA: Allyn and Bacon.

McGrew, K. S. (1997). Analysis of the major intelligence batteries according to a proposed comprehensive Gf-Gc framework. In D. P. Flanagan, J. L. Genshaft, & P. L. Harrison (Eds.), *Contemporary intellectual assessment: Theories, tests, and issues* (pp. 151–179). New York, NY: Guilford.

McGrew, K. S. (2005). The Cattell–Horn–Carroll theory of cognitive abilities. In D. P. Flanagan & P. L. Harrison (Eds.) *Contemporary intellectual assessment: Theories, tests, and issues* (2nd ed., pp. 136–181). New York, NY: Guilford Press.

McGrew, K. (2009). Editorial: CHC theory and the human cognitive abilities project: Standing on the shoulders of the giants of psychometric intelligence research. *Intelligence, 37*, 1–10. doi:10.1016/j.intell.2008.08.004

McGrew, K. (2010). *Applied psychometrics 101 brief #6: Understanding Wechsler IQ score differences—the CHC evolution of the Wechsler FS IQ score.* Retrieved from http://www.iqscorner.com/2010/02/ap101-brief-6-understanding-wechsler-iq.html

McGrew, K. S. (2012). IAP Applied Psychometrics 101 Brief Report # 11: What is the typical IQ and adaptive behavior correlation? *Intelligent Insights on Intelligence Theories and Tests (aka, IQ's Corner).* Retrieved from http://www.iqscorner.com/search/label/adaptive%20behavior

McGrew, K., & Bruininks, R. (1990). Defining adaptive and maladaptive behavior within a model of personal competence. *School Psychology Review, 19*, 53–73.

McGrew, K., & Flanagan, D. (1998). *The Intelligence Test Desk Reference (ITDR). Gf-Gc cross-battery assessment.* Boston, MA: Allyn & Bacon.

Mental Measurement Yearbook. Retrieved from http://buros.org/how-cite-reviews-buros-institutes-test-reviews-online

Naglieri, J. A., Das, J. P., & Goldstein, S. (2012). Planning, attention, simultaneous, successive: A cognitive-processing-based theory of intelligence. In D. Flanagan, & P. L. Harrison (Eds.), *Contemporary intellectual assessment: Theories, tests, and issues* (3rd ed., pp. 178–194). New York, NY: Guilford.

Neisser, U., Boodoo, G., Bouchard, T. J., Jr., Boykin, A. W., Brody, N., Ceci, S. J., ... Urbina, S. (1996). Intelligence: Knowns and unknowns. *American Psychologist, 51*, 77–101.

Phelps, L., McGrew, K. S., Knopik, S. N., & Ford, L. (2005). The general (*g*), broad, and narrow CHC stratum characteristics of the WJ III and WISC-III tests: A confirmatory cross-battery investigation. *School Psychology Quarterly, 20*, 66–88.

Ramos, E., Alfonso, V. C., & Schermerhorn, S. M. (2009). Graduate students' administration and scoring errors on the Woodcock-Johnson III Tests of Cognitive Abilities. *Psychology in the Schools, 46*, 650–657. doi: 10.1002/pits.20405

Raven, J. C. (1976). *Standard progressive matrices.* Oxford, England: Oxford Psychologists Press.

Reschly, D., Myers, T., & Hartel, C. (2002). *Mental retardation: Determining eligibility for social security benefits.* Washington, DC: National Academy Press.

Roid, G. H. (2003). *Stanford-Binet Intelligence Scale* (5th ed). Austin, TX: Pro-Ed.

Ryan, J. J., & Schnakenberg-Ott, S. D. (2003). Scoring reliability on the Wechsler Adult Intelligence Scale-Third Edition (WAIS-III). *Assessment, 10*, 151–159. doi: 10.1177/1073191103010002006

Sattler, J. (2001). *Assessment of children: Cognitive applications* (4th ed.). San Diego, CA: Jerome M. Sattler, Publisher, Inc.

Schalock, R. L., Buntinx, W. H. E., Borthwick-Duffy, S., Bradley, V., Craig, E. M., Coulter, D. L., Gomez, S. C., Lachapelle, Y., Luckasson, R. A., Reeve, A., Shogren, K. A., Snell, M. E., Spreat, S., Tassé, M. J., Thompson, J. R., Verdugo, M. A., Wehmeyer, M. L., & Yeager, M. H. (2010). *Intellectual disability: Definition, classification, and system of supports* (11th ed.). Washington, DC: American Association on Intellectual and Developmental Disabilities.

Schalock, R. L. & Luckasson, R. (2005). *Clinical judgment*. Washington, DC: American Association on Intellectual and Developmental Disabilities.

Schalock, R. L., Luckasson, R., Bradley, V., Buntinx, W., Lachapelle, Y, Shogren, K. A., Snell, M. E., Thompson, J. R., Tassé, M., Verdugo-Alonso, M. A., & Wehmeyer, M. L. (2012). *User's guide to mental retardation: Definition, classification, and systems of supports*. Washington, DC: American Association on Intellectual and Developmental Disabilities.

Schneider, W. J., & McGrew, K. (2012). The Cattell-Horn-Carroll model of intelligence. In D. Flanagan & P. Harrison (Eds.), *Contemporary intellectual assessment: Theories, tests, and issues*(3rd ed.; pp. 99–144). New York, NY: Guilford.

Singer, J. K., Licthenberger, E. O., Kaufman, J. C., Kaufman, A. S., & Kaufman, N. L. (2012). The Kaufman Assessment Battery for Children (2nd ed.) and the Kaufman Test of Educational Achievement (2nd e.d,) In D. Flanagan, & Harrison (Eds.), *Contemporary intellectual assessment: Theories, tests, and issues* (3rd ed.; pp. 178–194). New York, NY: Guilford.

Snow, R. E. (1998). Abilities and aptitudes and achievements in learning situations. In J. J. McArdle & R. W. Woodcock (Eds.), *Human cognitive abilities in theory and practice* (pp. 93–112). Mahwah, NJ: Erlbaum.

Sparrow, S. S., Cicchetti, D. V., & Balla, D. A. (2005). *Vineland—II: Vineland Adaptive Behavior Scales* (2nd ed.). San Antonio, TX: Pearson.

Spearman, C. E. (1904). "General intelligence," objectively determined and measured. *American Journal of Psychology, 15,* 201–293.

Spearman, C. E. (1927). *The abilities of man: Their nature and measurement*. London, England: Macmillan.

Sternberg, R. J., & Kaufman, J. C. (1998). Human abilities. *Annual Review of Psychology, 49,* 479–502.

Thurstone, L. L. (1938). Primary mental abilities. *Psychometric Monographs, 1.*

Thurstone, L. L. (1947). *Multiple factor analysis*. Chicago, IL: University of Chicago.

Thurstone, L. L., & Thurstone, T. G. (1941). Factorial studies of intelligence. *Psychometrics Monographs, 2.*

VandenBos, G. (2007). *APA dictionary of psychology*. Washington, DC: American Psychological Association.

Wasserman, J. D. (2012). A history of intelligence assessment: The unfinished tapestry. In D. Flanagan, & P. L. Harrison (Eds.), *Contemporary intellectual assessment: Theories, tests, and issues* (3rd ed.; pp. 3–55). New York, NY: Guilford.

Wechsler, D. (1997). *Wechsler Adult Intelligence Scale* (3rd ed.). San Antonio, TX: Pearson.

Wechsler, D. (1991). *Wechsler Intelligence Scale for Children* (3rd ed.). *New York: Psychological Corporation.*

Wechsler, D. (2003). *Wechsler Intelligence Scale for Children* (4th ed.). San Antonio, TX: Pearson.

Wechsler, D. (2008). *Wechsler Adult Intelligence Scale* (4th ed.). San Antonio, TX: Pearson.

Whitaker, S. (2008). The stability of IQ in people with low intellectual ability: An analysis of the literature. *Intellectual and Developmental Disabilities, 46*(2), 120–128. doi: 10.1352/0047-6765(2008)46[120:TSOIIP]2.0.CO;2

Woodcock, R., McGrew, K., & Mather, N. (2001). *Woodcock-Johnson III Normative Update*. Rolling Meadows, IL. Riverside.

8 | Intelligence Testing

Dale G. Watson

Nature of the Problem

The evaluation of intelligence is an essential component in establishing the diagnosis of an intellectual disability (ID). Clinical practice and professional standards require that, in high-stakes evaluations, an IQ test score be derived from an individually administered global measure of intellectual functioning. In most instances, this is represented by indexes of general cognitive (thinking) abilities (e.g., the full-scale IQ test score or its equivalent), though in certain circumstances, subcomponent elements or part scores may provide invaluable information.

In selecting a test to measure intellectual functioning or in understanding the adequacy of a test that has been administered, a number of important dimensions must be considered. For example, key considerations include the degree to which an IQ test score is saturated with a general factor of intelligence, known as "g," or is instead, a narrow measure of a more specific ability (e.g., fluid reasoning or crystallized intelligence—see Chapter 7); the number and mixture of specific intellectual abilities assessed by a particular IQ test; the influence of "practice effects" and norm obsolescence (Flynn effect) on the accuracy of the obtained scores (see Chapter 10); foundational psychometric characteristics such as reliability and validity (see Chapter 5); the adequacy of the standardization procedures; and the representativeness of the test norms. Additional issues relate to the use of current instruments, congruence of language between the test and the person to be assessed, the cultural fairness of the instrument, and the level of acculturation of the individual. The information presented in this chapter discusses these important issues related to IQ assessment, particularly as relevant to the diagnosis of ID.

Summary of Related Research

There are a multiplicity of definitions of intelligence and continuing debate over the nature of intelligence (Urbina, 2011; VandenBos, 2007). Most definitions recognize intelligence as a combination of cognitive abilities involved in the comprehension of complex ideas, problem solving, learning, reasoning, abstract thinking, and efficient adaptation to the environment (see also Chapter 7). For example, as described in the 11th edition of the American Association on Intellectual and Developmental Disabilities's *Intellectual Disability: Definition, Classification, and Systems of Supports* (Schalock et al., 2010), intellectual functioning is "best conceptualized and captured by a general factor in intelligence. [That is,] intelligence is a general mental ability. It includes reasoning, planning, solving problems, thinking abstractly, comprehending complex ideas, learning quickly, and learning from experience" (Schalock et al., 2010, p. 31).

The general factor of intelligence is correlated with a wide array of important individual characteristics and behavioral outcomes including, but not limited to: academic achievement measured by grade point average (GPA), risk of dropping out, and years of education; occupational achievement; risk for unemployment; risk for delinquency and criminal behavior (Gottfredson, 1997; Jensen, 1998); coping with ordinary life such as using maps, banking, and interpreting news articles; dealings with people (Gottfredson, 1997); biological characteristics including brain size, central nerve conductance velocity (Gignac, Vernon, & Wickett, 2003; Luders, Narr, Thompson, & Toga, 2009; Mackintosh, 2011; McDaniel, 2005), and efficiency of brain glucose metabolism (Haier, 2003); death rates from motor vehicle accidents (O'Toole, 1990); and life expectancy (Hart et al., 2003; Whalley & Deary, 2001; *cf.* Patja, Iivanainen, Vesala, Oksanen, & Ruoppila, 2000). A higher level of intelligence serves as a protective factor. In contrast, individuals with more limited intellectual resources are increasingly vulnerable to the vicissitudes of life.

IQ test scores, in the form of the composite full-scale IQ in particular, are commonly used to estimate and describe this general factor of intelligence. The dominant and most accepted view is that intellectual abilities are arranged in a hierarchical fashion with the general factor of intelligence at the apex, which in turn subsumes a number of broad intellectual abilities as well as more specific or narrow functions (Buckhalt, 2002; Carroll, 1993; Jensen, 1998; Mackintosh, 2011; Neisser et al., 1996; Schneider & McGrew, 2012; Spearman, 1927; *cf.* Stankov, 2005; *cf.* Sternberg & Grigorenko, 2002; see also Chapter 7).

Carroll's (1993) seminal meta-analytic study of the extant literature on the factor structure of intelligence identified the major components of general intelligence. This work was subsequently combined with that of Horn and Cattell to provide a structural model of intelligence termed the Cattell–Horn–Carroll (CHC) theory (Kaufman, 2009; McGrew & Flanagan, 1998; McGrew, 1997, 2005, 2009; Schneider & McGrew, 2012; see also Chapter 7). CHC theory posits a hierarchical structure of intelligence with a *general* ability factor (g) at the apex. In this taxonomy, abilities are differentiated at three different levels (referred to as strata) of generalization or breadth. The most specialized abilities are classified as *narrow* abilities. Narrow abilities, in turn, are subsumed under more *broad* intellectual abilities. All broad abilities are subsumed by the *general* ability of general intelligence (*g*). The broad cognitive ability factors include fluid intelligence (*Gf*), quantitative knowledge (*Gq*), crystallized intelligence (*Gc*), reading and writing (*Grw*), short-term memory (*Gsm*) or short-term working memory (*Gwm*), visual processing (*Gv*), auditory processing (*Ga*), long-term storage and retrieval (*Glr*), processing speed (*Gs*), and decision/reaction time/speed (*Gt*; Flanagan, Ortiz, & Alfonso, 2007; McGrew, LaForte, & Schrank, 2014).

Composite IQ test scores are highly correlated with the general factor of intelligence (Jensen, 1998; National Research Council [NRC], 2002), even though they are only approximate proxy measures for the underlying general dimension (Colom, Abad, Garcia, & Juan-Espinosa, 2002; Fiorello et al., 2007; Mackintosh, 2011; Schneider, 2013a). Full-scale composite IQ scores are derived, in general, from admixtures of tasks more or less saturated with the general factor of intelligence. However, different full-scale IQ scores are also impacted by the specific combination of broad and narrow intellectual abilities measured by different IQ tests (see Chapter 7). To the extent that an IQ test can be judged a valid measure of general intellectual functioning, it must reasonably and accurately measure general intellectual ability rather than isolated specific components of intelligence. The general factor of intelligence is of particular import inasmuch as it has a greater impact on functioning at lower levels of intelligence, whereas factors that are more specific tend to become significant in higher IQ ranges (Detterman & Daniel, 1989; Reynolds, Keith, & Beretvas, 2010; Wechsler, 2008). Moreover, individuals with a mild level of ID perform more poorly on subtests that are better measures of general intelligence (Spitz, 1988) though the presence of "splinter skills" may not be uncommon (Bergeron & Floyd, 2006; Fiorello, et al., 2007; Fiorello, Hale, McGrath, Ryan, Quinn, 2001). In addition, the diagnosis of ID has traditionally focused on composite full-scale IQ scores that serve as proxies for the general factor of intelligence.

The "intelligence" measured by one IQ test is not necessarily the same as that measured by another test (Daniel, 2000; Stankov, 2002, 2005; see Chapter 7). However, although the general factor of intelligence may be "colored" by the specific mixture of broad and narrow abilities measured by different tests, research studies have demonstrated that a similar higher-level general intelligence factor or ability emerges whenever a sufficiently large and diverse array of intellectual abilities are assessed, mostly independent of the specific battery utilized (Carroll, 1993; Floyd, Shands, Rafael, Bergeron, & McGrew, 2009; Jensen, 1980, 1998, 2002; Johnson, Bouchard Jr., Krueger, McGue, & Gottesman, 2004; Johnson, te Nijenhuis, & Bouchard Jr., 2008; Mackintosh, 2011; Thorndike, 1987). Nonetheless, this is not to say that IQ test scores will be identical across tests. IQ tests differ in how and the extent to which they measure general intellectual ability and the component parts of intelligence (see Chapter 7). IQ tests also differ along a number of other important dimensions.

Standards for Educational and Psychological Testing

The American Educational Research Association (AERA), the American Psychological Association (APA), and the National Council on Measurement in Education (NCME), published, in 2014, an updated version of the *Standards for Educational and Psychological Testing* (hereafter *Standards*). The purpose of these standards is "to provide criteria for the development and evaluation of tests and testing practices and to provide guidelines for assessing the validity of interpretations of test scores for the intended test uses" (AERA, APA, & NCME, 2014, p. 1). Standards have been established addressing issues of test construction, evaluation, and documentation; fairness in testing; and testing applications. The standards address issues of validity, reliability, normative standards, and other important criteria for the evaluation of tests. The standards also provide an overarching framework for examining issues relevant to test selection detailed below.

Normative Standards

IQ test scores reference an individual's relative standing in comparison to a large sample of individuals (the normative sample) selected to be representative of the general population. The IQ test scores obtained from psychometrically sound IQ tests are normally distributed, forming the well-known bell-shaped curve. Composite IQ test scores for all major contemporary IQ tests (see Chapter 7) are reported as standard scores that have a mean (average) of 100 and a standard deviation of 15. Individuals with ID will generally have composite IQ test scores that are approximately two standard deviations or more below the mean of the population on a recently normed test, that is, an IQ standard score of 65 to 75 (70 ± 5) or below, allowing for measurement error (American Psychiatric Association, 2013; Schalock et al., 2010).

IQ test scores are not 100% reliable. The degree of measurement error associated with an IQ test score is based on the reliability of the IQ test score. The standard error of measurement (*SEM*; see Chapter 5) provides a measurement of the degree of error. The *SEM* allows users to place a band of confidence around the obtained IQ test score, most commonly operationalized as ±5 IQ test score points (95% confidence band). The IQ test score criteria for the diagnosis of ID may then include scores of 75 or below, considering the *SEM*.

Normative samples for measures of intelligence typically have exclusion criteria eliminating individuals with sensory-motor impairment; limited English language skills; and histories of severe medical, psychiatric, or neurological dysfunction that might affect cognition. Normative samples must be large enough to provide meaningful stratification of the sample based on the subject characteristics of age, gender, socioeconomic status, levels of education, geographic location, and other variables.

The adequacy and representativeness of an IQ test's normative sample is a critical variable in the selection of an IQ test. The major IQ tests are generally constructed to match the United States Census in terms of key demographic variables including

TABLE 8.1. Normative Sample Sizes for Selected IQ Tests

Test/Sample Size	WAIS-IV	SB5	WJ III NU	RIAS
Overall Sample Size	2200	4800	8782	2438
Sample Size (Age > 17)	2000	1200	2997	1116
Sample Size by Age	1400	600	2530	982
(Age Range)	(18:0 – 64:11)	(17:0 – 59:11)	(18:0 – 59:11)	(17:0-74:11)
Intellectually Disabled Comparison Studies	104	119	93	26
Sample Size (Age Range)	(16:0 – 63:11)	(3 – 25	(< 19)	(18:0 +)

Note. WAIS-IV = Wechsler Adult Intelligence Scale–IV; WJ III NU = Woodcock-Johnson III Normative Update; SB5 = Stanford Binet 5; RIAS = Reynolds Intellectual Assessment Scales. Data are from the respective technical manuals.

gender, race/ethnicity, geographic region, and education (as a proxy for socioeconomic level). The sizes of the normative samples for the major IQ tests are generally considered adequate (see Bridges & Holler, 2007; also Crawford & Garthwaite, 2008). Norm sample sizes, within the relevant adult age groups (approximately 18–60 years old), range from about 600 for the Stanford-Binet 5 (SB5) to about 2500 for the Woodcock-Johnson III (WJ III; see Table 8.1). As also reported in Table 8.1, clinical samples of subjects with ID are sometimes reported in IQ test manuals.

As described in the AERA, APA, and NCME standards, test publishers are responsible for creating tests that provide valid score interpretations across diverse individuals (Standard 3.1):

> A test that is fair . . . reflects the same construct(s) for all test takers, and scores from it have the same meaning for all individuals in the intended population; a fair test does not advantage or disadvantage some individuals because of characteristics irrelevant to the intended construct. To the degree possible, characteristics of all individuals in the intended test population, including those associated with race, ethnicity, gender, age, socioeconomic status, or linguistic or cultural background, must be considered throughout all stages of development, administration, scoring, interpretation, and use so that barriers to fair assessment can be reduced. (AERA, APA, & NCME, 2014, p. 50)

Information relevant to these issues is commonly available in the test manual. Further, it is the responsibility of the examiner to determine if the examinee can reasonably be compared to the normative reference group (Standard 10.5). In this context, the adequacy of the individual's English language skills, the presence of sensory and motor limitations (especially hearing and vision), and their level of acculturation should be considered. However, the use of subgroup norms based on other demographic variables, such as gender, race, and education, commonly referred to as demographically adjusted norms (Heaton, Miller, Taylor, & Grant, 2004), while potentially appropriate for neuropsychological evaluation, cannot be used to diagnose ID because the diagnosis is dependent on a comparison to the larger normative reference group.

Standardization

The reliability and validity (discussed below and in Chapter 5) of an assessment for ID requires the use of standardized procedures for the administration and scoring:

> The usefulness and interpretability of test scores require that a test be administered and scored according to the developer's instructions. When directions, testing conditions, and scoring follow the same detailed procedures for all test takers, the test is said to be standardized. (AERA, APA, & NCME, 2014, p. 111)

There are a number of other relevant standards that are applicable to the appropriate administration of tests of intelligence. First, certain basic conditions relate to the environment in which the assessment takes place (e.g., quiet and free from distractions, absence of third-party observers, freedom of motion as needed for any task requiring motor movements) and deviations from these conditions should be considered during the interpretative process (Standard 10.8; American Academy of Clinical Neuropsychology [AACN], 2001; Axelrod et al., 2000; Committee on Psychological Tests and Assessment–American Psychological Association, 2007). Second, there is an apparent need for test administration and scoring to be accurate (Standard 9.5; AERA, APA, & NCME, 2014, p. 153). Third, accurate assessment assumes that the testee puts forth adequate effort (AERA, APA, & NCME, 2014, p. 154–155; Bush et al., 2005); this concern is particularly relevant in assessing individuals with ID (Dean, Victor, Boone, & Arnold, 2008; Salekin & Doane, 2009). The American Academy of Clinical Neuropsychology (2007) described relevant techniques for assessing motivation and effort:

> Approaches for assessing motivation and effort include: behavioral observations from interview or testing of behaviors such as avoidance, resistance, hostility, and lack of cooperation; examination of the pattern of performance among traditional neuropsychological measures; identification of cognitive profiles that do not fit with known patterns typical of brain disorder; and consideration of suspect performance on objective measures of effort. Clinicians utilize multiple indicators of effort, including tasks and paradigms validated for this purpose, to ensure that decisions regarding adequacy of effort are based on converging evidence from several sources, rather than depending on a single measure or method. (p. 221–222)

Reliability

Issues of test reliability are central to the selection of an appropriate test for the measurement of intelligence (see Chapter 5 for an extensive discussion of this issue). Reliability is "the ability of a measurement instrument (e.g., a test) to measure an attribute consistently..." (VandenBos, 2007, p. 786). Reliable tests provide consistent results over time and circumstances (Reynolds & Kamphaus, 2003). The scores obtained from IQ tests can be described by different forms of reliability; indices of internal consistency reliability and stability (or test-retest) reliability are presented here.

Internal consistency reliability addresses the degree to which items or subtests are homogeneous and measuring similar underlying abilities (Henson, 2001). The quantification of internal consistency relies on coefficients of the correlations between items or subsets of items. This type of reliability ensures that what is being measured is similar and provides the basis for valid interpretations of the underlying dimension or ability. Stability or test-retest reliability refers to the consistency of scores over time, that is, whether scores on a second administration of a test to the same group of individuals will be similar.

Reliability coefficients for the composite (full-scale) IQ test scores of the major intelligence tests are generally excellent with average or median coefficients in adults of .97 to .99. Reliability coefficients are generally higher for the full-scale scores than for part scores. Reliability coefficients should be .90 or greater for high-stakes decision making (Jensen, 1980; National Research Council [NRC], 2002; Wasserman & Bracken, 2012). The National Research Council observed, "Instruments used for the high-stakes purposes of diagnosing mental retardation . . . should approximate this minimal level of reliability, recognizing that the inverse of reliability is measurement error and that error only confounds correct decision making" (2002, p. 132). Reliabilities below .97 progressively widen the .95% confidence band beyond the ± 5 points generally seen as acceptable for diagnosing ID.

The *SEM* is a more relevant and convenient means of using reliability information than are reliability statistics (AERA, APA, & NCME, 2014). The *SEM* has an inverse relationship with measures of reliability and is computed from the reliability coefficient and the standard deviation of the scale (Roid, 2003b). A more reliable test will result in a smaller *SEM* (Wechsler, 2008). The *SEM* represents the error in estimating a theoretical true score based upon the actual score on a test (VandenBos, 2007; Wechsler, 2008). The true score is the theoretical score that would be found if it were possible to administer the test thousands of times to the same individual (absent practice effects; Kaufman, 2009).

Because all test scores include error, it is critical to be able to quantify the magnitude of the error—*SEM* serves this purpose. Because of measurement error, it is important to recognize that obtained IQ test scores only estimate the theoretical true score; the obtained IQ test score is the approximate midpoint of the range in which a score is likely to fall. For example, with an obtained score of 72 and an *SEM* of 2.12, the true score is likely to fall, with a 68% degree of confidence, within a band of ± 1 *SEM*, that is, approximately 70 to 74. Similarly, with a 95% degree of confidence, using ± 2 *SEM*s, the score is likely to fall between 68 and 76. The *Standards* state, "When a test score or composite score is used to make classification decisions (e.g., pass/fail, achievement levels), the standard error of measurement at or near the cut scores has important implications for the trustworthiness of these decisions" (AERA, APA, & NCME, 2014, p. 46). As the United States Supreme Court determined in *Hall v. Florida* (2014), the *SEM* of an IQ test score must be considered when making the diagnosis of ID in capital punishment cases. The use of "bright line" cutoffs for determining whether an individual has ID only reduces the trustworthiness of such decisions. Some instruments, notably the WAIS-IV and the SB5, use the standard error of estimate (*SEE*) instead of the *SEM* to construct confidence intervals. The *SEE* corrects for the probability that true scores are more likely to fall towards the middle of the distribution, i.e., regression to the mean effects. The *SEE* affects extreme scores to a greater extent than scores falling in the middle of the distribution and, thus, provides an asymmetrical confidence band around obtained IQ scores at the extremes (Roid, 2003b).

Validity

Validity refers to the accuracy with which a test measures the underlying dimension or ability it is designed to assess (AERA, APA, & NCME, 2014; VandenBos, 2007). Validity "is the degree to which all the accumulated evidence supports the intended interpretation of test scores for the proposed use" (AERA, APA, & NCME, 2014, p. 14). It is the interpretation and not the test itself that is valid (AERA, APA, & NCME, 2014).

Validity is supported by different lines of evidence that commonly include data related to test content, response processes, internal structure, relations to other variables and measures, and the consequences of testing (AERA APA, & NCME, 2014; Reynolds & Kamphaus, 2003; see Chapter 5 for a more extensive discussion of these issues). The test manuals for each of the major IQ test instruments provide the specific lines of evidence supporting the interpretations of the test. In general, there is substantial evidence that the major IQ tests discussed in this chapter are valid measures of intellectual abilities. Nonetheless, because these instruments measure (and conceptualize) intelligence in somewhat different ways, differences exist between tests.

Braden and Niebling (2012) have used the previous edition (1999) of the *Standards* to "articulate a framework for judging the validity evidence provided by test developers" (p. 739), specifically as applied to contemporary intelligence tests. The authors have evaluated the validity claims made by the test developers of the Wechsler Intelligence Scale for Children, Fourth Edition (WISC-IV), the SB5, the Woodcock-Johnson III Tests of Cognitive Abilities (WJ III Cog), the Kaufman Assessment Battery for Children, Second Edition (KABC-II), and the Reynolds Intellectual Assessment Scales (RIAS).

Exchangeability

Exchangeability refers to the degree to which IQs will be reasonably consistent across test batteries (Floyd, Bergeron, McCormack, Anderson, & Hargrove-Owens, 2005; Floyd, Clark, & Shadish, 2008; see also Chapter 7). The common assumption is that an IQ obtained on, for example, the WAIS-IV will be reasonably similar to an IQ obtained on another test. Such exchangeability can be broadly quantified by determining the degree to which the tests are measuring the same underlying abilities, that is, the proportion

TABLE 8.2. Select Composite Score Correlation Coefficients and Shared Variance Between IQ Tests

	WAIS-IV FSIQ	WAIS-III FSIQ	SB5 FSIQ	WJ III GIA	RIAS CIX
WAIS-IV		88%	—	—	—
WAIS-III	.94		67%	45%	56%
SB5	—	.82		61%/81%	—
WJ III	—	.67	.78/.90*		—
RIAS	—	.75	—	—	

Note. WAIS-IV = Wechsler Adult Intelligence Scale–IV; WAIS-III = Wechsler Adult Intelligence Scale-III; WJ III NU = Woodcock-Johnson III Normative Update; SB5 = Stanford Binet 5; and RIAS = Reynolds Intellectual Assessment Scales. FSIQ = Full-scale IQ; GIA = General intellectual ability; and CIX = Composite intelligence index.

Data are from each IQ test's technical manuals. Correlation coefficients are displayed below the shaded diagonal line and the percent of shared variance above the diagonal. Data for the WJ III are for the 2001 version rather than the Normative Update. Dashes indicate that data is unavailable in the respective test manuals.

*A study using the same five factors across the SB5 and WJ III Cog found a substantially higher correlation of .90 (Roid, 2003b).

of shared variance. Shared variance is calculated as the square of the correlation coefficients (r) between the measures of global intelligence, multiplied by 100. For example, the SB5 Full Scale IQ (FSIQ) and the WAIS-III FSIQ have approximately 67% shared score variance (r = .82; See Table 8.2). Stankov (2005) has noted that correlations lower than about .60 suggest that two tests are not measuring the same underlying abilities. Because of the magnitude of the typical correlations reported between tests, composite IQ test scores on average can differ between instruments to a significant degree (see Chapter 7 for more detailed discussion). See Table 8.3 for examples of reported IQ test score differences ranging from one to approximately nine points.

TABLE 8.3. Example Composite Score Mean Differences Between IQ Tests With Flynn Effect Corrections (Below Diagonal)

	WAIS-IV FSIQ	WAIS-III FSIQ	SB5 FSIQ	WJ III GIA	RIAS CIX
WAIS-IV		+2.9	—	—	—
WAIS-III	−.07		−3.6	−8.5	−.52
SB5	—	−1.8		+1.4	—
WJ III	—	−7.6	+.5		—
RIAS	—	+.98	—	—	

Note. WAIS-IV = Wechsler Adult Intelligence Scale–IV; WAIS-III = Wechsler Adult Intelligence Scale-III; WJ III NU = Woodcock-Johnson III Normative Update; SB5 = Stanford Binet 5; and RIAS = Reynolds Intellectual Assessment Scales. FSIQ = Full-scale IQ; GIA = General intellectual ability; and CIX = Composite intelligence index.

Data are from each IQ test's technical manual. The values are presented as *example differences* from single studies and are *not* to be interpreted as the best single estimate of typical score differences between the different IQ tests— estimates that would require the synthesis of all available specific pairs of IQ-IQ test comparison studies. Average differences are displayed above the shaded diagonal and are based on the reported calculations that have subtracted the IQ scores from the test in the left column from the IQ scores in the top row , e.g., the WAIS-III provided higher scores than the WAIS-IV (+2.9) but the WJ III provided lower scores than the WAIS-III (−8.5). Difference scores below the diagonal are Flynn effect adjusted scores (see Chapter 10) providing the difference once Flynn effect adjustments are made. Data for the WJ III are from the 2001 technical manual (McGrew & Woodcock, 2001). Dashes indicate that data was unavailable from the respective IQ test technical manuals used to construct this table.

IQ test score differences across instruments may stem from a variety of reasons (see Chapter 7 for further discussion). One major reason is that different IQ tests measure different mixes of abilities. The extant IQ-IQ test battery joint factor analysis research (see Keith and Reynolds, 2010) suggests that IQ tests measure somewhat overlapping broad intellectual abilities, but they also do not always measure the exact same set of parallel broad abilities. For example, the WAIS-IV has been found to measure the broad CHC abilities *Gf, Gc, Gv, Gsm,* and *Gs* (Lichtenberger & Kaufman, 2009). In contrast, the WJ III (Woodcock, McGrew, Schrank, & Mather, 2001, 2007) measures seven of the broad intellectual abilities identified by CHC theory (*Gf, Gc, Glr, Gv, Ga, Gs, Gsm, Grw,* and *Gq*; McGrew & Flanagan, 1998). Finally, the SB5 measures *Gf, Gc, Gq, Gv,* and *Gsm* (Keith & Reynolds, 2010; Roid, 2003b; Roid & Pomplun, 2012). Thus, exchangeability may be impacted by the degree to which an IQ test measures similar broad intellectual abilities as well as the balance between general intelligence versus more specific abilities (Floyd et al., 2008). Exchangeability is increased when instruments load highly on the general factor of intelligence (Floyd et al., 2008).

To summarize, despite evidence for a unitary general factor of intelligence across different IQ tests, within adult populations, different IQ tests measure somewhat different mixtures of intellectual abilities. As a result, different IQ tests will not always provide IQ test scores that are precisely the same (Floyd et al., 2008). IQ test scores between instruments are not perfectly "exchangeable." (See below for strategies to resolve apparent discrepancies across test batteries.)

Practice Effects

Practice effects refer to the potential for inflated IQ scores due to the repeated administrations of the same test to the same individual. Considerations regarding practice effects should play a prominent role in the selection of an appropriate IQ instrument in cases in which the same IQ test (or an earlier version of the IQ test) has previously been administered. When the same tests are administered in close proximity in time, there is likely to be a gain in the obtained IQs on the second administration. Schalock et al. (2010) noted, ". . . established clinical practice is to avoid administering the same intelligence test within the same year to the same individual because it will often lead to an overestimate of the examinee's true intelligence" (p. 38).

However, the magnitude of potential practice effects is frequently insufficiently considered. For example, substantial practice effects have been shown to occur on the Wechsler Adult Intelligence Scale–Revised (WAIS-R; Matarazzo & Herman, 1984) and the Wechsler Adult Intelligence Scale–Third Edition (WAIS-III; Basso, Carona, Lowery, & Axelrod, 2002), with an average increase of 6 points on the full-scale IQ over periods ranging from 2 weeks to 6 months. Practice effects for the WAIS-IV have also been reported to be substantial (over 7 points in some populations at a 6-month retest interval; Brooks, Sherman, Iverson, Slick, Strauss, 2011; Brooks, Strauss, Sherman,

Iverson, & Slick, 2009; Estevis, Basso, & Combs, 2012; Wechsler, 2008). Smaller practice effects have been reported for the SB5 (Roid, 2003b) and the RIAS (Reynolds & Kamphaus, 2003).

IQ tests show considerable stability over time at the group level, represented by relatively high stability (test-retest) correlation coefficients. However, considerably less consistency has been reported at the individual level, particularly within low IQ groups (Whitaker, 2008). Considerable caution must be exercised in repeating similar IQ tests or, when interpreting past test findings with lower results, assuming them to be invalid. Practice effects may also be magnified when similar instruments are administered on multiple occasions. This practice can lead to "progressive error" in which subsequent tests become less and less accurate (Kaufman, 2009).

Statistical procedures are available to assist in determining whether subsequent administrations of the same instrument represent real differences or simple statistical artifact. For example, various reliable change indices (RCI), based upon stability coefficients, have been developed that inform the user of the magnitude of change expected to be found on retesting (Basso et al., 2002; Brooks et al., 2009; Brooks et al., 2011; Estevis et al., 2012; Heaton et al., 2001; Lineweaver & Chelune, 2003; Temkin, Heaton, Grant, & Dikmen, 1999). In cases in which the same test has been administered, the application of RCIs adjusted for practice effects may be used to determine whether significant differences actually exist between the obtained scores (Estevis et al, 2012; Heaton et al., 2001; Pearson, 2009; Temkin et al., 1999). As Lineweaver and Chelune (2003) reported,

> . . . one cannot interpret scores from a repeat evaluation in the same manner and with the same meaning as those from an initial evaluation. The systematic bias inherent in retest scores, as well as measurement error, can dramatically alter the magnitude of the scores themselves, rendering them at best questionable and at worst misleading. (p. 332)

For some tests, scoring software is available to facilitate the calculation of RCIs.

Given the magnitude of practice effects, it is critically important to consider carefully the impact of repeat testing with the same test. Schalock et al. (2010) suggested avoiding the administration of the same intelligence test within the same year. However, data are limited as to the magnitude of practice effects over longer periods. Furthermore, retest interval time has not appeared to have a moderating effect across the intervals that have been studied (Basso et al., 2002; Estevis et al., 2012).

Multiple IQ Scores Over Time

It is not uncommon for individuals to have been administered multiple IQ tests over time. One might be tempted to simply average these scores to obtain a "true" IQ or conversely to adopt the highest score as the most accurate IQ. However, it is not psychometrically sound to simply average IQ scores in order to form a composite score (Schneider, 2012, 2013a, 2013b). Furthermore, it is inappropriate to simply accept, in a rote fashion, the higher score in the false belief that one can never score higher than their true IQ but can always score poorer in the face of limited effort. Instead, at a minimum, such scores should be examined to determine whether the confidence intervals for the obtained scores overlap or not.

It is also possible, in accordance with reliable scientific methods and professional standards, to combine composite IQ test scores across batteries when the correlations between the instruments can be reasonably determined or estimated and the reliabilities for all test scores are available. When this psychometric information is available for all relevant IQ tests that have been administered, it is then possible to calculate a psychometrically defensible estimated "true" IQ score (Schneider, 2012, 2013a, 2013b; see also *Hall v. Florida*). Such techniques may serve to resolve apparent discrepancies that can occur when different IQ tests have been administered. Further, this procedure allows one to avoid the statistically untenable action of simply averaging scores.

However, this psychometrically sophisticated procedure may not be practical to implement. Frequently, the intercorrelations between all IQ tests administered to the individual are not available in current or old test manuals (e.g., correlation between SB-IV and WAIS-IV) and it would be a daunting task to search the literature for all possible independent research studies to develop a methodologically sound meta-analytic estimate of the various IQ-IQ test correlation combinations. Nonetheless, the procedure outlined and implemented by Schneider (2012, 2013a, 2013b) does allow the software template to substitute reasonable estimates for correlations or reliabilities that are not easily found (or do not exist), but this option should only be used judiciously.

Given problems in locating all necessary input for the Schneider (2012) software, the next best practice for estimating an "average" of multiple IQ test scores is to use the median value of the collection of scores (Sattler, 2001). The use of the psychometric method of Schneider (2012, 2013a, 2013b) or the use of the median score to represent the "average" estimate of collection of scores should only be done when the variability of IQ test scores across time is minimal. Discrepant IQ test scores over time often reflect possible real changes in intelligence and may be due to a variety of factors (see Chapter 7 for discussion of reasons why IQ-IQ test score discrepancies occur). When scientific-based plausible explanations can explain vastly different IQ scores over time, attempting to estimate an "average" score is not recommended. It is only when a collection of IQ scores demonstrates a reasonable degree of convergence (e.g., 95% *SEM* confidence bands for all scores overlap or are not far apart), that estimating a composite IQ test score may be appropriate.

Norm Obsolescence: The Flynn Effect

The Flynn effect (see also Chapter 10) refers to the phenomenon of steady increases in intelligence levels within populations over time. This phenomenon has been acknowledged by the major publishers of intelligence tests since the early 1990s and is, in part, the rationale for updating versions of most IQ tests due to norm obsolescence (Wechsler, 1991; Wechsler, 2002a). Although there has been some controversy regarding the application of the Flynn effect in high-stakes evaluations (Hagan, Drogin, & Guilmette, 2010), the scientific and professional consensus is that the Flynn effect is a real phenomenon (Gresham & Reschly, 2011; Hagan et al.; Schalock et al., 2010; Weiss, 2010). Disagreements have centered on the magnitude of the Flynn effect, whether it is disappearing, whether it differentially affects lower and higher IQ groups equally, and whether it should be applied in litigation (Hagan et al.; Trahan, Stuebing, Fletcher, & Hiscock, 2014; Zhou, Zhu, & Weiss, 2010; see Chapter 10 for detailed discussion). Courts have also treated these issues with different outcomes, with some accepting the use of Flynn effect adjustments (e.g., *Ex Parte Eric Dewayne Cathey,* 2012; *People v. Superior Court (Vidal),* 2005, 2007; *United States v. Davis,* 2009; *United States v. Hardy,* 2010; *United States v. Wilson,* 2013; N. Haydt, personal communication, May 22, 2013) while others have prohibited its use (e.g., *Beckworth v. State,* 2009; *Butler v. Quarterman,* 2008; *Pizzuto v. Blades,* 2012; *Thorson v. State,* 2011; N. Haydt, personal communication, May 22, 2013).

Professional standards require that examiners use up-to-date tests and norms. As the *Standards* indicate, "test publishers should assure that up-to-date norms are readily available or provide evidence that older norms are still appropriate. However, it remains the test user's responsibility to avoid inappropriate use of norms that are out of date and to strive to ensure accurate and appropriate score interpretations" (Standard 5.11; AERA, APA, & NCME, 2014, pp. 104–105). Best practice and professional standards mandate the use of up-to-date versions of individually administered IQ tests. Thus, in order to provide accurate and appropriate test interpretations, test users cannot reasonably rely on norms that are out of date and should acknowledge the potential impact of the Flynn effect in the assessment of intellectual disability (Gresham & Reschly, 2011; Schalock et al., 2007; Schalock et al, 2010; *cf.* Loring & Bauer, 2010).

The procedure for computing an adjustment for the Flynn effect has generally involved calculating the time between the administration of a test and the midpoint of the year(s) of norming (which is often 1 to 4 years prior to publication), multiplying that number by .3 points, and subtracting this amount from the obtained full-scale IQ test score of the test in question. See Table 8.4 for the publication and norming dates required for these calculations.

A recent meta-analysis of the Flynn effect reported a "mean of about 3 and a SEM of about 1 [that] supports the correction and is consistent with the Flynn correction of 3 points per decade" (Fletcher, Stuebing, & Hughes, 2010, p. 472). Another such meta-analysis of the Flynn effect provided similar results (Trahan et al., 2014). Given these findings, calculations of the Flynn effect can reasonably incorporate the 0.30 points annual inflation rate as the appropriate magnitude for the Flynn effect. Norm obsolescence is discussed in greater detail in Chapter 10.

TABLE 8.4. Publication and Midyear Norming Dates for Selected IQ Tests

Test	Publication Date	Mid-Year Norming Dates
Wechsler Adult Intelligence Scale – IV	2008	2007
Wechsler Adult Intelligence Scale – III	1997	1995
Wechsler Adult Intelligence Scale – R	1981	1978
Wechsler Adult Intelligence Scale	1955	1954
Wechsler Abbreviated Scale of Intelligence – II	2011	2010
Wechsler Abbreviated Intelligence Scale	1999	—
Wechsler Intelligence Scale for Children – IV	2003	2001
Wechsler Intelligence Scale for Children – III	1991	1989
Wechsler Intelligence Scale for Children – R	1974	1972
Wechsler Intelligence Scale for Children	1949	1947–1948
Stanford – Binet 5	2003	2001
Stanford – Binet 4	1986	1985
Stanford – Binet LM (Updated Norms)	1973	1972
Stanford – Binet LM	1960	1952
Woodcock – Johnson IV	2014	2010/2011
Woodcock – Johnson III Normative Update	2007	2007
Woodcock – Johnson III	2001	1998
Woodcock – Johnson – Revised	1990	1987
Reynolds Intellectual Ability Scale	2003	2000

Note. Norming dates were calculated as the mid-year of the normative data collection dates from the respective test manuals and adapted from Flynn (2009). The date provided by Flynn for the norming of the WAIS-IV was corrected to that reported in the *Technical and Interpretive Manual* (Wechsler, 2008). Wechsler scales's publication dates are also, in part, from Coalson and Weiss (2002) and Wechsler (2008). Stanford–Binet publication and norming dates are from Becker (2003) and Roid (2003b). WJ-R, WJ III, and WJ III Normative Update dates are for the adult norms (McGrew, Werder, & Woodcock, 1991; McGrew & Woodcock, 2001; McGrew, Schrank, & Woodcock, 2007). The WJ III NU norms are an updated recalculation of norms originally collected between September 1996 and August 1999. The WJ IV sample was collected between December 2009 and January 2012 (K. McGrew, personal communication, August 21, 2014). Dashes represent data not available.

g-ness of IQ tests

The nature of the general factor of intelligence has remained elusive. Views have ranged from considering *g* to be an emergent property of the mind (Wechsler cited by Jensen, 1998) to little more than an artifact of factor analysis (Gould, 1996). Recent conceptualizations emphasize "the processes and abilities that define processing efficiency and capacity, such as processing speed, inhibition or control of processing, attention, and working memory" (Demetriou, 2002; *cf.* Detterman, 2002). Others suggest it to be the consequence of neural plasticity (Garlick, 2002), the result of elemental cognitive processes (Kranzler & Jensen, 1991), or the inter-relationships between basic cognitive processes (Detterman, 2002).

In any case, composite IQ test scores may differ in the extent to which they measure the general factor of intelligence and the manner in which they are calculated. For example, the full-scale IQ test scores for the WAIS-IV and the SB5 are derived from equally weighted subtest scores. In contrast, the WJ III General Index of Ability (GIA), which uses subtests that are only moderate measures of the general factor of intelligence, is derived from a combination of *g*-weighted subtests determined by a first principle component analysis. Such a procedure, according to the authors of the WJ III and consistent with Jensen (1998), "gives the best statistical estimate of general intelligence" (McGrew & Woodcock, 2001, p. 26).

There has additionally been disagreement as to how to best estimate the *g*-saturation of a particular IQ test battery (Flanagan, McGrew, & Ortiz, 2000). Most commonly, within-battery determination of the *g*-saturation of an instrument is based upon the proportion of variance derived from factor analytic studies. That is, the general factor is commonly estimated from the first unrotated principle factor or principle component in a factor analysis of the test battery (Flanagan et al., 2000; Roid, 2003b; Sattler & Ryan, 2009). However, Roid (2003b) estimated the proportion of variance attributed to *g* from the square of the overall average *g* loadings. Though such estimations are known to be downwardly biased and underestimate *g*-loadings (Maynard et al., 2011), they are nonetheless commonly reported. For example, Roid (2003b) estimated the *g*-saturation of the SB5 to range from 56% to 61%. In contrast, the WAIS-III was estimated to have 50% of its variance attributed to the general factor of intelligence (Roid, 2003b). Conversely, Jensen (1998) argued that this methodology would significantly underestimate the actual *g* saturation of an instrument. Jensen reported that, rather than representing the *g*-saturation of the composite score,

> The 'proportion of variance' attributed to a given factor in this case refers only to the average of the variances (the squared factor loadings) of each of the separate subtests. . . . The *g* loading of the *composite* score (i.e., the sum of the subtest scores), if it could be included in the same factor analysis with all the subtests without affecting their *g* loadings, would be much larger than the average of the *g* loadings of the separate subtests, assuming a fair number of subtests. (p. 103)

Completing the calculations suggested by Spearman (Jensen, 1998; Spearman, 1927), each of the major intelligence batteries have composite IQ *g*-loadings greater than .90 with the WAIS-IV, SB5, and WJ III Extended GIA having *g*-loadings greater than .95. However, though these estimates can provide comparative information, they are undoubtedly inflated due to the presence of correlated group factors (Jensen, 1998; Maynard et al., 2011). Jensen (1998) estimated the average *g*-loadings of standard IQ tests to be in the .80s. Ultimately, the true *g*-ness of composite measures must be determined by cross or joint factor analyses of multiple batteries and such data is currently limited, hence, it is difficult to know what value to place on this research. Nonetheless, given the apparent differences across tests in the degree to which the general factor of intelligence is assessed, consideration may need to be given to the relative importance of the *g*-saturation versus domain specific functions of each instrument.

Domain Specific Abilities and Part Scores

Because the general factor of intelligence is domain neutral (nonspecific), a greater depth of information regarding functioning may be revealed by analyzing the domain-specific patterns of neurocognitive abilities. When these abilities diverge markedly within the individual's profile, differences in functional outcome may be seen (Fiorello et al., 2007; *cf.* Reynolds & Kamphaus, 2003). That is, patterns of intellectual strengths and weaknesses may best be understood by moving beyond the general factor of intelligence and focusing on the underlying broad intellectual abilities (i.e., Fiorello et al., 2001). However, care must be taken in such an approach, as it has been argued that within-person comparisons at the subtest/factor level may lack reliability or add little to the interpretation of the composite full-scale measure for the Wechsler scales (Canivez, 2013; Lichtenberger & Kaufman, 2009; Watkins & Canivez, 2004; *cf.* Fiorello et al., 2001). Further, as noted above, IQ tests differ in the factors that they measure.

Two of the CHC broad cognitive ability factors are considered most relevant in the assessment of global intelligence—crystallized intelligence (*Gc*) and fluid intelligence (*Gf*). Crystallized intelligence (*Gc*) refers to primarily verbally mediated abilities reflecting the breadth and depth of culturally specific knowledge and processing abilities related to the use of that knowledge (Flanagan et al., 2007). These abilities, including knowledge of vocabulary, fund of information, and facility with language, are acquired during the course of life and education. In contrast, fluid intelligence (*Gf*) refers to a type of "on the spot" problem-solving ability that allows one to effectively deal with novel problems that cannot be dealt with routinely (Flanagan et al., 2007). As Jensen (2002) observed, "*Gf* is aptly defined as what you use when you don't know what to do" (p. 47). This ability includes the recognition of patterns, inferential thought, concept formation, analysis, and problem solving—which is often measured using nonverbal stimuli. These factors appear to have a degree of centrality in relationship to other intellectual abilities and are the broad ability factors most closely associated with the general factor of intelligence. *Gf* and *Gc* are measured by each of the major intelligence tests.

However, there may also be value in the extent to which an IQ test measures the broad array of CHC factors both in terms of the impact of such factors on the general factor and in terms of understanding an individual's functioning beyond the molar level represented by the general factor. The WJ III Normative Update (Woodcock et al., 2001, 2007) holds the distinction of measuring seven CHC factors, whereas the WAIS-IV and SB5 each measure five such factors. Brief IQ tests typically only measure two factors beyond the general factor—commonly *Gc* and *Gf*.

There has been a long-held view that ID is marked by "flat" cognitive profiles. The prevalence of significant discrepancies between factor scores decreases at lower levels of intellectual ability (Wechsler, 2008). Because of this finding, in instances in which there is "part-score" variability (i.e., significant differences between factor scores), some have asserted this to be inconsistent with the diagnosis of ID (Bergeron & Floyd, 2006).

However, in the face of certain neuropathologies, the domain-specific factors may dissociate such that discrepancies can occur between specific modular aspects of intellectual ability (Anderson & Miller, 1998).

Initial research with the WJ III has demonstrated that individuals with ID do not necessarily display a flat cognitive profile when assessed with comprehensive measures of CHC abilities, particularly when the measures vary in terms of g-saturation (Bergeron & Floyd, 2006; see also Van der Molen et al., 2010). These researchers found that, in children with ID, there were significantly greater intra-individual score ranges (scatter) than in average-achieving individuals. Given these findings, one should be hesitant to dismiss the diagnosis of ID because of profile scatter when the individual otherwise meets diagnostic criterion. As Bergeron and Floyd (2006) noted, regarding the diagnosis of ID in children, ". . . failing to make a diagnosis of mental retardation based on significant part score variability may do these children disservice when other ecologically valid evidence of mental retardation (e.g., adaptive behavior skill deficits) indicates genuine need" (p. 429). Therefore, the impact of specific, modular deficiencies may have broad impacts on behavior and adaptation consistent with ID.

Utilizing a neuropsychological model of intellectual functioning, in contrast to a psychometric model, it has been suggested that intellectual disability may arise from either a general deficit in thinking or as the result of more specific, modular impairments that function as gatekeepers to the development of broader intellectual abilities and adaptive functions (Anderson & Miller, 1998; Frith & Happé, 1998). Detterman (2002) used a systems explanation of general intelligence, noting

> . . . if a central process is congenitally weak or has been damaged, it will have a widespread effect on the system because so many other parts of the system rely on the central process. . . . [Deficits in general intellectual functioning may result] from a defect in one or more central processes. The damaged central process has the effect of lowering the efficiency of the entire system. In a sense, the damaged central process sets a limit on performance for the whole system. (p. 235)

By extension, in the case of brain dysfunction or deficiency, impairments in more specific, modular components of, for example, working memory, executive functions, or language functions, may compromise the overall functioning of the individual and alter their developmental trajectory—resulting in deficits in adaptive functioning and ID. In such instances, reliance on part scores may be appropriate when they have a meaningful relationship to the individual's adaptive functioning. Detailed recommendations for the proper use of part scores (when the validity of the full-scale general IQ score is questioned) are discussed in Chapter 7.

Comprehensive IQ Tests

There are only a limited number of IQ tests available that provide an assessment of the general factor of intelligence as well as multiple broad ability domains. The most widely used instruments, assuming an English-speaking adult without significant sensory or motor impairments, include the SB5 (Roid, 2003a), the WAIS-IV (Wechsler, 2008), and the WJ III (Woodcock et al., 2001, 2007). Clinical practice has generally supported the use of these comprehensive assessment instruments (see also Chapter 7).

Brief IQ Tests

The rationale for brief IQ tests is based upon the view that it may be most important to evaluate the general factor of intelligence and other central broad abilities, either verbal-crystallized or nonverbal-fluid factors, in terms of differential diagnosis and treatment planning (Glutting, Adams, & Sheslow, 2000). Some have suggested that multidimensional intelligence batteries lack sufficient reliability and validity at the subtest level to justify subtest level interpretation, and that brief measures can determine a full-scale IQ equally well and more efficiently (Canivez & Watkins, 2010; Nelson, Canivez, Lindstrom, & Hatt, 2007). Reynolds and Kamphaus (2003) wrote, "from our research, we have concluded that a strong measure of g coupled with strong measures of verbal and nonverbal intelligence, account for nearly all of the reliable and interpretable variance in the subtests of good intelligence measures" (p. 10). Still others have even questioned the multidimensional nature of tests such as the WAIS-IV as a measure of anything beyond the general factor of intelligence based upon divergent factor structures found with differing factor extraction methods (Canivez & Watkins, 2010).

Brief intelligence tests, such as the RIAS (Reynolds & Kamphaus, 2003), the Wide Range Intelligence Test (WRIT; Glutting et al., 2000), the Kaufman Brief Intelligence Test, Second Edition (KBIT-2; Kaufman & Kaufman, 2004), and the Wechsler Abbreviated Scale of Intelligence-II (WASI-II; McCrimmon & Smith, 2012; Wechsler, 2011), primarily provide evidence of intellectual functioning at the level of general intellectual ability without multidimensional elements of intellectual functioning beyond the broad verbal and nonverbal level. Careful consideration should be given to the role, if any, that such instruments might play in the comprehensive assessment of ID. These brief IQ tests may be most appropriate for screening purposes, to supplement the information from a comprehensive IQ test, or in circumstances in which restrictions to motor movements necessitate a test that has minimal motor demands. Considerable caution should be exercised in the use of brief IQ tests in the evaluation of ID. Because detailed reviews of these briefer tests are beyond the scope of this work, readers are referred to the specific test manuals and secondary works.

Alternative IQ Tests

Other instruments, focusing on domain-specific measures of intellectual functioning include the BETA-III (Kellogg & Morton, 1999), the Test of Non-Verbal Intelligence-4 (TONI-4; Brown, Sherbenou, & Johnson, 2010), the Comprehensive Test of Nonverbal Intelligence, Second Edition (CTONI-2; Hammill, Pearson, & Weiderholt, 2009), the General Ability Measure for Adults (GAMA; Naglieri & Bardos, 1997), and the Raven's

Progressive Matrices and related measures (Raven, Raven, & Court, 2000). These uni-dimensional instruments, if not "culture-fair," tend to be somewhat "culture-reduced." However, such instruments should only have a role in circumstances in which language or other issues preclude a comprehensive assessment of intelligence or as cognitive screeners (NRC, 2002). In addition, group IQ tests, because of uncertain administration parameters and limited breadth of coverage, should not be used as the primary source of information in the diagnosis of ID.

Other instruments have been developed to measure intelligence in non-English speaking populations, notably Spanish speakers. These instruments include the Escala de Inteligencia de Wechsler para Adultos–Tercera Edicion (EIWA-III; Wechsler, 2002b), a derivative of the WAIS-III with Puerto Rican norms; Batería III Woodcock-Muñoz (Muñoz-Sandoval, Woodcock, McGrew, & Mather, 2005), an alternative to the Woodcock-Johnson III; and Escalas de Inteligencia de Reynolds (Reynolds, Kamphaus, Fernández, & Pinto, 2009), a European Spanish translation of the RIAS with norms. Care must be exercised in the use of such instruments to ensure that the dialect spoken by the examinee matches that of the normative sample.

Summary and Conclusion

The assessment of intellectual functioning is the first of the three prongs in the diagnosis of ID. An understanding of the available instruments used for the measurement of intelligence is essential to fairly identifying those with ID. Contemporary practice has relied upon comprehensive, individually administered measures of intellectual functioning in making the determination of possible deficits in intelligence. In making the decision as to which instrument(s) to utilize, or in critiquing the adequacy of prior testing, instruments can be evaluated according to which general intellectual abilities and specific factors are assessed; the psychometric properties of the instrument; the adequacy of the normative sample size; how language, culture, and level of acculturation might affect the findings; and the specific application of practice effects and the Flynn effect to obtained scores.

More specifically, IQ instruments can be evaluated across a number of parameters. For example:

- Is the instrument an individually administered, reliable, and valid comprehensive measure of general intellectual functioning?
- Does the instrument measure at least three or more broad intellectual abilities as opposed to only the general factor of intelligence?
- Are the normative comparison samples large and adequately representative of the current population according to the demographic characteristics of age, race/ethnicity, gender, education, socioeconomic status, and geographic location?
- What is the impact that language and culture might have on obtained IQ test scores (see also Chapter 16)?

- Do the interpretive procedures avoid the use of demographically corrected sub-group norms, e.g., norms based on race/ethnicity, gender, and education (excepting age) in the determination of an IQ test score?
- Does the interpretive process allow for the use of composite (full-scale) IQ in order to provide the most reliable and valid information regarding an individual's general level of intellectual functioning as well as the use of subcomponent or part scores that may be of significance when they have meaningful relationships to the individual's adaptive functioning?

It is important to reiterate the fact that obtained IQ scores only approximate an underlying "true" score. Clinical, and now legal, standards emphasize consideration of the *SEM* when making diagnostic conclusions, and attention also should be given to potential practice effects as well as the influence of norm obsolescence in determining the accuracy of a given score. Finally, the results of IQ testing must be meaningfully integrated with the assessment of adaptive functions in order to accurately assess for the presence of ID.

References

American Academy of Clinical Neuropsychology. (2001). Policy statement on the presence of third party observers in neuropsychological assessments. *The Clinical Neuropsychologist*, 15(4), 433–439. http://dx.doi.org/10.1076/clin.15.4.433.1888

American Academy of Clinical Neuropsychology. (2007). American Academy of Clinical Neuropsychology (AACN) practice guidelines for neuropsychological assessment and consultation. *The Clinical Neuropsychologist*, 21(2), 209–231. http://dx.doi.org/10.1080/13825580601025932

American Educational Research Association, American Psychological Association, & National Council on Measurement in Education. (2014). *Standards for educational and psychological testing*. Washington, DC: American Educational Research Association.

American Psychiatric Association. (2013). *Diagnostic and statistical manual of mental disorders* (5th ed.; *DSM5*). Arlington, VA: American Psychiatric Association.

Anderson, M., & Miller, K. L. (1998). Modularity, mental retardation and speed of processing. *Developmental Science*, 1(2), 239–245. http://dx.doi.org/10.1111/1467-7687.00037

Axelrod, B., Barth, J., Faust, D., Fisher, J., Heilbronner, R., Larrabee, G., . . . Silver, C. (2000). Presence of third party observers during neuropsychological testing: Official statement of the National Academy of Neuropsychology. *Archives of Clinical Neuropsychology*, 15(5), 379–380. http://dx.doi.org/10.1093/arclin/15.5.379

Basso, M. R., Carona, F. D., Lowery, N., & Axelrod, B. N. (2002). Practice effects on the WAIS-III across 3- and 6-month intervals. *The Clinical Neuropsychologist*, 16(1), 57–63. http://dx.doi.org/10.1076/clin.16.1.57.8329

Becker, K. A. (2003). *History of the Stanford-Binet intelligence scales: Content and psychometrics. (Stanford-Binet Intelligence Scales, Fifth Edition Assessment Service Bulletin No. 1)*. Itasca, IL: Riverside Publishing. http://www.assess.nelson.com/pdf/sb5-asb1.pdf

Beckworth v. State, 2009 Ala. Crim. App. LEXIS 64, 61–62 (Ala. Crim. App. May 1, 2009).

Bergeron, R., & Floyd, R. G. (2006). Broad cognitive abilities of children with mental retardation: An analysis of group and individual profiles. *American Journal on Mental Retardation*, 111(6), 417–432. http://dx.doi.org/10.1352/0895-8017(2006)111[417:BCAOCW]2.0.CO;2

Braden, J. P., & Niebling, B. C. (2012). Using the Joint Test Standards to evaluate the validity evidence for intelligence tests. In D. P. Flanagan & P. L. Harrison (Eds.), *Contemporary intellectual assessment: Theories, tests, and issues* (3rd ed., pp. 739–757). New York, NY: Guilford Press.

Bridges, A. J., & Holler, K. A. (2007). How many is enough? Determining optimal sample sizes for normative studies in pediatric neuropsychology. *Child Neuropsychology*, 13, 528–538.

Brooks, B. L., Sherman, E. M., Iverson, G. L., Slick, D. J., & Strauss, E. (2011). Psychometric foundations for the interpretation of neuropsychological results. In M. R. Schoenberg & J. G. Scott (Eds.), *The little black book of neuropsychology* (pp. 893–922). New York, NY: Springer.

Brooks, B. L., Strauss, E., Sherman, E. S., Iverson, G. L., & Slick, D. J. (2009). Developments in neuropsychological assessment: Refining psychometric and clinical interpretive methods. *Canadian Psychology/Psychologie Canadienne*, 50(3), 196–209. http://dx.doi.org/10.1037/a0016066

Brown, L., Sherbenou, R. J., & Johnson, S. K. (2010). *Test of Nonverbal Intelligence, fourth edition (TONI-4)*. Austin, TX: Pro-Ed.

Buckhalt, J. (2002). A short history of *g*: Psychometrics' most enduring and controversial construct. *Learning and Individual Differences*, 13(2), 101–114. http://dx.doi.org/10.1016/S1041-6080(02)00074-2

Bush, S., Ruff, R., Troster, A., Barth, J., Koffler, S., Pliskin, N., . . . Silver, C. (2005). Symptom validity assessment: Practice issues and medical necessity–NAN Policy & Planning

Committee. *Archives of Clinical Neuropsychology, 20*(4), 419–426. http://dx.doi.org/10.1016/j.acn.2005.02.002

Butler v. Quarterman, 576 F. Supp. 2d 805, 812 (S.D. Tex. 2008).

Canivez, G. L. (2013, May 6). Incremental criterion validity of WAIS-IV Factor Index Scores: Relationships with WIAT-II and WIAT-III subtest and composite scores. *Psychological Assessment.* Advance online publication. http://dx.doi.org/10.1037/a0032092

Canivez, G. L. & Watkins, M. W. (2010). Investigation of the factor structure of the Wechsler Adult Intelligence Scale—Fourth edition (WAIS-IV): Exploratory and higher order factor analyses. *Psychological Assessment, 22*(4), 827–36.

Carroll, J. B. (1993). *Human cognitive abilities: A survey of factor-analytic studies.* New York, NY: Cambridge University Press.

Coalson, D., & Weiss, L. (2002, Spring). The evolution of Wechsler intelligence scales in historical perspective. *Assessment Focus Newsletter, 11,* 1–3. Retrieved May 26, 2013, from http://www.pearsonassessments.com/NR/rdonlyres/6F6A90D0-9EF9-41CC-BF21-EB3FE7E9A5B2/0/Assess_Focus_Spring_02.pdf

Colom, R., Abad, F. J., Garcia, L. F., & Juan-Espinosa, M. (2002). Education, Wechsler's Full Scale IQ, and *g. Intelligence, 30,* 449–462.

Committee on Psychological Tests and Assessment–American Psychological Association. (2007). *Statement on third party observers in psychological testing and assessment: A framework for decision making.* Retrieved from http://www.apa.org/science/programs/testing/third-party-observers.pdf

Crawford, J. R., & Garthwaite, P. H. (2008). On the "optimal" size for normative samples in neuropsychology: Capturing the uncertainty associated with the use of normative data to quantify the standing of a neuropsychological test score. *Child Neuropsychology, 14,* 99–117. doi: 10.1080/09297040801894709

Daniel, M. H. (2000). Interpretation of intelligence test scores. In R. J. Sternberg (Ed.), *Handbook of intelligence* (pp. 477–491). New York, NY: Cambridge University Press.

Dean, A., Victor, T., Boone, K., & Arnold, G. (2008). The relationship of IQ to effort test performance. *The Clinical Neuropsychologist, 22*(4), 705–722. http://dx.doi.org/10.1080/13854040701440493

Demetriou, A. (2002). Tracing psychology's invisible giant and its visible guards. In R. J. Sternberg & E. L. Grigorenko (Eds.), *The general factor of intelligence: How general is it?* (pp. 3–18). Mahwah, NJ: L. Erlbaum Associates.

Detterman, D. K. (2002). General intelligence: Cognitive and biological explanations. In R. J. Sternberg & E. L. Grigorenko (Eds.), *The general factor of intelligence: How general is it?* (pp. 223–243). Mahwah, NJ: L. Erlbaum Associates.

Detterman, D., & Daniel, M. (1989). Correlations of mental tests with each other and with cognitive variables are highest for low IQ groups. *Intelligence, 13*(4), 349–359. http://dx.doi.org/10.1016/S0160-2896(89)80007-8

Estevis, E., Basso, M. R., & Combs, D. (2012). Effects of practice on the Wechsler Adult Intelligence Scale-IV across 3- and 6-month intervals. *The Clinical Neuropsychologist, 26*(2), 239–254. http://dx.doi.org/10.1080/13854046.2012.659219

Ex Parte Eric Dewayne Cathey, Cause No. 713189-B (Dist. Ct. Harris County, TX 2012).

Fiorello, C. A., Hale, J. B., Holdnack, J. A., Kavanagh, J. A., Terrell, J., & Long, L. (2007). Interpreting intelligence test results for children with disabilities: Is global intelligence relevant? *Applied Neuropsychology, 14*(1), 2–12. doi: 10.1080/09084280701280338

Fiorello, C. A., Hale, J. B., McGrath, M., Ryan, K., & Quinn, S. (2001). IQ interpretation for children with flat and variable test profiles. *Learning and Individual Differences, 13*(2), 115–125. http://dx.doi.org/10.1016/S1041-6080(02)00075-4

Flanagan, D. P., McGrew, K. S., & Ortiz, S. O. (2000). *The Wechsler intelligence scales and Gf-Gc theory: A contemporary approach to interpretation.* Boston, MA: Allyn and Bacon.

Flanagan, D. P., Ortiz, S. O., & Alfonso, V. C. (2007). *Essentials of cross-battery assessment* (2nd ed.). Hoboken, NJ: John Wiley & Sons.

Fletcher, J. M., Stuebing, K. K., & Hughes, L. C. (2010). IQ scores should be corrected for the Flynn Effect in high-stakes decisions. *Journal of Psychoeducational Assessment, 28*(5), 469–473. http://dx.doi.org/10.1177/0734282910373341

Floyd, R. G., Bergeron, R., McCormack, A. C., Anderson, J. L., & Hargrove-Owens, G. L. (2005). Are Cattell-Horn-Carroll broad ability composite scores exchangeable across batteries? *School Psychology Review, 34*(3), 329–357.

Floyd, R. G., Clark, M. H., & Shadish, W. R. (2008). The exchangeability of IQs: Implications for professional psychology. *Professional Psychology: Research and Practice, 39*(4), 414–423. http://dx.doi.org/10.1037/0735-7028.39.4.414

Floyd, R. G., Shands, E. I., Rafael, F. A., Bergeron, R., & McGrew, K. S. (2009). The dependability of general-factor loadings: The effects of factor-extraction methods, test battery composition, test battery size, and their interactions. *Intelligence, 37*(5), 453–465. http://dx.doi.org/10.1016/j.intell.2009.05.003

Flynn, J. R. (2009). The WAIS-III and WAIS-IV: Daubert motions favor the certainly false over the approximately true. *Applied Neuropsychology, 16*, 98-104. doi: 10.1080/09084280902864360

Frith, U., & Happé, F. (1998). Why specific developmental disorders are not specific: On-line and developmental effects in autism and dyslexia. *Developmental Science, 1*(2), 267–272. http://dx.doi.org/10.1111/1467-7687.00041

Garlick, D. (2002). Understanding the nature of the general factor of intelligence: The role of individual differences in neural plasticity as an explanatory mechanism. *Psychological Review, 109*(1), 116–136. http://dx.doi.org/10.1037//0033-295X.109.1.116

Gignac, G., Vernon, P. A., & Wickett, J. C. (2003). Factors influencing the relationship between brain size and intelligence. In H. Nyborg (Ed.), *The scientific study of general intelligence: Tribute to Arthur R. Jensen* (pp. 93–106). Amsterdam, Netherlands: Pergamon.

Glutting, J., Adams, W., & Sheslow, D. (2000). *WRIT: Wide Range Intelligence Test manual.* Wilmington, DE: Wide Range.

Gottfredson, L. S. (1997). Why g matters: The complexity of everyday life. *Intelligence, 24*(1), 79–132. http://dx.doi.org/10.1016/S0160-2896(97)90014-3

Gould, S. J. (1996). *The mismeasure of man.* New York, NY: Norton.

Gresham, F. M., & Reschly, D. J. (2011). Standard of practice and Flynn Effect testimony in death penalty cases. *Intellectual and Developmental Disabilities, 49*(3), 131–140.

Hagan, L. D., Drogin, E. Y., & Guilmette, T. J. (2010). Science rather than advocacy when reporting IQ scores. *Professional Psychology: Research and Practice, 41*(5), 420–423. http://dx.doi.org/10.1037/a0021077

Haier, R. J. (2003). Positron emission tomography studies of intelligence: From psychometrics to neurobiology. In H. Nyborg (Ed.), *The scientific study of general intelligence: Tribute to Arthur R. Jensen* (pp. 41–51). Amsterdam, Netherlands: Pergamon.

Hall v. Florida, No. 12-10882, slip op. (U.S. May 27, 2014), http://www.supremecourt.gov/opinions/13pdf/12-10882_kkg1.pdf

Hammill, D. D., Pearson, N. A., & Weiderholt, J. L. (2009). *Comprehensive Test of Nonverbal Intelligence—Second Edition (CTONI-2).* Austin, TX: Pro-Ed.

Hart, C. L., Taylor, M. D., Smith, G. D., Whalley, L. J., Starr, J., Hole, D. J., . . . Deary, I. J. (2003). Childhood IQ, social class, deprivation, and their relationships with mortality and morbidity risk in later life: Prospective observational study linking the Scottish Mental Survey 1932 and the Midspan Studies. *Psychosomatic Medicine, 65*(5), 877–883. http://dx.doi.org/10.1097/01. PSY.0000088584.82822.86

Heaton, R. K., Miller, S. W., Taylor, M. J., & Grant, I. (2004). *Revised comprehensive norms for an expanded Halstead-Reitan Battery: Demographically adjusted neuropsychological norms for African American and Caucasian Adults.* Lutz, FL: Psychological Assessment Resources.

Heaton, R. K., Temkin, N., Dikmen, S., Avitable, N., Taylor, M. J., Marcotte, T. D., & Grant, I. (2001). Detecting change: A comparison of three neuropsychological methods, using normal and clinical samples. *Archives of Clinical Neuropsychology, 16*(1), 75–91. http://dx.doi.org/10.1093/arclin/16.1.75

Henson, R. K. (2001). Understanding internal consistency reliability estimates: A conceptual primer on Coefficient Alpha. *Measurement & Evaluation in Counseling and Development, 34*(3), 177–189.

Iverson, G. L. (2010). Detecting exaggeration, poor effort, and malingering in neuropsychology. In A. M. Horton, Jr. & L. C. Hartlage (Eds.), *Handbook of forensic neuropsychology, second edition* (pp. 91–135). New York, NY: Springer Pub.

Jensen, A. R. (1980). *Bias in mental testing.* New York, NY: Free Press.

Jensen, A. R. (1998). *The g factor: The science of mental ability.* Westport, CT: Praeger.

Jensen, A. R. (2002). Psychometric g: Definition and substantiation. In R. J. Sternberg & E. L. Grigorenko (Eds.), *The general factor of intelligence: How general is it?* (pp. 39–53). Mahwah, NJ: L. Erlbaum Associates.

Johnson, W., Bouchard, T. J., Jr., Krueger, R. F., McGue, M., & Gottesman, I. I. (2004). Just one g: Consistent results from three test batteries. *Intelligence, 32*(1), 95–107. http://dx.doi.org/10.1016/S0160-2896(03)00062-X

Johnson, W., te Nijenhuis, J., & Bouchard, T., Jr. (2008). Still just 1 g: Consistent results from five test batteries. *Intelligence, 36*(1), 81–95. http://dx.doi.org/10.1016/j.intell.2007.06.001

Kaufman, A. S. (2009). *IQ testing 101.* New York, NY: Springer Pub.

Kaufman, A. S., & Kaufman, N. L. (2004). *Kaufman Brief Intelligence Test* (2nd ed.). Bloomington, MN: Pearson.

Kellogg, C. E., & Morton, N. W. (1999). *Beta III.* San Antonio, TX: The Psychological Corporation.

Keith, T. Z., & Reynolds, M. R. (2010). Cattell–Horn–Carroll abilities and cognitive tests: What we've learned from 20 years of research. *Psychology in the Schools, 47*, 635–650. doi: 10.1002/pits.20496

Kranzler, J. H., & Jensen, A. R. (1991). The nature of psychometric g: Unitary process or a number of independent processes? *Intelligence, 15*(4), 397–422.

Lichtenberger, E. O., & Kaufman, A. S. (2009). *Essentials of WAIS-IV assessment.* Hoboken, NJ: Wiley.

Lineweaver, T. T., & Chelune, G. J. (2003). Use of the WAIS-III and WMS-III in the context of serial assessments. Interpreting reliable and meaningful change. In D. S. Tulsky, D. H. Saklofske, G. J. Chelune, R. J. Ivnik, A. Prifitera, R. K. Heaton, et al. (Eds.), *Clinical interpretation of the WAIS III and WMS III* (pp. 303–337). New York, NY: Academic Press.

Loring, D. W., & Bauer, R. M. (2010). Testing the limits: Cautions and concerns regarding the new Wechsler IQ and Memory scales. *Neurology, 74*(8), 685–690. http://dx.doi.org/10.1212/WNL.0b013e3181d0cd12

Luders, E., Narr, K. L., Thompson, P. M., & Toga, A. W. (2009). Neuroanatomical correlates of intelligence. *Intelligence, 37*(2), 156–163. http://dx.doi.org/10.1016/j.intell.2008.07.002

Mackintosh, N. J. (2011). *IQ and human intelligence* (2nd ed.). New York, NY: Oxford University Press.

Matarazzo, J. D., & Herman, D. O. (1984). Base rate data for the WAIS-R: Test-Retest stability and VIQ-PIQ differences. *Journal of Clinical Neuropsychology, 6*(4), 351–366. http://dx.doi.org/10.1080/01688638408401227

Maynard, J. L., Floyd, R. G., Acklie, T. J., & Houston, L., III. (2011). General factor loadings and specific effects of the Differential Ability Scale, Second Edition composites. *School Psychology Quarterly, 26*(2), 108–118. doi: 10.1037/a0023025

McCrimmon, A., & Smith, A. (2012). Review of the Wechsler Abbreviated Scale of Intelligence, Second Edition (WASI-II). *Journal of Psychoeducational Assessment.* Retrieved from http://jpa.sagepub.com/content/early/2012/12/04/0734282912467756.citation

McDaniel, M. (2005). Big-brained people are smarter: A meta-analysis of the relationship between in vivo brain volume and intelligence. *Intelligence, 33*(4), 337–346. http://dx.doi.org/10.1016/j.intell.2004.11.005

McGrew, K. S. (1997). Analysis of the major intelligence batteries according to a proposed comprehensive Gf-Gc framework. In D. P. Flanagan, J. Genshaft, & P. L. Harrison (Eds.), *Contemporary intellectual assessment: Theories, tests, and issues* (pp. 151–179). New York, NY: Guilford Press.

McGrew, K. S. (2005). The Cattell–Horn–Carroll theory of cognitive abilities. In D. P. Flanagan & P. L. Harrison (Eds.) *Contemporary intellectual assessment: Theories, tests, and issues* (2nd ed., pp. 136–181). New York, NY: Guilford Press.

McGrew, K. S. (2009). Editorial: CHC theory and the human cognitive abilities project: Standing on the shoulders of the giants of psychometric intelligence research. *Intelligence, 37,* 1–10. doi:10.1016/j.intell.2008.08.004

McGrew, K. S., & Flanagan, D. P. (1998). *The intelligence test desk reference (ITDR): Gf-Gc cross-battery assessment.* Needham Heights, MA: Allyn and Bacon.

McGrew, K. S., LaForte, E. M., & Schrank, F. A. (2014). *Technical manual. Woodcock-Johnson IV.* Rolling Meadows, IL: Riverside.

McGrew, K. S., Woodcock, R. W., & Schrank, K. A. (2007). *Woodcock-Johnson III normative update technical manual.* Rolling Meadows, IL: Riverside.

McGrew, K. S., Werder, J. K., & Woodcock, R. W. (1991). *Woodcock-Johnson technical manual.* Allen, TX: DLM.

McGrew, K. S., & Woodcock, R. W. (2001). *Technical manual. Woodcock-Johnson III Tests of Cognitive Abilities.* Itasca, IL: Riverside Pub.

Muñoz-Sandoval, A. F., Woodcock, R. W., McGrew, K. S., & Mather, N. (2005). *Batería III Woodcock-Muñoz.* Itasca, IL: Riverside Publishing.

Naglieri, J. A., & Bardos, A. N. (1997). *GAMA (General Ability Measure for Adults) manual.* Minneapolis, MN: National Computer Systems.

National Research Council. (2002). *Mental retardation: Determining eligibility for social security benefits* (Committee on Disability Determination for Mental Retardation—D. J. Reschly, T. G. Myers, & C. R. Hartel, Eds.). Washington, DC: National Academy Press.

Neisser, U., Boodoo, G., Bouchard, T. J., Boykin, A. W., Brody, N., Ceci, S. J., . . . Urbina, S. (1996). Intelligence: Knowns and unknowns. *American Psychologist, 51*(2), 77–101. http://dx.doi.org/10.1037//0003-066X.51.2.77

Nelson, J. M., Canivez, G. L., Lindstrom, W., & Hatt, C. V. (2007). Higher-order exploratory factor analysis of the Reynolds Intellectual Assessment Scales with a referred sample. *Journal of School Psychology, 45*(4), 439–456. http://dx.doi.org/10.1016/j.jsp.2007.03.003

O'Toole, B. I. (1990). Intelligence and behaviour and motor vehicle accident mortality. *Accident Analysis & Prevention, 22*(3), 211–221. http://dx.doi.org/10.1016/0001-4575(90)90013-B

Patja, K., Iivanainen, M., Vesala, H., Oksanen, H., & Ruoppila, I. (2000). Life expectancy of people with intellectual disability: A 35-year follow-up study. *Journal of Intellectual Disability Research, 44*(5), 591–599. http://dx.doi.org/10.1046/j.1365-2788.2000.00280.x

Pearson. (2009). *Advanced clinical solutions for WAIS-IV and WMS-IV: Administration and scoring manual.* San Antonio, TX: Author.

People v. Superior Court (Vidal), 129 Cal. App. 4th 434, 471 (Cal. App. 5th Dist. 2005)

People v. Superior Court (Vidal), 40 Cal. 4th 999, 1007 (Cal. 2007)

Pizzuto v. Blades, 2012 U.S. Dist. LEXIS 2786, 23–24 (D. Idaho Jan. 10, 2012)

Raven, J., Raven, J. C., & Court, J. H. (2000). *Manual for Raven's progressive matrices and vocabulary scales (including the parallel and plus versions)*. Oxford, England: OP Limited.

Reynolds, C. R., & Kamphaus, R. W. (2003). *RIAS (Reynolds Intellectual Assessment Scales) and the RIST (Reynolds Intellectual Screening Test): Professional manual*. Lutz, FL: Psychological Assessment Resources.

Reynolds, C. R., Kamphaus, R. W., Fernández, P. S., & Pinto, I. F. (2009). *RIAS: Escalas de Inteligencia de Reynolds y RIST: Test de Inteligencia Breve de Reynolds*. Madrid, Spain: TEA.

Reynolds, M. R., Keith, T. Z., & Beretvas, S. N. (2010). Use of factor mixture modeling to capture Spearman's law of diminishing returns. *Intelligence, 38*(2), 231–241. http://dx.doi.org/10.1016/j.intell.2010.01.002

Roid, G. H. (2003a). *Stanford–Binet Intelligence Scales, fifth edition*. Itasca, IL: Riverside Publishing.

Roid, G. H. (2003b). *Stanford–Binet Intelligence Scales, fifth edition, technical manual*. Itasca, IL: Riverside Publishing.

Roid, G. H., & Pomplun, M. (2012). The Stanford–Binet Intelligence Scales, fifth edition. In D. P. Flanagan & P. L. Harrison (Eds.), *Contemporary intellectual assessment: Theories, tests, and issues* (pp. 249-268). New York, NY: Guilford Press.

Salekin, K., & Doane, B. (2009). Malingering intellectual disability: The value of available measures and methods. *Applied Neuropsychology, 16*(2), 105–113. http://dx.doi.org/10.1080/09084280902864485

Sattler, J. (2001). *Assessment of children: Cognitive applications* (4th ed.). San Diego, CA: Jerome M. Sattler, Publisher, Inc.

Sattler, J. M., & Ryan, J. J. (2009). *Assessment with the WAIS-IV*. San Diego, CA: Jerome M. Sattler, Publisher, Inc.

Schalock, R. L., Borthwick-Duffy, S. A., Bradley, V. J., Buntinx, W. H., Coulter, D. L., Craig, E. M., Gomez, S. C., Lachapelle, Y., Luckasson, R., Reeve, A., Shogren, K. A., Snell, M. E., Spreat, S., Tasse, M. J., Thompson, J. R., Verdugo-Alonso, M. A., Wehmeyer, M. L., & Yeager, M. H. (2010). *Intellectual disability: Definition, classification, and systems of supports* (11th ed.). Washington, DC: American Association on Intellectual and Developmental Disabilities.

Schalock, R. L., Buntinx, W., Borthwick-Duffy, S., Luckasson, R., Snell, M., Tassé, M. J., & Wehmeyer, M. (2007). *User's guide: Mental retardation: Definition, classification, and systems of supports* (10th ed.). Washington, DC: American Association on Intellectual and Developmental Disabilities.

Schneider, W. J. (2012, January 13). *Can't decide which IQ is best? Make a composite IQ score* (Issue brief). Retrieved from http://assessingpsyche.wordpress.com/2012/01/13/cant-decide-which-iq-is-best-make-a-composite-iq-score/

Schneider, W. J. (2013a). What if we took our models seriously? Estimating latent scores in individuals. *Journal of Psychoeducational Assessment, 31*(2), 186–201. http://dx.doi.org/10.1177/0734282913478046

Schneider, W. J. (2013b). Principles of assessment of aptitude and achievement. In D. H. Saklofske, C. R. Reynolds, & V. L. Schwean (Eds.), *The Oxford handbook of child psychological assessment* (pp. 286–330). Oxford: Oxford University Press.

Schneider, W. J., & McGrew, K. (2012). The Cattell-Horn-Carroll model of intelligence. In D. Flanagan & P. Harrison (Eds.), *Contemporary intellectual assessment: Theories, tests, and issues* (3rd ed. pp. 99-144). New York, NY: Guilford.

Spearman, C. (1927). *The abilities of man; their nature and measurement.* New York, NY: Macmillan, reprinted by Kessinger Publishing.

Spitz, H. H. (1988). Wechsler subtest patterns of mentally retarded groups: Relationship to *g* and to estimates of heritability. *Intelligence, 12*(3), 279–297.

Stankov, L. (2002). *g*: The diminutive general. In R. J. Sternberg & E. L. Grigorenko (Eds.), *The general factor of intelligence: How general is it?* (pp. 19–37). Mahwah, NJ: L. Erlbaum Associates.

Stankov, L. (2005). *g* factor - Issues of design and interpretation. In O. Wilhelm & R. W. Engle (Eds.), *Handbook of understanding and measuring intelligence* (pp. 279–293). Thousand Oaks, CA: Sage Publications.

Sternberg, R. J., & Grigorenko, E. L. (Eds.). (2002). *The general factor of intelligence: How general is it?* Mahwah, NJ: L. Erlbaum Associates.

Tellegen, A., & Briggs, P. F. (1967). Old wine in new skins: Grouping Wechsler subtests into new scales. *Journal of Consulting Psychology, 31*(5), 499–506. http://dx.doi.org/10.1037/h0024963

Temkin, N. R., Heaton, R. K., Grant, I., & Dikmen, S. S. (1999). Detecting significant change in neuropsychological test performance: A comparison of four models. *Journal of the International Neuropsychological Society, 5*(4), 357–369. http://dx.doi.org/10.1017/S1355617799544068

Thorndike, R. (1987). Stability of factor loadings. *Personality and Individual Differences, 8*(4), 585–586. http://dx.doi.org/10.1016/0191-8869(87)90224-8

Thorson v. State, 76 So. 3d 667, 671-672 (Miss. 2011)

Trahan, L. H., Stuebing, K. K., Fletcher, J. M., & Hiscock, M. (2014, June 30). The Flynn effect: A meta-analysis. *Psychological Bulletin.* Advance online publication. http://dx.doi.org/10.1037/a0037173

United States v. Davis, 611 F. Supp. 2d 472, 488 (D. Md. 2009)

United States v. Hardy, 762 F. Supp. 2d 849, 866 (E.D. La. 2010)

United States v. Wilson, 2013 U.S. Dist. LEXIS 16872, 43-44 (E.D.N.Y. Feb. 7, 2013)

Urbina, S. (2011). Tests of intelligence. In R. J. Sternberg & S. B. Kaufman (Eds.), *The Cambridge handbook of intelligence* (pp. 20–38). Cambridge: Cambridge University Press.

VandenBos, G. R. (2007). *APA dictionary of psychology.* Washington, DC: American Psychological Association.

Van der Molen, M., Huizinga, M., Huizenga, H., Ridderinkhof, K., Van der Molen, M., Hamel, B., . . . Ramakers, G. (2010). Profiling Fragile X Syndrome in males: Strengths and weaknesses in cognitive abilities. *Research in Developmental Disabilities, 31*(2), 426–439. http://dx.doi.org/10.1016/j.ridd.2009.10.013

Wasserman, J. D., & Bracken, B. A. (2012). Fundamental psychometric considerations in assessment. In I. B. Weiner, J. R. Graham, & J. A. Naglieri (Eds.), *Handbook of Psychology, Volume 10: Assessment Psychology.* (2nd ed., pp. 153–229). Hoboken, NJ: John Wiley & Sons.

Watkins, M. W., & Canivez, G. L. (2004). Temporal stability of WISC-III subtest composite: Strengths and weaknesses. *Psychological Assessment, 16*(2), 133–138. http://dx.doi.org/10.1037/1040-3590.16.2.133

Wechsler, D. (1991) *Wechsler Intelligence Scale for Children, third edition (WISC-III): Manual.* San Antonio, TX: Psychological Corporation.

Wechsler, D. (2002a). *WAIS-III, Wechsler Adult Intelligence Scale, third edition: WMS-III, Wechsler Memory Scale, third edition: Technical manual. Updated.* San Antonio, TX: Psychological Corporation.

Wechsler, D. (2002b). *WAIS-III. Escala de Inteligencia para Adultos de Wechsler—Tercera Edición.* Buenos Aires, Brazil: Paidos.

Wechsler, D. (2008). *WAIS-IV: Technical and interpretive manual.* San Antonio, TX: Pearson.

Wechsler, D. (2011). *Wechsler Abbreviated Scale of Intelligence, Second Edition*. San Antonio, TX: NCS Pearson.

Weiss, L. G. (2010). Considerations on the Flynn effect. *Journal of Psychoeducational Assessment, 28*(5), 482–493. http://dx.doi.org/10.1177/0734282910373572

Whalley, L. J., & Deary, I. J. (2001). Longitudinal cohort study of childhood IQ and survival up to age 76. *British Medical Journal, 322*(7290), 819. Retrieved from http://www.ncbi.nlm.nih.gov/pmc/articles/PMC30556/pdf/819.pdf

Whitaker, S. (2008). The stability of IQ in people with low intellectual ability: An analysis of the literature. *Intellectual and Developmental Disabilities, 46*(2), 120–128. http://dx.doi.org/10.1352/0047-6765(2008)46[120:TSOIIP]2.0.CO;2

Woodcock, R. W., McGrew, K. S., Schrank, F. A., & Mather, N. (2001, 2007). *Woodcock-Johnson III normative update*. Rolling Meadows, IL: Riverside Pub.

Zhou, X., Zhu, J., & Weiss, L. G. (2010). Peeking inside the "black box" of the Flynn Effect: Evidence from three Wechsler instruments. *Journal of Psychoeducational Assessment, 28*(5), 399–411. http://dx.doi.org/10.1177/0734282910373340

9 | Variability of IQ Test Scores

Stephen Greenspan
J. Gregory Olley

Several possible causes of IQ test score variability are discussed in this chapter. These causes include (a) learning that occurs as a result of multiple test administrations, (b) developmental processes (positive and negative) in adults who are incarcerated, (c) test regression in populations which are disadvantaged, (d) examiner factors (bias, training, corruption or deviation from standard practice), (e) problems with test norms, (f) lack of equivalence across tests, (g) motivational factors (poor effort as well as very high effort), and (h) test unreliability (especially for individuals with low IQ test scores). Although some of these factors have been discussed in *Intellectual Disability: Definition, Classification, and Systems of Supports* (11th ed.; Schalock et al., 2010, Chapter 4) and are noted previously in this volume (see Chapters 7 and 8), this chapter offers an expanded discussion.

IQ test scores play a central role in judicial proceedings in determining whether a defendant meets the first prong (significant deficits in intellectual functioning) for diagnosing intellectual disability (ID) in an *Atkins* proceeding and it is common for such a defendant to have been tested multiple times. For example, testing may have occurred (a) in school, either because he or she was being evaluated for special education or as part of a routine screening; (b) during a placement for the juvenile justice system; (c) during a placement for the adult correctional system for a prior offense; (d) as part of an application for Social Security benefits or to join the military; and (e) during the period leading up to the *Atkins* proceeding (by psychologists hired by either the defense or prosecution). With multiple testing, some variability in obtained scores is inevitable.

Because IQ test scores of *Atkins* defendants often fall close to the conventional upper limit of 70–75, some scores are likely to fall above or below that range. There are multiple reasons for IQ test score fluctuation, with most of them not having to do with effort (a common factor cited by forensic expert evaluators in *Atkins* cases). These various explanations are briefly explored and practical implications for individuals involved in *Atkins* assessments are discussed.

Effect of Multiple Administrations

The term *practice effect* is used to describe the rise in scores that occurs as a result of repeated administrations of the same test within a too-short period of time. The explanation for this effect is that some learning occurs during the taking of an IQ test, with most of the learning involving performance or nonverbal subscales. Although verbal subscales are derived from, and are very similar to, tasks used in school curricula, in contrast, the nonverbal subscales involve novel tasks and manipulative materials both of which are tasks that likely have never been encountered before. For this reason, scores can increase with re-administration, although there is no empirically established rule to predict how much that increase would be for an individual with re-administration after a specified time. Any repeat administration of an IQ test should be interpreted with the practice effect in mind (Kaufman, 1994).

Following is one hypothetical example, which is similar to an actual case:

A defendant as a youth had frequently been moved from one residential facility to another over a period of a few years, and in every new placement he was given a new IQ test. Over an 8-year period, he was tested on the Wechsler Intelligence Scale for Children-Revised (WISC-R, Wechsler, 1974) six times, and his full-scale IQ score ranged from 72 (first testing) to 85 (last testing). Two years after the last WISC-R, he was tested on the Wechsler Adult Intelligence Scale-Revised (WAIS-R, Wechsler, 1981) and received a full-scale IQ of 72. At this point in time, he was 16 years of age, the age at which one transitions from the WISC to the WAIS.

Consistent with Kaufman (1994), a steady increase in WISC-R scores as reflected in the example can be the result of the learning that occurs from so many administrations of that test. From this perspective, the only test scores that should be given any weight in the previous example are the 72 from the first WISC-R and the same score from the WAIS-R 10 years later.

Concern about the practice effect has resulted in the admonition to wait either 6 months (Wechsler, 2008) or 1 year (Luckasson et al., 2002) before administering the same test to an individual. However, it is Kaufman's (1994) opinion that the practice effect can still be operative years and not just months later. One way to circumvent the practice effect is to switch, for example, from the WAIS-IV (Wechsler, 2008) to the Stanford-Binet-5 (Roid, 2003) for the second test, and another way is to have a motion filed for a continuance based on the inability to complete a valid assessment at that time.

Maturation During Incarceration

There is a literature base that suggests that significant brain maturation, particularly in the prefrontal area, often occurs in typically developing adults well past the age of majority (e.g., Lebel & Beaulieu, 2011). Furthermore, the course of intellectual development is not the same for all people, and for some individuals, it can continue well into the 30s or 40s (Schaie, 1996; 2013). If so, the fact that IQ has risen in a long-term incarcerated prisoner could reflect continued brain development, including plasticity (repair) of brain structures after cessation of drug use. Moreover, there may be some increase in measured intelligence that results from information acquired during incarceration. Opportunities for exposure to information include, but are not limited to, television, radio, written material, and communications with pen pals and other inmates. An individual's ability to read, although well behind age level, is very common in adults with higher functioning intellectual disability (Young, Moni, Jobling, & Kraayenoord, 2004). Further, incarcerated people with low IQ test scores may achieve improved literacy in prison (National Center for Educational Statistics, 1994).

For *Atkins* purposes, the relevance of raised or lowered intelligence in prison may not undermine the validity or weight given to scores obtained around the time of the crime or before the defendant's 18th birthday. As the *User's Guide to Intellectual Disability: Definition, Classification, and Systems of Supports* (Schalock et al., 2012) states, "the diagnosis of ID is not based on the person's 'street smarts,' behavior in jail or prison, or 'criminal adaptive functioning'" (p. 20).

Regression in Childhood

A negative developmental pattern may be observed in the early IQ test scores of some *Atkins* petitioners. In this pattern, IQ test scores from early primary grades are in the 80s, but then go progressively downhill as the individual ages, ending up and staying below the 70-75 ID ceiling by middle school, secondary school, and early adulthood. Such a pattern is especially common in youngsters who are disadvantaged (Breslau et al., 2001) where it is accompanied by a pattern of increasing failure in school, repeated grade retentions and, sometimes, special education placement, school dropout, and the beginnings of an arrest history.

This unfortunate pattern of cognitive and academic regression has been named the "Matthew Effect," after this famous passage in the New Testament's "Gospel According to Saint Matthew" (New Revised Standard Oxford Edition, 25:29): "For to all those who have, more will be given, and they will have an abundance; but from those who have nothing, even what they have will be taken away." This phenomenon has been used to explain widening gaps in class privilege, income (Reardon, 2011; Rigney, 2010), and educational achievement, particularly literacy (Fryer & Levitt, 2004; Hindman, Erhart, & Wasik, 2012; Stanovich, 1986). One reason given for this drop in IQ test scores is poor school attendance, which may have some impact, but is not the best or most accurate explanation for this phenomenon (Herbers et al., 2012). There are two likely explanations for why intelligence test scores often decline from early to later childhood in youngsters who are both disadvantaged and who have low (but slightly above the ID ceiling) IQ test scores. First, early childhood IQ test scores are not very reliable for various reasons, including variable state and limited attention or motivation in young children, and test items that are fewer in number and very different tests given at older ages. Consequently, test scores obtained by young children usually correlate weakly with IQ test scores in adolescence or adulthood (Weinert & Schneider, 1999). Second, in children from more advantaged families, the effects of brain-based risk factors, such as executive dysfunction, in lowering intelligence are lessened by good parental and other environmental supports. In children who are disadvantaged, the effect of brain-based impairments in lowering intelligence may be increased over time due to the effects of disorganized and nonsupportive environments (Ungar, 2004; Werner, 1992).

Examiner Bias and Competence

IQ tests are designed to be relatively robust, in the sense that they are intended to produce results that are unaffected by the identity of the examiner or the nature of the testing environment. That robustness is established during the test development process, in which the author and publisher are able to control how and by whom their test is administered. Furthermore, in the test development process, the examiner has no interest in the results of any individual test administration. In the real world, however, testing circumstances vary considerably and not all examiners are adequately qualified, careful, or willing to abide by the prescribed test procedures. In the latter case, clinicians may feel pressure to produce scores that meet the goals of others. For example, there has long been a push to keep children, especially minority children, out of special education (Codrington & Fairchild, 2012), and in the legal arena the pressure can originate from external sources (e.g., attorneys, members of the claimant's family, members of the victims family) who are invested in the outcome of testing and/or internal processes. These processes may be conscious or unconscious and may be related to the examiner's moral position in relation to the death penalty or perhaps a personal investment in a particular claimant.

When considering variability in test results, it is important to examine the possibility that examiner errors in administration, scoring, or interpretation occurred (Slate & Jones, 1989). A widely cited study (Moon, Blakey, Gorsuch, & Fantuzzo, 1991), involving the WAIS-R but applicable to more current tests, found that 33% of junior psychologists made testing and scoring errors, even after satisfactorily completing relevant training. Such errors impact the accuracy of obtained scores, and this could be true for both current and past test administrations. Individually or combined, these factors can account for some of the discrepancy in scores over time. Experts in such a high-stakes matter should not delegate IQ testing to underqualified (and sometimes unsupervised) assistants or junior psychologists, something that is undoubtedly done quite often.

In addition to the possibility that an examiner may not have been adequately qualified, there are other administrative factors that could invalidate the results of a test session. These factors may include (a) an examiner who begins the session in an adversarial manner (e.g., asking challenging questions about the alleged crime); (b) too many observers in the testing room (e.g., police, correctional officers, attorneys, or mitigation specialists); (c) an examiner who may administer the test in an overly curt or unfriendly manner; or (d) an examiner who deviates substantially from the test administration protocol (e.g., not administering all subscales, giving too much time, not enough time, or too much encouragement). In addition, testing conditions, especially in jail or prison settings, are often quite noisy and distracting, and this can obviously have an impact on test performance. One should attempt to determine the circumstances under which any given IQ test was administered before assuming that the result is valid.

In some states (e.g., North Carolina), statutes require that IQ testing in *Atkins* cases be carried out by a licensed, doctoral-level psychologist. Yet in the inherently retro-spective *Atkins* evaluation, records of school testing are heavily relied upon and many such tests in the past would likely have been conducted by master's-level school psy-chologists. If the testing is more than about 20 years old (when certification of school psychologists became common), the school testing might have been done by some-one with minimal qualifications in psychometrics. In such cases, the raw data and the opportunity to interview the person who did the testing may not be available. In fact, it may be that the only remaining documents are the report, the name of the test admin-istered, and/or a mere mention of an IQ test score.

Problems with Test Norms

IQ tests are *norm-based*, which means that standard scores are based on the individual's performance in comparison to that of others of the same age used in the standardiza-tion sample. The norms are intended to reflect the population of the larger society which, in the case of the Wechsler and Stanford-Binet tests, is the most recent census of the United States. Developing an adequate normative sample is an expensive and time-consuming process.

In spite of the effort put into the normative process, mistakes are sometimes made resulting in a test score that may be invalidly high or low. Flynn (2006) argued that a normative mistake is what happened with the WAIS-III. The publisher attempted to correct for the so called "tree stump" (floor effect) phenomenon with the predeces-sor WAIS-R (if you had administered the WAIS-R to a tree stump, you would have obtained a score in the 40s), which was caused by an absence of very low-functioning subjects in the normative sample. According to Flynn, the firm hired by the publisher to select the WAIS-III normative sample, over-corrected by recruiting too many low-functioning subjects, the result of which is that the WAIS-III produced scores that were 2.34 points too high (Flynn, 2006, p. 178).

Floor effect problems can, however, be found in other tests, most notably the second edition of the Test of Non-Verbal Intelligence (TONI-2; Brown, Sherbenon, & Johnson, 1990) and the first edition of the Comprehensive Test of Non-Verbal Intelligence (CTONI; Hammill, Pearson, & Wiederholt, 1997),which produced inflated scores for low-functioning subjects (Naglieri & Goldstein, 2009). As a result of correcting for this problem, scores obtained with the CTONI-2 (Hammill, Pearson, & Wiederholt, 2009) are lower for low-functioning subjects than would have been the case with the earlier tests cited previously.

James Flynn is the person primarily associated with the discovery of the so-called "Flynn effect" (Flynn, 1984; see Chapter 10). This term refers to norm obsolescence. Because of increasing competence in population performance on, especially, nonverbal subscales of IQ tests, test publishers re-norm successive editions of their tests, so that an individual will score roughly the same on a new edition as he or she did on the older edition. The re-norming process results in an average test score increase of 3 points per decade (see Chapter 10 for a full discussion of how the Flynn effect affects test score reliability).

In addition to the problems noted previously concerning construction problems or obsolescence of norms, a third issue is that test publishers may use incorrect statistical formulae or make other statistical mistakes, which have the effect of producing IQ test scores that cannot be interpreted. That is what happened with the Mexican version of the WAIS-III (e.g., Tulsky & Zhu, 2003). It is essentially identical to the U.S. version, except that the instructions and items are translated into Spanish. The IQ test scores obtained when using the Mexican norms were considerably higher than when using the U.S. norms provided for the same test. The publisher attributed this to differences between the U.S. and the Mexican populations. However, when examining the test's technical manual, Suen and Greenspan (2009) discovered many statistical and other mistakes (in addition to improper sampling methods) that were made when these norms were constructed.

Publication of these findings caused the test publisher to send out a notice steering purchasers away from using the Mexican norms and urging them to use the U.S. norms. The main lesson here is that translated versions of established intelligence tests may or may not have valid norms, and it is incumbent upon users of these tests to look into the validity data for any test they are relying upon and not to assume that all IQ norm tables are adequately constructed.

Lack of Test Equivalence

The concept of *validity* refers to the extent to which a test measures what the test authors say that it measures (see also Chapters 7 and 8). In the case of IQ tests, the construct that is purported to be measured is "intelligence," but that is a construct whose meaning is not universally agreed upon (Schalock et al., 2010; Sternberg & Detterman, 1986). One semiserious definition of intelligence is "that which is measured by IQ tests." Reflecting this, the most common approach to validating a new test is to select items so that a full-scale score on the new test correlates well with a full-scale score on another well-accepted test, such as one of the Wechsler scales. An alternative is to construct a test to conform to a theory of the nature of intelligence. Two such theories—the Cattell-Horn-Carroll (CHC) theory (McGrew, 2005, see Chapter 7) and the PASS (Planning, Attention-Arousal, Simultaneous and Successive) theory (Das, Kirby, & Jarman, 1975)—have been used to develop tests and to judge the extent to which other tests tap into components of those theories. These theories are discussed further in Schalock et al. (2010) and in Chapters 7 and 8.

Even assuming that a test correlates strongly with a "gold standard" test such as the WAIS-IV, one must consider the possibility that there are systematic differences in the obtained scores. That is because a significant correlation indicates only a similar rank ordering (i.e., subjects high on one test are also high on the other, and *vice versa*) but tests can show similar rank orderings and still produce different mean scores. An example of this can be found in the Reynolds Intellectual Assessment Scales (RIAS; Reynolds & Kamphaus, 2003), which Umphress (2008) found produces higher mean scores, especially in the nonverbal/performance domain, in spite of generally strong correlations with other tests. Of course, different does not mean inferior, but one must be aware of the possibility that an outlier score may have less to do with within-subject variability and more to do with between-test variability.

Motivational Factors

Motivational factors undoubtedly contribute to IQ test performance, although some examiners may be too quick to attribute score variability to malingering or poor effort without considering other possibilities or, for that matter, looking for direct indicators of "faking low" (see Chapter 18). As a rule, subjects often do not understand why they are being examined or what impact their performance might have on their legal case, and low-IQ subjects (whether or not they qualify as having ID) are generally bothered by the prospect of being labeled ID (Ali, Hassiotis, Strydom, & King, 2012; Werner, Corrigan, Ditchman, & Sokol, 2012). That said, a motivated subject who is trying his best will likely do better on an IQ test than the same subject would do if he were in an unmotivated state and was not putting forth an adequate effort.

Formal measures of effort or malingering have been developed and validated for use in evaluations for mental illness or in neuropsychological evaluations. However, their validity for use in *Atkins* evaluations remains unproven, and questionable in general (see Erin, 2011 and Chapter 18). Before the advent of formal measures of effort, the standard way of determining if a subject was putting forth an adequate effort was to rely on the clinical judgment of an experienced examiner who was taking into account such things as internal test consistency, time taken, congruence with other measures, and apparent engagement. As indicated by Drob, Meehan, and Waxman (2009), such an approach was less likely to result in false positives (misattributing malingering when there is none) than the current widespread reliance of formal measures.

According to Reynolds, Price, and Niland (2004), two factors—clinical observation and data convergence—are more valid indicators of effort on forensic cognitive tasks than are formal measures of effort (Reynolds et al. 2004). This skeptical view of formal effort tests in *Atkins* cases was confirmed by Salekin and Doane (2009), who cited data suggesting that such tests have poor validity when used with subjects with very low IQ test scores. (This issue is also addressed in Chapter 18 in this volume.)

A common belief is that motivational factors can only cause a test score to go down. That is because it is assumed that poor effort results in poor performance, whereas good effort (and the resulting score) is already maximized. There is research, however, that suggests that what we consider good effort is actually average (i.e., less than superior) effort, as reflected in research (e.g., Duckworth, Quinn, Lynam, Loeber, & Stouthamer-Loeber, 2011) that shows that paying a subject to do very well on an IQ test may cause his or her score to increase an average of 0.64 of a standard deviation (or almost 10 points). The effect of incentives on test performance, according to Kiefer and Goh (1981) is likely greater for subjects who are disadvantaged. The cliché that "you can fake low, but you cannot fake high" is widely believed, and sometimes causes lower scores in a variable sequence to be unfairly dismissed. In contrast, one should keep in mind that one cannot ever know definitively when there is optimal performance on an IQ (or any other) test, and there are many reasons (some covered earlier in this chapter) why a high score can be equally suspect.

Test Unreliability

Test *reliability* refers to the extent to which a test score obtained on the instrument is subject to error. IQ tests are among the most reliable of the psychological instruments, but they are still subject to error. This error can be approached in several ways, but for *Atkins* purposes, the most usual and important way of describing reliability is "test-retest" reliability which refers to the extent to which an IQ test score obtained on time 1 agrees with the IQ test score obtained on time 2 (factoring out the effect of practice). For the best IQ tests, such as the Wechsler and Stanford-Binet scales, the average index of test-retest variability, at the 95% confidence level, is approximately plus or minus 5 points. What this means is that on a typical basis, when a subject receives an IQ test score of say 80, his or her "true score" will fall 95% of the time within a range from 75 to 85.

This finding underlies the AAIDD (Schalock et al., 2010) definition indicating that IQ test scores of up to approximately 75 may be indicative of limitations in intellectual functioning. This definition, although reflected in criminal statutes and/or case law, is not endorsed in some states (e.g., Florida and North Carolina). These states have been referred to as "bright line states" in that they employ a strict cut off for the distinction between ID and not-ID. This bright line falls at an IQ of 70; a score of 71 makes the claimant death penalty eligible. This concern was a key focus of the U.S. Supreme Court ruling in *Hall v. Florida* (2014; see Chapter 1).

Standard error (addressed previously in Chapter 5, 7 and 8), is the standard deviation (an index of variability) of the sampling distribution of a set of data. The statistic describing a distribution is an estimate, because no two samples are entirely identical; nor are the samples perfect representations of the population from which they are drawn. In practical terms, the true value of a standard error is unknown, which is why it is considered an estimate. For this reason, confidence intervals are used to give an indication of the size of the uncertainty about the validity of an obtained score depending on the probability level (typically 95th percentile).

In asserting that a subject's true score falls 95 times out of a hundred within a certain range, it means that on occasion (one out of 20 times) his or her score could fall outside of that range, as a function of chance and not as a function of any systematic cause. Furthermore, the confidence interval will differ somewhat, depending on various factors, such as how the test was constructed and the characteristics of a particular sample.

The 5-point spread that is usually mentioned was obtained from normative sampling studies. Whitaker (2008; 2010) presented data showing that for subjects with low IQ test scores, test-retest reliability is considerably worse, with 14% of this population scoring plus or minus 10 points differently on a retest. Furthermore, for subjects with a low IQ test score, he found that when tested on the WAIS their scores averaged many points higher than when the same subjects were previously tested on the WISC.

A final consideration in terms of IQ test score variability relates to the health of the examinee. Experts should be aware of illnesses, either acute (e.g., influenza) or chronic (e.g., diabetes, with related fluctuation in blood-sugar level) and ways that such illnesses might affect test performance.

Discussion

There is a tendency among laypeople, but also among many mental health professionals, to reify IQ test scores; that is, to treat them as if they were fixed, immutable, and concrete. IQ test scores can and do differ across tests, examiners, time, and testing circumstances. In the future, intelligence measurements will likely be approached more holistically, with integration of information obtained from multiple measures, rather than relying heavily on IQ instruments whose basic intent (predicting performance in school) has not changed much since they were developed by Binet and Simon over a century ago.

Given how frequently the claim of malingering is made by testifying experts to explain IQ test score variability, it should be pointed out that there are other explanations (most of them covered in this chapter, Chapters 7 and 8, and in Schalock et al., 2010) that should also be considered. Contrary to the view that IQ test scores never change and that one IQ test score should be the same as every other one, thoughtful and competent forensic experts understand that is often not the case. Although *intelligence* is a concept representing a theoretically stable human trait, an IQ test is a measure of human performance at a particular time, and human performance, by definition, is variable. IQ tests do not tap a magical trait that is not influenced by internal or external factors that affect virtually every other form of human behavior. The factors described in this chapter illustrate why a more complex understanding is required.

References

Ali A., Hassiotis, A., Strydom, A., & King, M. (2012). Self stigma in people with intellectual disabilities and courtesy stigma in family careers: A systematic review. *Research in Developmental Disabilities, 33*(6), 212–240. doi: 10.1016/j.ridd.2012.06.013.

Breslau, N., Chilcoat, H. D., Susser, E. S., Matte, T., Kung-Yee, L., & Peterson, E. (2001). Stability and change in children's intelligence quotient scores: A Comparison of two socioeconomically disparate communities. *American Journal of Epidemiology, 154,* 711–717. doi: 10.1093/aje/154.8.711

Brown, L., Sherbenon, R. J., & Johnson, S. K. (1990). *TONI-2: Test of Nonverbal Intelligence—2nd edition.* Austin, TX: Pro-Ed.

Codrington, J., & Fairchild, H. F. (2012). *Special education and the mis-education of African-American children: A call to action.* Fort Washington, MD: Association of Black Psychologists.

Das, J. P., Kirby, J. R., & Jarman R. F. (1975). Simultaneous and successive syntheses: An alternative model for cognitive abilities. *Psychological Bulletin, 82,* 87–103.

Drob, S. L., Meehan, K. B., & Waxman, S. E. (2009). Clinical and conceptual problems in the attribution of malingering in forensic evaluations. *American Academy of Psychiatry and Law 37*(1), 98–106.

Duckworth, A. L., Quinn, P. D., Lynam, D. R. Loeber, R., & Stouthamer-Loeber, M. (2011). Role of test motivation in intelligence testing. *Proceedings of the National Academy of Sciences, 109,* 7716–7720. doi: 10.1073/pnas.1018601108

Erin, D. B. (2011). Symptom validity testing, effort, and neuropsychological assessment. *Journal of the International Neuropsychological Society, 18,* 632–642. doi: http://dx.doi.org/10.1017/S1355617712000252

Flynn, J. R. (1984). The mean IQ of Americans: Massive gains 1932 to 1978. *Psychological Bulletin, 95,* 29–51.

Flynn, J. R. (2006). Tethering the elephant: Capital cases, IQ and the Flynn effect. *Psychology, Public Policy, and Law, 12,* 170–189. doi:10.1037/1076-8971.12.2.170

Fryer, R. G., Jr., & Levitt, S. D. (2004). Understanding the Black-White Test Score Gap in the First Two Years of School. *Review of Economics & Statistics, 86*(2), 447–464. doi: 10.3386/w8975

Hall v. Florida (572 U. S., 2014; U.S. Supreme Court No. 12–10882).

Hammill, D. D., Pearson, N. A., & Wiederholt, J. L. (1997). *CTONI: Comprehensive Test of Nonverbal Intelligence.* Austin, TX: Pro-Ed.

Hammill, D. D., Pearson, N. A., & Wiederholt, J. L. (2009). *CTONI-2: Comprehensive Test of Nonverbal Intelligence,* (2nd ed.). Austin, TX: Pro-Ed.

Herbers, J. E., Cutuli, J. J., Supkoff, L. M., Heistad, D., Chan, C.-K., Hinz, E. & Masten, A. S. (2012). Early reading skills and academic achievement trajectories of students facing poverty, homelessness, and high residential mobility. *Educational Researcher, 41*(9), 366–374. doi: 10.3102/0013189X12445320

Hindman, A. H., Erhart, A. C., & Wasik, B. A. (2012). Reducing the Matthew Effect: Lessons from the "ExCELL" Head Start Intervention. *Early Education and Development, 23*(5), 781–806.

Kaufman, A. S. (1994). Practice effects. In R. J. Sternberg (Ed.), *Encyclopedia of intelligence* (Vol. 2; pp. 828–833). New York, NY: Macmillan.

Kaufman, A. S., & Kaufman, N. L. (2004). *Kaufman Brief Intelligence Test.* (2nd ed.; KBIT-2). Circle Pines, MN: American Guidance Service.

Kiefer, D. A., & Goh, D. S. (1981). The effect of individually contracted incentives on intelligence test performance of middle- and low-SES children. *Journal of Clinical Psychology, 37,* 175–179.

Lebel, C., & Beaulieu, C. (2011). Longitudinal development of human brain wiring continues from childhood into adulthood. *Journal of Neuroscience, 31,* 10937–10947. doi: 10.1523/JNEUROSCI.5302-10.2011

Luckasson, R., Borthwick-Duffy, S. A, Buntinx, W. H. E., Coulter, D. L., Craig, E. M., Reeve, A., Schalock, R. L., Snell, M. E., Spitalnik, D. M., Spreat, S.,& Tassé, M. J. (2002). *Mental retardation: Definition, classification, and systems of supports (10th ed.).* Washington, DC: American Association on Intellectual and Developmental Disabilities.

McGrew, K. S. (2005). The Cattell-Horn-Carroll theory of cognitive abilities: Past, present, and future. In D. P. Flanagan, J. L. Genshaft, & P. L. Harrison (Eds.), *Contemporary intellectual assessment: Theories, tests, and issues (*2nd ed.*; pp. 136–182). New York, NY: Guilford.

Moon, G. W., Blakey, W A., Gorsuch, R. L. & Fantuzzo, J. W. (1991). Frequent WAIS-R administration errors: An ignored source of inaccurate measurement. *Professional Psychology: Research and Practice, 22*(3), 256–258.

Naglieri, J. A., & Goldstein, S. (2009). *Practitioner's guide to assessing intelligence and achievement.* New York, NY: Wiley.

National Center for Educational Statistics. (1994). *Literacy behind prison walls.* Washington, DC: Author.

Reardon, S. F. (2011). The widening academic achievement gap between the rich and the poor: New evidence and possible explanations. In R. Murnane & G. Duncan (Eds.), *Whither opportunity? Rising inequality and the uncertain life chances of low-income children* (pp. 91–116). New York, NY: Russell Sage.

Reynolds, C. R., & Kamphaus, R. W. (2003). *Reynolds Intellectual Assessment Scales (RIAS).* Torrance, CA: Western Psychological Services.

Reynolds, C. R., Price, R. J., & Niland, J. (2004). Applications of neuropsychology in capital felony (death penalty) defense. *Journal of Forensic Neuropsychology, 3,* 89–123.

Rigney, D. (2010). *The Matthew effect: How advantage begets further advantage.* New York, NY: Columbia University Press.

Roid, G. H. (2003). *Stanford-Binet Intelligence Scales* (SB5, 5th ed.). Itasca, IL: Riverside.

Salekin, K. L., & Doane, B. M. (2009). Malingering intellectual disability: The value of available measures and methods. *Applied Neuropsychology, 16,* 105–113. doi: 10.1080/0908428090 2864485.

Schaie, K. W. (1996). Intellectual development in adulthood. In J. E. Birren & K. W. Schaie (Eds.), *Handbook of the psychology of aging* (pp. 266–286). San Diego, CA: Academic.

Schaie, K.W. (2013). *Developmental influences on adult intelligence: The Seattle longitudinal study.* New York, NY: Oxford University Press.

Schalock, R. L., Borthwick-Duffy, S. A., Bradley, V. J., Buntinx, W. H. E., Coulter, D. L., Craig, E. M., Gomez, S. C., Lachapelle, Y., Luckasson, R., Reeve, A., Shogren, K. A., Snell, M. E., Spreat, S., Tassé, M. J., Thompson, J. R., Verdugo-Alonso, M. A., Wehmeyer, M. L., & Yeager, M. H. (2010). *Intellectual disability: Definition, classification, and systems of supports (11th ed.).* Washington, DC: American Association on Intellectual and Developmental Disabilities.

Schalock, R. L., Luckasson, R., Bradley, V., Buntinx, W. H. E., Lachapelle, Y., Shogren, K. A., Snell, M. E., Thompson, J. R., Tassé, M. J., Verdugo-Alonso, M. A., and Wehmeyer, M. L. (2012). *User's guide to intellectual disability: Definition, classification, and systems of supports.* Washington, DC: American Association on Intellectual and Developmental Disabilities.

Slate, J. R., & Jones, C. H. (1989). Can teaching of the WISC—R be improved? Quasi-experimental exploration. *Professional Psychology: Research and Practice, 20,* 408–410.

Stanovich, K. E. (1986). Matthew effects in reading: Some consequences of individual differences in the acquisition of literacy. *Reading Research Quarterly, 10*(1), 360–407.

Sternberg, R. J., & Detterman, D. K. (1986). *What is intelligence?: Contemporary viewpoints on its nature and definition.* Norwood, NJ: Ablex.

Suen, H., & Greenspan, S. (2009). Serious problems with the Mexican norms for the WAIS-III when assessing mental retardation in capital cases. *Applied Neuropsychology, 16,* 214–222. doi: 10.1080/09084280903098786.

Tulsky, D., & Zhu, J. (2003). *Escala Wechsler de Intelligencia para Adultos-III.* Mexico, D. F.: Moderno.

Umphress, T. B. (2008). A comparison of low IQ scores from the Reynolds Intellectual Assessment Scales and the Wechsler Adult Intelligence Scale—Third Edition. *Intellectual and Developmental Disabilities, 46,* 229–233. doi: 10.1352/2008.46:229-233

Ungar, M. (2004). A constructionist discourse on resilience: Multiple contexts, multiple realities among at-risk children and youth. *Youth and Society, 35*(3), 341–365. doi: 10.1177/0044118X03257030

Wechsler, D. (1974). *Wechsler Intelligence Scale for Children—Revised.* New York, NY: Psychological Corporation.

Wechsler, D. (1981). *Wechsler Adult Intelligence Scale-Revised.* New York, NY: Psychological Corporation.

Wechsler, D. (2008). *Wechsler Adult Intelligence Scale—Fourth edition* (WAIS-IV). San Antonio, TX: Pearson Assessment.

Weinert, F. E., & Schneider, W. (Eds). (1999). *Individual development from 3 to 12: Findings from the Munich Longitudinal Study.* Cambridge, UK: Cambridge University Press.

Werner, E. E. (1992). The children of Kauai: Resiliency and recovery in adolescence and adulthood. *Journal of Adolescent Health, 13,* 262–268.

Werner, S., Corrigan, P., Ditchman, N., & Sokol, K. (2012). Stigma and intellectual disability: A review of related measures and future directions. *Research in Developmental Disabilities, 33*(2), 748–765. doi: 10.1016/j.ridd.2011.10.009

Whitaker, S. (2008). The stability of IQ in people with low intellectual ability: An analysis of the literature. *Intellectual and Developmental Disabilities, 46,* 120–128. doi: 10.1352/0047-6765(2008)46[120:TSOIIP]2.0.CO;2.

Whitaker, S. (2010). Error in the estimation of intellectual ability in the low range using the WISC-IVand WAIS-III. *Personality and Individual Differences, 48,* 517–521. doi: 10.1016/j.paid.2009.11.017

Young, L., Moni, K. B., Jobling, A., & Kraayenoord, C. E. (2004). Literacy skills of adults with intellectual disabilities in two community-based day programs. *International Journal of Disability, Development and Education, 51*(1), 83–97.

10 | Norm Obsolescence: The Flynn Effect

Kevin S. McGrew

Nature of the Problem

A person's IQ test score is based on the comparison of the person's tested performance to an age-appropriate norm reference group. The *norms* for an IQ test are developed to represent the snapshot of the general U.S. population (at each age level the test covers) at the time the norm or standardization data are collected (American Educational Research Association, American Psychological Association, & National Council on Measurement in Education [AERA, APA, NCME], 1999). (VandenBos, 2007, defines a norm as "a standard or range of values that represents the typical performance of a group or of an individual [of a certain age, for example] against which comparisons can be made" [p. 631]). The person's test performance is compared to this standard reference group. For example, the WISC-R IQ test was published in 1974 and the WISC-R norm data was gathered on children ages 6 through 16 from 1971 through 1973 (Wechsler, 1974). (1972 is thus considered the official date of the WISC-R norm/ standardization sample.) Thus, a child who is 7 years, 2 months old who was administered the WISC-R in 1974 would have the calculation of his or her IQ test score based on a comparison to the performance of children from ages 7 years, 0 months through 7 years, 3 months in the year 1972. (The WISC-R norm tables are provided in 3 month intervals within each year of age.) If the WISC-R was administered to a child of the same age (7 years, 2 months) in 1984, rather than being compared to other children of the same age in 1984, this child's performance would still be evaluated against similarly aged children from 1972. This second comparison results in a test-date/test-norm *mismatch* of 12 years (1984 – 1972 = 12). As explained next, comparing an individual's performance on an IQ test with outdated test norms results in *a comparison to a historical reference group from the past—not the person's contemporary peers*. This *norm obsolescence* problem is more commonly referred to as the *Flynn effect* (Flynn, 1984,

1985, 2000, 2006, 2007a, 2009). The Flynn effect produces inflated and inaccurate IQ test scores.

In simple terms, psychologists and psychological measurement experts typically describe the Flynn effect as the result of a "softening" of IQ tests norms with the passage of time. That is, individuals tested today on an IQ test normed many years earlier will obtain artificially inflated IQ test scores, because the older test norms reflect a level of overall performance that is lower than that of individuals in contemporary society. This is one of the primary reasons why authors and publishers of IQ tests make every effort to periodically provide "freshened" norms by collecting new nationally representative sample data for IQ test batteries. The professional consensus among test developers is that the "shelf life" of an IQ test's norms is approximately 10 years. According to Weiss (2010), Vice President of Pearson Clinical Assessment, the company and division that develops and publishes the various Wechsler IQ batteries, "there is no definition of when a test becomes obsolete. When asked privately, most Flynn effect researchers have 10 years in mind" (p. 492). If new norms are not provided, individuals tested using IQ tests with outdated norms will typically obtain inflated and inaccurate IQ test scores.

The Flynn effect recognizes that the normal curve distribution of intelligence shifts upward over time. Thus, the same raw score performance on an IQ test, when compared to outdated norms, will produce a markedly different IQ score when it is compared to updated norms based on a contemporary sample of abilities for a person of the same age. The person's tested performance (i.e., the number of correct responses across all parts of the IQ test) does *not* change, but the person's relative standing in the distribution of IQ scores across the population *does* change as a function of which norm reference group his or her performance is compared against. The same performance that is considered average in the contemporary norm sample, yielding an IQ test score of 100 in the distribution, will result in a higher IQ test score when using older norms (Schalock, 2012).

As a result of the Flynn effect, it is possible that one or more IQ test scores reported for an individual being considered for a diagnosis of intellectual disability (ID) may be inaccurate and inflated estimates. Given the high-stakes nature of *Atkins,* ID cases and their tendency to artificially focus on specific "bright line" cutoff scores, the impact of the Flynn effect must be recognized and an adjustment to the inflated scores is recommended.

Summary of Related Research

Origins of the Flynn Effect

Probably the first widely recognized scholarly report of IQ norm obsolescence was published by Lynn in 1983. Reflecting Lynn's early writings, some intelligence scholars refer to IQ norm obsolescence as the *Lynn-Flynn effect* (Woodley, 2012a). Recently, Lynn

(2013) provided evidence that 24 studies, the first being Runquist (1936), reported on the phenomenon of norm obsolescence before the "effect was rediscovered by Flynn" (1984). Lynn (2013) argued that the proper designation of IQ test norm obsolescence should be the "Runquist effect." Although Lynn (2013) provided a compelling argument (based on the customary practices in the history of science for naming phenomena), the term *Flynn effect* is used here given its prominent and frequent use in intelligence research and *Atkins* court cases.

Seventeen years prior to the 2002 *Atkins* decision, Flynn (1985) published an article in the *American Journal on Mental Deficiency* (now the *American Journal on Intellectual and Developmental Disabilities*). This article, titled "Wechsler Intelligence Tests: Do We Really Have Criterion of Mental Retardation?" first raised the issue of a possible "adjustment" in the context of an ID diagnosis. In hindsight, Flynn's 1985 article was the "canary in the coal mine" in that it first demonstrated that the Flynn effect may have a significant impact on the proportion of the population of individuals that would be identified as ID. At that time, Flynn proposed a form of adjusting for the softening of tests norms, although it was in a slightly different form than the current recommended Flynn effect adjustment procedure.

Flynn (1985) proposed that to account for the softening of test norms, an IQ test score of 70 on a "reference" IQ test (i.e., WAIS-R) would be set in as the *absolute criterion for mental retardation* (that is, on the intellectual functioning prong of the definition). Then, to account for norm obsolescence, each time a new IQ test was published there would be a lowering of the MR cutting line. Flynn's 1985 idea was that whenever a new IQ test was published, it would be given together with the established reference IQ test (e.g., WAIS-R) and the average mean IQ test score difference between the new test and the reference test would be used to "derive a new score equivalent to the old cutting line" (p. 243). Although different from what is now considered the standard Flynn effect adjustment approach (i.e., subtracting 3 IQ test score points from an individual's total IQ test score for every 10 years for which the test was administered to a person who was normed prior to the date of individual's testing), conceptually Flynn's 1985 proposal accomplished the same goal as the currently employed Flynn effect adjustment procedure.

Fifteen years later, and still 2 years prior to the *Atkins* decision, Flynn (2000) again sounded the alarm regarding the implication of norm obsolescence related to the diagnosis and classification of mental retardation:

> It is certain that over the past 50 years, literally millions of Americans evaded the label of mentally retarded designed for them by the test manuals. Whether this was good or bad depends on what one thinks of the label. Some will say millions avoided stigma. Others will say that millions missed out on needed assistance and classroom teachers were left unaided to cope with pupils for whom aid was needed (p. 197).

The potential impact of the Flynn effect on other diagnoses was also reported in 2001 and 2003. Truscott and colleagues (Sanborn, Truscott, Phelps, & McDougal, 2003; Truscott & Frank, 2001) reported on the impact of the Flynn effect on learning disability (LD) identification, not identification of individuals with ID. Although these authors did not offer or endorse any IQ test score adjustment procedure, these researchers concluded that

> A critical finding of this study is that the FE probably contributes to misdiagnosis of LD. If this research is combined with previous reports that academic achievement may be unaffected by the FE (Neisser, 1998) it strongly suggests that, over the life of a test version, IQ-achievement discrepancies, the most salient LD criterion, are exaggerated. One potential result of such an exaggeration of IQ-achievement discrepancies would be that, as test norms aged, fewer students would score in the mentally retarded range (Flynn, 2000) and more students would qualify for LD based on inflated severe discrepancies (p. 300).

In conclusion, the recognition of the impact of *norm obsolescence* (i.e., the Flynn effect) on IQ test scores, and more importantly, the potential for misdiagnosis of ID and other conditions (e.g., LD), has been recognized and documented as early as the 1980s. It continued to be discussed prior to and after the 2002 ID-related *Atkins* decision by researchers and professionals who did not anticipate nor were influenced by the 2002 *Atkins* decision. For obvious reasons (i.e., the life-or-death implications of the *Atkins* decision), there has been increased interest in the Flynn effect adjustment procedure since the *Atkins* decision. The facts indicate that the recognition of the impact of norm obsolescence on IQ test scores (and the idea of a norm obsolescence IQ test score adjustment) was established prior to the *Atkins v Virginia* (2002) U.S. Supreme Court decision.

Scientific Basis of the Flynn Effect

There is a scientific and professional consensus that the Flynn effect is a scientific fact. A complete reading of the extant Flynn effect research literature leads to the conclusion that, despite debates regarding the causes of the Flynn effect, differences in the rate of Flynn effect change in different countries. Whether the Flynn effect has started to plateau in Scandinavian countries or whether the Flynn effect differs by different levels of intelligence and different methodological issues in various studies, *the consensus of the relevant scientific community is that the Flynn effect is real* (Cunningham & Tassé, 2010; Fletcher, Stuebing & Hughes, 2010; Flynn, 2009; Greenspan, 2006, 2007; Gresham & Reschly, 2011; Kaufman, 2010a, 2010b; McGrew, 2010; Rodgers, 1999; Trahan, Stuebing, Fletcher, & Hiscock 2014; Weiss, 2010; Zhou, Zhu, & Weiss, 2010). The robustness of this conclusion may best be represented by Rogers' (1999) statement where, after raising valid methodological issues regarding various statistical analysis and conclusions across Flynn effect studies, that even with a "healthy dose of skepticism, the effect rises above purely methodological interpretation, and appears to have substantive import" (p. 354).

The research literature regarding the Flynn effect is extensive. Trahan et al. (2014) found over 4,000 articles in their comprehensive literature review. (Most all norm obsolescence references and articles can be found at the regularly updated *Flynn Effect Archive Project* [http://www.atkinsmrdeathpenalty.com/2010/01/atkins-mrid-capital-punishment-flynn_11.html]. As of 2014, this archive includes approximately 190 publications.) A thorough treatment of all this research is beyond the scope of the current chapter. Fortunately, key contemporary Flynn effect issues bearing on an ID diagnosis in the *Atkins* context were covered in a special 2010 issue of the *Journal of Psychoeducational Assessment* (*JPA*). A variety of invited scholars confirmed the scientific consensus regarding the validity of the Flynn effect. For example, Dr. Alan Kaufman (2010a), arguably the most prominent scholar on intelligence testing and interpretation of the various Wechsler IQ tests, stated that

> The Flynn effect (FE) is well known: Children and adults score higher on IQ tests now than they did in previous generations (Flynn, 1984, 2007, 2009b). The rate of increase in the United States has apparently remained a fairly constant 3 points per decade since the 1930s (p. 382).

The consensus of almost all authors who contributed to the *JPA* Flynn effect issue (Fletcher et al., 2010; Flynn, 2010; Hagan, Drogin, & Guilmette, 2010a; Kaufman, 2010a, 2010b; Kaufman & Weiss, 2010; McGrew, 2010; Reynolds, Niland, Wright, & Rosenn, 2010; Sternberg, 2010; Weiss, 2010; Zhou et al. 2010) was that IQ test norm obsolescence (i.e., the Flynn effect) is an established scientific fact. The following select quotes from recent peer-reviewed articles capture the essence of the convergence of opinion regarding the validity of the Flynn effect.

> The Flynn effect (FE) is real. The FE has been shown to be nearly 3 points per decade on average across a large number of studies, countries, and tests (Weiss, 2010, p. 491).

> The point is that a person tested on an outdated test will earn spuriously high scores as each year goes by, and the amount of the spuriousness amounts to about 3 points per decade for Americans (Kaufman, 2010b, p. 503).

> The FE, whatever its cause, is as real as virtually any effect can be in the social sciences. Studies have observed an increase of 0.3 points per year in average IQs; thus, for a test score to reflect accurately the examinee's intelligence, 0.3 points must be subtracted for each year since the test was standardized (Reynolds et al., 2010, p. 478).

> The Flynn effect is a well-established psychometric fact documenting substantial increases in measured intelligence test performance over time (Gresham & Reschly, 2011, p. 131).

Since the publication of the 2010 special *JPA* Flynn effect issue, many additional Flynn effect research and commentary articles have appeared (e.g., Battarjee, Khaleefa, Ali, & Lynn, 2013; Baxendale, 2010; Cunningham & Tassé, 2010; Hagan, Drogin, & Guilmette, 2010b; Kanaya & Ceci, 2011, 2012; Lynn, 2013; Nijenhuis, 2013; Nijenhuis, Cho, Murphy, & Lee, 2012; Nijenhuis, Murphy, & van Eeden, 2011; Nijenhuis & van der Flier, 2013; Pietschnig, Voracek, & Formann, 2011; Nijman, Scheirs, Prinsen, Abbink, & Blok, 2010; Rindermann, Schott, & Baumeister, 2013; Rönnlund, Carlstedt, Blomstedt, Nilsson, & Weinehall, 2013; Skirbekk, Stonawski, Bonsang, & Staudinger, 2013; Trahan et al., 2014; Wai & Putallaz, 2011; Woodley, 2011, 2012a, 2012b; Young, 2012). The continued flow of the Flynn effect related to peer-reviewed articles confirms the consensus that the Flynn effect is a scientifically important and studied phenomenon among intelligence scholars.

Adjusting IQ Test Scores for the Flynn Effect in Atkins *Cases Is Best Practice*

Not only is there a scientific consensus that the Flynn effect is a valid and real phenomenon, there is also a consensus that individually obtained IQ test scores derived from tests with outdated norms must be adjusted to account for the Flynn effect, particularly in *Atkins* cases. (The use of a Flynn effect correction in clinical settings is less of an issue given that psychologists in such settings typically have more leeway to interpret scores as ranges, invoke clinical judgment, and incorporate information regarding measurement error in interpretation of the scores when making a diagnosis. In contrast, certain high stakes settings [e.g., *Atkins* cases; eligibility for Social Security Disability benefits] may have strict point-specific cut-scores [i.e., "bright line" criteria] where examiners, or the recipients of the scores [e.g., the courts], do not allow for such clinical interpretation. Thus, the Flynn effect adjustment is more relevant, appropriate, and primarily discussed in literature and law dealing with this type of high stakes IQ testing.) The most prominent and relevant professional consensus-based guidelines for ID diagnosis (Schalock et al., 2007, 2010, and 2012) support a Flynn effect adjustment for scores based on obsolete IQ test norms. *Intellectual Disability: Definition, Classification, and Systems of Supports* (11th ed.; Schalock et al., 2010), based on an expert-consensus process, provides a written guideline that endorses the appropriateness of the Flynn effect adjustment in the diagnosis of ID. (The 11th edition was created using a group-based consensus process conducted by the AAIDD Ad Hoc Committee on Terminology and Classification [Schalock et al., 2010]). AAIDD recommends that psychologists use the most recent versions of IQ tests and, if scores are reported from an IQ test with outdated norms, a correction for the age of norms is warranted (Schalock et al., 2007). The 11th edition states

> As discussed in the *User's Guide* (Schalock et al., 2007) that accompanies the 10th edition of this *Manual*, best practices require recognition of a potential Flynn effect when older editions of an intelligence test (with corresponding older norms) are used in the assessment or interpretation of an IQ score. (p. 37)

As suggested in the *User's Guide to Mental Retardation: Definition, Classification, and Systems of Supports* (Schalock, 2007, pp. 20–21),

> The main recommendation resulting from this work [regarding the Flynn effect] is that all intellectual assessment must use a reliable and appropriate individually administered intelligence test. In cases of tests with multiple versions, the most recent version with the most current norms should be used at all times. In cases where a test with aging norms is used, a correction for the age of the norms is warranted. (p. 37)

The AAIDD's more recent *User's Guide to Intellectual Disability: Definition, Classification, and Systems of Supports* (Schalock et al., 2012) states

> The *Flynn effect* refers to the increase in IQ scores over time (i.e., about 0.30 points per year). The Flynn effect affects any interpretation of IQ scores based on outdated norms. Both the 11th edition of the manual and this *User's Guide* recommend that in cases in which a test with aging norms is used as part of a diagnosis of ID, a corrected Full Scale IQ upward of 3 points per decade for age of norms is warranted. (p. 23)

A consensus among the professional and scientific community of intelligence and ID scholars has emerged. This consensus is that given the high-stakes nature of *Atkins* ID cases and their tendency to artificially focus on specific "bright line" cutoff scores, *a Flynn effect correction to a person's scores in this setting is now considered best or standard practice.* This conclusion is supported by a significant number of scholars and researchers in the areas of intelligence and ID (Cunningham & Tassé, 2010; Fletcher et al., 2010; Flynn, 2006, 2007b; Flynn & Widaman, 2008; Greenspan, 2006, 2007; Gresham & Reschly, 2011; Kaufman, 2010b; McVaugh & Cunningham, 2009; Reynolds et al., 2010; Schalock , 2007; Schalock, 2012). One example of this support is the statement of Reynolds et al. (2010) that "as a generally accepted scientific theory that could potentially make the difference between a constitutional and unconstitutional execution, the Flynn effect must be applied in the legal context" (p. 480). Reynolds et al. (2010) go as far as to state that "the failure to apply the Flynn correction as we have described it is tantamount to malpractice. No one's life should depend on when an IQ test was normed" (p. 480).

A minority of scholars have offered a different approach to the issue of correcting IQ test scores due to the Flynn effect. Weiss (2010), while acknowledging the scientific validity of the Flynn effect, advocates that experts should simply inform the fact finder of what the research shows and the trier-of-fact should evaluate and decide if and how to apply it when interpreting individual scores. Hagan et al. (2010b) also agree with the need to consider the Flynn effect in capital cases but their disagreement "lies in how psychologists should convey IQ scores in light of the observation that mean scores drift over time" (p. 420). It is important to note that the more conservative positions of Weiss (2010) and Hagan et al. (2010a, 2010b) represent a minority position in the professional literature. More importantly, they do not argue against the scientific validity of the Flynn effect or even the need to consider the effect in *Atkins* cases. Rather, their difference of opinion with the majority is only as to whether a specified score adjustment should be made to the original score or whether testifying experts should instead address the Flynn effect in narrative form.

Recently, legal scholars have also supported the application of the Flynn effect correction in *Atkins* cases. Young's (2012) recent law review article ("A More Intelligent and Just *Atkins*: Adjusting for the Flynn Effect in Capital Determinations of Mental Retardation or Intellectual Disability") concluded that

> adjusting for the Flynn effect reflects a practice consistent with both *Atkins* and the known world of IQ measurements. While a freakish strike of lightning is difficult to avoid, the potentially deadly and unconstitutional consequences of refusing to account for the Flynn effect are wholly preventable. Thus, for the intelligent and just enforcement of *Atkins*, courts and juries should adjust IQ score from outdated tests for the Flynn effect. (p. 663)

What Is the Correct Flynn Effect Adjustment for Norm Obsolescence?

The AAIDDs' *User's Guide* (Schalock, 2012) recommends a Flynn effect correction of 3 points per decade (0.3 points per year). The 3 points per decade rule-of-thumb is consistent with the previously cited comments of Kaufman (2010a, 2010b) and Weiss (2010), and is also consistent with the recommendation of most scholars in the areas of intelligence and ID (e.g., Fletcher et al., 2010; Gresham & Reschly, 2011; Trahan, et al., 2014; Widaman, 2007).

The 3 points per decade rule-of-thumb is based primarily on Flynn's (2009) seminal article where he synthesized the results of 14 estimates of IQ test score gains over time. Flynn reported an average IQ test score change, across the 14 studies, of 0.311 points per year. An average mean score of 0.299 points was reported for the Wechsler comparisons only. Flynn concluded that "the evidence suggests that a rate of 0.30 is about right, and varying it from case to case lacks any rationale" (p. 104).

More recently Fletcher et al. (2010) applied more precise quantitative meta-analytic procedures to Flynn's (2009) data and reported a weighted mean of 2.80 points per decade. After removing two outlier studies, the weighted mean per decade was 2.96. These researchers concluded that "the level of precision we reported of a mean of about 3 and a *standard error of the mean* (SEM) of about 1 supports the correction and is consistent with the Flynn correction of 3 points per decade" (p. 472). In the most comprehensive meta-analysis research synthesis of 285 studies, Trahan et al. (2014) found that for modern intelligence tests the Flynn effect size was a similar 2.93 points per decade. These researchers concluded that their "findings are consistent with previous research and with the argument that it is feasible and advisable to correct IQ scores for the Flynn effect in high-stakes decisions" (p. 22).

The best available research syntheses consistently converge on a Flynn effect rule-of-thumb of 3 IQ test score points per decade (of IQ test norm obsolescence). Although scientific journals may report Flynn effect results to the second decimal place (e.g., 3.11 per decade or 0.311 per year), the psychometrics of IQ testing and research cannot partition human behavior with such precision. As noted by Widaman (2007), much of the variation between scores from different Flynn effect studies is due to sampling and measurement error. Using Flynn effect adjustment formulae that use numbers to the second decimal place would be akin to slicing butter with a laser beam. Consequently, the current best estimate of IQ norm obsolescence, and the recommended Flynn effect adjustment, is 3 IQ points per decade, or 0.3 points per year.

Researching the Flynn Effect "Black Box": Implications for Practice

Recently a significant portion of Flynn effect research has shifted from a focus on the secular changes in the global IQ test scores over time to changes on more specific intellectual abilities, possible differential effects by level of intelligence, and a search for the cause of the Flynn effect (Kaufman, 2010a). Zhou et al. (2010) characterized this shift to a focus on the "black box" of the Flynn effect.

The cause of the Flynn effect. In the context of the special articles in the 2010 *JPA* Flynn effect issue, Weiss (2010) stated that "Except for Flynn, there is general agreement . . . that we know precious little about the causes of the effect" (p. 487). Explanations and theories have touched on such causative variables as genetics, environmental factors (e.g., nutrition, education, improved public health, increased use of computer games), ethnicity, and different societal risks and benefits associated with different generations (Kaufman & Weiss, 2010; Weiss, 2010). Flynn (2007a), in his book *What Is Intelligence? Beyond the Flynn Effect*, suggests that the effect that bears his name is due to systematic shift in societies from concrete to abstract scientific thinking. Confounding the search for the cause(s) of the Flynn effect has been idiosyncratic and armchair-based speculations (Weiss, 2010).

In the current context, knowing that the Flynn effect exists trumps a lack of consensus regarding causation. The impact of norm obsolescence on IQ test scores is real and the professional consensus is that it should be accounted for in *Atkins* ID determination. Understanding the "why" of the Flynn effect is beyond the scope of the current chapter and is not necessary for recognizing the scientifically and professionally based consensus that IQ test scores suffering from norm obsolescence need to be adjusted in *Atkins* cases. As stated by Kaufman (2010b), "The Flynn effect is a fact, even if its cause is elusive, and it must be considered carefully when making high stakes decisions such as the death penalty" (p. 503).

Differential Flynn effects by specific intellectual abilities. The foundation of Flynn's (2007a) theoretical explanation of the Flynn effect is based primarily on the interpretation of differential rates of score changes as a function of different specific intellectual abilities (e.g., smaller gains on verbal and crystallized ability tasks and larger changes on visual-spatial and abstract fluid reasoning tasks—not a singular focus on the global IQ test score). If differential specific ability Flynn effects are eventually found to be valid, the potential implication is that different Flynn effect adjustments may be recommended for different composite or cluster "part" scores in IQ tests, and not just the global IQ score. This would introduce a new layer of complexity in the interpretation of IQ test scores (and part scores) in *Atkins* cases.

Although the recent methodologically sophisticated attempt by Zhou et al. (2010) to examine differential ability Flynn effects within the Wechsler tests represents an important step forward in this area of inquiry, their research produced inconsistent and contradictory findings. Although differential specific ability Flynn effect findings may eventually be identified, currently the supporting research results are sparse, mixed in results, and suffer from significant measurement and methodological flaws (McGrew, 2010). The foundation of Flynn effect causal theory, which hinges on the presence of differential specific ability Flynn effects, has been questioned on logical, theoretical, measurement and methodological grounds (Kaufman, 2010a, 2010b; McGrew, 2010; Weiss, 2010). Currently the extant research is not mature enough to support differential specific-ability Flynn effect adjustments in clinical or forensic contexts.

Differential Flynn effects by level of intelligence. The use of the 3 IQ test score points per decade Flynn effect adjustment rule-of-thumb has been questioned by research suggesting that the Flynn effect may not be uniform across all levels of general intelligence (Kanaya & Ceci, 2007; Kanaya, Ceci, & Scullin, 2003; Sanborn et al. 2003; Zhou et al., 2010). More important has been the suggestion that the Flynn effect may be larger at the IQ score range at the threshold for ID diagnosis. Cunningham and Tassé (2010) have referred to this research as the investigation of the Flynn effect in the "zone of ambiguity" (IQ test scores from 71–80). Studies reviewed by Cunningham and Tassé (2010) report IQ per decade changes ranging from roughly 4 to 5 points in the zone of ambiguity. Zhou et al. (2010) also reported differential Flynn effects by level of intelligence, but the results were inconsistent in the directions of the variation and may differ for different tests or age groups.

Similar to the differential Flynn effect by specific ability research, the ability-specific research has not been fully vetted through a sufficiently large number of studies and has been questioned on methodological grounds (McGrew, 2010; Widaman, 2007; Zhou et al., 2010). As summarized by Weiss (2010), "a small number of studies have suggested differential Flynn effect by ability level, but not enough is known about this at present" (p. 492). Reynolds et al. (2010) reinforce this conclusion, when after commenting on the Zhou et al. (2010 differential Flynn effects by levels of intelligence findings, that the results were inconsistent and "for now, best practice is the application of the Flynn correction as a constant by year across the distribution" (p. 480). Until more studies replicate the possibility of larger Flynn effects near the ID diagnostic threshold, the 3 points per decade Flynn effect rule-of-thumb should be employed across all levels of general intelligence.

Implications for Practice

The following implications are based on the integration of the content of the current chapter as well as the recommendations from the *User's Guide to the 10th edition*, the *11th edition*, and the *User's Guide to the 11th edition* (Schalock et al., 2007, 2010, 2012):

First, the potential problem of norm obsolescence can be minimized, but not always eliminated, by assessment professionals using IQ tests with the most up-to-date norms. When a new version of an IQ battery is published (e.g., WAIS-IV replaces WAS-III), assessment professionals should use the newest version (WAIS-IV) in *Atkins* cases. Assessment professionals have an ethical responsibility to stay abreast with the publication of new versions of IQ batteries and when the option exists to select among different IQ tests to administer to an individual. The relative degree of norm obsolescence of each possible IQ test should be one important factor incorporated into the IQ test selection decision.

Second, in cases where current or historical IQ test scores are impacted by norm obsolescence (i.e., Flynn effect), and the scores are to be used as part of the diagnosis of ID in *Atkins* or other high stakes decisions, the global scores impacted by outdated norms should be adjusted downward by 3 points per decade (0.3 points per year) of norm obsolescence.

Third, the recommended formula for the Flynn effect adjustment is: *FE adjustment = (Date test administered – date test was normed) × 0.3.* Stated simply, subtract the date the IQ test was normed (see point seven below) from the date the test was administered to the individual, multiply the obtained difference by 0.3. The obtained Flynn effect adjustment value should then be subtracted from the inflated obtained IQ score. The final Flynn effect adjustment value should be an integer value. Thus, the treatment of decimals in the final value should adhere to standard mathematical rules of "rounding to the nearest integer." The rationale for the particular rounding strategy employed should be described in the report. Current research does not support the application of different Flynn effect adjustment values for different part scores on IQ tests or at different levels of general intelligence. The best scientific evidence and professional consensus is that until sufficient research evidence produces evidence to the contrary, the 3 points per decade (0.3 points per year) adjustment rule-of-thumb should be used only on the global IQ test score and should be employed uniformly across all levels of general intelligence.

Fourth, both the original obtained (unadjusted) and Flynn effect adjusted scores should be included in all reports or court related statements or declarations provided by assessment professionals.

Fifth, the rationale for employing a Flynn effect correction should be described with supporting references. This chapter is intended to serve this function and can be cited as an authoritative source for the use of the Flynn effect adjustment in reports.

Sixth, when writing and discussing the Flynn effect, such as in psychological reports, legal declarations, or expert testimony, professionals should make frequent use of the term *norm obsolescence* when explaining the Flynn effect. Norm obsolescence is a much more descriptive and understandable means for conveying the essence of the Flynn effect.

Seventh, the calculation of the years of norm obsolescence should be based on the difference between the year the test was administered to an individual and the best estimate of the year the IQ test was *normed* (see also Chapters 7 and 8). The data of pub-lication of an IQ test does not accurately capture the time period when the test norm data were gathered. For example, the WISC-R IQ test was published in 1974 and the WISC-R norm data was gathered on children from 6 through 16 years of age from 1971 through 1973 (Wechsler, 1974). Thus, the middle most year of the actual norm data col-lection period is 1972. For the WISC-R, the year 1972 should be subtracted from the date of testing to determine the number of years of norm obsolescence. The test norm years reported for the different IQ tests by Flynn (2009) are recommended for unifor-mity purposes. For tests not reported in Flynn (2009), professionals need to consult the technical manuals for the IQ test in question and establish the best year estimate that is at the middle of the norm data collection period. If not readily available, professionals should seek the expertise of the test authors, publisher, or other intelligence test experts who may possess this information.

This chapter concludes with an example from an *Atkins* case. In 1998 an individual was administered the WAIS-R and obtained a Full Scale IQ of 80. Despite knowing that the WAIS-R had been revised and published as the WAIS-III in 1997, the psychologist administered the WAIS-R despite 20 years of norm obsolescence. The WAIS-R was published in 1981 and the best estimate of the date the actual test norms were gathered, as per the recommended procedures above, is 1978. Thus, the difference between the date of WAIS-R testing (1998) and date of test norming (1978) was 20 years, Using the 0.3/year Flynn effect adjustment, the best estimate of the magnitude of IQ test score inflation due to norm obsolescence is 6 IQ test score points ($0.3 \times 20 = 6.0$). Thus, this individual's Flynn effect adjusted WAIS-R score is 74 ($80 - 6 = 74$). This example represents one of the most dramatic instances of norm obsolescence (20 years) and also reflects the fact that the examiner did not engage in proper practice by administering the WAIS-III which was available at the time the individual was assessed.

References

American Educational Research Association, American Psychological Association, & National Council on Measurement in Education. (1999). *Standards for educational and psychological testing.* Washington, DC: American Educational Research Association.

Atkins v. Virginia, 536 U.S. 304, 122 S. Ct. 2242 (2002).

Batterjee, A. A., Khaleefa, O., Ali, K., & Lynn, R. (2013). An increase in intelligence in Saudi Arabia, 1977–2010. *Intelligence, 41*(2), 91–93. doi: 10.1016/j.intell.2012.10.011

Baxendale, S. (2010). The Flynn effect and memory function. *Journal of Clinical and Experimental Neuropsychology, 32*(7), 699–703. doi: 10.1080/13803390903493515

Cunningham, M. D., & Tassé, M. J. (2010). Looking to science rather than convention in adjusting IQ scores when death is at issue. *Professional Psychology: Research and Practice, 45*(5), 413–419. doi: 10.1037/a0020226

Fletcher, J., Stuebing, K., & Hughes, L. (2010). IQ scores should be corrected for the Flynn effect in high stakes decisions. *Journal of Psychoeducational Assessment, 28*(5), 469–473.

Flynn, J. R. (1984). The mean IQ of Americans: Massive gains 1932 to 1978. *Psychological Bulletin, 95*, 29–51.

Flynn, J. R. (1985). Wechsler Intelligence Tests: Do we really have a criterion of mental retardation? *American Journal of Mental Deficiency, 90*(3), 236–244.

Flynn, J. R. (2000). The hidden history of IQ and special education: Can the problems be solved? *Psychology Public Policy and Law, 6*(1), 191–198.

Flynn, J. R. (2006). Tethering the elephant: Capital cases, IQ, and the Flynn effect. *Psychology, Public Policy, and Law, 12*, 170–189. doi:10.1037/1076-8971.12.2.170

Flynn, J. R. (2007a). *What is intelligence? Beyond the Flynn effect.* New York: Cambridge University Press.

Flynn, J. R. (2007b). Capital offenders and the death sentence: A scandal that must be addressed. *Psychology in Mental Retardation and Developmental Disabilities, 32(3)*, 3–7.

Flynn, J. R. (2009). The WAIS-III and WAIS-IV: *Daubert* motions favor the certainly false over the approximately true. *Applied Neuropsychology, 16*, 98–104. doi: 10.1080/09084280902864360

Flynn, J. R., & Widaman, K. F. (2008). The Flynn effect and the shadow of the past: Mental retardation and the indefensible and indispensible role of IQ. In L. M. Glidden (Ed.), *International review of mental retardation* (Vol. 35, pp. 121–149). Boston, MA: Elsevier.

Greenspan, S. (2006). Issues in the use of the "Flynn effect" to adjust IQ scores when diagnosing MR. *Psychology in Mental Retardation and Developmental Disabilities, 31*(3), 3–7.

Greenspan, S. (2007). Flynn-adjustment is a matter of basic fairness: Response to Roger B. Moore, Jr. *Psychology in Mental Retardation and Developmental Disabilities, 32*(3), 7–8.

Gresham, F., & Reschly, D. J. (2011). Standard of practice and Flynn effect testimony in death penalty cases. *Intellectual and Developmental Disabilities, 49*(3), 131–140. doi: 10.1352/1934-9556-49.3.131

Hagan, L. D., Drogin, E. Y., & Guilmette, T. J. (2010a). IQ Scores should not be adjusted for the Flynn effect in capital punishment cases. *Journal of Psychoeducational Assessment, 28*(5), 474–476. doi: 10.1177/0734282910373343

Hagan, L. D., Drogin, E. Y., & Guilmette, T. J. (2010b). Science rather than advocacy when reporting IQ scores. *Professional Psychology Research and Practice, 41*(5), 420–423.

Kanaya, T., & Ceci, S. J (2007). Mental retardation diagnosis and the Flynn effect: General intelligence, adaptive behavior, and context. *Child Development Perspectives, 1*(1), 62–63. doi: 10.1111/j.1750-8606.2007.00013.x

Kanaya, T., & Ceci, S. J (2011). The Flynn effect in the WISC subtests among school children tested for special education services. *Journal of Psychoeducational Assessment, 29*(2), 125–136. doi:10.1177/0734282910370139

Kanaya, T., & Ceci, S. (2012). The impact of the Flynn effect on LD diagnoses in special education. *Journal of Learning Disabilities, 45*(4), 319–326. doi: 10.1177/0022219410392044

Kanaya, T., Ceci, S. J., & Scullin, M. H. (2003). The rise and fall of IQ in special ed: Historical trends and their implications. *Journal of School Psychology, 41*(6), 453–465. doi:10.1016/j.jsp.2003.08.003

Kaufman, A. (2010a). "In what way are apples and oranges alike?": A Critique of Flynn's interpretation of the Flynn effect. *Journal of Psychoeducational Assessment, 28*(5), 382–398. doi: 10.1177/0734282910373346

Kaufman, A. (2010b). Looking through Flynn's rose-coloured scientific spectacles. *Journal of Psychoeducational Assessment, 28*(5), 494–505. doi: 10.1177/0734282910373573

Kaufman, K., & Weiss, L. (2010). Guest editor's Introduction to the special issue of *JPA* on the Flynn effect. *Journal of Psychoeducational Assessment, 28*(5), 379–381. doi:10.1177/0734282910373344

Lynn, R. (1983). IQ in Japan and the United States shows a growing disparity. *Nature, 306*, 291–292.

Lynn, R. (2013). Who discovered the Flynn effect? A review of early studies of the secular increase in intelligence. *Intelligence,41*(6), 765–769. doi: 10.1016/j.intell.2013.03.004

McGrew, K. (2010). The Flynn effect and its critics: Rusty linchpins and "lookin' for *g* and Gf in some of the wrong places." *Journal of Psychoeducational Assessment, 28*(5), 448–468. doi:10.1177/0734282910373347

McVaugh, G. S., & Cunningham, M. D. (2009). Atkins v. Virginia: Implications and recommendations for forensic practice. *The Journal of Psychiatry and Law, 37*, 131–187.

Nijenhuis, J. T. (2013). The Flynn effect, group differences, and *g* loadings. *Personality and Individual Differences*, 55, 224–228. doi:10.1016/j.paid.2011.12.023

Nijenhuis, J. T., Cho, S. H., Murphy, R., & Lee., K. H. (2012). The Flynn effect in Korea: Large gains. *Personality and Individual Differences, 53*(2), 147–151. doi: 10.1016/j.paid.2011.03.022

Nijenhuis, J. T., Murphy, R., & van Eeden, R. (2011). The Flynn effect in South Africa. *Intelligence, 39*(6), 456–467.

Nijenhuis, J. T., & van der Flier, H. (2013). Is the Flynn effect on g? A meta-analysis. *Intelligence*, 41, 802–807.

Nijman, E. E., Scheirs, J. G., Prinsen, M. J., Abbink, C. D., & Blok, J. B. (2010). Exploring the Flynn effect in mentally retarded adults using a nonverbal intelligence test for children. *Research in Developmental Disabilities, 31*, 1404–1411. doi: 10.1016/j.ridd.2010.06.018

Reynolds, C., Niland, J., Wright, J., & Rosenn, M. (2010). Failure to apply the Flynn correction in death penalty litigation: Standard practice of today maybe, but certainly malpractice of tomorrow. *Journal of Psychoeducational Assessment, 28*(5), 477–481.

Rindermann, H., Schott, T., & Baumeister, A, (2013). Flynn effect in Turkey: A comment on Kagitcibasi and Biricik (2011). *Intelligence, 41*, 178–180. doi: 10.1016/j.intell.2013.02.003

Rodgers, J. L. (1999). A critique of the Flynn effect: Massive IQ gains, methodological artifacts, or both? *Intelligence, 26*(4), 337–356.

Rönnlund, M., Carlstedt, B., Blomstedt, Y., Nilsson, L. G., & Weinehall, L. (2013). Secular trends in cognitive test performance: Swedish conscript data 1970–1993. *Intelligence, 41*(1), 19–24.

Runquist, E. A. (1936). Intelligence test scores and school marks in 1928 and 1933. *School and Society, 43*, 301–304.

Sanborn, K. J., Truscott, S. D., Phelps, L., & McDougal, J. L. (2003). Does the Flynn effect differ by IQ level in samples of students classified as learning disabled? *Journal of Psychoeducational Assessment, 21*(2), 145–159.

Schalock, R. L., Buntinx, W. H. E., Borthwick-Duffy, S. A., Luckasson, R., Snell, M. E., Tassé, M. J., & Wehmeyer, M. L. (2007). *User's guide to mental retardation: Definition, classification, and systems of supports (10th ed.).* Washington, DC: American Association on Intellectual and Developmental Disabilities.

Schalock, R. L., Borthwick-Duffy, S. A., Bradley, V. J., Buntinx, W. H. E., Coulter, D. L., Craig, E. M., Gomez, S. C., Lachapelle, Y., Luckasson, R., Reeve, A., Shogren, K. A., Snell, M. E., Spreat, S., Tassé, M. J., Thompson, J. R., Verdugo-Alonso, M. A., Wehmeyer, M. L., & Yeager, M. H. (2010). *Intellectual disability: Definition, classification, and systems of supports (11th ed.).* Washington, DC: American Association on Intellectual and Developmental Disabilities.

Schalock, R. L., Luckasson, R., Bradley, V., Buntinx, W. H. E., Lachapelle, Y., Shogren, K. A., Snell, M. E., Thompson, J. R., Tassé, M. J., Verdugo-Alonso, M. A., and Wehmeyer, M. L. (2012). *User's guide to intellectual disability: Definition, classification, and systems of supports.* Washington, DC: American Association on Intellectual and Developmental Disabilities.

Skirbekk, V., Stonawski, Bonsang, E., & Staudinger, U. M. (2013). The Flynn effect and population aging, *Intelligence, 41*(3), 169–177. doi: 10.1016/j.intell.2013.02.001

Sternberg, R. (2010). The Flynn effect: So what? *Journal of Psychoeducational Assessment, 28*(5), 434–440. doi: 10.1177/0734282910373349

Trahan, L. H., Stuebing, K. K., Fletcher, J. M., & Hiscock, M. (2014, June 30). The Flynn effect: A meta-analysis. *Psychological Bulletin.* Advance online publication. http://dx.doi.org/10.1037/a0037173

Truscott, S. D., & Frank, A. J. (2001). Does the Flynn effect affect IQ scores of students classified as LD? *Journal of School Psychology, 39*(4), 319–334.

Wai, J., & Putallaz, M. (2011). The Flynn effect puzzle: A 30-year examination from the right tail of the ability distribution provides some missing pieces. *Intelligence, 39*(6), 443–455. doi:10.1016/j.intell.2011.07.006

Wechsler, D. (1974). *The Wechsler Intelligence Scale for Children—Revised (WISC-R).* San Antonio,TX: Psychological Corporation.

Weiss, L. G. (2010). Considerations on the Flynn effect. *Journal of Psychoeducational Assessment, 28*(5), 482–493. doi: 10.1177/0734282910373572

Widaman, K. (2007). Stalking the roving IQ score cutoff: A commentary on Kanaya and Ceci (2007). *Child Development Perspectives,1*(1),57–59. doi: 10.1111/j.1750-8606.2007.00011..x

Woodley, M. A. (2011). Heterosis doesn't cause the Flynn effect: A critical examination of Mingroni (2007). *Psychological Review, 118*(4), 689–693. doi: 10.1037/a0024759

Woodley, M. A. (2012a). A life history model of the Lynn-Flynn effect. *Personality and Individual Differences, 53*(2), 152–156. doi: 10.1016/j.paid.2011.03.028

Woodley, M. A. (2012b). The social and scientific temporal correlates of genotypic intelligence and the Flynn effect. *Intelligence, 40*(2), 189–204. doi:10.1016/j.intell.2011.12.002

Young, G. W. (2012). A more intelligent and just *Atkins:* Adjusting for the Flynn effect in capital determinations of mental retardation or intellectual disability. *Vanderbilt Law Review*, 615–755.

Zhou, X., Zhu, J., & Weiss, L. (2010). Peeking inside the "blackbox" of the Flynn effect: Evidence from three Wechsler instruments. *Journal of Psychoeducational Assessment, 28*(5), 399–411.

Vandenbos, G. (2007). *APA dictionary of psychology.* Washington, DC: American Psychological Association.

PART II
Assessment Considerations
C. Adaptive Behavior

11 | Evolving Concepts of Adaptive Behavior

Stephen Greenspan

Adaptive Behavior (AB) is the second prong of the definition of intellectual disability (ID). Although prongs 1 (intellectual functioning) and 3 (age of onset) may also often be contested, the majority of *Atkins* outcomes hinge on whether or not prong 2 has been met (Blume, 2010). There are problems with the way in which this prong has been addressed methodologically (Tassé, 2009; see also Chapter 12), but this chapter focuses on a more fundamental problem concerning the meaning of adaptive functioning/behavior.

Development of the Adaptive Behavior Construct

This section reviews the history of AB, since it was first introduced in the ID definition in the late 1950s (see Heber, 1961). Specifically, this chapter discusses its evolution from a construct lacking any theory, to one based on a list of 10 broad adaptive skill areas, to one using a tripartite theory based on the existing factor analytic research on AB.

Early Introduction of the Concept

Although to some extent the confusion over the meaning of AB reflects a failure to understand the relevant sections in the respective AAIDD manuals (Luckasson et al., 2002; Schalock et al., 2010), the problem is exacerbated by the fact that the definition of AB is still evolving and there is not yet full consensus about the construct's meaning. The lack of consensus can be best understood if one considers its history (see Greenspan & Switzky, 2006, for a comprehensive historical overview).

The term was first used by animal behavior researchers to refer to the ability of mammals to cope in their natural environments rather than in artificial research tasks, such as a rat maze (Hull, 1937). It was introduced by the American Association on Mental

Deficiency (AAMD), the precursor of the American Association on Intellectual and Developmental Disabilities (AAIDD), in its diagnostic manual (Heber, 1959, 1961). Its inclusion was to emphasize that, when diagnosing ID, one should consider how an individual functions and solves problems in the real world, rather than just on an intelligence test. The current iteration of this concept is ecological validity. A problem with using a newly conceptualized psychological construct (i.e., adaptive behavior) is that a measure developed to quantify this newly identified trait may not always be based in theory. Then, the said measure is eventually factor-analyzed, and definitions (along with subsequent measures) of the construct are further refined post hoc based on the factors derived from the first developed measure. That in fact is the history of the concept of AB as well as other psychological constructs, such as intelligence. This is not to deny that the first measures of AB reflected some ideas regarding what they thought it to be. The questions which concern the field today are (a) whether that conceptualization was fully adequate, and (b) what we can do to further clarify the construct?

One apparent limitation is that if items reflecting important aspects of AB are not included in the assessment measures, they will not emerge as factors, and thus, will not be included in conceptual definitions derived from the analyses. The only way out of this circularity is to ask "what is the essential nature of intellectual disability, and what are salient considerations that adaptive behavior is supposed to be capturing?" Of course, intellectual disability itself is a social construct.

The Heber (1961) manual in which AB became part of the definition, was preceded by a preliminary version (Heber, 1959) published as a journal supplement. The earlier version referred to impairments in the three areas of *maturation, learning,* and *social adjustment.* Maturation was described as self-help skills usually acquired in early childhood; learning was described as academic skills usually acquired in middle childhood; and social adjustment was described as interpersonal skills usually acquired early, but reaching fullest development in adolescence and adulthood, as manifested in successful work, relationships, and socially appropriate law-abiding behavior.

Instead of applying a single, integrated construct at all life stages, one was to apply only one of the three constructs, depending on whether the individual in question was a young child, an older child, or an adolescent/young adult. In spite of this work, few clinicians ever used these preliminary constructs. This pattern continued to be largely the case for a decade or more with the 1961 replacement construct of AB (which incorporated the three previously mentioned domains into a single construct intended to be applied at all subject ages). This failure of clinicians to use AB undoubtedly contributed to the decision by AAMR to drop the "Borderline" (IQ 71–85) subcategory 12 years later (Grossman, 1973). Tassé et al. (2012) pointed out that although the field of ID has veered into different directions with respect to defining adaptive behavior, 50 years after Heber (1959) the field has essentially returned to defining AB with the same original framework: conceptual skills (learning), social skills (social adjustment), and practical skills (maturation).

Resistance to the Second Criterion

The force driving the development of what was then termed the *dual criteria* definition of ID (i.e., IQ & AB) was concern about the problem of "false positives" in the overassignment to self-contained special education classes of low socioeconomic status children of ethnic minority groups. This group was described as "six-hour retarded children"; that is, they were identified as having an ID while in school, but not outside of school. This phenomenon reflected two things: (a) the sole reliance on full-scale IQ scores as the basis for assigning the ID label, and (b) the (typically reported) lower IQ scores of low socioeconomic status minority children. Thus, the introduction of the AB prong can be seen as reflecting a desire to ground ID diagnosis on real-world functioning and to be less culturally biased than measures of intelligence, particularly at the same time.

The insertion of AB into the diagnostic criteria of ID triggered a great deal of debate, most dramatically expressed in a polemic by Clausen (1972), whose article title—"Quo Vadis, AAMD?" (translation: "Where are you going, AAMD?")—suggested that an attempt to move beyond exclusive reliance on IQ had caused the field to lose its way. A decade later, Zigler, Balla, and Hodapp (1984) expressed concern that clarifying the social construct of ID was unlikely to be achieved by embedding within it unknown and ill-defined psychological construct of AB. The opposition to AB was so strong that Zigler et al. (1984) proposed a radical alternative: eliminate entirely the subcategory of *mild ID*, with the reasoning that people who have an IQ test score of 50 or less are so globally impaired that there would be no need for a second criterion. In fact, in some state *Atkins* statutes, an IQ test score under 55 or 60 (IQ test score under 65 in Arkansas) is considered *prima facie* evidence of ID, and the requirement to show AB deficits is essentially waived.

Although the suggestion to eliminate the subcategory might have simplified the task of diagnosing ID, it would have ignored the plight of the many children and adults (a great many with biologically based syndromes) whose significant need for supports would have gone unmet. Another problem is that it would have strengthened what many consider the unhealthy trend towards defining ID solely or mainly on the statistical units of standard deviation. The larger question had to do with whether ID should be viewed as a *disability* (where reliance on statistical cut-offs may be appropriate) or whether it should be viewed as a *disorder* (where such reliance is less appropriate). This divergence in approaches is addressed in a paper by the working group that proposed a new name and definition of ID for the World Health Organizations' forthcoming ICD-11 (Salvador-Carulla et al., 2011).

Absence of a Community Focus

A problem with the construct of AB prior to the existence of a coherent theory is that the construct will become defined by the early instrument used to measure it. In the case of AB, that instrument was the AAMD Adaptive Behavior Scale (ABS; Nihira Foster,

Shellhaas, & Leland, 1969). (The ABS should not be confused with the much-later developed Adaptive Behavior Assessment Scale [ABAS; Harris & Oakland, 2000]). There were two issues with the ABS which limited its utility. The first was the absence of population-derived standard scores, reflecting a preference by the authors for a profile approach useful less in diagnosis (not critical for an institutionalized population) and more in guiding programming interventions. Utility for programming of habilitation goals, in fact, continues to be the major purpose of current measures, which is why AAIDD decided to develop the Diagnostic Adaptive Behavior Scale (DABS; Tassé et al., in press).

The second was the emphasis in the ABS (again, repeated later in other scales) on low-level, self-help skills (such as feeding, toileting, and dressing).This emphasis reflected the fact that the ABS was developed at a Kansas institution with a population comprised primarily of individuals in residential facilities and absent inclusion of those persons with ID in the community or those who were less significantly disabled. This focus on low-level skills was especially problematic in that the largest segment of the ID population—those who have ID at the upper end of the range—were relocating in the community: with parents, in small group homes, or their own apartments. Although such individuals still need substantial supports, these are different in nature and severity from the supports tapped by the ABS and needed by people living at the facility where it was developed.

The definition of adaptive behavior underlying the ABS had three major components: (a) education-related skills (e.g., language, reading, telling time); (b) self-help skills (e.g., cooking, cleaning, dressing, hygiene, work) required to live semi-independently; and (c) social skills needed to get along with others. The last of these components was particularly problematic, in that it focused less on the possession of social skills and more on the absence of *maladaptive* behaviors (e.g., acting out against others, self-abuse). Such an emphasis on maladaptive behavior reflected the reality that in a setting such as the institution in which the ABS was developed, extreme forms of *maladjustment* (reflecting, for example, brain conditions and severe environmental deprivation) were commonplace. It also reflected the absence of a sophisticated model of social competence, one that is grounded not in absence of mental illness but in presence of interpersonal understandings and skills. Such a model, might have oriented AB instruments and definitions more toward behaviors reflecting social awareness and perspective-taking and less toward behaviors reflecting emotional stability or "niceness."

Confounding of ID With Mental Illness

Challenges in the definition of adaptive behavior have been (a) the absence of agreement regarding the core essence of ID, (b) the connection between AB and the essence of ID, and (c) the lack of emphasis on AB deficits most common among people who have ID, as opposed to people with other disorders (e.g., mental illness). This is not to deny that many people with ID have mental illness, but merely to point out that many people with ID do not have mental illness. It thus follows that it is a mistake to embed within the definition of AB (and, thus, the diagnostic criteria for ID) deficits that are not specific to the core essence of ID. That essence is composed of deficits in intelligence applied broadly to all aspects of life, including dealings with others.

Greenspan (1979) suggested that AB, and by extension ID, should be based on a theory of what Gardner (1983) termed *multiple intelligences*. The rationale behind this argument was that as the natural taxon (phenotype) for ID was low intelligence, AB should be tied more closely to this taxon. A tripartite model of intelligence was generated and embedded in a broader model of *personal competence*, which has since been found to have considerable construct validity (McGrew, Bruininks, & Johnson, 1996).

The model of multiple intelligences suggested for this purpose was a three-factor framework first proposed by E. L. Thorndike (1920). The three factors were what Thorndike termed *abstract intelligence* (retitled conceptual intelligence), *mechanical intelligence* (retitled practical intelligence) and *behavioral intelligence* (retitled social intelligence). This model has been accepted and promoted in varied forms by a variety of major intelligence scholars, including several who contributed to Sternberg and Detterman's (1986) book *What Is Intelligence?* The idea proposed originally was that IQ test scores (along with other indices of prong 1, including executive functioning and achievement scores) would be covered by conceptual intelligence, whereas the other two forms of intelligence—practical and social—would be substituted for the two forms of adaptive functioning tapped by the ABS and succeeding adaptive behavior scales. In this way, IQ would no longer be the only index of intelligence, and AB would cease to exist as a separate (and subsidiary) index. AB would thus become more central to the essence of ID as a condition marked by significant impairments in broadly defined intelligence. Of course, deficits in "everyday intelligence" are also found in people with severe mental illness. An emphasis on cognitive (as opposed to motivational) aspects of daily functioning could be an improvement because it would provide a basis for saying that noncognitive items (such as "has pleasant breath," an item in the ABAS-2, Harrison & Oakland, 2003) have no place in diagnosing ID. Such items may have value in determining habilitation goals but have limited discrimination power as it relates to diagnosing ID.

Ten Adaptive Skill Areas

The 10 skill areas specified in the Luckasson et al. (1992) AB model were: communication, community use, functional academics, home living, health and safety, leisure, self-care, self-direction, social, and work. The standard specified for meeting the criteria for prong 2 was the presence of deficits in at least two of the 10 skill areas, with no extra weight given to any particular skill area. One standardized adaptive behavior measure, the Adaptive Behavior Assessment Scale (ABAS; Harris & Oakland, 2000), adopted the list of 10 adaptive skill areas from *Mental Retardation: Definition, Classification, and Systems of Supports* (9th ed.; Luckasson et al., 1992) as its basis. As it was intended to be used at all age levels (with different norms for subject age and kind of rater), the work skill was made optional, as many younger subjects never work or some raters might lack knowledge of work skills. The 10-item list approach was not continued in the *Mental Retardation: Definition, Classification, and Systems of Supports* (10th ed.; Luckasson et al., 2002), when the tripartite model was more fully adopted (see following section), although it continued (in its 11-item form) in the 2000 DSMIV-TR, and in many state *Atkins* statutes that are based on DSMIV-TR rather than on AAIDD criteria, even though DSM-5 (American Psychiatric Association, 2013) has since adopted the tripartite model..

Tripartite Competence Model

Departing from the 9th edition in 1992, a different framework for defining ID (and AB) was embedded in the *10th edition* (Luckasson et al., 2002); this framework remained unchanged in the *Intellectual Disability: Definition, Classification, and Systems of Supports* (11th ed.; Schalock et al., 2010). The tripartite model of conceptual, practical, and social domains became the conceptual basis for AB. The three domains included attention to the 10 skill areas as reflected in the previous 1992 edition. Consistent with both the 2002 and 2010 books, a diagnosis of ID requires significant deficits in one of these three respective domains.

While the list of 10 adaptive skill areas (Luckasson et al., 1992) were not determined empirically, factor analysis supported the notion that the structure of adaptive behavior consisted of 3 factor clusters in which these areas would fall—in particular, within-conceptual skills, social skills, and practical skills (Luckasson et al., 2002). Some elements of the list of 10 adaptive skill areas (Luckasson et al., 1992), for example self-direction, appear to be like personality and motivational constructs, which—however useful for the success of people with ID—are not unique to ID. Social deficits, which are believed by many practitioners to pose especially critical problems for people with ID (Duffy & Greenspan, 2006) continue to be relatively underemphasized in current AB instruments, as reflected for example in the fact that the Social domain on the ABAS-2 has by far the fewest items.

In the original tripartite theory, social was one of three domains and was equal in importance to the other two. Certainly, that is how it should be, given that problems in understanding people and social situations lie at the heart of the concerns for persons with ID. In the list, however, Social was one of 10 skill areas, perhaps reflecting the traditional tendency in the ID field to underappreciate the importance of social competence. In addition, social items on most adaptive behavior scales tend to focus on aspects of character (e.g., niceness) and temperament (e.g., stability) rather than judgment. This explains an anomaly in *Atkins* assessments, as defendants with profound histories of poor social judgment may receive a misleadingly high score on Social skill, whether using the ABAS-2 or the Vineland-2 (Sparrow, Cicchetti & Balla, 2005).This problem was exacerbated by combining Social with Leisure (much of it involving solitary play activities) in the new Social domain described in the next section. Many defendants who may be ID in capital cases may be described as nice, but also with limited social perception. (If they participate in a killing, often it is because of impulsivity, gullibility, or the lack of complex planning consistent with ID). Unfortunately, although adaptive behavior instruments do a good job of identifying "niceness" and its absence, they may not be as effective in identifying this social perceptual aspect.

Hegelian Synthesis Solution

Although the *10th edition* (Luckasson et al., 2002) and *11th edition* (Schalock et al., 2010) books went far toward acting on the suggestion to base AB on the tripartite model, they deviated significantly in one major respect from what had been originally suggested. The original proposal (Greenspan, 1979) had been to ground ID in a tripartite model of *adaptive intelligence*, with IQ incorporated into the fold as a measure (not necessarily the only one) of *conceptual intelligence*. Instead, in what Schalock (1999) termed a Hegelian synthesis, the framework morphed into a tripartite model of AB, as opposed to the suggested model of *adaptive intelligence*. As mentioned previously, if the original proposal had been implemented, it would have folded IQ into conceptual intelligence, and replaced adaptive behavior with practical and social intelligence (thus keeping ID grounded in its natural phenotype of "everyday lack of intelligence"). In the process, the definition of ID would be similar to the one used prior to the invention of the IQ test, when everyday functioning (and the perception that someone lacked everyday intelligence) was the reason that someone needed supports.

The decision to construct a tripartite model of AB rather than a tripartite model of intelligence had the major consequence of keeping *intelligence* and *adaptive behavior* separate and unequal. Intelligence (which continues to be incorrectly thought of largely as IQ) is central to the essence of ID, whereas AB, without a clear cognitive grounding, continues to sometimes be viewed as more peripheral to the essence of ID. One likely reason is that there was concern over the absence of psychometrically sound and generally accepted alternative measures of intelligence. Tassé (personal communication, 2012) noted, "there was concern [about] introducing yet another theoretical construct with no objective way of assessing these latent traits."

Although this concern is understandable (especially given the preference for standardized measures), the synthesis solution had the apparent effect of keeping AB in a subordinate position and from better tapping into the core (cognitive) essence of ID. Some might argue that this concern is overstated, given that deficits in prong 2 are necessary for the ID diagnosis. In practice, however, prong 1 is typically the starting point, and experts may fail to gather information about prong 2 if an IQ test score is somewhat above the usual 70-75 threshold. In *Hall v. Florida*, the Supreme Court affirmed that states could not exclude AB evidence in defining ID.

New Directions in Approaching Adaptive Behavior

This concluding section addresses efforts to move the concept of adaptive behavior forward, particularly as it relates to its importantance in *Atkins* cases. Specifically, this section discusses (a) the development of an instrument (the Diagnostic Adaptive Behavior

Scale) that keeps the tripartite model but frees it from the list of 10, (b) the effort to rethink adaptive behavior in relation to a deeper understanding of why people with ID need supports, and (c) a move from a general-trait to a micro-situational focus on handling of challenges.

Freeing Tripartite Model from List of 10

AAIDD is coming full circle, in that it was the initial publisher of the prototype adaptive behavior instrument, known as the AAMD Adaptive Behavior Scale (ABS) and it is the publisher of the newest (and also prototypical) measure, the Diagnostic Adaptive Behavior Scale (DABS; Tassé et al., 2012; Tassé et al., in press). The ABS was published so that the newly conceptualized prong 2 could be implemented as a diagnostic and programming framework, while the DABS is being published so that the now well-established prong 2 could be better implemented as a purely diagnostic framework.

DABS uses item response theory (see Chapter 5) to construct an instrument intended to reliably and validly discriminate between individuals with and without ID. The instrument also differs from other AB measures in that items across age groups were selected based on their ability to statistically discriminate between individuals with and without ID at the cut-off area (significant deficits or no significant deficits). Such an instrument will have great utility in *Atkins* proceedings where qualifying on prong 2 is, literally, a matter of life and death. In relation to the preceding discussion, one way of thinking about DABS is that it has kept the tripartite framework, but not the 1992 10-item list that had been folded into that framework without an empirical justification.

The basic method used in developing the DABS was to generate a large pool of items (including through solicitation from many authorities) for each of the three domains, and then use field-testing of the item pool and statistical methods to winnow the items down to those which best discriminated developmentally and categorically. Of particular interest is that gullibility items (which have not been represented in current instruments, except for one item added to the Vineland-2) were not only strong developmental discriminators but were also strong categorical (ID vs. non-ID) discriminators–but only at the adolescent and young adult level (note: the DABS covers ages 4 to 21). The reason for this last finding is that all children are gullible (it is why they are prevented from entering into contracts), but adults with ID remain gullible. The only weakness of the DABS for use in *Atkins* proceedings is the age range covered (4 to 21), which limits its use. Most states require some indicator of adaptive deficits at the time of the crime, which in most cases is over age 21. However, as many jurisdictions (e.g., California) rely almost exclusively on evidence of ID before the age of 18, the DABS—used retrospectively—can still be very useful in *Atkins* cases.

Essence of Adaptive Behavior

The conceptualization of prong 2 was intended to move diagnosis of ID somewhat away from indirect (IQ) and artificial (standard deviation) predictor criteria, and toward more natural (functioning) and outcome (supports) criteria. That effort has only been partially realized possibly due to (a) the failure to ground the construct sufficiently in behaviors that reflect vulnerabilities specific to the disorder and (b) the persistence of a belief that standard scores are what make the ID field (and forensic psychology, for that matter) legitimate.

Greenspan, Loughlin, and Black (2001) have noted that people with ID are universally gullible (i.e., susceptible to being duped and manipulated by others). This insight came from pre-*Atkins* involvement in a capital case, involving Richard Lapointe (Greenspan, 1995). Lapointe, who was born with Dandy-Walker syndrome, illustrated gullibility in the context of a confession; he was described by one family member as "the most gullible person on the planet."

Understanding the role of gullibility (or *credulousness*) was common among 19th-century scholars writing about *imbecility*, but by the 20th-century it had disappeared from the literature on ID. Gradually, this has started to change as Luckasson et al. (2002) indicated that gullibility was one of the forms that deficient social adaptive functioning could take. Clinicians were in fact encouraged to collect descriptive information on gullibility, reasoning that it was not being tapped in 2 two instruments. As mentioned previously, a number of gullibility items are now contained in DABS. This in part reflects committee members' experience with gullibility in persons with ID as described by informants (e.g., childhood peers and family members).

Clearly, ID authorities have increasingly acknowledged that gullibility—along with other forms of social incompetence—is a common problem in people with ID. However, there is reluctance to declare it a universal (as opposed to an optional) characteristic. This reluctance probably reflects two factors: (a) it would create a precedent which goes against the current polythetic approach in which one does not need to be incompetent in all domains; and (b) a belief that gullibility, although a common occurrence, is not observable all of the time or in all subjects who legitimately have ID. A solution to this latter problem is to embed gullibility in a broader construct of "foolish" handling of situations involving risk.

A Shift from Traits to Situations

A basic theme in the AAIDD position over the years (Greenspan & Switzky, 2006) is that the disability of people with ID is partially context-specific. People with ID may function well in routine environments calling on well-learned schemas, but may function poorly in novel or complex situations that depend less on learning and more on "thinking." The context contributor to disability is, in fact, why adaptive functioning in prison should not be used to rule out ID, as prison life is tightly regulated and there are few opportunities to encounter ambiguity or to make choices.

Taking the situational view of disabilty further, one could argue that the essence of ID is a failure to recognize risk, whether that risk is practical (carelessly crossing a busy street or heating oil in a pan) or social (gullibly falling for a scam or agreeing to help carry out a crime). Such events can be very infrequent occurrences, which is why they do not always manifest when an observer is present. But, when they do occur and are not skillfully dealt with, the result can have catastrophic outcomes, ranging from death to death row.

Recognition of risk is another term for what is colloquially called "common sense." Behavior that shows an absence of common sense (i.e., which fails to take account dangerous social or practical risk) can also be termed "foolish" (Greenspan, 2009). Greenspan et al. (2011) have argued that ID can be considered a *Common Sense Deficit Disorder*. Gullibility can be described as "induced socially foolish action"; induced, in that it is brought on by pressure from another. Socially foolish action can be noninduced as well, as when one initiates a very inappropriate verbalization or course of action. This analysis explains why gullibility is not always described (assuming, of course, that an investigator asks the right questions) in AB interviews, given that socially induced foolishness is not an everyday occurrence. However, by locating gullibility within a broader framework of risk-unaware conduct, it reflects that people with ID may exhibit a propensity to show poor judgment.

The previous situation-based analysis also can accommodate a key notion expressed in the 2002 *Atkins* decision: a characterization of people with ID as "impulsive" and "lacking rationality." On the surface, impulsivity would seem to be a personality characteristic which can vary considerably for people with ID. However, one can put an evaluative and cognitive interpretation on impulsivity and describe it as a tendency to quickly make bad decisions because of an inability to understand the possible negative consequences of those decisions.

Haydt (2012) compiled a database of nearly 200 *Atkins* cases and analyzed the nature of the crimes for which the defendants were convicted or charged. Although many of these crimes involved gullibility in relation to a more competent co-defendant, by far the largest category of these homicides can be described as impulsive. A representative example (involving both gullibility and impulsivity) involved John Eley, a condemned Ohio prisoner granted gubernatorial clemency in 2012. Eley, a man with likely ID, had no substantial history of violence, but was talked into using a gun to hold up a convenience store by a much younger man. Eley had no intention of shooting the victim, but panicked when the victim went for a gun. Eley's actions (agreeing without reflecting on the crime and then responding automatically by shooting without considering alternatives) lacked rationality (common sense) as demonstrated by his failure to appreciate the physical risk posed to the victim and the social risk posed to himself. Eley's absence of common sense was also manifested when he turned down a 6-year sentence offered by the prosecutor in exchange for his testimony against the initiator, which played a big part in his being granted clemency.

The chapter concludes with an additional perspective regarding the importance of adaptive behavior within the diagnosis of intellectual disability. In his widely cited early definition of ID (then termed mental deficiency), Edgar Doll defined it as "social incompetence, due to mental subnormality, which has been developmentally arrested, which obtains at maturity, is of constitutional origin, and which is essentially incurable" (1941, p. 215). Substituting adaptive functioning or adaptive behavior for social incompetence, one could envisage the concept of ID along similar lines as "a disability marked by poor adaptive functioning in situations of social or physical risk, stemming from brain-based cognitive limitations in the ability to recognize and avoid such risk." A useful analogy suggested by Woods (personal communication 2012) is to think of the ID prongs not as a decision tree starting with intelligence, but rather as the three legs in a stool. The idea here is that one should always assess AB, regardless of what the data seem to indicate for other domains of functioning, in that all three legs of a stool are equally important.

There is general agreement that there is a need to place less emphasis on test score cut-offs, and more emphasis on exploring an individual's overall functioning and the cognitive and other factors which contribute to that functioning. In many *Atkins* proceedings, a large amount of time has typically been devoted to the examination of IQ test scores and a relatively small amount of time devoted to trying to understand who the person is and why he might be deserving of special treatment (as ID) by the legal system. If greater definitional prominence were given to AB, especially if it were worded with an emphasis on strengths or deficits in *Atkins*-relevant situational judgments, it is likely that forensic experts would acquire, and communicate, a much better understanding of the people whom they are describing and trying to categorize.

References

American Psychiatric Association (2000). *Diagnostic and statistical manual of mental disorders, fourth edition, text revision (DSMIV-TR)*. Arlington, VA: Author.

American Psychiatric Association (2013). *Diagnostic and statistical manual of mental disorders, fifth edition (DSM-5)*. Arlington, VA: Author.

Blume, J. (2010). *An empirical look at Atkins v. Virginia and its application in capital cases*. Paper presented at the 134th AAIDD Annual Meeting, June, 2010, Providence, RI.

Clausen, J. (1972). Quo Vadis AAMD? *Journal of Special Education, 6*(1), 51–60.

Doll, E. A. (1941). The essentials of an inclusive concept of mental deficiency. *American Journal of Mental Deficiency, 46*, 214–229.

Duffy, S., & Greenspan, S. (2006). *Views of mild mental retardation held by experienced practitioners*. Paper presented at the 130th AAMR Annual Meeting, May, 2006, Montreal, Quebec.

Gardner, H. (1983). *Frames of mind: A theory of multiple intelligences*. New York, NY: Basic Books.

Greenspan, S. (1979). Social intelligence in the retarded. In N. R. Ellis (Ed.), *Handbook of mental deficiency, psychological theory and research* (2nd ed., pp. 483–531). Hillsdale, NJ: Erlbaum.

Greenspan, S. (1995). There is more to intelligence than IQ. In D. C. Connery (Ed.), *Convicting the innocent* (pp. 112–137). Cambridge, MA: Brookline Books.

Greenspan, S. (2009). Foolish action in adults with intellectual disabilities: The forgotten problem of risk unawareness. In L. M. Glidden (Ed.), *International review of research in mental retardation* (pp. 147–194). New York, NY: Elsevier.

Greenspan, S., Loughlin, G., & Black, R. (2001). Credulity and gullibility in persons with mental retardation. In L. M. Glidden (Ed.), *International Review of Research in Mental Retardation* (pp. 101–135). New York, NY: Academic Press.

Greenspan, S., & Switzky, H. N., (2006). Forty-four years of AAMR manuals. In H. N. Switzky & S. Greenspan (Eds.), *What is mental retardation?: Ideas for an evolving disability in the 21st century* (pp. 3–28). Washington, DC: American Association on Mental Retardation.

Greenspan, S., Switzky, H. N. & Woods, G. W. (2011). Intelligence involves risk-awareness and Intellectual Disability involves risk-unawareness: Implications of a theory of common sense. *Journal of Intellectual & Developmental Disability, 36*(4), 1–33.

Grossman, H. J. (Ed.). (1973). *Manual on terminology in mental retardation* . Washington, D. C.: American Association on Mental Deficiency.

Harris, S., & Oakland, T. (2000). *Adaptive Behavior Assessment System*. San Antonio, TX: Psychological Corporation.

Harrison, P. L., & Oakland, T. (2003). *ABAS II: Adaptive behavior assessment system* (2nd ed.). San Antonio, TX: The Psychological Corporation.

Haydt, N. (2012, July). *Some findings from a database of Atkins litigation*. Paper presented at the International Association for the Scientific Study of Intellectual Disability, Halifax, Nova Scotia.

Heber, R. (1959). A manual on terminology and classification in mental retardation: A monograph supplement. *American Journal of Mental Deficiency, 64*, 1–111.

Heber, R. (1961). *A manual on terminology and classification in mental retardation (2nd ed.)*. Washington, DC: American Association on Mental Deficiency.

Hull, C. L. (1937). Mind, mechanism, and adaptive behavior. *Psychological Review, 44*(1), 1–32.

Luckasson, R., Borthwick-Duffy, S. A., Buntinx, W. H. E., Coulter, D. L., Craig, E. M., Reeve, A., Schalock, R. L., Snell, M. E., Spitalnik, D. M., Spreat, S., & Tassé, M. J. (2002). *Mental retardation: Definition, classification, and systems of supports (10th ed.)*. Washington, DC: American Association on Intellectual and Developmental Disabilities.

Luckasson, R., Coulter, D. L., Polloway, E. A., Reiss, S., Schalock, R. L., Snell, M. E., . . . Stark, J. A. (1992). *Mental retardation: Definition, classification, and systems of supports (9th ed.)*. Washington, DC: American Association on Mental Retardation.

McGrew, K. S., Bruininks, R. H., & Johnson, D. R. (1996). Confirmatory factor analytic investigation of Greenspan's model of personal competence. *American Journal on Mental Retardation, 100* (5), 533–545.

Nihira, K., Foster, R., Shellhaas, M., & Leland, H. (1969). *AAMD Adaptive Behavior Scale*. Washington, DC: American Association on Mental Deficiency.

Salvador-Carulla, L., Reed, G. M., Vaez-Azizi, L. M., Cooper, S. A., Martinez-Leal, R., Bertelli, M., . . . Saxena, S. (2011). Intellectual developmental disorders: Towards a new name, definition and framework for "mental retardation/intellectual disability" in ICD-11. *World Psychiatry, 10*(3), 175–180.

Schalock, R. L. (1999). Adaptive behavior and its measurement: Setting the future agenda. In R. L. Schalock (Ed.), *Adaptive behavior and its measurement: Implications for the field of mental retardation* (pp. 209–219). Washington, DC: American Association on Mental Retardation.

Schalock, R. L., Borthwick-Duffy, S. A., Bradley, V. J., Buntinx, W.H.E., Coulter, D. L., Craig, E. M., Gomez, S. C., Lachapelle, Y., Luckasson, R., Reeve, A., Shogren, K. A., Snell, M. E., Spreat, S., Tassé, M. J., Thompson, J. R., Verdugo-Alonso, M. A., Wehmeyer, M. L., Yeager, M. H. (2010). *Intellectual disability: Definition, classification, and systems of supports (11th ed.)*. Washington, DC: American Association on Intellectual and Developmental Disabilities.

Sparrow, S., Cicchetti, D. V. & Balla, D. A. (2005). *Vineland adaptive behavior scales, second edition* (Vineland-II). Indianapolis: Pearson Assessment.

Sternberg, R. J., & Detterman, D. K. (1986). *What is intelligence? Contemporary viewpoints on its nature and definition*. Norwood, NJ: Ablex.

Tassé, M. J. (2009). Adaptive behavior assessment and the diagnosis of mental retardation in capital cases. *Applied Neuropsychology, 16*, 114–123.

Tassé, M. J., Schalock, R. L., Balboni, G., Bersani, H., Bothwick-Duffy, S. A., Spreat, S., . . . Zhang, D. (2012). The construct of adaptive behavior: Its conceptualization, measurement, and use in the field of intellectual disability. *American Journal on Intellectual and Developmental Disabilities, 117*, 291–303.

Tassé, M., Schalock, R. L., Balboni, G., Borthwick-Duffy, S. A., Bersani, H., Jr, Spreat, S., . . . Zhang, D. (in press). *Diagnostic Adaptive Behavior Scale (DABS)*. Washington, DC: American Association on Intellectual and Developmental Disabilities.

Thorndike, E. L. (1920). Intelligence and its uses. *Harper's Magazine, 140*, 227–235.

Zigler, E., Balla, D., & Hodapp, R. (1984). On the definition and classification of mental retardation. *American Journal on Mental Deficiency, 89*, 215–230.

Acknowledgement: The author is grateful to Marc Tassé for his many helpful comments on this manuscript.

12 | Adaptive Behavior Instruments

J. Gregory Olley

As noted in Chapter 11, the interest in adaptive behavior (AB) and its measurement grew remarkably after Heber's (1961) *Manual on Terminology and Classification in Mental Retardation* included "associated . . . impairment in adaptive behavior" in the definition of the disability. Since that time, many scales of AB have been published, and the 2010 American Association on Intellectual and Developmental Disabilities (AAIDD) publication, *Intellectual Disability: Definition, Classification, and Systems of Supports* (11th ed.; Schalock et al., 2010) emphasized the importance of using standardized measures of adaptive functioning. Today there are three well established instruments and one forthcoming scale that promise to be very useful in *Atkins* cases. The three contemporary scales, in order of their publication dates, are the Scales of Independent Behavior–Revised (SIB-R; Bruininks, Woodcock, Weatherman, & Hill, 1996); the Adaptive Behavior Assessment System (2nd ed.; ABAS-II; Harrison & Oakland, 2003); and the Vineland Adaptive Behavior Scales (2nd ed.; Sparrow, Cicchetti, & Balla, 2008a, 2008b). The forthcoming instrument is the Diagnostic Adaptive Behavior Scale (DABS; Tassé et al., in press) to be published by AAIDD.

The current AAIDD 11th edition (Schalock et al. , 2010) and the recent *User's Guide* to the 11th edition (Schalock et al., 2012) have urged the use of standardized instruments in the concurrent assessment of AB, but they have not directly addressed their use in *Atkins* cases in which the assessment is retrospective by its nature. That is, such scales were normed and standardized by asking the respondent to rate that individual's current functioning. In *Atkins* cases, raters are asked to rate the defendant based on the examiner's memory of the defendant's functioning in the past–usually pre-18 and often at the time of the crime. Given that defendants are incarcerated at the time of the evaluation, current adaptive community functioning cannot be measured. As is pointed out in the 11th edition (Schalock et al., 2010) and the *User's Guide* (Schalock et al, 2012),

AB is typical functioning in one's community. It is about independent functioning, which cannot be known for a defendant in an *Atkins* case whose freedom is severely limited. Further, courts in different states have ruled differently regarding the relevant time in the defendant's life for which impaired functioning must be demonstrated (see Chapter 14).

As AB scales have developed, researchers and clinicians have also recognized the importance of drawing AB information from many sources. Gresham (1983) described the multitrait, multimethod approach applied to the assessment of adaptive and other functioning. In addition to standardized scales using ratings from people who knew the defendant well, a thorough assessment must rely on other sources, such as records, interviews, and other instruments (Olley & Cox, 2008; Schalock et al., 2012; Tassé, 2009).

Format of This Chapter

This chapter reviews the contemporary instruments that are used to assess adaptive functioning so they can be carefully considered when reviewing the records and considers using adaptive behavior scales to assess adaptive functioning retrospectively. The chapter concludes with a discussion of the implications for practice. As noted earlier, adaptive behavior assessment should include information from as many sources as is feasible; a review of the strengths and weaknesses of several sources that may complement standardized tests is provided.

Tests That Are not Suitable

Although in the *11th edition* and the *User's Guide* (Schalock et al., 2010, 2012) AAIDD recommended using standardized measures of AB, not all instruments that purport to assess this construct are suitable for determining intellectual disability (ID; e.g., screening tests, checklists, or short versions of the tests described in this chapter). Spreat (1999) noted the existence of "well over 200 scales, each purporting to measure adaptive behavior" (p. 103). For the purpose of diagnosing ID in the context of *Atkins* cases, it may be possible that there are appropriate instruments in addition to those reviewed here. However, the choice of instrument should be guided by Spreat's (1999) distinctions among the purposes of adaptive behavior measures. The choice of instrument should be one that is designed for diagnosis or classification, rather than documenting progress, describing strengths or weaknesses, program evaluation, or other purposes. The chosen measure should also reflect the psychometric standards for AB measures described by Spreat. Tests of adaptive behavior designed for other populations, such as individuals with dementia, that have not been standardized to include people with ID (e.g., Independent Living Scales, Loeb, 1996) do not have demonstrated validity for the diagnosis of ID.

The Street Survival Skills Questionnaire (SSSQ; Linkenhoker & McCarron, 1993) has an appealing name, but it is essentially a nonverbal picture test of practical skills. It was designed as part of a larger battery of vocational assessments and is not an adequate stand-alone test of AB. The SSSQ reveals some *knowledge* of everyday practical functioning, but it does not measure actual AB in conceptual, social, or practical areas. The test is a good example of the difference between *knowledge* of adaptive behavior and actual behavior and is an inappropriate test for the diagnosis of ID; (see review by Denkowski & Denkowski, 2008). Several other examples of inappropriate measures could be listed, and some have been admitted as evidence in court, but the careful expert will apply Spreat's (1999) criteria for the selection of an AB scale.

Scales Standardized on Children

An examination of AB scales reveals that many (such as the forthcoming DABS; Tassé et al., in press) have been standardized only on children. In *Atkins* cases, the evidence from AB scales comes primarily from childhood records containing AB scores or from AB scales administered retrospectively and based on childhood functioning. In either instance, the reliance on childhood norms is appropriate. Other scales reviewed in this chapter are standardized to age 80 or older, which allows ratings of adults where needed.

Validity Problems in Assessing Current Functioning in Prison

Although, as noted earlier, current functioning cannot be validly assessed for a person who is incarcerated, judges may require that current functioning be assessed in *Atkins* cases. There are validity limitations when conducting such an evaluation. For instance, the administration of an AB scale to an individual who is familiar with the defendant's prison behavior (e.g., corrections officers, the defendant) would not yield a valid measure of adaptive behavior. Many items on AB scales cannot be answered for incarcerated individuals, and thus incarcerated persons were not included in the standardization sample of these scales (see also Chapter 13).

Current Standardized Measures

The following scales are in current use; meet contemporary standards for standardization, reliability, and validity; and have many common features. For example, they have reasonably objective wording that focuses on behavior, rather than potential. They are also intended to be administered to someone who has known the individual over time and observed him or her across settings. The scales require that person to rate the individual with regard to how independently he or she performs each task. This method is necessary, because the examiner cannot directly observe the individual in varied community settings over time in order to determine what AB is typical. The standards for choosing an informant are discussed further by Olley and Cox (2008), Schalock (2012), Tassé (2009), and in Chapter 13 of this book.

Although some earlier AB measures were simple checklists, contemporary measures emphasize using an interview format to complete rating scales. For some measures, it is possible to simply give the form to an experienced rater and ask him or her to fill it out. However, in *Atkins* evaluations, it is preferred that AB scales be administered as part of a face-to-face interview, which allows the examiner to clarify items when needed. This clarification is useful, because even teachers can misunderstand items or be influenced by their feelings toward the individual (Evans & Bradley-Johnson, 1988). Reading each item aloud assures fewer misunderstandings of item content or scoring.

All of the scales yield standard scores with a mean of 100 and a standard deviation of 15, which allows the examiner to apply the usual cutoff of approximately 2 standard deviations below the mean. Each scale also produces an overall standard score as well as subtest scores representing specific skill areas.

Despite these common features and strong psychometric properties, the scales do not contain exactly the same content and are not, strictly speaking, interchangeable. Doane and Salekin (2009) reported preliminary information on the susceptibility of the ABAS-II to malingering of ID.

Scales of Independent Behavior–Revised (1996)

The Scales of Independent Behavior–Revised (SIB-R; Bruininks et al., 1996) is a revision of the 1984 scale by the same name and by the same authors. The SIB-R yields scores in 14 areas of AB grouped in four clusters and standardized for individuals from ages infancy to 80 plus years. The four clusters are Motor Skills, Social Interaction and Communication, Personal Living Skills, and Community Living Skills. It includes a Short Form, an Early Development Form, and a Problem Behavior Scale. However, the Adaptive Behavior Full Scale is the only appropriate scale to use for the diagnosis of ID. It can be administered as an interview or a checklist. Administration and scoring recognize basal and ceiling items, which makes administration more efficient.

The original Scales of Independent Behavior (SIB) were standardized on 1,764 individuals in the United States, and the revised scales added 418 normative subjects in order to account for the revised items and to make the sample comparable to the demographics of the 1990 United States Census. The method of scale development was item response theory (IRT, described in Chapter 5 of this book). The SIB-R yields age equivalents, percentile ranks, and standard scores with means of 100 and standard deviations of 15 (similar to other scales) for Cluster scores and a composite score called Broad Independence. The standard error of measurement (SEM) for Broad Independence is 3 at ages 5 years, 8 months and below, and 2 for ages 5 years, 9 months and above.

Given that the SIB-R subtests are IRT scaled, people who receive scores near the bottom of a subtest or near the top of the subtest will have scores that are subject to greater error than people whose scores fall near the middle (Bruininks et al., 1996; McGrew,

Werder, & Woodcock, 1991). However, SIB-R cluster scores, which are based on combinations of subtests, do not retain this IRT ability-related SEM feature. As Bruininks et al. (1996) noted, SIB-R cluster scores will reflect the average SEM across the entire ability range of scores for a cluster. The differential ability-related SEM characteristics of subtests is present in all subtests on psychological tests, but if classical test theory (CTT; see chapter 5) methods are used for item calibration, the subtests will not reflect this empirical reality and will typically report the average SEM across all possible subtest raw scores.

Adaptive Behavior Assessment System, Second Edition (2003)

The Adaptive Behavior Assessment System, Second Edition (ABAS-II; Harrison & Oakland, 2003) is a revision of the 2000 scale of the same name by the same authors. Although a third edition of the Adaptive Behavior Assessment System will be available in 2015, the available research is on the second edition. The ABAS-II yields scaled scores in 10 areas of AB that correspond to the *Mental Retardation: Definition, Classification, and Systems of Supports* (10th ed.; Luckasson et al., 2002) and the *Diagnostic and Statistical Manual (DSM-IV-TR)* of the American Psychiatric Association (APA; 2000). Those 10 areas include Communication, Community Use, Functional Academics, Home Living, Health and Safety, Leisure, Self-Care, Self-Direction, Social, and Work. (The DSM-IV-TR split Health and Safety into separate categories.) Administration of the Work items is optional, depending on the individual's work history. The scaled scores for these 10 scales have a mean of 10 and a standard deviation of 3. The ABAS-II also yields four Composite Scores, each with a mean of 100 and standard deviation of 15. These scores include Conceptual, Social, and Practical, which correspond to the AAIDD (Schalock et al., 2010) system for clustering adaptive behaviors. The fourth Composite Score is the General Adaptive Composite. Summary scores expressed in these ways are practical in that they correspond to the AAIDD standards and to many statutes and/or legal precedents from various state and federal courts.

The ABAS-II has forms for Infant-Preschool, School Age, and Adult. In the standardization process, the Infant-Preschool Scale (ages birth to 5 years, 11 months) was administered to 750 teachers or daycare providers and 1,350 parents or primary caregivers. The School-Age Form (ages 5–21) was administered to 1,690 teachers and 1,670 parents. The Adult Form (ages 16–89) was administered to 990 individuals who rated themselves and 920 individuals who rated others.

The average standard error of measurement for the General Adaptive Composite score on each form across rating groups is: Daycare Providers (2.12), Teachers (1.57), Primary Caregivers (2.94), Parents (1.97), Adult Self-Report (1.60 without the Work scale, 1.50 with the Work scale), and Adults rated by others (1.50 with or without the Work scale). Although the ABAS-II is the only one of the contemporary scales to provide norms for self-report, the test manual advises that only "individuals who display a high level of functioning may complete the forms themselves" (p. 16). The authors did not intend that people of low intelligence should provide information regarding their own diagnosis. Much more information on the use of the ABAS-II appears in Oakland and Harrison (2008).

Vineland Adaptive Behavior Scales, Second Edition (2008)

The Vineland Adaptive Behavior Scales, Second Edition (Sparrow et al., 2008a, 2008b) is a revision of the 1984 scale by the same name by the same authors. The original Vineland Social Maturity Scale developed by Edgar Doll in 1935 was groundbreaking in its time, but resembles the current scale in name only. The Vineland-II has the advantage of containing items that reflect more current community functioning than the previously mentioned scales. Thus, in a retrospective assessment, the expert should consider the year in which the rater is asked to provide information. The Vineland-II or DABS may be well suited for ratings of behavior in recent years; whereas, the SIB-R or ABAS-II may be the better choice when rating behavior from earlier years.

The Vineland-II assesses skill performance in four broad domains, each with several subdomains. The broad domains are Communication, Daily Living Skills, Socialization, and Motor Skills. Motor Skills are assessed only for ages 0–6. Like the SIB-R, the Vineland-II includes a Maladaptive Behavior domain, although the score does not contribute to the assessment of AB in either instrument. Information about maladaptive behavior is not relevant to a diagnosis of ID, although it may be useful in forensic evaluations for other purposes.

The Vineland-II format offers Survey Forms (Survey Interview Form and Parent/Caregiver Rating Form), a Teacher Rating Form, and an Expanded Interview Form. The Expanded Interview Form contains more items within the same four domains and allows an opportunity to explore adaptive functioning in greater depth. For this reason, the authors stated a strong preference for the administration of the longer interview format over the rating format.

The language and the examples are more up to date in the Vineland-II than the earlier scales (e.g., they contain references to computers and e-mail). The standard error of measurement for the Adaptive Behavior Composite for the Survey Forms between the ages of 16 and 90 is 2.48 to 4.23 standard score points, depending on age. For the Expanded Interview Form, it is 1.6 to 2.7. Although the scale is long, it is arranged by age or difficulty level. By establishing a basal and ceiling, not every item must be administered.

Diagnostic Adaptive Behavior Scales (in press)

The Diagnostic Adaptive Behavior Scales (DABS) (Tassé et al., in press) is a new instrument to be published by AAIDD and is not a revision of the AAMR Adaptive Behavior Scale–School (2nd ed., Lambert, Nihara, & Leland, 1993) or the AAMR Adaptive Behavior Scale–Residential and Community (2nd ed.; Nihira, Leland, & Lambert, 1993). The DABS was standardized on a sample of 1,058 individuals between the ages of 4 and 21. Thus, administration to individuals older than 21 uses the age 21 norms and relies on the assumption that adaptive functioning does not change substantially after age 21.

The DABS is an up-to-date instrument in several respects. It was constructed using IRT (also called modern test theory; see Chapter 5), and contains some content that is not represented in earlier scales (e.g., technology related items). For some time, Greenspan (2009) has emphasized the importance of judgment and naiveté (or gullibility, what he has termed "foolish action," or "risk-unaware" behavior) in the diagnosis of ID. The DABS is the first scale to include such items.

The scale items are arranged by age group with 75 items per age group—25 each for the areas of Conceptual, Social, and Practical Skills. Special attention has been given in the selection of items that are sensitive around the cutoff point for determining significant impairment in AB. This feature should be especially valuable in *Atkins* evaluations.

Unlike the scales previously described, the DABS is a diagnostic scale, rather than a dual-purpose scale for diagnosis and program planning. It has a Spanish version normed in Spain and an Italian version normed in Italy, which include some of the same and some different items.

Retrospective Use of Standardized Adaptive Behavior Scales in *Atkins* Cases

The assessment of AB in *Atkins* cases focuses on behavior in childhood through the time of the crime and is, thus, inherently retrospective. The examiner must draw information from as many sources as possible and give each source its appropriate weight, using clinical judgment to arrive at a diagnostic conclusion (Schalock & Luckasson, 2005). Among the most common and potentially most valuable sources are interviews with family members and others who have known the individual well in varied community settings. Multiple informants who have known the individual at different ages before the pertinent crime can provide consensual validity regarding adaptive functioning.

The importance of clinical judgment is especially great in *Atkins* evaluations, because the various sources of AB information are subject to many kinds of bias. For instance, interviewing several informants who have known the defendant at different times can be helpful in judging the potential bias of any particular source. Parents are the most common source for interviews and the administration of AB scales, but they may also be biased in providing information that could contribute to the death penalty for their son or daughter. Bias may also influence their reporting in a different way. That is, they may exaggerate accomplishments or deny impaired functioning in order to avoid the stigma of the disability. If the information that they provide is congruent with information from other sources, the validity of their information is strengthened.

Given the fact that adaptive behavior assessment for adults in the criminal justice system is likely to necessitate having a retrospective component, examiners can complement the administration of an adaptive behavior scale in which the informant is asked to rate the individual's behavior at a specific time before the crime with interviews that also focus on the relevant areas of adaptive functioning. Further information related to retrospective assessment is provided in Chapter 18.

Other Sources of Adaptive Behavior Information.

Although it is standard practice to include as many sources of information as possible in a thorough AB assessment (Schalock et al., 2012), clinical judgment is necessary in assessing the value or validity of those sources. The following are some sources and related cautions.

1. **School records** (see also Chapter 20) may be the most common and the most valuable source of historical information, but they usually require interpretation. It is valuable to have a school official who worked in the school or in the school system at the time that the defendant was in attendance review the records and provide a context for interpretation.

    a. *Standardized tests of achievement* are objective but vary in their standardization quality. For instance, they may be standardized on a national sample or a local or state sample. They may provide standard scores based on grade norms or age norms, which result in different findings.

    b. *School performance* in the form of grades may be highly variable and subjective. Especially in special education programs, some teachers grade based on their expectations for their students or on attitude, effort, and motivation, but not necessarily on academic progress. (See also Chapter 20.)

    c. *Special education* placement and curriculum (Individualized Education Programs) should be standard in compliance with federal law, but this is not always true, especially for students who attended classes before the implementation of the Education for All Handicapped Children Act in 1977. For individuals who attended racially segregated schools, standards are even more idiosyncratic.

    d. Reports of *earlier adaptive behavior assessments* may also be part of school records, even if the student was found ineligible for special education services. These assessments may vary in their thoroughness or adherence to standard practices. For instance, the administration of the Vineland Adaptive Behavior Scales to a parent may be considered an adequate AB evaluation for school placement purposes, but it would be only one piece of a complex puzzle in an *Atkins* evaluation.

    e. *Teacher comments* may be informative but may be very subjective. The comments may be unrealistically favorable in order to give encouragement or unfavorable due to individual bias. Teacher comments are redacted from records by some school systems.

    f. *Participation in extracurricular activities* may or may not be included in school records. Teachers who supervised such activities may be good sources for interview information.

2. **Work records** are often valuable, because they were produced before the capital offense and address more objective standards of performance. For instance, they

may provide information about the type and length of employment, responsibilities, advancement or lack of advancement, reprimands or commendations, reasons for leaving the job, and name of supervisor. They may also contain the original job application, which the defendant might or might not have filled out independently. Performance on prison jobs would be informative if the defendant had significant difficulty, but most prison jobs are within the capabilities of an individual who would otherwise qualify for *Atkins* status. Reports of adequate work in prison are not informative with regard to adaptive functioning, but should be obtained in order to discuss if the issue is brought up during direct or cross-examination.

3. **Social Security records** may include adaptive behavior testing conducted months or years before the time of the pertinent crime, as well as qualitative information based on interviews with family members. Reports of evaluations conducted for Social Security eligibility can be very useful for *Atkins* hearings, because the standards for eligibility under Social Security (see Reschly, Myers, & Hartel, 2002) are very close to the standards used by the AAIDD (Schalock et al., 2010) and the American Psychiatric Association (2013). Social Security records may also be secondary sources for other records no longer available from primary sources.

4. In appellate cases, **affidavits, declarations,** or **records of interviews** with lay witnesses may have been gathered in connection with earlier court proceedings.

5. In order to gather information that is as thorough as is feasible, the current assessment should include **interviews** with individuals who knew the defendant well, especially in childhood. These individuals may include family members, friends, neighbors, teachers, employers, pastors, coaches, and others. As noted earlier, people who knew the individual well in childhood are also likely to be the most knowledgeable; however, they may also be biased. The interviewer should exercise great care in such circumstances.

6. Records of **therapeutic programs** may include objective testing and subjective comments. Such programs are usually structured, which should enhance performance. Further, these records are not true measures of typical community functioning because the programs provide supervision and support.

7. **Mental health programs,** group homes, social services, and substance abuse programs may also offer structure that is intended to improve performance, but they also may limit access to independent community functioning. Reports from such programs must be judged individually.

8. **Medical records** (including, as relevant, maternal pregnancy records) may have information about birth, early development, illnesses, exposure to toxins, and a wide variety of other causes, risk factors, or symptoms of ID. It should be noted, however, that a diagnosis of ID does not require a medical or organic etiology, and often medical records contain little objective information about intellectual or adaptive functioning.

9. Earlier **criminal justice records** seldom contain an objective evaluation of adaptive functioning but may contain informative comments about deficits in functioning in prison. Comments about functioning while incarcerated have limited value in assessing community functioning (see Chapter 13.). When considering information about functioning in prison, it is especially important to keep in mind that a finding of significant impairment in AB is based on the existence of deficits. The existence of competence in some areas does not disprove a diagnosis of ID or somehow counter the existence of a deficit.

10. A thorough *Atkins* evaluation should contain an **interview with the defendant;** however, individuals with low intelligence are often not valid reporters of their own functioning. As Schalock et al., (2012) noted, defendants in *Atkins* hearings may have incentive to minimize their accomplishments in order to avoid the death penalty or to exaggerate their accomplishments in order to avoid the stigma of the label of ID. Self-report of AB in an interview or resulting from the administration of an AB scale would yield information of unknown validity. Self-report information gained in an interview may be used to guide the search for reliable informants who may or may not provide similar information. Self-report used to complete an AB scale and produce standard scores risks introducing information to the court that is based on poor science. Once again, convergence of information strengthens the argument for or against the diagnosis of ID.

11. An assessment of AB may include tests of the **defendant's performance,** but for the purpose of an *Atkins* evaluation, few skills can be validly tested in a prison or jail setting. Even performance on simple, practical tasks, such as using a telephone book, a map, or a ruler may not generalize to community functioning and should be interpreted with caution.

12. **Prison records and interviews with corrections officers** can be useful, especially if they substantiate impaired functioning, but reports of adequate adaptive functioning in the restricted environment of prison may be impossible to interpret. Clinical judgment is required to answer several questions: Do people with ID perform well in this predictable, low-demand environment, or is their performance further depressed by the stress and unfamiliarity of it? Are letters or forms with the defendant's name on them valid measures of academic functioning or did the defendant copy them from another source or receive assistance in completing these tasks?

13. Other sources of information frequently presented in *Atkins* hearings are the **facts of the specific crime or the defendant's past criminal behavior.** Schalock et al. (2010, 2012) have taken the clear position that past criminal behavior is not an indicator of one's level of adaptive functioning and that "the diagnosis of ID is not based on the person's 'street smarts,' behavior in jail or prison, or 'criminal adaptive functioning'" (2012, p. 20). This position is supported by the

definition of adaptive functioning that requires examination of typical behavior in one's community. As noted earlier, isolated examples of relative strengths are expected. It is difficult to prove that specific examples of criminal behavior are typical or representative of one's overall adaptive functioning. Further, Schalock and colleagues (2010, 2012) have noted that research shows that *maladaptive behavior* (e.g., criminal behavior) is not the same as *impaired adaptive behavior*. Research in this area has been reviewed by Harrison (1987) and Thompson, McGrew, and Bruininks (1999).

14. Regardless of the source of adaptive functioning information, some **distinguishing features of people with** ID can be considered in the assessment. These features include such things as difficulty in independent living; dependence on a benefactor to assist with everyday responsibilities; the need for prompting or reminding; motivation by short-term rather than long-term goals; excessive approval seeking; difficulties in decision making and problem-solving (especially under stress); naiveté, gullibility, or credulity (often manifested by a history of exploitation); poor employment history or history of work in unskilled tasks; and difficulty learning by experience (Snell et al., 2009). None of these characteristics alone is a definitive indicator of ID, but all are worthy of investigation.

15. One must keep in mind the distinction between **acquisition deficits** (not having acquired the necessary knowledge or skill) and **performance deficits** (failure to use the acquired knowledge or skill when needed; Schalock et al., 2010). Without such a distinction, AB assessments may fall prey to the error of assuming that because the individual can recite the right answer or has demonstrated the skill at some time, he or she has no deficit in that area.

16. **Lay witnesses** can provide helpful information in adaptive behavior assessment. However, significant care is needed to assure the independence of information received from each informant. Further, it is likely that a given informant may only know the defendant in certain circumstances and consequently cannot provide valid information for all sections of an adaptive behavior scale. Nevertheless, the data they may provide, even if limited to only certain sections of adaptive behavior instruments, can be helpful. Information from multiple informants, however, should not be combined into one test protocol.

Interpretation and Clinical Judgment

In most *Atkins* cases, the expert will be required to integrate findings in a report and present them orally in testimony. In light of the emphasis on gathering information from as many sources as possible and then interpreting the information in relation to the varied validity of each source, it is expected that there will be variability in scores and contradictions in obtained information. Interpretation of such variability must rely on clinical judgment (Schalock & Luckasson, 2005). Ratings on AB scales can vary in several ways. Caution in the selection of raters and administration of scales can reduce variability. However, the reality is that AB scores depend on the memory of the rater, and raters are purposely chosen to report on the defendant's functioning at different ages and in different circumstances. Although the AB scales described in this chapter meet the minimum standards for a psychometrically strong instrument suitable for *Atkins* cases, they have different item content, and they cluster scores in different ways. Their methods of administration and scoring differ; therefore, scores from different scales would be expected to differ.

In addition to scores obtained from AB scales, the expert will integrate other information obtained from the varied sources discussed in this chapter. Multiple sources of adaptive behavior information must be considered, and examiners must give appropriate weight to the various sources of information. Given that a diagnosis of intellectual disability requires the presence of deficits in everyday functioning, evidence of a pattern of deficits is critical. The expert must exercise clinical judgment in informing the court about the AB findings in order to reach accurate conclusions regarding the defendant's typical community adaptive functioning.

References

American Association on Mental Retardation. (1992). *Mental retardation: Definition, classification, and systems of supports* (9th ed.). Washington, DC: Author.

American Psychiatric Association. (2000). *Diagnostic and statistical manual of mental disorders* (4th ed., Rev.). Washington, DC: Author.

American Psychiatric Association. (2013). *Diagnostic and statistical manual of mental disorders* (5th ed.). Washington, DC: Author.

Bruininks. R. H., Woodcock, R. W., Weatherman, R. F., & Hill, B. K. (1996). *Scales of Independent Behavior–Revised: Comprehensive manual.* Chicago: Riverside.

Denkowski, G. C., & Denkowski, K. M. (2008). Misuse of the street survival skills questionnaire (SSSQ) for evaluating the adult adaptive behavior of criminal defendants with intellectual disability claims. *Intellectual and Developmental Disabilities, 46,* 144–149.

Doane, B. M., & Salekin, K. L. (2009). Susceptibility of current adaptive behavior measures to feigned deficits. *Law and Human Behavior, 33,* 329–343. doi: 10.1007/s10979-008-9157-5

Doll, E. A. (1935). A genetic scale of social maturity. *American Journal of Orthopsychiatry, 5,* 180–190. doi: 10.1111/j.1939-0025.1935.tb06339.x

Evans, L. D., & Bradley-Johnson, S. (1988). A review of recently developed measures of adaptive behavior. *Psychology in the Schools, 25,* 276–287. doi: 10.1002/1520-6807(198807)25:3 <276::AID-PITS2310250309>3.0.CO;2-2

Greenspan, S. (2009). Foolish action in adults with intellectual disabilities: The forgotten problem of risk-unawareness. In L. M. Glidden (Ed.), *International review of research in mental retardation* (Vol. 36, pp. 147–194). New York, NY: Elsevier.

Gresham, F. M. (1983). Multitrait-multimethod approach to multifactored assessment: Theoretical rationale and practical application. *School Psychology Review, 12,* 26–34.

Harrison, P. L. (1987). Research with adaptive behavior. *Journal of Special Education, 21,* 37–68. doi: 10.1177/002246698702100108

Harrison, P. L., & Oakland, T. (2003). *Adaptive Behavior Assessment System (2nd ed.): Manual.* San Antonio, TX: Psychological Corporation.

Heber, R. (1961). *A manual on terminology and classification in mental retardation* (Rev.ed.). Washington, DC: American Association on Mental Deficiency.

Lambert, N., Nihira, K., & Leland, H. (1993). *AAMR Adaptive Behavior Scale–School* (2nd ed.). Austin, TX: Pro-Ed.

Linkenhoker, D., & McCarron, L. (1993). *Adaptive Behavior: The Street Survival Skills Questionnaire.* Dallas, TX: McCarron-Dial Systems.

Loeb, P. A. (1996). *Independent Living Scales.* Minneapolis, MN: Pearson.

Luckasson, R., Borthwick-Duffy, S. A., Buntinx, W. H. E., Coulter, D. L., Craig, E. M., Reeve, A., Schalock, R. L., Snell, M. E., Spitalnik, D. M., Spreat, S., & Tassé, M. J. (2002). *Mental retardation: Definition, classification, and systems of supports (10th ed.).* Washington DC: American Association on Intellectual and Developmental Disabilities.

McGrew, K. S., Werder, J. K., & Woodcock, R. W. (1991). *WJ-R technical manual.* Chicago, IL: Riverside.

Nihira, K., Leland, H., & Lambert, N. (1993). *AAMR Adaptive Behavior Scale–Residential and Community* (2nd ed.). Austin, TX: Pro-Ed.

Oakland, T., & Harrison, P. L. (Eds.). (2008). *Adaptive Behavior Assessment System-II: Clinical use and interpretation.* San Diego, CA: Elsevier.

Olley, J. G., & Cox, A. W. (2008). Assessment of adaptive behavior in adult forensic cases: The use of the Adaptive Behavior Assessment System-II. In T. Oakland & P. L. Harrison (Eds.),

Adaptive Behavior Assessment System-II: Clinical use and interpretation (pp. 381–398). San Diego, CA: Elsevier.

Reschly, D. J., Myers, T. G., & Hartel, C. R. (Eds.). (2002). *Mental retardation: Determining eligibility for Social Security benefits.* Washington, DC: National Academy Press.

Schalock, R. L., Borthwick-Duffy, S. A., Bradley, V. J., Buntinx, W.H.E., Coulter, D. L., Craig, E. M., Gomez, S. C., Lachapelle, Y., Luckasson, R., Reeve, A., Shogren, K. A., Snell, M. E., Spreat, S., Tassé, M. J., Thompson, J. R., Verdugo-Alonso, M. A., Wehmeyer, M. L., Yeager, M. H. (2010). *Intellectual disability: Definition, classification, and systems of supports (11th ed.).* Washington, DC: American Association on Intellectual and Developmental Disabilities.

Schalock, R. L., Luckasson, R., Bradley, V., Buntinx, W. H. E., Lachapelle, Y., Shogren, K. A., Snell, M. E., Thompson, J. R., Tassé, M. J., Verdugo-Alonso, M. A., and Wehmeyer, M. L. (2012). *User's guide to intellectual disability: Definition, classification, and systems of supports.* Washington, DC: American Association on Intellectual and Developmental Disabilities.

Schalock, R. L., & Luckasson, R. (2005). *Clinical judgment.* Washington, DC: American Association on Mental Retardation.

Snell, M. E., & Luckasson, R., with Borthwick-Duffy, S., Bradley, V., Buntinx, W. H. E., Coulter, D. L., Craig, E. M., Gomez, S. C., . . . Yeager, M. H. (2009). Characteristics and needs of people with intellectual disability who have higher IQs. *Intellectual and Developmental Disabilities, 47,* 220–233. doi:10.1352/1934-9556-47.3.220

Sparrow, S. S., Cicchetti, D. V., & Balla, D. A. (2008a). *Vineland Adaptive Behavior Scales (2nd ed.): Expanded Interview Form manual.* Minneapolis, MN: Pearson.

Sparrow, S. S., Cicchetti, D. V., & Balla, D. A. (2008b). *Vineland Adaptive Behavior Scales (2nd ed.): Survey Forms manual.* Minneapolis, MN: Pearson.

Spreat, S. (1999). Psychometric standards for adaptive behavior assessment. In R. L. Schalock (Ed.), *Adaptive behavior and its measurement: Implications for the field of mental retardation* (pp. 103–117). Washington, DC: American Association on Mental Retardation.

Tassé, M. J. (2009). Adaptive behavior assessment and the diagnosis of mental retardation in capital cases. *Applied Neuropsychology, 16,* 114–123. doi:10.1080/09084280902864451

Tassé, M. J., Schalock, R. L., Balboni, G., Borthwick-Duffy, S. A., Bersani, H., Jr., Spreat, S., . . . Zhang, D. (in press). *Diagnostic Adaptive Behavior Scale.* Washington, DC: American Association on Intellectual and Developmental Disabilities.

Thompson, J. R., McGrew, K. S., & Bruininks, R. H. (1999). Adaptive and maladaptive behavior: Functional and structural characteristics. In R. L. Schalock (Ed.), *Adaptive behavior and its measurement: Implications for the field of mental retardation* (pp. 15–42). Washington, DC: American Association on Mental Retardation.

13 | Challenges in the Assessment of Adaptive Behavior of People Who Are Incarcerated

Caroline Everington
Gilbert S. Macvaugh III
Karen L. Salekin
Timothy J. Derning

In capital cases, *Atkins* claims can be brought forward at many points in the judicial process (e.g., pretrial, sentencing, appeal), but in order to be brought forward, the *Atkins* claimant must inject the intellectual disability (ID) issue into the proceedings. Once injected, the *Atkins* claimant moves forward in accordance with procedures dictated by the jurisdictional state. In proving their cases, *Atkins* claimants must show that they have met all three prongs of the diagnosis; it is the second prong (i.e., adaptive behavior) that is often the most challenging to demonstrate, and it is this prong that is the focus of this chapter.

As noted in previous chapters, two definitions of ID are typically used by the judiciary in *Atkins* cases: the American Association on Intellectual and Developmental Disabilities (AAIDD) and the American Psychiatric Association (APA). Although different in some respects, what is similar between the two definitions is that *adaptive behavior* (AB) refers to an individual's typical level of independence, across multiple domains of personal functioning, meeting life demands in the context of community settings. *Atkins* experts using either definition face the challenge of demonstrating that the data gathered during the evaluation satisfies (or does not satisfy) the adaptive prong establishing the presence of ID.

The diagnostic criteria for ID are fixed and are not a relative standard based on whether the individual is in prison or not. However, the assessment can be helped or hindered by the context in which it is carried out. In an *Atkins* case, the assessment of ID is particularly difficult because the context prevents or limits the use of data typical to community assessments. For example, a satisfactory assessment of AB is not possible in a prison context because the individual has no opportunities to demonstrate the presence or absence of adaptive skills typical in day-to-day life. Inmates do not cook, choose clothing, or make independent choices about their day-to-day existence. By design, correctional settings remove virtually all personal control from the individual, and, as such, practical behaviors pertinent to the diagnosis cannot be demonstrated. What can be observed in these types of environments , however, is an individual's ability to follow orders, to learn simple daily routines, and to learn how to negotiate simple tasks required to meet their needs (e.g., how to order and/or purchase items from commissary; how to communicate with the outside world). Although information such as this is important, it is not adequate to satisfy the diagnostic requirements for ID. In fact, adequate functioning within a restricted environment, such as a prison, is expected of individuals with ID, as they may appear to function better in highly structured, less demanding environments.

In addition to problems related to a prison context, *Atkins* assessments are hindered by the questions asked by the trier-of-fact. Unlike typical evaluations of AB done in the community, which are focused on abilities here and now, triers-of-fact are interested in status at times in the past, specifically, at the time of the crime and additionally, prior to the age of 18 because this is a required prong of the ID diagnosis. Although current status is of interest to some, and perhaps mandated by others, it is these prior points of time that are often the focus of *Atkins* proceedings (see for example, Tenn. Code Ann. § 39-13-203, 2011). Both of these points of time are in the past and, as such, all *Atkins* evaluations, regardless of the age of the defendant or level of proceedings, require the most challenging investigation—one that requires collecting credible historical data, and analysis of the retrospective data. (See also Chapter 14.)

Nature of the Problem

As previously noted, there are two primary hindrances to the assessment of AB in the context of an *Atkins* case: (a) context and (b) retrospective investigation to two time points. This section begins with a discussion of problems related to context and retrospective investigation, followed by a brief review of the literature on the assessment of adaptive skills, and concludes with some suggestions for practice.

Context

The *Atkins* claimant is incarcerated and necessary third-party informants are in the community. According to AAIDD guidelines in *Intellectual Disability: Definition, Classification, and Systems of Supports* (11th ed.) (Schalock, 2010), significant limitations in adaptive functioning should be established through the use of standardized norm-referenced assessments administered to persons who know the individual well, who have known him/her for some time, and who have had the opportunity to observe the person function across community settings and across time. Appropriate reporters include family members, teachers, employers, and friends. Based on these prerequisites, correctional personnel and/or other inmates within the institution are not ideal informants. In situations where the individual has been incarcerated for an extended period of time and/or estranged from his/her family, more desirable informants may no longer be accessible.

Although there is no standard of practice for addressing this situation, it is inappropriate to administer an AB measure to a respondent who is not qualified to provide accurate and credible adaptive information. Examples of such individuals include, but are not limited to, some employers (single context, often limited duration of contact, limited breadth and depth of information), some neighbors (limited breadth and depth of information), and correctional officers (single context; limited breadth and depth of information; structured noncommunity setting). Finding informants who can meet the standard is often difficult in assessing individuals who have been incarcerated for years.

When more appropriate informants are available, concerns may exist regarding the veracity of the information obtained from them because of the forensic context of *Atkins* litigation. For example, it is possible that informants may attempt to exaggerate and/or fabricate the person's deficits to prevent a death sentence from being imposed. Although attempts to fabricate adaptive deficits by informants are often transparent and insufficient, vigilance and corroboration are always required. Validity concerns also arise in non-*Atkins*, nonforensic evaluations, as explicitly addressed by AAIDD (see Schalock et al., 2010, p. 47).

Retrospective Investigation

Standardized adaptive behavior assessments. Retrospective evaluations present unique challenges that can threaten the reliability and validity (the trustworthiness) of the AB assessment results. There is no uniform agreement on the use of standardized AB instruments for retrospective assessment. For instance, Greenspan and Switzky (2006) described the challenges of *retroactive assessment* of adaptive behavior (i.e., difficulties related to identifying two or more informants familiar with the individual's functioning during the relevant time frame), but advocate this practice. The use of retrospective assessment in *Atkins* cases has been endorsed in AAIDD's *User's Guide to Intellectual Disability: Definition, Classification, and Systems of Supports* (Schalock et al., 2012) and the 11th edition (Schalock et al., 2010) . Olley and Cox (2008) recommend the use of a particular instrument, the *Adaptive Behavior Assessment System–Second Edition* (ABAS-II; Harrison & Oakland, 2003) for retrospective assessment in *Atkins* cases. Other commentators, however, have questioned the retrospective use of AB instruments as they were designed to measure current functioning, and there is insufficient research regarding the reliability of these instruments when used retrospectively (Bonnie & Gustafson, 2007; Brodsky & Galloway, 2003; Stevens & Price, 2006). Tassé et al. (2012) addressed this issue by recommending collating results with records, using multiple informants in multiple contexts, and recognizing that adaptive behavior refers to typical and actual functioning and not to capacity or maximum functioning.

Records. All psychological evaluations, forensic or nonforensic, current or retrospective, include a review of considerable information about an individual's past experiences. One of the best sources of such information is records. In an *Atkins* case, the onus is on the examiner to request all records that may shed light on the issue. Examples of such records include, but are not limited to: employment history; social security evaluations; legal records (e.g., affidavits, declarations, or records of interviews by lay witnesses); police reports; school records (e.g., individualized education program evaluations, report cards, standard scores on achievement tests); mental health records; birth, pediatric, and adult medical records; military and discharge history; all present and past prison records (e.g., evaluations, vocational and school training, disciplinary records); and relevant history and records for family members.

In many situations, records are requested but cannot be located or are known to have been destroyed. Difficulties related to obtaining necessary records are a common issue in both pretrial and postconviction cases. In some states, special education records are destroyed at a specified date (e.g., 5 years after school departure). Department of Human Services records are often redacted to protect the privacy of third parties. Medical/mental health records also may not be available (or complete) for a variety of reasons. Each case comes with unique challenges. Because of this, the role of investigation (and investigators) is a critical aspect of an *Atkins* assessment. Requests for records, including failed efforts, should be documented and recorded by the *Atkins* examiner.

Although some records may contain evaluations of ID within the community setting, many do not; even in those that exist, standardized test scores and/or protocols are often unavailable for review. In addition, when reviewing prison records, examiners are likely to discover a number of documents (e.g., medical request forms, letters, grievances) reportedly produced by the *Atkins* claimant, especially one who has a history of incarcerations. However, it is not uncommon for illiterate inmates to obtain the assistance of other inmates who are higher functioning to prepare medical request forms and/or other correspondences; authorship should be investigated and confirmed (Macvaugh & Cunningham, 2009).

Literature Base

In spite of the aforementioned constraints, the clinician is still faced with the issue of reaching a valid and reliable finding on adaptive functioning. Although the literature on *Atkins* assessment is limited at this time, there is an extensive literature base on assessment of adaptive behavior that spans over 70 years beginning with the work of Edgar Doll in 1935 (Bierne-Smith, Patton, & Kim, 2006; Tassé et al., 2012) and the incorporation of the adaptive behavior into the mental retardation definition in 1959 (Nihira, 1999). Professional associations such as AAIDD and the National Association for School Psychologists (NASP) have articulated best practices for assessment of adaptive skills. Although the contextual issues discussed necessitate some deviations from established practice, adherence to established standards, as closely as possible, will result in a more valid finding. The purpose of this section is to reiterate several key principles that should followed in *Atkins* evaluations.

The first issue is that of context. Authoritative sources agree that adaptive behavior assessment involves evaluating the individual's typical functioning in *community* settings and the degree of consistent independence achieved across conceptual, practical, and social skill areas (Luckasson et al, 2002; Schalock et al., 2010; Tassé, 2009). These are skills that were acquired and demonstrated on a consistent basis in the individual's day-to-day life outside of an institutional setting (Cohen & Spenciner, 2011; Harrison & Raineri, 2008).

The constraints presented in *Atkins* cases may tempt many examiners to ignore these guidelines. It must be emphasized that best practice precludes the use of the current environment—the prison—as the primary source of information on adaptive functioning (Blume, Johnson, & Seeds, 2009; Young, Boccaccini, Conroy, & Lawson, 2007) as well as the use of estimates of adaptive functioning based on (a) claimant's knowledge of a skill, (b) examiner's attribution of claimant's potential, or (c) perceived lack of motivation. The AAIDD guidelines in the 11th edition (Schalock et al., 2010) are clear that adaptive behavior focuses on typical performance, not isolated examples of maximum performance or estimations of potential. Examiner attributions of motivational issues are not valid indicators, unless those issues can be substantiated from reliable information.

The second issue is the choice of assessment instruments. As previously mentioned, authoritative sources recommend the use of norm-referenced assessments designed specifically for the purpose of diagnosing intellectual disability (Cohen & Spenciner, 2011; Overton, 2009; Salvia, Ysseldyke, & Bolt, 2010; Tassé et al., 2012; Taylor, 2009; Widaman & Siperstein, 2009) in combination with structured interviews with informants (Harrison & Raineri, 2008; Schalock, 1999). The retrospective issues discussed earlier necessitate the use of multiple informants and, in some cases, a stronger emphasis on information gained from structured interviews (Tassé et al., 2012).

Finally, having first-hand professional experience and knowledge of the characteristics of individuals with intellectual disability at the upper end of the range is critical for interpretation of the adaptive information gathered through this process (American Psychological Association, 2012; Schalock & Luckasson, 2005). Reschly (2009) pointed out that the evaluator needs to understand that (a) intellectual disability at the upper end of the range affects performance in social roles and settings and (b) typical performance can include academic skills up to 4th–6th grade level, employment in unskilled tasks, and independent community mobility (e.g., obtaining a driver's license). (See also Baroff & Olley, 1999; Beirne-Smith et al., 2006; Drew & Hardman, 2007).

In summary, best practice in assessment of adaptive behavior in any context means that (a) the evaluation focuses on the degree of independence displayed in community settings, (b) a standardized instrument designed for that purpose is used, and (c) the evaluation is performed by a professional with extensive experience in intellectual disability. These principles apply to *Atkins* evaluations as well.

Applying Assessment Principles for Incarcerated Individuals

An important challenge in assessment is the application of appropriate principles for individuals who are already in the criminal justice system and have been incarcerated. Central to the task is the reliability and validity of diagnostic conclusions. The overarching principle for obtaining a valid and reliable finding is convergent validity (Reschly, 2009). Convergent validity is achieved by integrating multiple sources of information. In this unique situation, special attention must be given to the substantiation of level of adaptive functioning within the community context as well as using the current context for corroboration. These two considerations are discussed in the following section.

As previously stated, the community environment is the most important source of information related to adaptive functioning. The challenge is to *substantiate adaptive behavior within this community context* while the individual is now residing outside of the community. It is important to use multiple informants who knew the *Atkins* claimant at different points in his life span and observed his or her functioning in different contexts (e.g., school, work, family). As Tassé (2009) noted, no single source can provide a complete understanding of adaptive behavior. Informants may be difficult to locate so effort may be needed to find and interview informants with sources including the *Atkins* claimant; families; social histories; and school, mental health, medical, and employment records.

Upon locating informants, the next critical consideration is to determine their credibility because the accuracy of the assessment is dependent on it. Certainly, the information obtained will be of limited value if provided by biased informants (positive or negative) or individuals who did not know the individual well and/or had little contact. For example, useful information concerning general abilities and personality traits can come from family members, younger siblings, and teachers with recollections from early schooling. Beneficial information can be obtained from teachers who taught the individual in high school or articulate family members or friends who had frequent and regular contact who may be able to provide anecdotes on functioning during that developmental period. When available, the most useful data will come from independent, unbiased, sources who knew the person well due to regular and frequent contact of over a year or more. These sources would include those who knew the individual in a professional capacity such as articulate daily care providers, teachers, family friends, or employers who can support their perspectives with clear, convincing anecdotes. The task is to consider the information that has been obtained in terms of possible themes and commonalties. Given the importance of convergent validity as noted previously, the more consistent the information (i.e., convergence of the data), the greater the confidence that can be placed in the findings.

The determination of possible deficits in adaptive behavior as the second prong of the diagnosis of ID requires that the information reviewed references skills in the conceptual, practical, and social adaptive behavior domains. Attention to all three domains as identified in the AAIDD definition (Schalock et al., 2010) ensures that assessment will not concentrate solely on practical skills (e.g., use of the telephone, transportation skills, making small purchases), but will also focus on social and conceptual skill areas (Greenspan, 1999), which are more commonly indicative of intellectual disability at the upper end of the ID spectrum.

When using norm-referenced adaptive scales retrospectively to measure community functioning, the principle of convergent validity is again of importance. Appropriate practice in AB assessment calls for the administration of the instrument to more than one informant who is familiar with the *Atkins* claimant's functioning during the time period and compare the information obtained across informants to determine levels of agreement (Widaman & Siperstein, 2009). Olley and Cox (2008) indicated that the period of time should be selected during which informant(s) had the most contact with the examinee. Given that appropriate practice also would require interviewing informants separately as a measure of interrater reliability (see *United States of America v. Joseph Smith*, 2011), if the results of multiple ratings for a particular time period (e.g., pre-18) are congruent (i.e., within one standard deviation of each other), increased confidence can be placed in those findings (Everington & Olley, 2008).

Reliability is enhanced when informants provide concrete examples of relevant behaviors to support their rating decisions (Everington & Olley, 2008; Olley & Cox, 2008). This process provides the triers-of-facts with clear and convincing evidence supporting scores and ratings, and serves as a way to weigh an informant's reliability. This principle holds true for informal interviews as well. For example, whereas data may indicate that the defendant had a job for 8 years, more useful information would relate to how the claimant obtained the job, the specific duties performed and how well, and the level of supervision and assistance needed (see *United States of America v. Joseph Smith*, 2011).

As also discussed in Chapter 20, an important aspect of AB assessment that provides a retrospective perspective comes from school records. As noted in that chapter, these data have to be placed in an appropriate context. When considering, for example, determinations regarding special education eligibility (Widaman & Siperstein, 2009), it is important to note that guidelines for special education assessments and classification vary considerably by state and year, as do local standards for grading across school districts (Reschly, 2009). Further, state policies regarding the classification of children as having ID vary widely from state to state and decade to decade (Scullen, 2006). Olley (2007) noted that educational professionals from the individual's school district may be able to assist in the interpretation of school records and understand the policies and practices in place at the time.

The second data set that is relevant for the assessment of individuals who are incarcerated is information on *current functioning that can be a source of corroborative data.* An initial consideration is that information pertaining to conceptual adaptive skills that may be found in records and learned through informant interviews can be supplemented with direct measures of functioning based on contemporary academic and language assessments (see Everington & Olley, 2008; e.g., Wide Range Achievement Test 4 [WRAT-4; Wilkinson & Robertson, 2006]; Woodcock-Johnson-III [Woodcock, Schrank, McGew, & Mather, 2007]; Test of Adolescent and Adult Language 4th ed. [TOAL-4; Hammill, Brown, Larsen, & Wiederholt, 2007]; and Peabody Picture Vocabulary Test, 4th ed. [PPVT-4; Dunn & Dunn, 2007]. Findings from these assessments can also be used to determine if documents allegedly written by an inmate during the course of incarceration are consistent with measured abilities. Because some inmates may acquire a seemly sophisticated vocabulary (e.g., repeating jargon and over-learned phrases), the use of standardized language assessments will establish an accurate normative perspective of true skills.

Information regarding practical adaptive skills can be corroborated by asking the examinee to complete certain tasks, such as using a telephone book or reading a map (Olley & Cox, 2008). This information can be used to make cautious inferences about the person's functioning in the community, although such tasks will necessarily be selective of a wide range of behaviors and also may not speak directly to what the person might do in a real life setting when the behavior is necessary. However, if the individual cannot perform the task and has no strategy to successfully complete the task, such current information may corroborate information from informants.

The potential informants who have most current contact with the individuals being assessed are death row correctional personnel who consequently may provide corroborative information. These officers or prison staff (e.g., teachers, vocational supervisors) from previous and current prison placements may have observed functioning, such as the need for close supervision on a simple job, failure to learn, difficulty with completing canteen forms, or interactive functioning with, and also possible exploitation by, other inmates. At the same time, it should be acknowledged that corrections officers may have limited knowledge of a claimant's abilities due to rotating shift assignments, limited opportunities to witness an array of applied skills due to the highly restricted setting, and biased perspectives. Most important, their observations regarding inmates' adaptive behavior within a highly structured maximum security prison do not correlate with the demands and skills that are found in the typical community environment.

One final source of corroborative information may be other inmates who may have observed the individual's level of functioning. Individuals with ID often have what Edgerton (1993) termed a "benefactor, " someone who assists them with academic tasks (reading and writing mail, reading legal documents, completing forms) and may intercede on the his behalf in social situations. These individuals may provide examples of claimant behavior (Everington & Keyes, 1999).

The assessment of individuals who are in a prison setting presents unique challenges. The task of applying the adaptive behavior assessment information is to seek convergent validity for the information obtained. This requires an integration of information from all sources and the use of clinical judgment to achieve a finding that is as accurate as possible (Schalock & Luckasson, 2005). Clinical judgment is enhanced by systematic inquiry methods, adherence to professional standards, and a comprehensive knowledge of the characteristics of the disability, based on training and experience with this population (American Psychological Association, 2012). In the final analysis, discretion and clinical judgment are always warranted regarding the interpretation of the results of adaptive behavior. Conducting a thorough assessment of adaptive deficits will provide the triers-of-fact with a comprehensive, informed, unbiased, and validated evaluation.

References

American Psychological Association. (2012). Guidelines for assessment of and interventions with persons with disabilities. *American Psychologist, 67*, 43–62. doi: 10.1037/a0025892

Baroff, G. S., & Olley, J. G, (1999). *Mental retardation: Nature, causes, and management.* Philadelphia, PA: Taylor & Francis.

Blume, J. H., Johnson, S. L., & Seeds, C. (2009). Of *Atkins* and men: Deviations from clinical definitions of mental retardation in death penalty cases. *Cornell Journal of Law and Public Policy, 18*, 689–733. Retrieved from http://0-www.lexisnexis.com.library.winthrop.edu/hottopics/lnacademic/?

Beirne-Smith, M., Patton, J. R., & Kim, S. (2006). *Mental retardation: An introduction to intellectual disability* (7th ed.). Upper Saddle River, NJ: Merrill Prentice Hall.

Bonnie, R. J., & Gustafson, K. (2007). The challenge of implementing *Atkins v. Virginia*: How legislatures and courts can promote accurate assessments and adjudications of mental retardation in death penalty cases. *Richmond Law Review, 41*(4), 811–860.

Brodsky, S. L., & Galloway, V. A. (2003). Ethical and professional demands for forensic mental health professionals in the post-*Atkins* era. *Ethics and Behavior, 13*, 3–9.

Cohen, L.G., & Spenciner, L. J. (2011). *Assessment of children and youth with special needs* (4th ed.). Boston, MA: Pearson.

Drew, C. J., & Hardman, M. L. (2007). *Intellectual disabilities across the lifespan* (9th ed.). Upper Saddle River, NJ: Pearson.

Dunn, L. M., & Dunn, D. M. (2007). *Peabody Picture Vocabulary Test* (4th ed.). Minneapolis, MN: Pearson.

Edgerton, R. B. (1993). *The cloak of competence: Revised and updated.* Berkeley, CA: University of California Press.

Everington, C., & Keyes, D. (1999). Diagnosing mental retardation in criminal proceedings: The importance of documenting adaptive behavior. *Forensic Examiner, 8,* 31–34.

Everington, C., & Olley, J. G. (2008). Implications of *Atkins v. Virginia*: Issues in defining and diagnosing mental retardation. *Journal of Forensic Psychology Practice, 8*(1), 1–23.

Greenspan, S. (1999). A contextualist perspective on adaptive behavior. In R. L. Schalock & D. L. Braddock (Eds.), *Adaptive behavior and its measurement* (pp. 61–80). Washington, DC: American Association on Mental Retardation.

Greenspan, S., & Switzky, H. N. (2006). Lessons from the *Atkins* decision for the next AAMR manual. In H. N. Switzky & S. Greenspan (Eds.), *What is mental retardation? Ideas for an evolving disability in the 21st century* (pp. 283–302). Washington, DC: American Association on Mental Retardation.

Hammill, D. D., Brown, V. L., Larsen, S. C., & Wiederholt, J. L. (2007). *Test of Adolescent and Adult Language* (4th ed.). Austin, TX: Pro-Ed.

Harrison, P. L., & Oakland, T. (2003). *ABAS II: Adaptive behavior assessment system* (2nd ed.). San Antonio, TX: The Psychological Corporation.

Harrison, P. L., & Raineri, G. (2008). Best practices in the assessment of adaptive behavior. In A. Thomas & J. Grimes (Eds.), *Best practices in school psychology V* (Vol. 2, pp. 605–615). Washington, DC: National Association of School Psychologists.

Luckasson, R., Borthwick-Duffy, S. A., Buntinx, W. H. E., Coulter, D. L., Craig, E. M., Reeve, A., Schalock, R. L., Snell, M. E., Spitalnik, D. M., Spreat, S., & Tassé, M. J. (2002). *Mental retardation: Definition, classification, and systems of supports (10th ed.).* Washington DC: American Association on Intellectual and Developmental Disabilities.

Macvaugh, G. S., & Cunningham, M. D. (2009). *Atkins v. Virginia*: Implications and recommendations for forensic practice. *Journal of Psychiatry & Law, 37,* 131–187.

Nihira, K. (1999). Adaptive behavior: A historical overview. In R. L. Schalock & D. L. Braddock (Eds.), *Adaptive behavior and its measurement* (pp. 7–14). Washington, DC: American Association on Mental Retardation.

Olley, J. G. (2007). The assessment of adaptive behavior in adult forensic cases: Part 3: Sources of adaptive behavior information. *Psychology in Mental Retardation and Developmental Disabilities, 33,* 3–6.

Olley, J. G., & Cox, A. W. (2008). Assessment of adaptive behavior in adult forensic cases: The use of the Adaptive Behavior Assessment System–II. In T. Oakland & P. L. Harrison (Eds.), *Adaptive Behavior Assessment System II: Clinical use and interpretation* (pp. 381–398). San Diego, CA: Elsevier.

Overton, T. (2009). *Assessing learners with special needs: An applied approach,* (6th ed.). Upper Saddle River, NJ: Pearson.

Reschly, D. J. (2009). Documenting the developmental origins of mild mental retardation. *Applied Neuropsychology, 16,* 124–134. doi:10.1080/09084280902864469

Salvia, J., Ysseldyke, J. E., & Bolt, S. (2010). *Assessment in special education and inclusive education* (11th ed.). Belmont, CA: Wadsworth.

Schalock, R. L. (1999). The merging of adaptive behavior and intelligence: Implications for the field of mental retardation. In R. L. Schalock & D. L. Braddock (Eds.), *Adaptive behavior and its measurement* (pp. 43–59). Washington, DC: American Association on Mental Retardation.

Schalock, R. L., Borthwick-Duffy, S. A., Bradley, V. J., Buntinx, W.H.E., Coulter, D. L., Craig, E. M., Gomez, S. C., Lachapelle, Y., Luckasson, R., Reeve, A., Shogren, K. A., Snell, M. E., Spreat, S., Tassé, M. J., Thompson, J. R., Verdugo-Alonso, M. A., Wehmeyer, M. L., Yeager, M. H. (2010). *Intellectual disability: Definition, classification, and systems of supports (11th ed.).* Washington, DC: American Association on Intellectual and Developmental Disabilities.

Schalock, R. L., & Luckasson, R. L. (2005). *Clinical judgment.* Washington, DC: American Association on Mental Retardation.

Schalock, R. L., Luckasson, R., Bradley, V., Buntinx, W. H. E., Lachapelle, Y., Shogren, K. A., Snell, M. E., Thompson, J. R., Tassé, M. J., Verdugo-Alonso, M. A., and Wehmeyer, M. L. (2012). *User's guide to intellectual disability: Definition, classification, and systems of supports.* Washington, DC: American Association on Intellectual and Developmental Disabilities.

Scullen, M. H. (2006). Large state-level fluctuations in mental retardation classifications related to introduction of renormed intelligence tests. *American Journal on Mental Retardation, 111,* 322–335. doi: 10.1352/0895-8017(2006)111[322:LSFIMR]2.0.CO;2

Stevens, K. B., & Price, J. R. (2006). Adaptive behavior, mental retardation, and the death penalty. *Journal of Forensic Psychology Practice, 1,* 1–29.

Tassé, M. J. (2009). Adaptive behavior assessment and the diagnosis of mental retardation in capital cases. *Applied Neuropsychology, 16,* 114–123.

Tassé, M. J., Shalock, R. L., Balboni, G., Bothwick-Duffy, S. A., Bersani, H., Jr.,Spreat, S., Widaman, K. F., & Zhang, D. (2012). The construct of adaptive behavior: Its conceptualization, measurement, and use in the field of intellectual disability. *American Journal on Intellectual and Developmental Disabilities, 117,* 291–303. doi: 10.1352/1944-7558-117.4.291

Taylor, R. L. (2009) *Assessment of exceptional students* (8th ed.). Upper Saddle River, NJ: Pearson.

Tenn. Code Ann. § 39-13-203 (2011).

United States of America v. Joseph Smith (United States District Court: Eastern District of Louisiana June 23, 2011).

Widaman, K. F., & Siperstein, G. N. (2009). Assessing adaptive behavior of criminal defendants in capital cases: A reconsideration. *American Journal of Forensic Psychology, 27*(2), 5–32.

Wilkinson, G.S., & Robertson, G.J. (2006). *Wide Range Achievement Test 4.* Lutz, FL: Psychological Assessment Resources.

Woodcock, R.W., Schrank, F.A., McGrew, K.S., & Mather, N. (2007). *Woodcock-Johnson III,* Itasca, IL: Riverside.

Young, B., Boccaccini, M. T., Conroy, M. A., & Lawson, K. (2007). Four practical and conceptual assessment issues that evaluators should address in capital case mental retardation evaluations. *Professional Psychology: Research and Practice, 38*(2), 169–178. doi: 10.1037/0735-7028.38.2.169

14 | Time at Which Disability Must Be Shown in *Atkins* Cases

J. Gregory Olley

In writing for the majority in the *Atkins v. Virginia* (2002) decision, Justice Stevens stated with regard to people with intellectual disability (ID) (previously known as mental retardation) that "their deficiencies do not warrant an exemption from criminal sanctions, but they do diminish their personal culpability" (p. 14). Thus, the task of an expert in an *Atkins* proceeding is to gather evidence pertinent to the presence or absence of such "deficiencies."

In its landmark decision, however, the Supreme Court left many details regarding the establishment of such deficiencies unspecified. Justice Stevens wrote, "We leave to the State[s] the task of developing appropriate ways to enforce the constitutional restriction upon its execution of sentences" (p. 12). Among these details that affect the conduct of an assessment and testimony in an *Atkins* proceeding is the time at which the disability must be shown to be present.

As a practical matter, there are three times in the defendant's life in which a diagnosis of ID could be made: in childhood, at or near the time of the relevant crime, and at the present time. The Court opinion gives some guidance in this matter, but as the opinion indicated, the final decision is up to the individual states, the federal court, or the military court that holds jurisdiction.

Impairment in Childhood

The *Atkins* opinion made reference (albeit in a footnote) to definitions of ID in *Mental Retardation: Definition, Classification, and Systems of Supports* (9th ed.; Luckasson et al., 1992) and *Diagnostic and Statistical Manual of Mental Disorders* (4th ed., Rev.; APA, 2000) in establishing a diagnosis and noted that the definitions of most states conformed closely to these clinical definitions. An essential component of these definitions is the establishment of the disability in childhood (defined as before age 18). The *Intellectual Disability: Definition, Classification, and Systems of Supports* book (11th ed.; Schalock et al. 2010) and the accompanying *User's Guide to Intellectual Disability: Definition, Classification, and Systems of Supports* (Schalock et al. 2012) made clear that when making a retrospective diagnosis (looking back from adulthood), a formal diagnosis made in childhood is not required. It is simply required that the disability existed in childhood.

Reschly (2009) (see also Chapter 18) described the challenges in establishing the presence of impairment in childhood retrospectively. They have pointed to informative sources such as records from school, social services, medical, and psychological services. They have also suggested using information from parents, teachers, classmates, relatives, and friends. Of course, not all of these sources are likely to be available (e.g., school systems have varied policies on the destruction of records) and some may be compromised by factors such as the reluctance of schools to use the ID classification for students who do not have a clear medical syndrome (Reschly, 2009). Health and human services agencies are less likely to destroy records, although their record-keeping systems vary widely in their comprehensiveness. In some cases, a court order will be necessary for agencies to release records. Information from all of these sources should be examined as part of a thorough retrospective assessment of adaptive behavior.

Impairment at the Time of the Crime

The *Atkins v. Virginia* (2002) opinion appears to base its rationale for less moral culpability for people with ID on their impairment at the time of the crime. The opinion noted that, "because of their disabilities in areas of reasoning, judgment, and control of their impulses . . . they do not act with the level of moral culpability that characterizes the most serious adult criminal conduct" (p. 1). Further, with reference to criminal acts, the opinion described people with ID in the present tense, stating for instance, "in group settings, they are followers rather than leaders" (pp. 13–14).

Establishing impairment at the time of the crime is often difficult, but an argument may be made on the basis of the assumption that ID is a trait that continues throughout life. If the condition was established in childhood, it was likely to have continued to the time of the crime.

Schalock et al., (2010) pointed out the possibility that a person with the ID diagnosis, who is currently receiving appropriate supports, could improve his or her functioning to the point that he or she would no longer meet diagnostic criteria; however, the underlying disability would remain. Such a change would require that the defendant experienced educational or social enrichment to such a degree that his or her functioning significantly improved. The implications of this distinction are significant in *Atkins* cases if there is evidence of such change.

If an *Atkins* evaluation is completed soon after the crime, it is possible that the examiner would administer an intelligence test and conduct an appropriate adaptive behavior evaluation and that this information would be relevant and valid in establishing the defendant's functioning level at or near the time of the crime. Again, the assessment must look back from the time of the assessment to the time of the crime. If the assessment takes place in preparation for a trial, it may be looking back as little as a year or less to determine functioning at the time of the crime. However, if the assessment is carried out as part of an appellate process for a person on death row, it may require looking back 20 or more years. Thus, the assessment is inherently retrospective. As Schalock and colleagues (2012) and Olley and Cox (2008) pointed out, there are other circumstances in which mental health professionals are required to offer opinions about earlier functioning in a legal context and such assessments require clinical judgment. Examples include "testamentary capacity" (competence to make a will at the time of signing), eligibility for adult rehabilitation services or Social Security benefits, guardianship petitions, competence determinations, or issues of sentencing eligibility as described by Schalock and Luckasson (2005).

Impairment at the Current Time

In addition to requiring that ID be proven in childhood and at the time of the crime, most of the current 32 death penalty states, the U.S. government, and U.S. military require that the disability be shown at present. This requirement may be written into state statute or established by precedent. If the court looks to the wording of the *Atkins* opinion for guidance, it may appear that the justices expected the defendant to show impaired functioning at the present time, because, as noted in the previous section, the descriptions of ID are in the present tense. These statements may have occurred simply because it is a more convenient form of writing, or it may reflect the Court's assumption that ID is a lifelong condition.

Justice Stevens's exact intentions in this regard may never be known, but if a judge instructs an expert to conduct an evaluation of current functioning, the expert's options are limited. He or she may administer an intelligence test that would satisfy the requirement to show significant impairment in general intellectual functioning at the present. However, with regard to the assessment of current adaptive behavior, the expert cannot assess typical community functioning in multiple contexts for a person who is incarcerated.

The available choices for assessing current adaptive functioning include (a) prison records, (b) interviews with people who have observed the defendant's daily functioning (e.g., corrections officers, other inmates, prison health and mental health professionals), (c) interview with the defendant, and (d) direct testing of the defendant's performance. It is essential to keep in mind that a diagnosis of ID requires evidence of significant impairment of functioning. Each of these alternatives could provide such information, but each has limitations to its validity; issues regarding these limitations should be conveyed to the court. Evidence of adequate functioning in jail or prison does not validly generalize to typical community functioning and does not rule out a diagnosis of ID.

With regard to an expert's direct testing or observation of performance, prisons differ in the access allowed for observation and the types of materials that experts are allowed to bring into the prison. Laptop computers are often prohibited without court orders; anything that can be used or made into a weapon or a means for escape is also prohibited. As discussed in Chapters 12 and 13, current academic functioning can be assessed through standardized tests and informal tasks, such as writing a letter, or using a ruler, a map, or a telephone book. These tasks provide helpful information, although they do not fully assess functional academics as described in Luckasson et al., (1992) or by APA (2000). Other aspects of community functioning cannot validly be assumed on the basis of prison behavior. The Independent Living Scales (Loeb, 1996) can be administered directly to the defendant in prison and is composed of five scales: Memory/Orientation, Managing Money, Managing Home and Transportation, Health and Safety, and Social Adjustment. The ILS provides a sample of adaptive behavior and knowledge of adaptive behavior, although its emphasis is on instrumental activities of daily living.

As Chapters 12 and 13 and Greenspan and Switzky (2006) have noted, an interview with corrections officers who have known the defendant in prison may document significant impairment within the limited demands of prison particularly for death row inmates. If corrections officers report that the defendant shows no impaired functioning, one cannot know whether the report would be the same if the defendant were living and functioning in the community.

It is common practice to interview a defendant; however, a defendant's self-report of adaptive functioning in or outside of prison should be viewed with caution. Further, the process of interviewing an individual with ID in any circumstances presents problems of validity. As described by Olley (2012),

> Research has identified many pitfalls in interviewing people with ID (Finlay & Lyons, 2001, 2002; Perry, 2004). . . further interviews may be influenced by the communication limitations of the defendant (e.g., difficulty understanding the questions, particularly those of a conceptual nature, or difficulty responding to open-ended questions) or the tendency to try to hide one's limitations (i.e., the cloak of competence). (p. 232)

The purpose of interviews is to gather information about a defendant's performance in order that the expert can form an opinion regarding that defendant's diagnosis of ID. It is quite inappropriate to ask lay witnesses or the defendant "Do you think that [the defendant] has an intellectual disability?" Such a question injects bias into the interview, and, of course, those being interviewed are not qualified to make a diagnosis. The expert offers an opinion and the final decision lies with the court.

Research has not addressed the possible changes that may occur in intelligence or adaptive functioning for people with ID (or lower functioning that approximates ID) while incarcerated. Haney and Specter (2001) addressed the stressful, perhaps traumatic effects of incarceration and the increased vulnerability of many special populations. Xenitidis, Fotiadou, and Murphy (2010) noted that there are many factors that put people with ID at a disadvantage in prison. At the same time, it should be noted that the prison experience is not uniform. Would the general vulnerability of people with ID make them more likely to be traumatized or otherwise further impaired by the prison experience? Would the predictable and structured nature of prison life make the person with ID appear to be functioning well? Would the prison experience with healthy meals, exercise, social contacts, absence of drugs and alcohol, proper medical care, and possibly formal education (e.g., GED classes) or cable television be likely to result in improved scores on IQ tests?

All of these uncertainties make it impossible for the expert to know with full confidence the validity of an evaluation of current functioning for a defendant who is incarcerated.

Conclusion and Implications for Practice

This chapter has focused on the question of the time when ID must be shown. Three timeframes were discussed, including in childhood, at the time of the crime, and at the present time. Given these three time frames, it is important that court expectations be established regarding which of these three timeframes are necessary in order to confirm the disability.

Due to the fact that ID must meet a developmental criterion (see Chapter 6), it can be assumed that ID must have been present during childhood (before the age of 18). Although it is not necessary that a formal assessment be available from that time period, there must be a demonstration that the condition of intellectual disability did exist in childhood. Chapter 12 provides a detailed discussion of the sources of information that can inform the expert's opinion regarding adaptive behavior.

The court may also seek information on the other two respective timeframes. With regard to the time of the commission of the crime, assessments of intellectual functioning and adaptive behavior administered at or near that time are preferable. Otherwise, retrospective assessment will be needed; Chapter 18 provides further guidance. Finally, if the court requires assessment of current functioning of an individual who is incarcerated, it is important that the examiner and the court be aware of the limitations of assessing adaptive behavior within this restricted environment.

References

American Psychiatric Association. (2000). *Diagnostic and statistical manual of mental disorders* (4th ed., Rev.). Washington, DC: Author.

Atkins v. Virginia, 536 U.S. 304 (2002).

Finlay, W. M. L., & Lyons, E. (2001). Methodological issues in interviewing and using self-report questionnaires with people with mental retardation. *Psychological Assessment, 13*, 319–335. doi: 10.1037/1040-3590.13.3.319

Finlay, W. M. L., & Lyons, E. (2002). Acquiescence in interviews with people who have mental retardation. *Mental Retardation, 40*, 14–29.

Greenspan, S., & Switzky, H. N. (2006). Lessons from the *Atkins* decision for the next AAMR manual. In H. N. Switzky & S. Greenspan (Eds.) *What is mental retardation? Ideas for an evolving disability in the 21st century* (Rev. ed., pp. 283–302). Washington, DC: American Association on Mental Retardation.

Haney, C., & Specter, D. (2001). Vulnerable offenders and the law: Treatment rights in uncertain legal times. In J. Ashford, B. Sales, & W. Reid (Eds.), *Treating adult and juvenile offenders with special needs* (pp. 51–79). Washington, DC: American Psychological Association.

Loeb, P. A. (1996). *Independent Living Scales*. San Antonio, TX: Pearson.

Luckasson, R., Coulter, D. L., Polloway, E. A., Reiss, S., Schalock, R. L., Snell, M. E., . . . Stark, J. A. (1992). *Mental retardation: Definition, classification, and systems of supports (9th ed.)*. Washington, DC: American Association on Mental Retardation.

Olley, J. G. (2012). The death penalty, the courts, and intellectual disability. In J. K. Luiselli (Ed.), *The handbook of high-risk challenging behaviors: Assessment and intervention* (pp. 229–240). Baltimore, MD: Brookes.

Olley, J. G., & Cox, A. W. (2008). Assessment of adaptive behavior in adult forensic cases: The use of the Adaptive Behavior Assessment System-II. In T. Oakland & P. L. Harrison (Eds.), *Adaptive Behavior Assessment System-II: Clinical use and interpretation* (pp. 381–398). San Diego, CA: Elsevier.

Perry, J. (2004). Interviewing people with intellectual disabilities. In E. Emerson, C. Hatton, T. Thompson, & T. R. Parmenter (Eds.), *International handbook of applied research in intellectual disabilities* (pp. 115–131). West Sussex, England: Wiley.

Reschly, D. J. (2009). Documenting the developmental origins of mild mental retardation. *Applied Neuropsychology, 16*, 124–134. doi:10.1080/09084280902864469

Schalock, R. L., Borthwick-Duffy, S. A., Bradley, V. J., Buntinx, W. H. E., Coulter, D. L., Craig, E. M., Gomez, S. C., Lachapelle, Y., Luckasson, R., Reeve, A., Shogren, K. A., Snell, M. E., Spreat, S., Tassé, M. J., Thompson, J. R., Verdugo-Alonso, M. A., Wehmeyer, M. L., & Yeager, M. H. (2010). *Intellectual disability: Definition, classification, and systems of supports (11th ed.)*. Washington, DC: American Association on Intellectual and Developmental Disabilities.

Schalock, R. L., Luckasson, R., Bradley, V., Buntinx, W. H. E., Lachapelle, Y., Shogren, K. A., Snell, M. E., Thompson, J. R., Tassé, M. J., Verdugo-Alonso, M. A., and Wehmeyer, M. L. (2012). *User's guide to intellectual disability: Definition, classification, and systems of supports*. Washington, DC: American Association on Intellectual and Developmental Disabilities.

Schalock, R. L., & Luckasson, R. (2005). *Clinical judgment*. Washington, DC: American Association on Mental Retardation.

Xenitidis, K., Fotiadou, M., & Murphy, G. H. (2010). People with intellectual disabilities in prison. In S. Wilson (Ed.), *Psychiatry in prisons: A comprehensive handbook* (pp. 107–124). London, England: Jessica Kingsley.

15 | The Briseño Factors

Stephen Greenspan

The Briseño factors are named after Jose Briseño, whose *Atkins* case (*Ex Parte Briseño*, 2004) was the first one addressed by the Texas Court of Criminal Appeals. It consists of a list of seven questions that the Texas high court indicated should be asked when determining whether or not a petitioner meets prong 2 (adaptive behavior; prong 1 refers to intellectual deficits, while prong 3 refers to developmental period onset). This diagnostic scheme was devised outside of, and with no reference to, any official clinical manuals (e.g., AAIDD and DSM). Because the Briseño factors emerged out of a purely legal context (what the late evolutionary theorist Stephen Jay Gould (1982) termed a *punctuated* or *branched* development), this (essentially alternative adaptive behavior) formulation is addressed in this chapter, rather than, for example, in Chapter 11 which discusses the gradual professional evolution of conceptions of adaptive behavior.

Few if any intellectual disability (ID) scholars, representative bodies, or specialists consider that the Briseño factors provide a valid diagnostic framework. However, several courts have accepted them or found them credible not only in Texas but also in other jurisdictions (e.g., 2012 ruling by the Pennsylvania Supreme Court [*Commonwealth v. Jose DeJesus, 2012*]) .

In Chapter 22 and also in an earlier article by MacVaugh and Cunningham (2009), an important observation is made about the Briseño factors: that they are grounded in the lay stereotype of ID as what would historically be considered *moderate* or *severe*, rather than ID at the upper end of the spectrum. More broadly, the authors urged experts in an *Atkins* case to ask if "the assessment of adaptive functioning has been distorted by focusing on verbal behavior, criminal conduct, stereotypes of intellectual [disability], and/or strengths rather than deficits?" With regard to the Briseño factors, unfortunately the answer is *yes* to all four of these tendencies.

Briseño Factors Listed

The Briseño factors were published in 2004 by the Texas Court of Criminal Appeals. An apparent intent was to make attaining *Atkins* relief more difficult for petitioners whose impairments were not in line with the court's common sense (i.e., more severe) conception of the characteristics of people with ID.

In the Briseño decision, the intent to make obtaining *Atkins* relief more difficult was explicitly stated when the court indicated that the Texas statutory ID definition (based on national clinical standards) used in determining eligibility for residential or habilitative services was intended to cast a wide safety net. In contrast, the court believed that the citizens of Texas, through their judicial system (note: there is no Texas *Atkins* statute) are entitled to cast a narrower net when determining exemption from the death penalty. (Many would argue, to the contrary—that given the seriousness of a death sentence, one should set the eligibility bar lower in a capital case.) It is interesting that the court noted that Lenny, the impaired central character in Steinbeck's (1937) *Of Mice and Men* and who probably had an IQ around 45 or 50, "might" be considered to be *Atkins*-eligible for his obvious limitations in reasoning ability. In contrast, the court asserted that there are many others who are less obviously impaired than Lenny who could legitimately be found to not have ID by judges presiding in Texas *Atkins* cases, even if they had been found to have ID by a Texas human services eligibility office.

There was no scientific or legal source provided for the Briseño factors, which were devised to narrow the ID population to people who, like Lenny, have ID at the lower end of the spectrum. No justification was provided for this framework other than a stated belief that it helps to clarify a confusing construct. Nor did the Court provide an explanation regarding why it believed persons who could perform the behaviors specified in the Briseño factors should not be eligible for *Atkins* relief. Therefore, the factors reflect an intuitive or common sense belief by the Texas Court of Criminal Appeals as to what the subset of the ID population deserving *Atkins* protection is "like" or, more to the point, is "not like."

In rejecting the *Atkins* petition by Jose Briseño, the court (*Ex Parte Briseño, 2004*) declared that the criteria for assessing adaptive behavior were too subjective, and provided a list of questions that a judge or jury should consider and that they believed were more objective. Implicit in this list is the idea that if the answer is *yes* to some or all of these factors, then the petition should be denied. The Briseño factors questions to be asked are:

- Did those who knew the person best during the developmental stage—his family, friends, teachers, employers, authorities—think he had MR (ID) at that time, and, if so, act in accordance with that determination?
- Has the person formulated plans and carried them through or is his conduct impulsive?
- Does his conduct show leadership or does it show that he is led around by others?

- Is his conduct in response to external stimuli rational and appropriate, regardless of whether it is socially acceptable?
- Does he respond coherently, rationally, and on point to oral or written questions or do his responses wander from subject to subject?
- Can he hide facts or lie effectively in his own or others' interests?
- Putting aside any heinousness or gruesomeness surrounding the capital offense, did the commission of that offense require forethought, planning, and complex execution of purpose?

The Implicit Taxon Underlying the Briseño Factors

It is estimated that the majority of defendants in capital cases who qualify for a diagnosis of ID fall at the upper end of the spectrum. Virtually all *Atkins* claimants, whether successful in their petition or not, can be found in the pool of people who have impairment severity levels that fall in, or just above, the upper end of the ID spectrum. People with moderate levels of severity (previously defined as having IQ test scores between roughly 40–55) are typically not subjected to *Atkins* proceedings, as most are so obviously impaired that diversion from execution (or, for that matter, from being tried at all) is almost automatic. However, as mentioned frequently throughout this book, ID at the upper end of the spectrum is a somewhat hidden disability, as many individuals who apply for *Atkins* relief do not stand out in appearance or behavior in routine (especially brief) settings as obviously impaired. Most of these individuals exhibit competence profiles that are fairly mixed, which conflicts with the lay conception of people with ID as globally deficient. Certainly, when the *Intellectual Disability: Definition, Classification, and Systems of Supports* (11th ed., Schalock et al., 2010) and the *Diagnostic and Statistical Manual of Mental Disorders* (4th ed. Rev., [DSM 4 TR], American Psychiatric Association [APA], 2000) manuals prescribed that one need be significantly impaired in only 1-out-of-3 (Schalock et al., 2010) or 2-out-of-11 (APA, 2000) skill areas, the obvious implication is that one could be competent in other adaptive domains without jeopardizing one's ID status. The *Diagnostic and Statistical Manual of Mental Disorders* (5th ed., [DSM-5], APA, 2013) adopted the 2010 AAIDD-11 formula of 1-out-of-3 adaptive domain deficits. It follows, therefore, that the clinical standards that are used in most jurisdictions do not specify any prong 2 deficits that "make or break" an ID diagnosis.

The Briseño factors diverge from this mixed profile emphasis, in that certain prong 2 behaviors (e.g., carrying on a coherent and focused conversation) are believed by the Texas court to rule out a diagnosis of ID in a criminal manner. Whether a state legislature or high court can redefine ID in an idiosyncratic manner that diverges substantially from professional norms is a question that has begun to be raised in the courts. In *Chester v. Thaler* (2011), attorneys for the Texas condemned prisoner Elroy Chester argued that the Briseño factors did not provide an appropriate basis for rejecting their clients' petition for ID status. That claim was rejected by the Federal courts, and the U.S. Supreme Court in 2012 refused to hear the case. An Oklahoma case, *Hooks v. Workman* (2012) is also relevant, in that the 10th Circuit Court of Appeals accepted the state's claim that evidence of strengths (something central to the Briseño factors) could be a basis for denying a claim of ID by condemned prisoner Victor Wayne Hooks. Other cases, involving a more fully developed challenge to the Briseño factors, are likely to be filed in the future. The U.S. Supreme Court will likely have to decide whether or not the Briseño framework creates an obvious conflict with clearly established federal law.

Analyzing the Seven Briseño Factors

As previously noted, the Briseño factors—which lack any theoretical or empirical basis-reflect a view of the disorder that is inappropriate for most of the incarcerated ID population. In this section, the focus is on each of the seven factors and on two questions that the Texas high court did not ask: (1) Does this factor have any support either in research or clinical experience as a reasonable criterion for ruling ID in or (more relevantly) out?, and (2) Is it possible to collect information about this factor in a manner that is measurable and valid?

Factor 1: Being Labeled or Referred to as Having ID During the Developmental Period

Two kinds of labeling are covered by this factor: (a) official labeling (e.g., by a school district or a human services agency), and (b) informal labeling (e.g., by peers, neighbors, employers, or family members).

First, being officially labeled ID, for example by a school system, is dependent on many extraneous factors. These factors include (a) economics (ID services are expensive), (b) family preference and sophistication (many families may oppose the label or fail to appreciate its need), (c) legal rulings (in California, because of *Larry P. v. Riles,* 495 F. Supp. 926, 1979, minority children are rarely labeled ID and never administered IQ tests), (d) culture (as a rule, the problems of almost all poor minority children are attributed to upbringing, even when there are overt signs of brain abnormalities), and (e) professional competence (it is not uncommon to find general and special educators who lack any training in ID and thus may operate on basic misconceptions concerning ID when testifying about one of their former students).

Although the majority of *Atkins* petitioners have a clear history of school failure and nonachievement, many of them (including many whose *Atkins* petitions were ultimately successful) were never labeled ID in school. A more common pattern seen in many case files is for a student to have been repeatedly retained in grade as many as three or four times, or given an alternative label. Learning disability is the label most typically designated, even when the official criteria (near average or average IQ and deficits in isolated academic areas) are not met.

Unofficial labeling (such as being called "retard" by peers or family members) is undoubtedly more common than official labeling for individuals with ID, but it is by no means universal. This is another area in which cultural and familial processes must be considered. For example, the individual may have grown up in a family in which there are parents, siblings, and peers who have significant cognitive limitations, and within such a community context, the defendant may not appear noticeably different or deficient. Although perceptions of others, gathered from a formal rating instrument such as the Adaptive Behavior Assessment System, 2nd edition (ABAS-2; Harrison & Oakland, 2003), should be part of the diagnostic process, there may be a disconnect between how a professional views an individual and the words used to describe that individual. For example, a special educator in one case stated that she did not think of the defendant as having ID, yet her ABAS ratings were extremely low and very much in line with other professionals who were willing to use the ID label. She stated that her reason for not viewing him as having ID was because he had friends from his neighborhood who were nondisabled who came to wait for him when his (special) school got out. It was her mistaken belief that adolescents with ID never have typically developing friends. The friends whom she saw coming for him after school had grown up on the same block as the defendant and saw him as a surrogate sibling. Thus, while having been seen as significantly impaired as a child or adolescent is a common experience for adults with ID, it is not a universal one and should not be used to conclude that a person does not have a legitimate claim to ID status.

Factor 2: Formulating Plans as Opposed to Being Impulsive

Impulsivity is one characteristic mentioned by the U.S. Supreme Court in its *Atkins* decision as a reason why individuals with ID deserve exemption from imposition of the ultimate penalty. It appeared to have been intended as illustrative and not as a diagnostic criterion, in that the court avoided any mention of a definition of ID (other than pointing to the AAIDD and DSM for guidance). Impulsivity is an almost universal indicator of brain impairment (Einfeld & Aman, 1995) and is a common behavioral characteristic of people with a variety of psychiatric and cognitive disorders (Webster & Jackson, 1997). It is especially characteristic of individuals with attention deficit hyperactivity disorder (ADHD), although the diagnostic focus with ADHD is really on disordered attention rather than impulsivity (Barkley, 1997). Impulsivity has never been a part of any official definition of ID for the obvious reason that impulsivity is a dimension of one's personality and people with ID vary widely in their personalities. Although many, if not most, people with ID may behave impulsively (in part because of the high co-occurrence of brain damage), to argue that a person who does *not* exhibit marked impulsivity cannot have ID is simply incorrect, given that many people with ID have calm and deliberative modes of functioning.

Another problem with using the absence of impulsivity to dispute a diagnosis of ID is that even highly impulsive people do not exhibit impulsivity all of the time or in every situation. As with the other six Briseño factors, one needs to look at the context in which the impulsive or non-impulsive conduct occurred. Impulsivity can take many forms and have various causes, but the aspect most relevant to diagnosing ID involves cognitive confusion as to how to proceed in a given situation rather than a general absence of response inhibition. Making too abrupt a decision (e.g., whether to accept an invitation to participate in a crime) is less a matter of impulsivity and more a matter of an inability to make intelligent judgments. Approached as a personality style and not as a reflection of intellectual (including executive functioning) limitations, this Briseño factor is therefore not, a reliable basis for diagnosing ID.

Planning is worded in this factor as if it is the opposite of impulsivity, but that is not the case. Even persons who are highly impulsive (and cognitively impaired) can and do make plans (e.g., go the movies, retire for the night early). The relevant questions here pertain to how one defines planning, and how much planning a person can exhibit before one can say the person cannot have ID. Furthermore, even if it were established that people with ID cannot make multistep plans, it is typically difficult if not impossible to know how much help, if any, a person may have had in formulating and carrying out a given plan. The research basis for such a generalization in the real-world is far from clear-cut; on neuropsychological measures, such deficits are more clearly identifiable. This factor, like several others, provides a basis not for greater clarity but for increased confusion and debate.

Factor 3: Showing Leadership as Opposed to Being Led

Social vulnerability, including gullibility, in people with ID has become an important research interest (e.g., Greenspan & Love, 1997). It is increasingly being recognized that people with ID tend to adapt to (and to some extent cover up) their cognitive limitations by following the lead of others. That is especially likely to be the case in complex situations where the correct course of action is unclear. Therefore, of all of the seven Briseño factors, this one has the most validity.

As with any outcome that one might consider a sign of social competence, however, there are multiple ways of achieving a higher status (e.g., through shooting vs. persuading rivals); therefore, attaining a high status should be viewed in terms of certain questions. These questions pertain to (a) specific context (i.e., who are the people being led, and is it all the time or just on one occasion?), (b) the supports the individual may have had (i.e., are there others who perform some of the functions that leaders might normally be expected to perform?), and (c) whether deeper investigation might show that what looks like leadership may actually be a sign of following (i.e., did someone let the individual think he was a leader by giving him a gun and telling him to rob a victim so that he would be culpable if the plan went awry?).

In the *Atkins* literature, there is a term *the myth of the kingpin* (Lohman, 2012) that relates to the fact that individuals who are alleged to be leaders (an impression sometimes advanced by their own need to tell others how important they are), often turn out to have played no, or a very minor, role in the gang or other enterprise in which they are allegedly involved.

A problem with how this factor is interpreted or implemented is that occasionally asserting oneself or saying *no,* is not incompatible with being gullible or passive on many other occasions. An expert opinion in court testimony that someone is gullible may be challenged by pointing out several occasions in which the individual did not exhibit gullibility. However, it is important to note that (a) gullibility manifests when there is coercive pressure, and in many instances it may be cited that there is no coercion present; and (b) being gullibly misled, even in people with ID, can be a relatively low-frequency event, that one only has to manifest occasionally in very dangerous situations in order to seriously jeopardize the person's survival or future well-being. It can, therefore, be totally misleading to focus on a seemingly contrary example and assert that the person lacks the vulnerability that generally characterizes the social functioning of people with ID.

Factor 4: Conduct in Response to External Stimuli Is Rational and Appropriate

Rationality is a poorly defined concept, in both law and psychology. Most definitions are circular (e.g., "uses reason") and do not clarify the core ability or deficit that is involved. Rationality is a concept more applicable to mental illness where the focus is on deviant behavior driven more by emotion than capacity, but even there, it is a subject that has proven resistant to definition or measurement. The concept of *appropriateness* is also vague, as it incorporates both adherence to convention (such as table manners) as well as acting in accordance with, or against, one's interests. Both rationality and appropriateness are situation-specific, as individuals can behave appropriately and seemingly rationally in some situations and non-rationally and inappropriately in others. To imply that people with ID act inappropriately and without rationality in any and all circumstances is to exhibit a limited understanding of the characteristics of people with ID.

In Chapter 11, in discussing the Utah definition of prong 2 as non-rationality and impulsivity, it was noted that non-rationality has diagnostic relevance for ID if one reframes it as obliviousness to social or physical risk. (For a discussion of risk-unawareness as a diagnostic indicator, see Greenspan, Switzky, & Woods, 2011.) Even when risk-unawareness is manifested, such poor judgment is likely to be noted on occasion, and most often in non-obvious and ambiguous situations.

Factor 5: Oral and Written Communication Is Coherent, Rational, and On Point

Of all the Briseño factors, written and oral communication may be the aspect of everyday functioning that most ties into the popular stereotype that characterizes people with ID. That stereotype, which derives from the functioning of people with *moderate* or *severe ID*, is reinforced in popular portrayals on television (e.g., Mickey Rooney as Bill Sackler, a real-life formerly institutionalized man said to have an IQ of 50, who ran a coffee stand at the University of Iowa) or film (e.g., Sean Penn in *I Am Sam*, who played a fictionalized single parent with ID facing the possibility of losing custody of his daughter). Such a stereotype calls to mind people who speak in simple sentences—with impaired syntax, vocabulary, and grammar—or who write (if they do so at all) at an early elementary school level. Although people with ID at the upper end of the spectrum do often have communication deficits, these characteristics are more likely to appear on formal measures of complex syntax and comprehension, rather than in superficial conversations or simple written communications (Abbeduto, 2003).

Even outside of or prior to Briseño, such stereotypes often have been used in *Atkins* proceedings when evidence of seemingly "typical" oral or written communication was sometimes used to argue that a petitioner could not possibly have ID. Regarding oral communication, Kernan and Sabsay (1988, 1992) have shown in their research that adults with ID at the upper end of the spectrum have relatively normal syntax, vocabulary, and grammar. Therefore, listening to a recorded phone conversation can be misleading to a judge or jury, who may lack experience with adults with this type of disability and therefore do not understand that a diagnosis of ID cannot reliably be based on a sample of verbal behavior, no matter how "normal" it might sound.

People with ID at the upper end of the spectrum typically do have communication deficits, but these are more in the area of sociolinguistics (i.e., referential aspects of language, as in how one recognizes and corrects a mistaken understanding) than psycholinguistics (i.e., formal aspects of language, as in how grammatically correct an utterance is; Rosenberg & Abbeduto, 1993, pp. 137–138). Thus, the wording of the factor in terms of communicative adequacy is not entirely groundless. The problem is in how it is defined and measured. In terms of perspective-taking (i.e., the aspect of social intelligence most involved in referential communication adequacy), communicative deficits are most likely to appear when (a) the speaker and listener have different informational needs, (b) communication goes off track and needs to be repaired, or (c) communication is inappropriate to the attainment of some larger goal. A common example is the defendant discussing his legal case on the phone, in spite of repeatedly being warned not to do that. In stereotypic situations, such as bantering with a spouse or friend, circumstances likely to shed light on sociolinguistic inadequacies are typically not present.

Written letters or correctional complaints are another form of communication in which the functioning of adults with ID at the upper end of the spectrum may come into conflict with stereotypic notions held by laypeople. First, it is necessary to understand that some writing and reading skills are well within the behavioral repertoire of most people with this disability. Even so, it is common for inmates who are cognitively limited, even those on death row, to receive help from more competent peers to produce letters or legal documents that seem relatively polished and coherent. Once such a document is produced, it becomes a template that the defendant uses to produce such written documents repeatedly. Sometimes, this verges on *hypergraphia*, an overwhelming urge to write constantly that is often associated with brain damage, particularly in the temporal lobe (Schacter, Holmes, & Kasteleijn-Nolst Trenite, 2008). Inmates with hypergraphia can write thousands of letters to family members, attorneys, jailers, judges, or news outlets, often making the same points repeatedly. Such a pattern may give the formal appearance of being coherent and rational, whether or not it should be considered a sign of social effectiveness or communicative competence.

This factor is worded entirely in expressive aspects of language, but receptive language is not addressed. Receptive language is often impaired in adults with ID, but that ability area must be assessed as part of a formal overall battery, not estimated by interpretation of an action on a given day.

Factor 6: Lies or Hides Facts Effectively in Advancing One's Own or Others' Interests

Lying is virtually a universal behavior that starts early in childhood; it may begin around age 2 or 3, although understanding that one is lying starts around age 4. It occurs for the same reason that adults lie—that is, to obtain some objective or to avoid getting in trouble. Just as most children lie, it should not be surprising that many adults with ID lie. The question is whether they can lie *effectively*, as the wording of this factor emphasizes.

There is no doubt that young children do not lie effectively, as in the classic story of a 3-year-old who, when asked by her mother if she produced the puddle at her feet replied, "No, it was my shoes that did it." The main reason why young children do not lie effectively is that they lack the ability to take the perspective of others (Selman, 1971) and, thus, do not understand that listeners may possess knowledge (such as that shoes do not urinate) that enables them to know when the lie is not credible.

Perspective-taking in typically developing children develops at about the time they enter kindergarten or first grade (Chandler, Greenspan, & Barenboim, 1974). There is no question that adults with ID can and do lie effectively in many situations, but it is probably the case (given their lesser degree of social intelligence) that they are more likely to lie ineffectively in other situations. Aside from the lack of scientific support for this factor (there is little or no research on the topic), it also leads to two questions: (1) How do we decide when lying is "effective?" (the fact that a deceptive effort is transparent suggests it may not be so effective), and (2) Is a single instance of seemingly effective lying enough to prove that the person does not, and cannot, have ID? To answer *yes* to this last question would make it almost impossible to find any *Atkins* petitioner to have ID.

Factor 7: The Capital Offense Showed Forethought, Planning, and Complexity

In a pretrial *Atkins* hearing, testifying experts conducting *Atkins* evaluations are generally prohibited from asking the defendant about the facts of the alleged crime because of the strong possibility that this would interfere with a petitioner's right against self-incrimination (*Centeno v. California Superior Court*, 2004). As the petitioner in a pre-trial proceeding has not yet been convicted of anything, using the alleged facts of the crime is by necessity based on police reports and prosecutorial allegations.

In a postconviction *Atkins* case or when using facts from previous criminal convictions, utilizing details of an offense may be less problematic from a legal standpoint, but can still be problematic in terms of informational adequacy for diagnostic purposes. That is because crime facts are not typically revealed in sufficient detail to know the exact sequence of events, including the possible role of others in planning or helping the individual to carry out the crime. An example of this is the case of Walter Centeno (*Centeno v. Califonia Supreme Court*, 2004), who died in his jail cell on the morning his pre-trial *Atkins* hearing was to commence. It was argued that a person with ID could not have planned and carried out the robberies (one of which turned deadly) of beauty parlors and small female-run retail stores. However, it was unknown whether the defendant received any training from a more competent member of a gang with which he was affiliated. Furthermore, robberies may become homicidal when the script goes awry and the perpetrator panics. In *Centeno v. Califonia Supreme Court* (2004) and other similar cases, there was insufficient information to know whether or not a crime, which on the surface appeared to be a sign of competence, may in fact have been a sign of incompetence. For example, in a survey of approximately 200 cases, Haydt (2012) found that in the majority of the capital crimes allegedly or actually committed by *Atkins* petitioners, many of them involving some degree of planning contained a strong element of impulsivity. Consequently, how can it be determined if a crime is sufficiently sophisticated to activate this Briseño factor?

An additional point is that even when people who may have ID commit a homicide according to a plan (and most crimes involve some planning), the plans may be inept in both nature and execution. It has been argued that the essence of ID is an absence of common sense (i.e., unawareness of risk due to generally poor judgment; see Greenspan, Switzky & Woods, 2011). To argue that evidence of planning rules out ID, without considering whether the plan made sense, is to make this perhaps the least defensible of the Briseño factors.

Citing such considerations, in addition to the absence of research-based norms for determining whether or not people with ID are capable of, for example shooting a gun, imposing their will on victims, or carrying out robberies, the AAIDD's *User's Guide to Mental Retardation: Definition, Classification, and Systems of Supports* (Schalock et al., 2007) argued strongly against using crime facts as a basis for determining whether or not a person has or does not have ID.

As for the complexity, forethought, and planning of such crimes, the same reasons for questioning the applicability of Briseño factor #2 (i.e., planning vs. impulsivity) applies here. In part, that is because a strong lesson of the "community revolution in ID services" (Bradley & Knoll, 1995, pp. 5–6) is that we have come to learn that people with ID are more capable of many age-relevant activities (such as employment and independent living) than previously appreciated, and there is no reason to think that the ability to carry out crimes is exempt from such a finding.

Conclusion

A basic principle underlying the professional/clinical approach to prong 2 is that people with ID, especially ID at the upper end of the spectrum, have strengths mixed with deficits. This means that (a) one can be competent in some domains even while incompetent in others, and (b) even in domains where one is generally competent, there can be occasions of marked incompetence, sometimes as a function of the complexity of specific situational demands. The Briseño factors essentially argue that people with ID are uniformly incompetent, and therefore that any instance of competence means that the person cannot have ID.

In addition to the lack of research validity that incompetence on any of the Briseño factors are universal definers of the behavioral phenotype for ID, there are three practical problems with using these factors as an exclusionary template in *Atkins* cases. The first is that there is limited appreciation of the role of context (especially complexity) of the situation in which the behavior occurred. People with ID are generally less competent in complex or demanding situations, and one can find examples of people with ID doing well in noncomplex or nondemanding situations.

A second point concerns confusion regarding where one draws the line in terms of the relative frequency of a behavior. In other words, is a single example of an apparently coherent conversation (regardless of context) enough to decide a person should be found non-ID on factor 5, or does the person have to have coherent conversations all of the time? Related to this is the question of how many Briseño factor questions have to be answered *yes*. Is one factor enough to rule out ID or is a greater number required?

A third point pertains to the relative lack of definition of many, if not most, of the terms that are used in the factors. For example, few terms in psychology or law are more vague or subject to interpretation than *rationality,* and one can find occasional instances of apparent rationality even in people with more significant levels of ID.

The debate over the validity of the Briseño factors would be an academic exercise were it not for the empirical finding (Blume, Johnson, & Seed, 2010; Tobolowsky, 2011) that reliance upon the factors results in a much higher than average rejection of *Atkins* claims. As pointed out by Macvaugh (personal communication, February 12, 2013), the debate over the Briseño factors also reveals that *Atkins* rulings are psycho-legal decisions rather than psycho-diagnostic decisions. Psycho-legal decisions (such as whether to find a defendant incompetent or legally insane) are affected by a jurisdiction's political milieu, as reflected in the fact that states vary widely in their courts' and jurors' willingness to consider mitigating or exempting criminal responsibility due to mental factors. The use of the Briseño factors directly relates to the question of whether or not defendants who have an intellectual disability will continue to be exempted from the death penalty.

References

Abbeduto, L. (Ed.). (2003*). International review of research in mental retardation: Language and communication in mental retardation.* San Diego, CA: Academic/ Elsevier.

American Psychiatric Association. (2000). *Diagnostic and statistical manual of mental disorders* (4th ed., Rev.). Washington, DC: Author.

American Psychiatric Association. (2013). *Diagnostic and statistical manual of mental disorders, fifth edition: DSM-5.* Washington, DC: Author.

Barkley, R. A. (1997). Behavioral inhibition, sustained attention, and executive functions: Constructing a unifying theory of ADHD. *Psychological Bulletin, 121*(1), 65–94.

Blume, J. H., Johnson, S. L., & Seeds, C. (2010). *Implementing (or nullifying) Atkins: The impact of state procedural choices on outcomes in capital cases where intellectual disability is at issue.* Retrieved from Social Science Research Network http:ssrn.com/abstract=1670108

Bradley, V. J., & Knoll, J. A. (1995). Switching paradigms in services for people with developmental disabilities. In O. C. Karan & S. Greenspan (Eds.), *Community rehabilitation services for people with disabilities* (pp. 5–19). Newton, MA: Butterworth-Heinemann.

Chandler, M. J., Greenspan, S., & Barenboim, C. (1974).The assessment and training of role-taking and referential communication skills in institutionalized emotionally disturbed children. *Developmental Psychology, 10,* 546–533.

Chester v. Thaler, 666 F.3d 340 (5th Cir. 2011).

Centeno v. California Superior Court, No. B170615, March 2004.

Commonwealth v. Jose DeJesus, No. 546 CAP, No.547 CAP), 2012.

Einfeld, S. L., & Aman, M. (1995). Issues in the taxonomy of psychopathology in mental retardation. *Journal of Autism and Developmental Disorders, 25*(2), 143–167.

Ex Parte Briseño, 135 S.W.3d 1, 2004.

Gould, S. J. (1982). Punctuated equilibrium: A different was of seeing. *New Scientist, 94 (1301),* 137–141.

Greenspan, S. (1979). Social intelligence in the retarded. In N. R. Ellis (Ed.), *Handbook of mental deficiency: Psychological theory and research.* (2nd ed., pp. 483–531). Hillsdale, NJ: Erlbaum.

Greenspan, S., & Love, P. F. (1997). Social intelligence and developmental disorder: Mental retardation, learning disabilities and autism. In W. F. MacLean, Jr. (Ed.), *Ellis' handbook of mental deficiency* (3rd ed., pp. 311–342). Mahwah, NJ: Erlbaum.

Greenspan, S., Switzky, H. N., & Woods, G. W. (2011). Intelligence involves risk-awareness and intellectual disability involves risk-unawareness: Implications of a theory of common sense. *Journal of Intellectual & Developmental Disability, 36*(4), 1–33.

Harrison, P. L. & Oakland, T. (2003). *ABAS-II: Adaptive behavior assessment system* (2nd ed.). Torrance, CA: Western Psychological Services.

Haydt, N. (2012, July). *Some findings from a database of* Atkins *litigation.* Paper presented at the International Association for the Scientific Study of Intellectual Disability. Halifax, Nova Scotia.

Hooks v. Workman. 10th Circuit, No. 07-6152, 2012.

Kernan, K. T., & Sabsay, S. (1988). Communication in social interaction: Aspects of an ethnography of mildly mentally handicapped adults. In M. Beveridge, G. Conti-Ramsden, & I. Leudar (Eds.), *Language and communication in mentally handicapped people* (pp. 239–253). London, England: Chapman & Hall.

Kernan, K. T., & Sabsay, S. (1992). Discourse and conversational skills of mentally retarded adults. In A. M. Bauer (Ed.), *Students who challenge the system* (pp. 145–185). Norwood, NJ: Ablex.

Larry P. v. Riles, 793 F.2d 969 (9th Cir. 1979).

Lohman, J. (2012, July). *The myth of the kingpin in* Atkins *cases.* Paper presented at the International Academy for Law and Mental Health, Berlin, Germany.

MacVaugh, G. S., & Cunningham, M. D. (2009). *Atkins v. Virginia*: Implications and recommendations for forensic practice. *Journal of Psychiatry and Law*, *37*, 131–187.

Rosenberg, S. & Abbeduto, L. (1993). *Language and communication in mental retardation.* Hillsdale, NJ: LEA.

Schacter, S. C., Holmes, G. L., & Kasteleijn-Nolst Trenite, D. (2008).*Behavioral aspects of epilepsy: Principles and practice.* New York, NY: Demos.

Schalock, R. L., Borthwick-Duffy, S. A., Bradley, V. J., Buntinx, W. H. E., Coulter, D. L., Craig, E. M., Gomez, S. C., Lachapelle, Y., Luckasson, R., Reeve, A., Shogren, K. A., Snell, M. E., Spreat, S., Tassé, M. J., Thompson, J. R., Verdugo-Alonso, M. A., Wehmeyer, M. L., & Yeager, M. H. (2010). *Intellectual disability: Definition, classification, and systems of supports (11th ed.).* Washington, DC: American Association on Intellectual and Developmental Disabilities.

Schalock, R. L., Buntix, W. H. E., Borthwick-Duffy, S. A., Luckasson, R., Snell, M. E, Tassé, M. J., & Wehmeyer, M. (2007). *User's guide: Mental retardation: Definition, classification and systems of support* (10th ed.). Washington, DC: American Association on Intellectual and Developmental Disabilities.

Selman, R. L. (1971).Taking another's perspective: Role-taking development in early childhood. *Child Development*, *42*(6), 1721–1734.

State of Utah v. Roberto Miramontes Roman, Crim. No. 111300712, 2012.

Steinbeck, J. (1993/1937*). Of mice and men.* New York, NY: Penguin Group.

Tobolowsky, P. M. (2011). A different path taken: Texas capital offenders' post-*Atkins* claims of mental retardation. *Hastings Constitutional Law Quarterly*, *39*(1), 1–178.

Webster, C. D., & Jackson, M. A. (Eds.). (1997). Impulsivity Theory, assessment and treatment. New York, NY: Guilford Press.

Acknowledgement: The author is grateful to Gilbert Macvaugh, III for extensive and thoughtful comments on an earlier draft.

PART III
Related Topics

16 | Consideration of Cultural and Linguistic Factors

Richard Ruth

Nature of the Problem

The American Psychological Association (APA) establishes consensually accepted aspirational principles, enforceable standards, and practice guidelines for psychological evaluations of members of ethnic and language minority groups (American Psychological Association Task Force, 1990) and evaluations in forensic contexts (American Psychological Association, 2013). Both sets of the profession's expectations of best practices share common values, in line with APA's ethics code (American Psychological Association, 2010). The aspirational principles, the required standards, and the guidelines they frame recognize that culturally sensitive evaluations can be difficult to accomplish and draw on specific psychologist competencies (see Table 16.1).

It can take considerable effort to find psychologists with appropriate knowledge about a client's culture and subculture and about the technical and professional issues involved in doing assessments with people of the client's cultural and language background and in cross-cultural circumstances. Such effort is necessary, but often not sufficient, to guarantee reliable and valid assessment findings (Acevedo-Polakovich et al., 2007; Arnold & Matus, 2002; Dana, 2005; Hambleton, Merenda, & Spielberger, 2005; Roysircar, 2005). Cognitive and adaptive abilities are not totally or neatly separable from culture. Any person's abilities should be ascertained within the context of the person's cultural and community backgrounds (Allison & Strydom, 2009; Hatton, 2004). Concepts of intellectual disability are also culturally nested; an evaluation of a member of a cultural minority group must address both functioning within the culture in which the client grew up and capacity for functioning in the mainstream U.S. society (Cummins, 1980; Hatton, 2004). Cultures have within-group diversity; thus, evaluations must address issues of the client's specific community and subculture, and

TABLE 16.1. Excerpts from APA Ethics Code and Practice Guidelines

Excerpts from the "Ethical Principles of Psychologists and Code of Conduct: Including 2010 Amendments" (American Psychological Association (2010).

Principle E

. . . Psychologists are aware of and respect cultural, individual and role differences, including those based on age, gender, gender identity, race, ethnicity, culture, national origin, religion, sexual orientation, disability, language and socioeconomic status and consider these factors when working with members of such groups.

Standard 2.01 Boundaries of Competence

. . . (b) Where scientific or professional knowledge in the discipline of psychology establishes that an understanding of factors associated with age, gender, gender identity, race, ethnicity, culture, national origin, religion, sexual orientation, disability, language or socioeconomic status is essential for effective implementation of their services or research, psychologists have or obtain the training, experience, consultation or supervision necessary to ensure the competence of their services, or they make appropriate referrals.

. . . (d) When psychologists are asked to provide services to individuals for whom appropriate mental health services are not available and for which psychologists have not obtained the competence necessary, psychologists with closely related prior training or experience may provide such services in order to ensure that services are not denied if they make a reasonable effort to obtain the competence required by using relevant research, training, consultation or study. . . .

Standard 9.02 Use of Assessments

. . . (b) Psychologists use assessment instruments whose validity and reliability have been established for use with members of the population tested. When such validity or reliability has not been established, psychologists describe the strengths and limitations of test results and interpretation. (c) Psychologists use assessment methods that are appropriate to an individual's language preference and competence, unless the use of an alternative language is relevant to the assessment issues.

Excerpts from the "Guidelines for Providers of Services to Ethnic, Linguistic, and Culturally Diverse Populations" (American Psychological Association Task Force, 1990).

. . . 2d. Psychologists consider the validity of a given instrument or procedure and interpret resulting data, keeping in mind the cultural and linguistic characteristics of the person being assessed. Psychologists are aware of the test's reference population and possible limitations of such instruments with other populations.

Psychologists interact in the language requested by the client and, if this is not feasible, make an appropriate referral.

. . . 6a. Problems may arise when the linguistic skills of the psychologist do not match the language of the client. In such a case, psychologists refer the client to a mental health professional who is competent to interact in the language of the client. If this is not possible, psychologists offer the client a translator with cultural knowledge and an appropriate professional background. When no translator is available, then a trained paraprofessional from the client's culture is used as a translator/culture broker.

b. If translation is necessary, psychologists do not retain the services of translators/paraprofessionals that may have a dual role with the client to avoid jeopardizing the validity of evaluation or the effectiveness of intervention.

. . . 9. Psychologists working with culturally diverse populations should document culturally and sociopolitically relevant factors in the records.
   a. number of generations in the country
   b. number of years in the country
   c. fluency in English
   d. extent of family support (or disintegration of family)
   e. community resources
   f. level of education
   g. change in social status as a result of coming to this country (for immigrant or refugee)
   h. intimate relationship with people of different backgrounds
   i. level of stress related to acculturation

Excerpt from "Specialty Guidelines for Forensic Psychology" (American Psychological Association, 2013).

10.03 Appreciation of Individual Differences

When interpreting assessment results forensic practitioners consider the purpose of the assessment as well as the various test factors, test-taking abilities, and other characteristics of the person being assessed, such as situational, personal, linguistic, and cultural differences that might affect their judgments or reduce the accuracy of their interpretations (Ethical Principles of Psychologists and Code of Conduct Standard 9.06). Forensic practitioners strive to identify any significant strengths and limitations of their procedures and interpretations.

cannot make assumptions that all members of a specific minority culture function similarly (Acevedo-Polakovich et al., 2007; Allison & Strydom, 2009; Cummins, 1980; Roysircar, 2005).

Capital cases involving people considered to have an intellectual disability often hinge on fine distinctions between intellectual disability at the upper end of the spectrum and borderline average functioning; therefore, evaluations have to meet the demanding standards by which such distinctions are made. These distinctions can be harder to achieve in the assessment of members of cultural and linguistic minorities. Baseline evaluations of intellectual or adaptive abilities during the developmental period or behaviorally precise reporting from collateral informants about relevant domains of functioning are often not available for immigrants from underdeveloped countries or people from underprivileged communities. When available psychometric tests are only an imperfect fit with the client's cultural and linguistic background, the professional will have to make technical and clinical judgments that are carefully parsed and scientifically justified.

Although an extensive and highly technical literature exists on cross-cultural and bilingual psychological assessment issues, relatively little attention has been directed to assessment of people with intellectual disability within the context of culture. Relevant guidelines acknowledge the need for informed professional judgment (Schalock & Luckasson, 2005).

Peer-reviewed Practices

Cross-cultural assessment practices are nested within consensual values shared by all the mental health professions about clinical work across boundaries of ethnicity, race, and language (Kirmayer et al., 2003; Lum, 2010; Sue, 2006). These are in line with the ethical values that psychologists place on providing professional services to diverse populations with competence and respect (American Psychological Association, 2010).

To demonstrate that evaluating psychologists have met ethical standards regarding culture and assessment, reports must document efforts taken to meet aspirations and enforceable standards of the APA ethics code (American Psychological Association, 2010; American Psychological Association Task Force, 1990). Professionally relevant knowledge of culture and language is a matter of documented professional background and demonstrable competencies, not of values and sympathies (American Psychological Association Task Force,, 1990; Cummins, 1980; Dana, 2005; Hambleton et al., 2005; Roysircar, 2005; Suzuki & Ponterotto, 2007).

Assessments should address cognitive and adaptive functioning within the client's culture of origin and also how well the client is acculturated and functioning compared to age and/or education peers in the mainstream U.S. culture, to the extent possible

(Arends-Toth & van de Vijver, 2006; Cummins, 1980; Dana, 2005; Groth-Marnat, 2009; Hambleton et al., 2005; Roysircar, 2005; Schalock, 2004; Suzuki & Ponterotto, 2007). To the extent possible, evaluations should address how intellectual disability is conceived in the client's culture of origin and what educational and habilitative background and formal or informal supports the client had during the developmental years (Hatton, 2002, 2004). This may mean taking and documenting appropriate efforts to interview credible informants. Evaluations must address issues of within-culture diversity, such as the area(s) where the client grew up; socioeconomic background and changes in socioeconomic background during the developmental years; and relevant issues of subculture, such as whether the client's religion or ethnicity shaped education and adaptive development in specific ways (Cummins, 1980; Dana, 2005; Hatton, 2004; Suzuki & Ponterotto, 2007). It would also be relevant to consider, and document, whether the client is part of a language or ethnic U.S. minority group (e.g., Mexican-American), a first-generation immigrant, or a second- or third-generation immigrant (see Table 16.2).

The field has expected best practices and in some cases standards and guidelines for test selection with cultural and linguistic minorities (Acevedo-Polakovich et al., 2007; American Psychological Association, 2010, 2013; Arnold & Matus, 2002; Hambleton & Patsula, 1998; International Test Commission, 2010; Roysircar, 2005). If available tests of cognitive and adaptive abilities are imperfect fits with the client's cultural and linguistic background, the field's expectation is that practitioners will state the limitations and address the specifics of how they may have affected test findings (Dana, 2005; Groth-Marnat, 2009; Hambleton et al., 2005; Suzuki & Ponterotto, 2007).

Empirical research findings and associated professional best-practices consensus address assessment of acculturation (Arends-Toth & van de Vijver, 2006), relevant where a client has immigrated or otherwise moved over the course of their personal development from one cultural orientation/context to another; assessment of language dominance, preference, and usage in bilingual people (Cummins, 2000); and selection and interpretation of neuropsychological tests in cross-cultural assessments (Judd & Beggs, 2005). Similarly, the field has consensual views on best practices, informed by empirical research findings, in situations where no linguistically and culturally competent psychologist can be identified and an interpreter must be used (Tribe & Raval, 2003). It is recognized that, while use of a bilingual psychologist familiar with the client's culture and subculture is desirable, it is not always possible (American Psychological Association Task Force, 1990); when this is the case, however, the expectation will be that the psychologist is thoroughly familiar and compliant with specific guidelines involved when doing assessment through a translator (Kirmayer et al., 2003; Tribe & Raval, 2003), and that this will be reflected in the psychologist's written findings, including acknowledgement of any resulting constraints or limitations on the findings.

TABLE 16.2. Examples of Statements Regarding Culture and Language in Psychological Reports

Mr. A. is originally from Guatemala and is of Mam ethnicity. He speaks Mam as his first and strongest language, and Spanish as a second language. His education, as will be discussed further in this report, was limited, and was in both Mam and Spanish. The evaluator is fluent in Spanish and bicultural, and has general familiarity with Central American culture and with psychological evaluations of people of indigenous ethnicity from the region. No psychologist fluent in Mam was identified after careful search. In the course of this assessment, with Mr. A.'s informed consent, the evaluator sought consultation from an anthropologist (Dr. B.) and a linguist (Dr. C.) familiar with Mam culture and language. Limitations in this assessment due to language and cultural factors will be noted in relevant sections of the findings and recommendations of this report. The quality of Mr. A.'s interaction in Spanish with the evaluator will be described in the *Behavioral Observations* section of this report, along with any resulting limitations and constraints on the findings.

Ms. B. is originally from Cameroon. She was brought to the United States at age 10. Prior to this, she spoke an indigenous language as a young child (she did not know the name of the language, nor did any collateral informant interviewed), and then began using French—one of Cameroon's two official languages—as the language of her primary school education, and the primary language she used with friends and family. Ms. B. was not identified in Cameroon as having an intellectual disability and received no special education or habilitative service there. Formal assessment of her current skills in French and in English is included among the test findings in this report. After coming to the United States, Ms. B. had 5 years of English as a Second Language instruction. By the time she graduated from high school, in a program for students with mild intellectual disability, she was assessed as having solid basic interpersonal communication skills in English but limited formal/academic language skills in both English and French, which the school system considered a result of her intellectual disability. In Cameroon, Ms. B. lived in the country's capital; her parents' work as civil servants gave her a relatively advantaged standard of living in Cameroonian terms. After careful interview of collateral informants, more detailed information about her socioeconomic background in Cameroon could not be learned. After coming to the United States, Ms. B. lived with an aunt in a middle-class African-American community until the time of her imprisonment. Both the aunt and Ms. B. consider Ms. B bicultural, equally comfortable in Cameroonian immigrant and African-American contexts. Ms. B. does not follow an organized religion, nor, by credible report, did her family of origin in Cameroon or the aunt who raised her here.

Cultural and Linguistic Assessment Best Practices

Various standards should be addressed and best practices should be followed when assessments are conducted with people from diverse cultural or linguistic backgrounds. These standards and best practices represent appropriate expectations of psychologists in ensuring accurate assessments.

The initial consideration is the expertise of the examiner. This person preferably should have demonstrated training in cross-cultural assessment and specific skills and experiences for assessing people of the client's culture, subculture, and preferred or dominant language(s) (American Psychological Association Task Force, 1990). Such demonstration includes a statement of language capability and cultural competence, as well as documentation of the professional's training, experience, and relevant range of competencies. In some instances, it may be impossible to identify an examiner with the specific training and skills desirable in assessment of people from certain low-frequency cultural/linguistic minorities. The examiner, however, should be familiar with professional principles, standards, and guidelines for assessing people with low-frequency conditions (American Psychological Association 2010, 2013; Groth-Marnat, 2009) and seek appropriate consultation (American Psychological Association , 2010, 2013).

An examiner may have the appropriate cultural competence, but may lack appropriate intellectual disability or forensic assessment skills (American Psychological Association, 2013). In this case, evaluations should be done by a team including other professionals with appropriate training and background, in compliance with American Psychological Association (2010) ethical standards.

A critical standard and expected practice is that examiners need to select culturally and linguistically appropriate assessment instruments that are reliable and valid for people of the client's culture and subculture (Acevedo-Polakovich et al., 2007; Arnold & Matus, 2002; Cummins, 1980, 2000; Dana, 2005; Hambleton et al., 2005; Hambleton & Patsula, 1998; International Test Commission, 2010; Roysircar, 2005; Suzuki & Ponterotto, 2007) and for the purpose for which the assessment is being conducted (American Psychological Association, 2010, 2013).

Further, test findings need to be complemented with extensive qualitative interview data regarding not just generalities but specifics of cultural background. Considerations include socioeconomic class, living conditions, education (including nature of curriculum and educational system), and immigration history (e.g., voluntary/involuntary, age at immigration, conditions of immigration), if relevant (Acevedo-Polakovich et al., 2007; American Psychological Association Task Force, 1990; Arends-Toth & van de Vijver, 2006; Dana, 2005; Lum, 2010; Roysircar, 2005; Suzuki & Ponterotto, 2007). When obtained with professional thoroughness and care, these data constitute an important part of a cross-cultural evaluation.

It is important that language competence be established rather than assumed during cross-cultural evaluations in which issues of bilingualism are involved. Clarifying which language is the client's native language may not be apparent or intuitive (Cummins, 1980, 2000). Further, appropriate evaluations will address the individual's level of education in the native language; the manner in which the second language was acquired; the individual's education in any other languages; the nature of acquisition of second language(s) (e.g., whether through formal instruction or not); and native language and second language competencies, to include basic interpersonal communication skills vs. formal/academic language competencies (Acevedo-Polakovich et al., 2007; Cummins, 2000; Dana, 2005; Suzuki & Ponterotto, 2007). Additional considerations include attention to (a) the extent of habilitative services and formal and informal developmental supports a client has received (Hatton, 2002, 2004); (b) how others in the home culture/community assessed the client's adaptive abilities (Schalock, 2004); and (c) how these align with U.S. standards. Examiners should be specific in differentiating impact of limited acculturation to mainstream norms (Arends-Toth & van de Vijver, 2006) versus cognitive and adaptive deficits as such.

Clinical (American Psychological Association, 2010) and forensic (American Psychological Association, 2013) ethical and professional principles and standards mandate careful attention to documentation (Luepker, 2012), which has particular salience in cross-cultural assessments of persons with suspected intellectual disability in death-penalty cases. Evaluators will often be discussing information outside the usual frames of reference of consumers of their reports, and may be using less familiar tests and approaches. Thus, reports must make accessible and clear how the information and conclusions being reported were derived.

Conclusion

Evaluations of people from diverse cultural and linguistic backgrounds with possible ID in death-penalty cases have high stakes and are rightly viewed according to rigorous principles, standards, and guidelines. They therefore deserve the time, adequate resource, and meticulous professionalism needed to do a careful job. When attorneys and psychologists are in agreement about the need for such considerations, and evaluations are done with care, they have the potential to bring best professional values, aspirations, and practices to an important sociopolitical sphere (American Psychological Association, 2010, 2013; American Psychological Association Task Force, 1990).

References

Acevedo-Polakovich, I. D., Reynaga-Abiko, G., Garriott, P. O., Derefinko, K. J., Wimsatt, M. K., Gudonis, L. C., & Brown, T. L. (2007). Beyond instrument selection: Cultural considerations in the psychological assessment of U.S. Latinas/os. *Professional Psychology: Research and Practice, 38,* 375–384. doi: 10.1037/0735-7028.38.4.375

Allison, L., & Strydom, A. (2009). Intellectual disability across cultures. *Transcultural Psychiatry, 8,* 355–357. doi: 10.1016/j.mppsy.2009.06.008

American Psychological Association. (2010). Ethical principles of psychologists and code of conduct: Including 2010 amendments. Retrieved from http://www.apa.org/ethics/code/.

American Psychological Association (2013). Specialty guidelines for forensic psychology. *American Psychologist, 68,* 7–19. doi: 10.1037/a0029889

American Psychological Association Task Force on Delivery of Services to Ethnic Minority Populations. (1990). Guidelines for providers of services to ethnic, linguistic, and culturally diverse populations. Retrieved from http://www.apa.org/pi/oema/resources/policy/provider-guidelines.aspx

Arends-Toth, J., & van de Vijver, F. J. (2006). Assessment of acculturation. In D. L. Sam & J. W. Berry (Eds.), *The Cambridge handbook of acculturation psychology (*pp. 142–160). New York, NY: Cambridge University Press

Arnold, B. R., & Matus, Y. E. (2002). Test translation and cultural equivalence methodologies for use with diverse populations. In I. Cuellar & F. A. Paniagua (Eds.), *Handbook of multicultural mental health (*pp. 121–136.*)* San Diego, CA: Academic Press.

Cummins, J. (1980). Psychological assessment of immigrant children: Logic or intuition? *Journal of Multilingual and Multicultural Development, 1,* 97–111.

Cummins, J. (2000). BICS and CALP: Origins and rationale for the distinction. In C. B. Paulston & G. R. Tucker (Eds.), *Sociolinguistics: The essential readings (*pp. 322–328). Malden, MA: Blackwell.

Dana, R. H. (2005). *Multicultural assessment: Principles, applications, and examples.* Mahwah, NJ: Erlbaum.

Groth-Marnat, G. (2009). *Handbook of psychological assessment* (5th ed.). New York, NY: Wiley.

Hambleton, R. K., Merenda, P. F., & Spielberger, C. D. (2005). *Adapting educational and psychological tests for cross-cultural assessment.* New York, NY: Routledge Academic.

Hambleton, R. K., & Patsula, L. (1998). Adapting tests for use in multiple languages and cultures. *Social Indicators Research, 45,* 153–171.

Hatton, C. (2002). People with intellectual disabilities from ethnic minority communities in the United States and the United Kingdom. *International Review of Research on Mental Retardation, 25,* 209–239.

Hatton, C. (2004). Cultural factors. In E. Emerson, C. Hatton, T. Thompson, & T. R. Parmenter (Eds.), *The international handbook of applied research in intellectual disabilities* (pp. 133–160). New York, NY: Wiley.

International Test Commission. (2010). International Test Commission guidelines for translating and adapting tests. Retrieved from http://www.intestcom.org/upload/sitefiles/40.

Judd, T., & Beggs, B. (2005). Cross-cultural forensic neuropsychological assessment. In K. H. Barrett & W. H. George (Eds.), *Race, culture, psychology & law (*pp. 141–162.*)* Thousand Oaks, CA: Sage.

Kirmayer, L. J., Groleau, D., Guzder, J., Blake, C., & Jarvis, E. (2003). Cultural consultation: A model of mental health service for multicultural societies. *Canadian Journal of Psychiatry / La Revue Canadienne de Psychiatrie, 48,* 145–153.

Luepker, E. (2012). *Record keeping in psychotherapy and counseling: Protecting confidentiality and the professional relationship* (2nd ed). New York, NY: Routledge.

Lum, D. (2010). *Culturally competent practice: A framework for understanding diverse groups and justice issues.* Belmont, CA: Brooks/Cole.

Roysircar, G. (2005). Culturally sensitive assessment, diagnosis, and guidelines. In M. G. Constantine & D. W. Sue (Eds.), *Strategies for building multicultural competence in mental health and educational settings* (pp. 19–38). New York, NY: Wiley.

Schalock, R. L. (2004). Adaptive behavior: Its conceptualization and measurement. In E. Emerson, C. Hatton, T. Thompson, & T. R. Parmenter (Eds.), *The international handbook of applied research in intellectual disabilities* (pp. 116–31). New York, NY: Wiley.

Schalock, R. L., & Luckasson, R. (2005). *Clinical judgment.* Washington, DC: American Association on Mental Retardation.

Sue, S. (2006). Cultural competency: From philosophy to research and practice. *Journal of Community Psychology, 34,* 237–245. doi: 10.1002/jcop.20095

Suzuki, L. A., & Ponterotto, J. G. (Eds.) (2007). *Handbook of multicultural assessment: Clinical, psychological, and educational applications* (3rd ed.). San Francisco, CA: Jossey Bass.

Tribe, R., & Raval, H. (2003). *Working with interpreters in mental health.* New York, NY: Brunner-Routledge.

17 | Competence to Waive *Miranda* Rights and Competence to Stand Trial

Karen L. Salekin
Caroline Everington

Because of the nature of the disability, competence issues are particularly germane to people with intellectual disability (ID). Whereas no single, universally accepted definition exists, incompetence is a status through which a person is deemed to be lacking the comprehension, capacity, or ability to perform certain acts or make specific decisions. The evaluation of competence is context-specific and relates directly to the nature of the acts or decisions that need to be performed. This chapter considers two of the most commonly encountered issues—competence to confess and competence to stand trial.

Competence to Waive *Miranda* Rights

To discuss the issue of waiving of *Miranda* rights in cases of people with ID, the assumption has to be that the Court has made the determination that the person has met the legal criteria for intellectual disability. To the degree that people show similar deficits in functioning, but do not meet criteria for intellectual disability, the concerns regarding the ability to make a valid waiver remain the same. The ultimate question that must be addressed is whether the defendant made a knowing, voluntary, and intelligent decision to waive their rights, as outlined in *Miranda v. Arizona* (1966).

The Supreme Court of the United States has made it clear that presence of a disorder is not sufficient to rule a waiver invalid. Instead, a review of case law demonstrates that judges are mandated to look at the "totality of the circumstances" with no one factor being dispositive on the issue (see, e.g., *Dickerson v. U.S.*, 2000; *Fare v. Michael C.*, 1979; *Miranda v. Arizona*, 1966). For instance, people with low intellectual ability may present with characteristics associated with ID, including poor decision making, heightened gullibility, the tendency to acquiesce to authority, impaired memory, and limited cognitive ability, all of which render a person vulnerable to police tactics, but none of which, de facto, rules a confession inadmissible (see, e.g., *Bevel v. Florida,* 983 So. 2d 505 [Fla. 2008]).

To begin, it is important to understand that a fundamental right protected by the holding in *Miranda v. Arizona* (1966) is the right against self-incrimination in the face of police coercion in custodial situations. The following is an excerpt from *Dickerson v. United States* 530 U.S. 428, 120 S.Ct. 2326, 147 L.Ed.2d 405 (2000) that delineates the basis of this decision:

> In *Miranda,* we noted that the advent of modern custodial police interrogation brought with it an increased concern about confessions obtained by coercion. . . . Because custodial police interrogation, by its very nature, isolates and pressures the individual, we stated that "[e]ven without employing brutality, the 'third degree' or [other] specific stratagems, . . . custodial interrogation exacts a heavy toll on individual liberty and trades on the weakness of individuals. . ." We concluded that the coercion inherent in custodial interrogation blurs the line between voluntary and involuntary statements, and thus heightens the risk that an individual will not be "accorded his privilege under the Fifth Amendment . . . not to be compelled to incriminate himself. . . ." Accordingly, we laid down "concrete constitutional guidelines for law enforcement agencies and courts to follow. . . ." Those guidelines established that the admissibility in evidence of any statement given during custodial interrogation of a suspect would depend on whether the police provided the suspect with four warnings. These warnings (which have come to be known colloquially as "*Miranda* rights") are: a suspect has the right to remain silent, that anything he says can be used against him in a court of law, that he has the right to the presence of an attorney, and that if he cannot afford an attorney one will be appointed for him prior to any questioning if he so desires.

Gullibility and Suggestibility: Evaluating Voluntariness in Absence of Observable Coercion

The assumption cannot be made that officers always purposely employ coercive tactics to elicit confessions. For people with intellectual disability, the intent to deceive or manipulate is not relevant; the fact is that people with intellectual disability are often gullible and fall prey to suggestion, even in the absence of intent. Gullibility and suggestibility are well-established characteristics associated with intellectual disability, and some scholars would say that they are hallmarks of the disorder (Greenspan, Loughlin, & Black, 2001; Greenspan, Switzky, & Woods, 2011).

There is a debate as to whether the issue of suggestibility is relevant to the issue of waiver of rights, with some scholars stating that it is (see, e.g., Frumkin, 2000; Frumkin & Garcia, 2003) whereas others have argued that it is not (see, e.g., Grisso, 2003; Oberlander et al., 2003; Rogers & Shuman, 2005). Grisso (2003) took a firm stance on the issue and essentially eliminated suggestibility from consideration in his model of the assessment of waiver. According to Grisso, "information about a defendant's susceptibility to making false confessions may be important for purposes of the weight that judges or juries should place on a defendant's confession. But the issue of false confessions requires separate inquiry from the legal question of capacity to waive *Miranda* rights voluntarily, knowingly, and intelligently" (p. 150). In short, suggestibility, as defined by Gudjonsson (1997), is a characteristic that makes people more susceptible to coercion after they have waived their rights and relates directly to the reliability of the statement itself. What is not known, though perhaps assumed by proponents, is whether that same characteristic makes people more vulnerable to coercion when making the decision to waive or not waive their rights. Research should focus on a different process from that associated with voluntarily making a statement. In contrast, Brodsky and Bennett (2005), Frumkin (2000), Frumkin and Garcia (2003), Frumkin (2008) and Roesch, McLachlan, and Viljoen (2008) consider suggestibility to be relevant to the assessment of waiver of *Miranda* rights and endorse the use of the Gudjonsson Scales of Suggestibility (GSS; Gudjonsson, 1997) as an appropriate measure of voluntariness.

With regard to the assessment of suggestibility, there is no established method, but as just mentioned, some scholars support the use of the GSS. In brief, the GSS is a test that is administered by an examiner and begins with the recitation of a complex story. The defendant is first told that the GSS is a test of memory and that the defendant will be asked to recall the story as well as possible. There are two time-points of recall, initial and 50-minute delay: the 50-minute delay is not administered to people with poor initial recall, which may be an issue for some defendants with ID. To evaluate a person's tendency to change a response to leading questions, the examinee is administered 20 questions, 15 of which are leading or misleading; the sum of the number of times the examinee yields to misleading questions produces the Yield 1 score. Regardless of their true score, the examiner informs the examinee that the responses produced a number of errors and that the procedure must be repeated. This admonition is stated in a firm voice, and the examinee is informed that the examinee must work harder to provide correct answers. The sum of the number of times the examinee yields to misleading questions on the second administration produces the Yield 2 score. Yield 2 is used to calculate the Shift score. The Shift score is the sum of the number of times that the person changed the response after the first administration. Suggestibility, as measured by the GSS, is measured by looking at the tendency of a person to *yield* to leading questions and the tendency of a person to *shift* in response to negative feedback.

Studies that have looked at waiver of *Miranda* rights with the GSS (e.g., Everington & Fulero, 1999; O'Connell, Garmoe, & Goldstein, 2005) have found that adults with intellectual disability demonstrate poor comprehension and tend to change their responses when provided with feedback on their success. Of interest, the results of the study conducted by O'Connell and colleagues (2005) demonstrated that participants with intellectual disability showed increased suggestibility to friendly feedback, over and above both unfriendly and neutral. In their discussion, the authors stated that this finding has important policy implications and has the potential to influence judicial decisions on admissibility. Specifically, it is the first study to demonstrate that adults with ID are potentially more susceptible to the influence of others when the message is relayed in a kind and supportive manner.

The judiciary has been mixed with regard to the admissibility of data produced by the GSS. Several courts have found the results to be inadmissible and have raised issues related to its poor psychometric properties (see, e.g., *Soares v. Massachusetts,* 2001; *Misskelly v. Arkansas,* 1996) and its lack of scientific support (e.g., *Summers v. Wisconsin,* 2001). Rogers et al. (2010) provided citations for two appellate court decisions in which testimony on the GSS was permitted, but the courts did not conduct a critical evaluation of the scientific admissibility of the measure or its relationship to voluntariness (see *Oregon v. Romero,* 2003; *New Jersey v. King,* 2006). These authors also cited two cases in which the GSS was determined to be admissible; in one opinion, the Court noted that the results of the GSS were admitted because the measure has general acceptability in the scientific community and the experts were qualified to administer it (*New York v. Raposo,* 1998); and in the other opinion, the Court stated that the experts were qualified to conduct the evaluation and that procedures used to access voluntariness were acceptable (*Genaro v. California,* 2007).

They Agreed to Talk, but Did They Do So Knowingly and Intelligently?

As noted in *Morane v. Burbine,* 475 U.S. 412 (1986), not only does a waiver need to be made voluntarily, but also it must be made "with a full awareness of both the nature of the right being abandoned and the consequences of the decision to abandon it" (p. x). It is here that people with intellectual disability have the most difficulty. Research has convincingly demonstrated that a strong relationship exists between measured IQ and comprehension of *Miranda* rights (Everington & Fulero, 1999; Fulero & Everington, 1995; Grisso, 1998; McLachlan, Roesch, & Douglas, 2011; O'Connell et al., 2005). The relationship, however, is not linear throughout the IQ spectrum, but instead plateaus within the average range of intellectual ability. In the lower range of intellectual ability, comprehension of *Miranda* rights steeply declines alongside measured IQ (Grisso, 1998).

Though there is no definition of the word *knowing* in the context of *Miranda* waivers, review of relevant literature and case law suggests that people have to (a) know that they have the rights delineated by *Miranda,* (b) understand the meaning of these rights in a custodial situation, and (c) understand what it means to relinquish them (*Godinez v. Moran,* 509 U.S. 389 (1993); *Patterson v. Illinois,* 487 U.S. 285 [1988]. The difference between this term and that of *intelligently* within this context appears to be, at least in part, the ability of the defendants to apply their knowledge and understanding of these rights to their specific case (see, e.g., *In re Patrick W.* (1978) 84 Cal. App. 3d 520 [148 Cal.Rptr. 735]). More recently, the Courts appear to be merging the concepts of "totality of the circumstances" and the intelligent component of the waiver decision. For example, in *Iowa v. Tovar* (2004), the court stated that "the information a defendant must possess in order to make an intelligent election, our decisions indicate, will depend on a range of case-specific factors, including the defendant's education or sophistication, the complex or easily grasped nature of the charge, and the stage of the proceeding" (p. 88).

Miranda-*Specific Assessment Tools*

Instruments for Assessing Understanding and Appreciation of *Miranda* Rights. Only two measures exist for assessing the understanding of *Miranda* rights. The first is the Instruments for Assessing Understanding and Appreciation of *Miranda* Rights (Grisso, 1998). The measure comprises four separate scales: (1) Comprehension of *Miranda* Rights (CMR), (2) Comprehension of *Miranda* Rights–Recognition (CMR-R), (3) Comprehension of *Miranda* Vocabulary (CMV), and (4) Function of Rights in Interrogation (FRI). Only four studies have examined comprehension of *Miranda* rights for people with ID using this measure, all of which have found substantial deficits in comprehension for people with ID when compared to their counterparts without ID (Cloud, Shepard, Barkoff, & Shur, 2002; Everington & Fulero, 1999; Fulero & Everington, 1995; O'Connell et al., 2005). The following is a brief overview of each of the four scales:

1. **Comprehension of *Miranda* Rights (CMR):** This scale involves presenting the defendant with each of the four *Miranda* warnings, one at a time, and asking the examinee to paraphrase the meaning of the warning. Answers are scored zero, 1, or 2, with 2 representing an adequate level of comprehension, 1 = questionable; zero = inadequate. The range of scores for this scale is from zero to 8 based on responses to the four warnings.

2. **Comprehension of *Miranda* Rights–Recognition (CMR-R):** This scale is comprised of 12 items that measure the ability of the defendant to discern whether interpretations of the *Miranda* warnings are the same or different from the warning presented. The benefit of this scale is that people do not have to paraphrase their understanding, but instead simply state whether the two statements convey the same meaning. Items are scored as either zero or 1, with 1 point given for each correct response. Scores on this scale range from zero to 12.

3. **Comprehension of *Miranda* Vocabulary (CMV):** This scale assesses the ability of the defendant to define six words that are often included in *Miranda* warnings. The defendant is presented with a word, is then read a sentence that uses that word, and is then asked to provide a definition of that word. Similar to the CMR, responses are scored on a scale of zero, 1, or 2, with 2 representing an adequate level of understanding. The range of scores on this measure is from zero to 12.

4. **Function of Rights in Interrogation (FRI):** The FRI goes beyond the understanding of the *Miranda* rights themselves to assess the defendant's grasp of the

significance of the warnings in three areas: (a) Nature of Interrogation, (b) Right to Counsel, and (c) Right to Silence. The FRI uses four pictorial representations of an individual who is sitting at a table having a discussion with two officers. Each picture is accompanied by a brief vignette that tells a story about the suspect who is currently under arrest. Following the reading of each vignette, defendants are asked a set of questions that assess their grasp of the significance of the three areas of interest in this section. Similar to the other scales, the FRI is scored on a scale from zero to 2, with 2 representing an adequate level of comprehension. The range of scores on this scale is from zero to 30.

Standardized Assessment of *Miranda* Abilities. The second measure of comprehension of *Miranda* rights and waivers is the Standardized Assessment of *Miranda* Abilities (SAMA; Rogers, Sewell, Drogin, & Fiduccia, 2012). According to the manual, the measure is designed to assess comprehension of *Miranda* rights, as well as decision-making abilities specific to this context; the key elements addressed by the SAMA are knowledge, misconceptions, and decision making.

The SAMA comprises five measures that are to be administered in the following order: (1) the *Miranda* Quiz (MQ); (2) the *Miranda* Rights Measure (MRM) Interview Form; (3) the *Miranda* Comprehension (MCT); (4) the *Miranda* Acquiescence Quiz (MAQ); and (5) the *Miranda* Vocabulary Scale (MVS). The following are brief descriptions of each of the scales of the SAMA:

1. *Miranda* **Quiz (MQ):** The MQ is a 1-page questionnaire that includes 25 true-false questions. It is self-administered, with short sentences that are noted to be easy for the majority of pretrial defendants to read and understand. According to the manual, defendants with a reading level of 6th grade or higher are generally able complete this measure without difficulty.

2. *Miranda* **Rights Measure (MRM):** This measure uses open-ended inquiries and probes that focus on decision making and knowledge of rights. The MRM was designed to overcome some of the problems associated with a retrospective evaluation by examining people's recall of their thoughts and reasoning at the time they relinquished the *Miranda* rights. The focal issue is their memory of their experience, rather than their thoughts about the content of the warnings.

3. *Miranda* **Comprehension (MCT):** The MCT is a tool designed to assess defendants' memory of the exact warning that was administered at the time of their arrest. The MCT incorporates modality of administration (i.e., oral, written, both), content of the warnings, and the time elapsed between administration of the warning and the waiver. Administration requires that the examiner recreate the exact context of the advisement and the waiver(s); as such, the onus is on the examiner to obtain all records and other materials (e.g., audiotapes or videotapes) pertaining to both the arrest and custody of the defendant, as well as the warning(s) and subsequent waiver.

4. ***Miranda* Acquiescence Quiz (MAQ):** The MAQ comprises 64 true-false items that assess acquiescence through oppositely worded pairs. This measure can be helpful in determining defendants' beliefs about their rights and the roles of law enforcement at the time of interrogation. The MAQ is similar in structure to the MQ, but is longer and more complex. In addition to assessing beliefs, this measure also assesses attitudes of trust and distrust within the context of police questioning.

5. ***Miranda* Vocabulary Scale (MVS):** The MVS is a 36-item measure that assesses defendants' understanding of *Miranda*-relevant words. Each word is placed within the context of a standardized question, and probes are available to clarify ambiguous or vague responses. Because of concerns that presentation of such words may distort free recall, the MVS is usually the final measure administered.

Applying Competence-to-Confess Principles

The literature related to competence to confess provides guidance for applications to practice. Although a relative dearth of measures exists to assess *Miranda* comprehension and waiver, many tools can be put together to develop a valid assessment. The goal is to evaluate knowledge and waiver in a way that best approximates the conditions under which the *Miranda* warnings were administered because what is at issue is not current understanding and beliefs, but beliefs that were in place at the time of advisement and waiver.

Relevant for cases of intellectual disability, data that are available from the assessment of ID will include scores on intelligence tests, adaptive behavior scales, achievement tests, and measures of linguistic abilities (e.g., oral and receptive language; reading). Reading level is important in cases where the mode of administration is written (no concurrent recitation by an officer), and receptive language skills and short-term memory in cases in which the mode was solely oral. Frequently, these two modes of administration occur simultaneously or consecutively and, as such, all this information would be relevant. Readability statistics can be calculated on the exact admonition and review of transcripts, and tapes will assist in evaluating both oral and written comprehension, including the use of complex sentences, the use of words outside of the person's range of understanding, and a rate of speech that might impair comprehension on the basis of short-term memory capacity and receptive language skills.

Though neither measure of comprehension of *Miranda* and waiver (as discussed earlier) were normed on, or specifically designed for, people with ID, the results of either the SAMA (Rogers et al, 2012) or the Grisso (1998) test can provide a way to evaluate the defendant's capacity to understand and comprehend *Miranda* rights in comparison to a normative sample that includes people with a range of intellectual ability. The benchmark of interest is not this person's ability in comparison to others with ID, but instead to a national sample of people who vary on this characteristic. For both measures, it is possible that the ability to assess understanding through written word will be difficult in cases where the person has ID; consequently, what will be of importance will be the totality of information collected for the assessment and the determination of whether some scales can be used to inform the Court. If only parts of the measures are used, then an acknowledgment would be necessary that the measure was used in a nonstandardized manner and, as such, comparison to the norms is impossible. In addition to the use of a formal measure of *Miranda*, an interview of the defendant augments the objective data by allowing for an evaluation unconstrained by wording and structure that may be unsuitable for the particular defendant.

As previously mentioned, the construct of suggestibility has not been accepted by all scholars or practitioners. Because of the inherent characteristics of gullibility and naivety, however, suggestibility may play a larger role in investigation of confessions in defendants with ID. Fulero (2010) asserted that the GSS meets the "general acceptance" criteria of the *Daubert* and *Frye* standards for admissibility of testimony because GSS is mentioned in major forensic texts, studies appear in relevant peer-reviewed journals, and the usage of the scale is increasing. Qualitative investigation into the person's typical response pattern (e.g., easily led vs. not easily led) through collateral sources (e.g., third party informants; records) can supplement the GSS and can be used in concert with other information.

Though perhaps not as detailed as other forensic evaluations, a comprehensive biopsychosocial evaluation of the defendant's background that dates from birth to present informs the assessment process. Particular areas of importance including investigations into functional abilities within the school, work, and interpersonal domains will either buttress or not support deficits or abilities that are directly pertinent to the assessment of waiver. Knowledge of prior assessment and intervention for ID or other mental health issues is relevant, as is knowledge of known etiology, such as traumatic brain injury before the age of 18 years or a genetic condition.

One of the most important aspects of a waiver evaluation is the retrospective nature of the assessment. The data obtained at the time of the evaluation do not necessarily reflect understanding and comprehension at the time of waiver; therefore, a comprehensive analysis requires a review of all data relevant to the arrest, custody, and waiver , including video, audio, and transcripts of recordings, along with all other data available to the examiner. If the individual has been incarcerated since the time of arrest, jail records may contain relevant data (e.g., notations from medical or correctional staff); and officers who are in regular contact with the defendant and the attorneys that represent the defendant may provide additional information. Such data can assist in getting a sense of how much learning about *Miranda* and waiver has occurred since the time of arrest or incarceration, which has importance with regard to the final opinions regarding the validity of the waiver decision.

Competence to Stand Trial

The doctrine of competence to stand trial goes back to a legal foundation of fairness established in English Common Law that the defendant must be present in the trial.

Trying a defendant who cannot comprehend the proceedings is a violation of due process and fundamental fairness (Melton, Petrila, Poythress, & Slobogin, 2007). Competence to stand trial is a critical issue for defendants with ID because of the deficits they display in cognition, abstract thinking, reasoning, and language processing (Bonnie, 1992; Grisso, 2003).

Research on characteristics of defendants evaluated for competence to stand trial shows that incompetent defendants are more likely to have lower IQs (Everington, 1989; Nicholson & Kugler, 1991) and psychiatric disorders (Mumley, Tillbrook, & Grisso, 2003; Rosenfeld & Wall, 1998). These are important findings because many of the defendants with ID are dually diagnosed with a psychiatric disorder (Smith & O'Brien, 2004) (see also Chapter 19) and either condition can make the likelihood of effective trial participation more difficult. For example, people with less severe levels of ID may have some level of understanding of the process and roles, but delusional and paranoid thinking may inhibit their ability to work with their attorneys, and cognitive deficits may cause further difficulties in reasoning. Further, there is evidence that language skills are strongly related to competence abilities in people with ID (Ericson & Perlman, 2001; Everington, DeBerge, & Mauer, 2001). Deficits in expressive and receptive language cause difficulties in comprehension and problems with effective client-attorney communication.

Criteria for Competence to Stand Trial

The criteria for judging competence to stand trial was articulated in the 1960 Supreme Court decision *Dusky v. United States*. Whereas most states have their own standard, all closely follow the language of *Dusky*. *Dusky* states that to be competent to stand trial, defendants must have a "rational and factual understanding of the proceedings" and be able to consult with their attorneys with a "reasonable degree of rational understanding" (p. 402). There are three prongs to the *Dusky* standard, all of which must be met for a finding of competency. Not only must the defendants have a factual understanding of the proceedings, but they must also display a rational ability to consult with their attorney and a rational understanding of the proceedings (Rogers & Johansson-Love, 2009). It is the next two prongs that present difficulties for defendants with ID.

Many defendants with ID can recite the roles of the courtroom players (e.g. judge, prosecutor, the defendant's attorney), know the basic processes of the trial (testimony, cross examination), and can provide surface-level definitions for possible outcomes (e.g., acquittal) and pleas (e.g., guilty, not guilty by reason of insanity). What is particularly problematic for defendants with ID, however, is active and meaningful participation in the trial process. Having a surface level of understanding of trial proceedings has been referred to as "competence to proceed" and has been deemed a lower level cognitive skill than the reasoned and logical understanding of the proceeding required for true participation (Mumley et al., 2003). A rational understanding of the proceedings means defendants understand how these processes apply to their own situation (Viljoen, 2007). For example, that they can appreciate the implications of choices such as pleading not guilty, raising the issue of insanity or diminished responsibility, or firing their attorney.

For defendants with ID, the rational ability to consult with their attorney is an area of difficulty (Kalbeitzer & Benedetti, 2009). Working with their attorney requires the ability to relate the relevant facts of the case in a coherent, organized, manner, and to identify potential witnesses, and to provide critical evidence relevant to their case. More important, working with an attorney requires the ability to understand defense strategies and to weigh alternatives with a full understanding of the pros and cons of each. This type of understanding has been referred to as decisional competency and was highlighted in the Supreme Court decision in *Godinez v. Moran* (1993). In *Godinez*, the Court indicated that decision-making abilities (re: entering a plea of guilty) were encompassed in competence to stand trial (Grisso, 2003). Given the difficulties with problem-solving and abstract thought, it is easy to see how this can prove difficult even for defendants with ID whose impairment is not severe.

Determination of Competency

The issue of competency can be raised by either side and is typically determined pre-trial, and status (i.e., competent or incompetent) is determined by a judge rather than a jury. There is evidence to indicate the issue of competence to stand trial is not raised for many defendants with ID (Kalbeitzer & Benedetti, 2009; Mumley et al. 2003). Kalbeitzer and Benedetti (2009) hypothesized that this may result from two factors: (a) many evaluators focus more on psychopathology and less on cognition, and (b) defendants with ID of less severity do not often present as having deficits in understanding. Although little has been done to address this issue, first raised in 1985 by Ellis and Luckasson, Smith and Hudson (1995) found that a brief measure, which rates defendant responses to four words (i.e., *testify, plead, strategy,* and *jury*), may provide a reliable screen for the need to follow through with a comprehensive evaluation.

Best practice suggests that competence evaluations focus on the defendant's understanding and capacity relative to the psycholegal issue (Melton et al., 2007). Although information on intellectual and psychological functioning must be included in the evaluation, neither should be the determining factor in a competence evaluation. Put another way, IQ alone does not determine competence. Having said that, it is unlikely that a person with an IQ below 55 would be competent in any situation—assuming the IQ assessment is valid.

Assessments of Competence to Stand Trial

According to Rogers, Jackson, Sewell, Tillbrook, and Martin (2003), one of the greatest challenges when conducting evaluations of competence to stand trial is operationalizing the *Dusky* criteria so as to produce a systematic and reliable assessment. Contemporary practice in assessment of competence to stand trial suggests the use of validated instruments in combination with clinical interviews and other relevant assessments (Melton et al., 2007). In cases involving people with ID, information on intellectual functioning is essential. Other assessments that tap related skills, such as cognition (e.g., Wechsler Memory Scale; WMS-IV, 2009) and language (e.g., *OWLS: Oral and Written Language Scales II*; Carrow-Woolfolk, 2011), and assessments like the *Peabody Picture Vocabulary Test–Third Edition* (Dunn & Dunn, 2007) and the *TOAL-4: Test of Adolescent and Adult Language–Fourth Edition* (Hammill, Brown, Larsen, & Wiederholt, 2007), can provide good supportive information on defendant capacity.

Three of the most commonly used assessments of competence to stand trial are the *MacArthur Competence Assessment Tool–Criminal Adjudication* (MacCAT-CA; Hoge, Bonnie, Poythress, & Monahan, 1999), the *Evaluation of Competency to Stand Trial–Revised* (ECST-R; Rogers, Tillbrook, & Sewell, 2004), and the *Competence Assessment for Standing Trial for Defendants with Mental Retardation* (CAST-MR; Everington & Luckasson, 1992). A brief discussion regarding the utility of each assessment for people with ID is provided in the following sections. For more information on psychometric properties of these instruments, the reader is referred to the following research: Everington (1990) and Everington and Dunn 1995) for the CAST-MR; Poythress, Bonnie, Monahan, Otto and Hoge (2002) for the MacCAT-CA; and Rogers et al. (2003) for the ECST-R.

1. **The Competence Assessment for Standing Trial for Defendants With Mental Retardation (CAST-MR):** The CAST-MR (Everington & Luckasson, 1992), the oldest of the three measures, remains the only instrument developed specifically for use with people with ID. The instrument has three sections: (a) Basic Legal Concepts (25 items), (b) Skills to Assist Defense (15 items), and (c) Understanding Case Events (10 items). Sections I and II consist of multiple-choice questions. The multiple-choice format was chosen because it provides a quick, reliable means of assessing defendant understanding. Section III assesses defendants/ability to relate important information regarding their own legal circumstances through an open-ended questioning format. The CAST-MR is a "first generation" competence instrument as it focuses more on defendant's factual understanding and less on appreciation and reasoning (Poythress et al., 2002). Section II, Skills to Assist in Defense, and Section III, Understanding Case Events, however, provides information on defendants' rational understanding of their circumstances and capacity for decision making in their own defense (Grisso, 2003). The CAST-MR authors provide a caveat in the manual stating that the results should always be supplemented with additional information relevant to a defendant's competence. The CAST-MR can be useful as a screening tool for gauging the defendant's level of understanding of the proceedings and some aspects of decisional competence, for a defendant who has ID.

2. **The MacArthur Competence Assessment Tool—Criminal Adjudication (MacCAT-CA):** The MacCAT-CA (Hoge et al., 1999) is designed primarily around the notion of decisional competence. The instrument is composed of three scales: (a) Understanding (8 items), (b) Reasoning (8 items), and

(c) Appreciation (6 items). The MacCAT-CA uses what the authors refer to as "vignette methodology" by asking the examinee to make decision about a hypothetical case involving two defendants: Fred and Reggie (Poythress et al., 2002). The first two sections assess understanding and reasoning through questions about the legal system and options available to Fred. The third section, Appreciation, assesses the rationality of defendants' beliefs about their own case (Poythress et al., 2002). The strong concentration on decision making and rational understanding makes the MacCAT-CA a possible option for assessing competence in defendants with ID, as impaired reasoning is central to the disability. Although the conceptual approach to this instrument is relevant to this population, there are two concerns regarding the use of the instrument with people with ID. The primary concern is that it has not been normed on people with IQs under 70. We found no research-supported findings on the MacCAT-CA with this population. Because of this lack of normative data, we do not recommend this instrument as a primary assessment of competence to stand trial. Second, there has been some critique that the vignette methodology may not provide sufficient information on defendants' ability to make rational decisions in their own situations (Ackin, 2012). Should the examiner choose to use the MacCAT-CA, the findings must be supplemented with other information on defendants' rational decision making in their own situations and with the administration of a second instrument that has an established research base with people with ID.

3. **The Evaluation of Competency to Stand Trial–Revised (ECST-R):** The ECST-R (Rogers et al., 2004) purports to measure all three prongs of the *Dusky* standard. It contains three sections: (a) Consult with Counsel (6 items), (b) Factual Understanding of the Courtroom Proceedings (6 items), and (c) Rational Understanding of the Courtroom Proceedings (7 items). Unlike the other instruments, the ECST-R contains feigning scales. Feigning is assessed through the Atypical Presentation scales, which are organized around psychotic, non-psychotic, and purported impairment categories (Rogers & Johansson-Love, 2009). Unlike the MacCAT-CA, the norming sample of the ECST-R included people with ID. According to the manual, the ECST-R has been "validated on defendants with a range of cognitive abilities" (p. 9) and is appropriate for use with defendants with measured IQs of 60 or greater. A word of caution, however, is necessary here because the IQ scores were derived from the Shipley Institute of Living Scale (SILS; Zachary, 1986), and there is no indication that these people represented a sample of people who had been diagnosed as having ID. The concern regarding the IQ estimate is how close it is to an IQ obtained by a comprehensive measure of intelligence. According to the manual, the SILS "is not appropriate for individuals who have suspected mental retardation or have suffered profound cognitive deterioration due to neurological or severe psychological disturbances. Rather, it is intended as a screening device for the

broad band of near-average intelligence" (p. 2).

Defendant responses on the competence scales are scored using a 5-point rating scale, which centers on the degree of psychopathology: zero, not observed; 1, questionable clinical significance; 2, mild impairment unrelated to competence; 3, moderate impairment that will affect but not by itself impair competence; and 4, severe impairment that substantially impairs competence. Use of this type of scale with people with ID who do not present with a secondary psychiatric diagnosis may be less reliable and useful for interpretation than assessments ratings that are more closely aligned with the concept being tested. There is no published research beyond the norming sample on actual use and interpretation of the ECST-R with people with ID. The instrument, however, has strong psychometric properties and enjoys wide acceptance in the forensic community.

Regardless of the assessment used, a determination of competence is highly contextual. The complexity of a capital case will likely require a more sophisticated level of understanding and participation.

Findings of Incompetence

A finding of incompetence is often problematic for people with ID. Because of the severity of impairments, the majority of people with ID will not be restorable (i.e., trained to the point that they meet the minimum standard for competence). Defendants who are considered restorable receive treatment in institutional or outpatient settings, and this is true for defendants with ID. There are two primary problems with the application of these programs for defendants with ID. The first is that they are typically used for people with major mental illnesses that respond well to psychotropic medication; that is, as the interfering symptomatology (e.g., psychosis) abates, amenability to intervention increases. Intellectual disability does not fit this paradigm; and, as such, competence restoration programs must be different from the mainstream and focus on training in light of relatively unchanging cognitive status. The second problem is that these restoration programs concentrate on teaching factual understanding of the system, which is important, but does not deal with the two areas of primary concern for this population; working with their attorneys and having a rational understanding of the proceedings. Rational understanding is generally considered a higher-order ability than factual understanding and communication with one's attorney requires adequate receptive, expressive and social skills in addition to decision-making skills (Viljoen, 2007).

While there is a paucity of published research on competence training with ID, treatment centers report some success in teaching persons with intellectual disability at the upper end of the range (Anderson & Hewitt, 2002). Some programs are beginning to address decisional competency. Although administration is oral for the Grisso test, the test booklet is presented to the examinee to allow him or her to follow along via reading. There is no research on the value of the visual aid, but it is possible that this allows for better processing as it removes the need to retain information in memory.)

The Slater Method (Wall, Krupp & Guilmette, 2003), an outpatient-training program for incompetent defendants with ID, combines knowledge-based training with what the authors call "understanding-based training." Understanding-based training focuses on understanding consequences and decision-making in the context of the defendant's case. However, outcomes are limited to case examples. Although this appears promising, it is unclear if this training can improve one's rational understanding and rational ability to assist in own defense in the actual legal context. It is suggested that independent evaluations be conducted on individuals who have successfully completed restoration programs to insure that all aspects of the standard are met.

Applying Competence-to-Stand-Trial Principles

In a similar way as with the competence to confess, the relevant literature related to competence to stand trial provides guidance for applications to practice. A number of implications derive from the work in this area.

An initial focus has to do with the evaluation of the defendant's knowledge and ability relative to the presenting psycholegal issue. A key concern has to do with operationalizing the functional abilities relative to the referral question, which may consist of a vague statement such as difficulty in understanding and communicating with the attorney (Kalbeitzer & Benedetti, 2009). Several assessment procedures are relevant. Interviewing the attorney and reviewing client-attorney written communication may assist in pinpointing the focus of the evaluation. Such interviews, along with input from significant others, can also provide examples of communication difficulties, such as frequent misunderstandings of conversations and provide a foundation for the evaluation. A semi-structured interview with the defendant provides further understanding of the critical concepts relative to the case.

A second important consideration is the use of questioning and interview techniques that are appropriate for use with people with ID. Best practice in forensic evaluations dictates comprehensive clinical interviews (Melton et al., 2007). Of particular importance with defendants with ID are the critical characteristics of the person that can bias interview results. These may include the tendency to mask deficits by providing minimal verbal responses, the feigning of understanding, and the tendency of people with ID toward acquiescence. These problems can be exacerbated by the use of yes/no responses while they can be avoided by requesting defendants to restate concepts in their own words.

A third consideration is the use of competence-assessment measures that contain normative data on people with ID, as discussed previously. Clinical interviews can be supported by results from a standardized, norm-referenced competence assessment, which are helpful because the use of such assessments is recognized as good practice (because it keeps the focus on the psycholegal abilities; Grisso, 2003), and also because, given that many defendants with ID do not present as impaired, comparisons to the typical population are important for the court's understanding of this disability. Using an instrument that contains normative data on people with ID, as discussed earlier (e.g., the CAST-MR), provides an added benefit because a subset of people with intellectual disability is competent to proceed. Group performance data on people with ID provide an important reference point.

Fourth, collateral information (e.g., assessments of intellectual, academic, linguistic, and cognitive functioning) provides important supplements in the process of assessing defendant functioning. These data may confirm defendant competence deficits and may provide data to counter (or support) malingering claims. Third-party adaptive behavior interview information can also be useful in assessing possible deficiencies in understanding, memory, and reasoning.

Conclusion

Two important considerations within the criminal justice system that have particular relevance for defendants who have an intellectual disability are competence to confess and competence to stand trial. Careful consideration of competence to confess requires the use of appropriate assessment procedures that relate directly to an individual's understanding of the *Miranda* warning and waiver. Consideration of competence to stand trial requires assessment in order to determine whether). Competence to stand trial is a critical issue for defendants with ID because of the importance of determining whether they possess the level of cognition, abstract thinking, reasoning, and language processing to understand and participate fully in the legal processes.

References

Ackin, M. W. (2012). The forensic clinician's Toolbox I: A review of competency to stand trial (CST) instruments. *Journal of Personality Assessment, 94,* 220–222. http://dx.doi.org/10.108 0/00223891.2011.627970

Anderson, S. D., & Hewitt, J. (2002). The effect of competency restoration training on defendants with mental retardation found not competent to proceed. *Law and Human Behavior, 26,* 343–351. doi: 10.1023/A:1015328505884

Bevel v. Florida, 983 So. 2d 505 (Fla. 2008).

Bonnie, R. J. (1992). The competence of defendants with mental retardation to assist in their own defense. In R. W. Conley, L. Luckasson, & G. N. Bouthilet (Eds.), *The criminal justice system and mental retardation* (pp. 79–96). Baltimore, MD: Paul H. Brooks.

Brodsky, S. L., & Bennett, A. D. (2005). Psychological assessments of confessions and suggestibility in mentally retarded suspects. *Journal of Psychiatry & Law, 33,* 359–366.

Carrow-Woolfolk, E. (2011). *OWLS: Oral and Written Language Scales: Second Ed.* Minneapolis, MN: Pearson Assessments.

Cloud, M., Shepard, G. B., Barkoff, A. N., & Shur, J. (2002). Words without meaning: The constitution, confessions, and mentally retarded suspects. *Chicago Law Review, 69,* 495–624.

Dickerson v. United States, 530 U.S. 428, 120 S.Ct. 2326, 147 L.Ed.2d 405 (2000).

Dunn, L. M., & Dunn, D. M. (2007). *Peabody picture vocabulary test: Third edition. PPVT-III.* San Antonio, TX: Pearson.

Dusky v. United States, 362 U.S. 402 (1960).

Ellis, J., & Luckasson, R. (1985). Mentally retarded criminal defendants. *George Washington Law Review, 53,* 414–492.

Ericson, K. L., & Perlman, N. B. (2001). Knowledge and legal terminology and court proceedings in adults with developmental disabilities. *Law and Human Behavior, 25,* 529–544.

Everington, C. (1989, fall/winter). Demographic variables associated with competence to stand trial referral and evaluation of criminal defendants with mental retardation. *The Journal of Psychiatry and Law,* 627–640.

Everington, C. (1990). The competence assessment for standing trial for defendants with mental retardation (CAST-MR): A validation study. *Criminal Justice and Behavior, 17,* 147–168.

Everington, C., DeBerge, K., & Mauer, D. (2001). The relationship between language skills and competence to stand trial abilities in persons with mental retardation. *The Journal of Psychiatry and Law, 28,* 475–492.

Everington, C., & Dunn, C. (1995). A second validation study of the competence assessment for standing trial for defendants with mental retardation. *Criminal Justice and Behavior, 22,* 44–59.

Everington, C., & Fulero, S. M. (1999). Competence to confess: Measuring understanding and suggestibility of defendants with mental retardation. *Mental Retardation, 37,* 212–220.

Everington, C., & Luckasson, R. (1992). *The competence assessment for standing trial for defendants with mental retardation (CAST-MR).* Worthington, OH: IDS.

Fare v. Michael C., 442 U.S. 707 (1979).

Frumkin, B. (2000). Competency to waive *Miranda* rights: Clinical and legal issues. *Mental and Physical Disability Law Reported, 24,* 326–331.

Frumkin, B. (2008). Psychological evaluation in *Miranda* waiver and confession cases. In R. L. Denney & J. P. Sullivan (Eds.), *Clinical neuropsychology in the criminal forensic setting* (135–175). New York, NY: Guilford Press.

Frumkin, B., & Garcia, A. (2003). Psychological evaluations and the competency to waive *Miranda* rights. *The National Association of Criminal Defense Lawyers Champion, 27,* 11–22.

Fulero, S., & Everington, C. (1995). Competency to waive *Miranda* rights in defendants with mental retardation. *Law and Human Behavior, 19*, 533–543.

Genaro v. California, 2007 WL 934886 (2007).

Goldstein, N. E., Condie, L. O., Kalbeitzer, R., Osman, D., & Geier, J. (2003). Juvenile offenders' *Miranda* rights comprehension and self-reported likelihood of offering false confessions. *Assessment, 10*, 359–369. doi: 10.1177/1073191103259535

Godinez v. Moran, 509 U.S. 389 (1993).

Greenspan, S., Loughlin, G., & Black, R. S. (2001). Credulity and gullibility in people with developmental disorders: A framework for future research. In L. M. Glidden (Ed.), *International review of research in mental retardation* (pp. 101–135). New York, NY: Academic Press.

Greenspan, S., Switzkey, H. N., & Woods, G. W. (2011). Intelligence involves risk-awareness and intellectual disability involves risk-unawareness: Implications of a theory of common sense. *Journal of Intellectual and Developmental Disability, 36*, 246–257. doi:10.3109/13668250.2011.626759

Grisso, T. (1998). *Instruments for Assessing Understanding & Appreciation of* Miranda *Rights*. Sarasota, FL: Professional Resource Press.

Grisso, T. (2003). *Evaluating competencies: Forensic assessments and instruments* (2nd ed.). New York, NY: Kluwer Academic/Plenum Publishers.

Gudjonsson, G. H. (1997). *Gudjonsson Suggestibility manual*. East Sussex, UK: Psychology Press.

Hammill, D. D., Brown, V. L., Larsen, S. C., & Wiederholt, J. L. (2007). *TOAL4: Test of Adolescent and Adult Language* (4th ed.). Minneapolis, MN: Pearson Assessments.

Hoge, S. K., Bonnie, R. J., Poythress, N. G., & Monahan, J. (1999). *MacArthur Competence assessment tool—Criminal adjudication*. Sarasota, FL: Professional Resource Press.

In re Patrick W. (1978), 84 Cal. App. 3d 520 [148 Cal.Rptr. 735]

Iowa v. Tovar, 541 U.S. 77, 124 S.Ct. 1379, 158 L.Ed.2d 209 (2004).

Kalbeitzer, R., & Benedetti, R. (2009). Assessment of competency to stand trial in individuals with mental retardation. *Journal of Forensic Psychology Practice, 9*, 237–248. doi:10.1080/15228930902809955

McLachlan, K., Roesch, R., & Douglas, K. S. (2011). Examining the role of interrogative suggestibility in *Miranda* rights comprehension in adolescents. *Law and Human Behavior, 35*, 165–177. doi: 10.1007/s10979-009-9198-4

Melton, G. B., Petrila, J., Poythress, N. G., & Slobogin, C. (2007). *Psychological evaluations for the courts: A handbook for mental health professionals and lawyers*. New York, NY: Guilford Press.

Miranda v. Arizona, 384 U.S. 436 (1966).

Misskelly v. Arkansas, 323, Ark., 449, 915 S. W. 2d 702 (1996).

Morane v. Burbine, 475 U.S. 412 (1986).

Mumley, D. L., Tillbrook, C. E. & Grisso, T. (2003). Five year research update (1996–2000): Evaluations for competence to stand trial (adjudicative competence). *Behavioral Sciences and the Law, 21*, 329–350. doi: 10.1002/bsl.534

New Jersey v. King, 904 A.2d 808 (2006).

New York v. Raposo, 1998 WL 879723 (1998).

Nicholson, R. A., & Kugler, K. E. (1991). Competent and incompetent defendants: A quantitative review of competency research, *Psychological Bulletin, 109*, 355–370.

Oberlander, L. B., Goldstein, N. E., & Goldstein, A. M. (2003). Competence to confess. In A. M. Goldstein (Ed.), *Handbook of psychology: Forensic psychology, vol 11* (pp. 335–357). Hoboken, New Jersey, NJ: Wiley.

O'Connell, M. J., Garmoe, W., & Goldstein, N. (2005). *Miranda* comprehension in adults with mental retardation and the effects of feedback style on suggestibility. *Law and Human Behavior, 29*, 359–369. doi: 10.1007/s10979-005-2965-y

Oregon v. Romero, 81 P.3d 714 (2003).

Patterson v. Illinois, 487 U.S. 285 (1988).

Poythress, N. G., Bonnie, R. J., Monahan, J., Otto, R., & Hoge, S. K. (2002). *Adjudicative competence: The MacArthur studies.* Washington, DC: American Psychological Association.

Roesch, R., McLachlan, K., & Viljoen, J. L. (2008). *The capacity of juveniles to understand and waive arrest rights.* In R. Jackson (Ed.), *Learning forensic assessment* (pp. xii, 265–289, 618). New York: Routledge/Taylor & Francis.

Rogers, R., Jackson, R. L., Sewell, K. W., Tillbrook, C. E., & Martin, M. A. (2003). Assessing dimensions of competency to stand trial: Construct validation of the ECST-R. *Assessment, 10,* 344–351.

Rogers, R., & Johansson-Love, J. (2009). Evaluating competency to stand trial with evidence-based practice. *Journal of the American Academy of Psychiatry and Law, 37,* 450–460.

Rogers, R., Rogstad, J., Gillard, N., Drogin, E., Blackwood, H., & Shuman, D. (2010). "Everyone knows their *Miranda* rights": Implicit assumptions and countervailing evidence. *Psychology, Public Policy, and the Law, 17,* 264–285.

Rogers, R., Sewell, K. W., Drogin, E. Y., & Fiduccia, C. E. (2012). *Standardized Assessment of Miranda Abilities (SAMA) professional manual.* Odessa, FL: Psychological Assessment Resources.

Rogers, R., & Shuman, D. W. (2005). *Fundamentals of forensic practice: Mental health and criminal law.* New York, NY: Springer Science and Business Media.

Rogers, R., Tillbrook, C. E., & Sewell, K. W. (2004). *Evaluation of Competency to Stand Trial–Revised* (ECST-R). Odessa, FL: Psychological Assessment Resources.

Rosenfeld, B., & Wall, A. (1998). Psychopathology and competence to stand trial. *Criminal Justice and Behavior, 25,* 443–462.

Smith, A. H. W., & O'Brien, G. (2004). Offenders with dual diagnosis. In W. R. Lindsay, J. L. Taylor, & P. Strumey (Eds.), *Offenders with developmental disabilities* (pp. 241–263). West Sussex, England: Wiley.

Smith, S. A., & Hudson, R. L. (1995). A quick screening test of competency to stand trial for defendants with mental retardation. *Psychological Reports, 76,* 91–97.

Soares v. Massachusetts, 51 Mass.App.Ct. 273, 745 N.E. 2d 362 (2001).

Summers v. Wisconsin, 246 Wis.2d 672, 630 N.W. 277 (2001).

Viljoen, J. L. (2007). Prospects for remediating juvenile's adjudicative incompetence. *Psychology, Public Policy, and Law, 13,* 87–114. doi: 10.1037/1076-8971.13.2.87

Wall, B. W., Krupp, B. H., & Guilmette, T. (2003). Restoration of competency to stand trial: A training program for persons with mental retardation. *Journal of the American Academy of Psychiatry and Law, 31,* 189–201.

Wechsler, D. (2009) *Wechsler Memory Scale WMS IV.* San Antonio, TX: Pearson.

Zachary, R. A. (1986). *The Shipley Institute of Living Scale–Revised Manual.* Los Angeles, CA: Western Psychological Services.

18 | Retrospective Diagnosis and Malingering

Denis W. Keyes
David Freedman

This chapter focuses on two types of validity concerns that can occur in the assessment of intellectual disability (ID): retrospective diagnosis and malingering. Retrospective diagnoses are necessary when a person is older than the neurodevelopmental age period in which ID develops (before age 18). This assessment may be the necessary consequence of diagnostic error during the developmental period, especially in schools; legitimate concerns about stigma and labeling children who function at the higher end of ID; cultural or ethnic differences; or immigration from a place where testing is not routine or norms do not exist for testing instruments.

The chapter also considers the scientific and legal questions related to the possibility that some people may attempt to malinger ID. To that end, this chapter reviews the current status and accuracy of methods to determine evidence of malingering, provides information on problems related to measures of malingering identification, and relates these considerations to retrospective diagnosis.

Retrospective Diagnosis

Forensic assessments of ID, particularly in the context of death penalty litigation, require in-depth investigations, past and present, of both intellectual functioning and adaptive behavior. The requirements for competent and effective forensic assessment of neurobehavioral functioning, including that which should be done in cases where ID is hypothesized, was recently set out (Woods, Freedman, & Grenspan, 2012). The comprehensive approach to assessment means that the mental health professional must consider the validity and reliability of any and all previous assessments (and diagnoses), as well as the possibility of various types of errors or inaccuracies in past testing protocols, in interviews with the subject's family, in reviewing often subjective school records, and even in the various social contexts in which the individual was raised. In most situations, possibly dating back to an individual's enrollment in K–12 education, the lack of any original testing data may be a strong reason for arguing that consideration of a retrospective diagnosis is necessary.

Identifying the existence of intellectual disability may cause significant problems for assessment professionals, especially those whose clinical judgment may be lacking as a result of limited background in the field of intellectual disability (Schalock et al., 2010). An additional challenge is that each state has developed its own statutes that relate to diagnostic standards; such diversity of statutes presents the concern that certain children may be identified as having intellectual disability in some states (or even different school districts within the same state), but not in others (Heward, 2013; Reschly, 1996; Tassé, 2014). This reality also relates to the definitional issues of individual states given the way that the U.S. Supreme Court framed the decision in *Atkins v. Virginia* (2002), although they have recently been prevented from ignoring scientific protocol (*Hall v. Florida*, 2014).

Retrospective assessments raise issues at two time points in relation to the clinical judgment and specialized training of the assessor. The current evaluator needs to have the training and skills to assess the testing, records, and functioning of the person in question. In addition, the current evaluator must consider whether the prior evaluator(s) had the clinical training and judgment to conduct an evaluation and reach valid opinions. Further, the current evaluator must consider the context, social and cultural, of the prior assessment, and take into consideration the purpose and goals of the prior evaluation. If, for example, the prior evaluation arose because a child was viewed as acting out in the classroom, it is important for the current evaluator to understand the possible causes of the behavior (e.g., familial abuse, poverty and hunger, bullying), as well as to gain information about the options and resources that were available within the school to assess and ameliorate the referral question. It is often the case that the referral question was not ID, and the assessment and intervention plan did not consider ID, even when a qualifying score may have been obtained.

To respond to the previous concerns, the current evaluator must obtain raw testing data (when possible) to determine what specifically has been done to reach opinions, and to check and recalculate scoring. It is often found that out-of-date instruments were used by school psychologists or educational diagnosticians, and the Flynn effect has rarely been considered in juvenile cases (Flynn, 2006; Flynn & Widaman, 2008; Chapter 10); or that partial test forms or screening tests were administered and resulting scores estimated or prorated; or that substantial calculation errors occurred in summing and converting raw scores to scaled scores (Kuentzel, Hetterscheidt, & Barnett , 2011; *U.S. v. Antun Lewis*, 2010). Obtaining raw testing data is essential to evaluating the prior testing that occurred, the reliability of that testing, and whether the conclusions and opinions reached at the time were supported by an adequately trained and experienced evaluator, who made proper use of the test materials and had sufficient collateral social and family information to support his or her conclusion.

Research has identified certain defensive characteristics of people with ID in which they minimize symptoms (associated with ID) that may confound accuracy in a retrospective diagnostic process. The stigma associated with being labeled with ID leads many people to attempt to hide their condition, to minimize and underreport symptoms so as to appear higher functioning and to otherwise seek to appear more competent at a task than they may actually be. This characteristic of some people with ID makes an accurate diagnosis more difficult, tending to systematically underidentify those with ID (Edgerton, 1967; Edgerton, Bollinger & Herr, 1984). This feature has been termed the "Cloak of Competence," in which a person who truly has ID may sometimes be successful at appearing to have average functioning (sometimes referred to as "masking"), answering questions as if the person understands the question or has some information about the topic to appear better functioning and avoid the stigma of low cognitive ability.

The Cloak of Competence ruse can make attorneys, judges, and juries believe that the defendant cannot be intellectually impaired because, as one psychiatrist in a Florida case (i.e., *Hayes v. Florida,* 1991) testified, "He doesn't look retarded. … He has that 'spark of intelligence' in his eyes." Such behaviors, even in the face of serious consequences, speaks to the power of the self-stigma and the fear of being publicly labeled as a person with ID (Ali, Hassiotis, Strydom, & King, 2012). For forensic assessments, where the labeling is public and the risk of imprisonment bears potentially additional consequences for being labeled, stigma and the Cloak of Competence can make assessments significantly more difficult, particularly for those professionals not experienced in working with those who have ID.

Diagnoses of children who have ID may be erroneous for many reasons; but one significant reason is parental reluctance to accept, and teacher/psychologist reluctance to give, a label (e.g., "mentally retarded") that may persist throughout a child's life and may have many negative consequences associated with it. Educators may not always be willing to use terms that are considered derogatory and of limited educational value, in favor of seemingly less objectionable titles, such as "developmentally learning disabled" (*Hayes v. State of Florida*, 1991). A related reason for such determinations may be the historical overrepresentation of children of minority backgrounds in special education (Arnold & Lassmann, 2003; *Larry P. v. Riles*, 1972).

In circumstances where a child is likely to be diagnosed with ID, the diagnostic process often begins in school, when a child's development may be determined as significantly below the level expected of other children of the same age. This can occur in several areas, including intellectual capacity and adaptive behavior, and both of these areas figure prominently in the diagnosis of ID (see Chapter 2). Yet, children with ID who have higher IQ test scores (i.e., high 60s) may perform marginally adequately, meaning comparatively within the range of their peer group, for the first several years of elementary school and therefore may not be identified early in school. Children with ID commonly have a different developmental trajectory than peers without ID, with a shallower developmental slope, and plateaus sooner and lower than their peers without disabilities. Therefore, over time, as tasks and expectations for functioning become more complex, the impairments become ever more obvious and the differences in functioning become more pronounced. An additional concern is that IQ tests are less reliable and less stable for children, with wider confidence intervals, which concern can make early childhood diagnosis of those in the higher range of ID considerably more difficult.

After initial efforts are made to determine the possible need for more formal assessment (see Fuchs & Fuchs, 2005), school psychologists and special education teachers may be the first professionals who are asked to examine and evaluate the functioning of children for possible learning disabilities or ID. For the professional in a forensic setting, evaluating the accuracy and legitimacy of previous testing requires two important considerations: first, that school districts may not have had adequate resources to obtain the services of highly qualified and certified school psychologists, and had to resort to less-than-adequately prepared diagnosticians, or even teachers or counselors with a minimum of training in administering the instruments necessary for identifying ID in the upper ranges in children; and second, that parents (and even some multidisciplinary teams), as noted above, are sometimes reluctant to identify children as having ID, even when such diagnosis is clearly incontrovertible. As such, children may go through school receiving special services for children with disabilities, yet still not be *correctly* diagnosed or identified for a variety of reasons (Arnold & Lassmann, 2003; MacMillan & Reschly, 1998). Because of assessment inadequacies, some children may not be identified at all or may be labeled as, for example, having learning disabilities or emotional disturbance, rather than ID.

In those situations where the original diagnosis was, if not erroneous, obfuscated or watered down, other seemingly less branding labels, such as "developmentally delayed," "developmentally disabled" or "learning disabled" may have been substituted for what was then referred to as *mentally retarded*. This mislabeling also happened in cases where parents objected to their child being stigmatized by having been labeled as having ID, and in cases of perceived overrepresentation of minority children in special education when the use of the label was discouraged (Macmillan & Siperstein, 2002). When these same children, who may or may not have received adequate special education services to prepare them for life after school, have legal difficulties later in life, the original inaccurate diagnosis may finally come into question, possibly even thwarting justice (*Arizona v. Kyle Allegria*, 2013; *Arizona v. Shawn Grell*, 2011; *Commonwealth of Kentucky v. Brian Crabtree*, 2011; *Hayes v. State of Florida*, 1991; *Missouri v. Alys Ben Johns*, 2003; *Oklahoma v. Joshua Durcho*, 2012). The courts are then left to sort out which is the correct diagnosis, based on past records and testimony of various teachers, school psychologists (should any of them still be alive), and experts from both side of the bar (who may or may not have had any substantive clinical experience with people who have ID).

When people who have disabilities are involved in criminal court proceedings, the burden of proof, as noted in *Atkins v. Virginia* (2002), clearly rests with the defense, but in cases of misdiagnosis, the only option may be retrospective diagnosis, based on proof that the original diagnosis—if any was made—was in error (Macmillan & Siperstein, 2002). It is possible that a child with ID may have been "socially promoted" through elementary, middle school, and even high school, yet never properly diagnosed or identified as having ID (*Oklahoma v. Joshua Durcho*, 2012). In such cases, school and other records, a comprehensive social history that identifies difficulties encountered during school years, and interviews with those who knew the client well become crucial to an accurate determination (see also Chapter 20).

It is noteworthy to consider that when a defense strategy places the burden of proof on the defendant, it creates a significant challenge in instances when the claim is made that the individual has ID. In particular, when this is taken to the point of proving intellectual disability *beyond a reasonable doubt*, then considerations of both retrospective assessment, and/or malingering (discussed later in the chapter), could be seen as sufficient to raise the jurors' and the court's level of doubt (see Chapter 4). In such instances, the lack of corresponding documentation that indicates the defendant experienced functional difficulties during early childhood, school or in subsequent social relationships, can make it challenging to form an accurate retrospective diagnostic finding. This problem is more significant in the face of federal privacy laws that encourage schools to destroy many records after 5 years of leaving school (Family Educational Rights and Privacy Act [FERPA], 1974).

A special problem in diagnosis relates to the use of current adaptive behavior assessment data obtained from a person in a prison environment. For example, a particular case in Florida required that adaptive skills could be determined only at the *present* time (often after months or even years in prison), with no consideration of previous circumstances and impaired adaptive functioning of the defendant (*Jones v. State of Florida*, 2007). This lack of acknowledgment of the past does not permit any consideration of the fact that incarceration drastically increases the structure in one's life, and that high structure imposed on adults with ID will, generally, increase one's *apparent* adaptive functioning (Keyes & Edwards, 1996). This practice is inconsistent with accepted methodology in the field (see Schalock et al., 2010).

In situations where the goal is to place assessment data within a retrospective context, the value of documentation and records that effectively chronicle the defendant's past is significant. This is particularly true for medical, educational, psychological, employment-vocational, and juvenile justice records. State agency records, such as those from welfare and children's protection divisions, may also help to shed light on crucial behavioral facts that might, otherwise, go unreported. For those defendants who were identified as having some form of disability, school files may include psychoeducational reports, individualized education programs (IEPs), and, though rare, even raw data from past evaluations. These files are more likely to be available for younger defendants, because, as mentioned previously, subsequent privacy laws (i.e., *FERPA*) have served to hasten the destruction of school records, usually within 5 years of the year the student was supposed to graduate. In the event that school records have already been destroyed, the state department of education may still hold documentation as a result of legislative requirements of the Individuals with Disabilities Education Act (IDEA; *20 USC at 1400, et seq.*, 1991). Every school district in each state is required to submit a 100-day report outlining how many children receive services under Part B (school age) of IDEA, thus accounting for disbursed funds. In many instances, such documentation includes the names of children being served and the disability area under which they are being served. Chapter 20 in this volume discusses the role of school records in more significant detail.

If accurate retrospective diagnosis is to be successful, several factors must come into play. First, the defense must have adequate resources to acquire an experienced investigator who can concentrate on finding all-important documentation of prior functioning. This would include records illuminating the defendant's prior personal behavior, difficulties during school (both academic and social), prior assessments, and educational services (particularly under the auspices of special education), medical and hospital records, social and child protection service records, welfare records, and any prior interactions within the criminal justice system that may (or may not) indicate a lack of ability to conform one's maladaptive behaviors to accepted standards. Second, experts are better prepared when able to interview people who have known the defendant well during the developmental period. Interviewing various family members, including parents, siblings, and possibly former partners or spouses, is but a beginning to this endeavor. Friends are typically important interviewees and often may enlighten certain personal aspects overlooked by others, particularly possible social skill deficits. In these interviews, anecdotes can help to make the judge or jury aware of the defendant's concrete thinking processes. For example, in one case, the defendant's mother was asked to give an example of her son's behavior. She stated, "One night, when he was about 12, it was real hot in the apartment, and I told him to go and 'crack the door' a little. He got up, went in the kitchen and got a hammer, and started banging on the door to crack it" (*Allen v. State*, 2001).

Teachers, administrators, and school psychologists are among the most important interviews when trying to make an accurate retrospective diagnosis because several of them may have been involved in prior diagnostic processes during school. In some cases, the testimony of teachers has been the central testimony, such as with teachers even stating that, at the time of the original assessment, they knew the disability label being applied was inaccurate, and that the child actually had ID (*South Carolina v. Robert Nance*, 2012). In such circumstances, the existing documentation may be even more vital, since it may indicate that there was dissonance among team members in determining an accurate diagnosis. In addition, a careful reading of the defendant's IEP from school may reflect a behavioral level that disputes a diagnosis of learning disability, and supports a diagnosis of intellectual disability (Everington & Keyes, 1999; Keyes, 1997; Keyes & Edwards, 1995b).

Considerations of Malingering

Determining Intent

To accurately develop a proper diagnosis from any assessment, psychologists must determine that the level of cooperation presented meets the standard expected of a person who is being assessed. Therefore, the second area of concern for both current and retrospective assessments is whether or not the person is malingering ID. The American Psychiatric Association's *Diagnostic and Statistical Manual* (DSM-V, 2013) defines malingering as "the intentional production of false or grossly exaggerated physical or psychological symptoms, motivated by external incentives" (p. 726). As Conroy and Kwartner (2006) stated, "the difference between malingering and simple unreliable reporting is a matter of the individual's intent. Malingering, by definition, is deliberate" (p. 30). The definition of malingering is important because the concept is often confused with effort and attention. Malingering is a specific attempt to deceive so as to gain some advantage, not a loss of focus or disinterest or simply not trying very hard.

In Justice Scalia's dissent from the U.S. Supreme Court's decision in *Atkins v. Virginia* (2002), he warned that the courts would be filled with death row inmates claiming "mental retardation" as grounds for appeal:

> One need only read the definitions of mental retardation adopted by the American Association of Mental Retardation and the American Psychiatric Association to realize that the symptoms of this condition can readily be feigned. And whereas the capital defendant who feigns insanity risks commitment to a mental institution until he can be cured (and then tried and executed), the capital defendant who feigns mental retardation risks nothing at all. The mere pendency of the present case has brought us petitions by death row inmates claiming for the first time, after multiple habeas petitions, that they are retarded. See, e.g., *Moore v. Texas*, 535 U.S. (2002) (Scalia, J., dissenting from grant of applications for stay of execution, (*Atkins v. Virginia*, 2002).

As noted by Blume and Salekin (in Chapter 4), Justice Scalia's prediction that virtually all of the inmates who are on death row would subsequently claim that they were mentally retarded has proven to be unjustified. Contrary to Scalia's prophecy of a flood of new appeals, Blume, Johnson, and Seeds (2012) reported that only approximately 7% of those inmates previously sentenced to death ultimately raised claims in which they alleged that they had ID and, consequently, were ineligible for execution.

A case example that might seem inconceivable should be mentioned: At least one condemned murderer on death row who was identified as having ID through his school years refused to cooperate in an evaluation because he did not want anyone to know he was "retarded" (*Arizona v. Auturo Cañez*, 2003). In another case, a defendant refused to be tested before trial because he did not want his public defender to pursue an *Atkins* defense (*Arizona v. Kyle Allegria*, 2013).

Detecting Malingering

Malingering has not been well researched, particularly with regard to people with ID (Keyes, 1994; Macvaugh, Cunningham, & Tassé, 2014; Salekin & Doane, 2009). Simply put, until relatively recently, the extant research focused on feigning ID has been limited (e.g., Keyes, 1994; Salekin & Doane, 2009). Malingering may be suspected as a result of possible confusion related to a combination of psychiatric symptoms, neurological symptoms, and cognitive deficits, especially likely for those practitioners who have little or no clinical experience or background training with people who have ID.

A significant amount of attention has been focused in recent years on developing tools to identify malingered psychiatric symptoms, and many of those tools have been applied, with poor results and little quantitative support, to assessing malingered ID. The use of test instruments to detect malingering has not been reliably demonstrated as valid for use with those who have ID, and research only to a limited degree supports the use of symptom validity indicators (that is, tests that ask for self-reported symptoms of illness in which a person excessively or unusually reports) for any population, because of serious validity and reliability concerns (Bigler, 2012; Salekin & Doane, 2009). A number of reviews of test instruments commonly used to assess malingering of psychiatric illnesses have found that these instruments are not valid and reliable (An et al., 2012; Armistead-Jehle & Buican, 2012; Bigelow, 2012), and are not valid or reliable when administered to people with ID (Graue et al., 2007; Salekin & Doane 2009; Shandera et al., 2010). Many of the approaches to detecting malingering make assumptions that are inappropriate for testing people with ID, although this problem is not specific to people with ID (Silver, 2012). Problems with the assessment tools and processes are discussed below.

First, and most obviously, many test instruments are not normed for people with ID, particularly those with language and learning deficits. Developing normative data for a test is expensive, and rarely are sufficient numbers of people with ID included in test sampling pools such that adequate population data can be obtained. Some test instruments are simply written at a level inappropriate for people with ID; for instance, the reading level required to complete the test is too high (Keyes, 2004; Salekin & Doane, 2009). Further, norming studies that focused on malingering ID specifically asked students to fake ID while completing the test. This procedure likely means that the students acted according to social and cultural biases about what ID *looks like*, creating false standards against which to measure people with ID. Other test "norms" are generated by samples of convenience such as, for instance, institutionalized case subjects who are not typical of, and do not adequately reflect, the broad range of abilities and functional potential of many people with ID. Such biased comparison samples are based on ill-conceived stereotypes, and thus are inappropriate and lead to invalid inferences.

Common tests that have been used to attempt to assess malingering include the *Test of Memory Malingering* (Tombaugh, 1996), the *Rey Memory Test* (1964), the *Dot Counting Test* (Rey, 1941), the *Validity Indicator Profile* (VIP-NV; Frederick, 1997), and the *Minnesota Multiphasic Personality Inventory-2* (MMPI-2; Butcher et al., 2001). These tests may have shown some usefulness in determining feigned performances in research settings, often with psychology students asked to feign a specific type of illness or condition, but the use of the original normative data for these tests is inaccurate because the standardization sampling representation typically did not include a group of people with ID. Reviews of these tests have indicated that their reliability and validity are highly suspect (Salekin & Doane, 2009).

Salekin and Doane (2009) concluded that the assessment instruments being used to evaluate malingering on tests of intellectual functioning had poor validity, particularly when used with examinees having low IQ. Thus, so-called *symptom validity tests* (SVT) could not be considered sensitive enough or truly effective in determining those people who really do have ID, as opposed to those who do not. Subsequently, diagnostic errors, either false negatives or false positives, in cases where the SVT results had ostensibly confirmed that malingering actually had or had not taken place, would result in two kinds of mistakes: putting people who really have ID at risk of being sentenced to death, or identifying those who really do not have ID as ineligible for being sentenced to death. The researchers indicated that "there exists virtually no support for the use of effort tests (e.g., forced-choice symptom validity test) or embedded indicators (Mittenburg et al., 2001) for assessing malingering of ID, particularly when using standard scoring procedures; and the bulk of the available data suggest that these methods are prone to error" (p. 106).

An example of a problematic assessment is the *MMPI-2* (Butcher et al., 2001). The *MMPI-2* (now revised, MMPI-RF), which although held in significant esteem among many clinical psychologists, has nevertheless been determined to be of little or no use in identifying malingering of ID. For instance, after *Atkins*, the Mississippi Supreme Court initially made a series of rulings (*Foster v. State,* 848, So.2d 172, [2003]) that required the *MMPI* be administered to prove the examinee was not malingering. This was the law until it was made clear to the Court that the *MMPI* was not intended for, and is an inappropriate choice for, distinguishing people who are malingering from those who really do have ID (Keyes, 2004); and the Court later overturned this requirement (*Chase v. State,* 873 So.2d 1013; Miss. 2004).

Second, many people with ID prefer to endorse psychiatric symptoms, rather than be uncovered as having ID, and often overendorse psychiatric symptoms as a result (Boone, 2007). Out of context and with limited information, this may look like malingering on symptom validity measures of feigning, or like invalid profiles on other tests. This may explain at least part of the finding that one commonly used test of feigned psychiatric illness has substantial numbers of false positives when given to people with ID (Weiss, Rosenfeld, & Farkas, 2011). Further, as noted in Chapter 19, comorbid psychiatric conditions are common for people with ID, and testing that addresses only how a person performs on cognitive tests and malingering tests will likely misdiagnose the accurate reporting of comorbid symptoms as malingering.

Third, effort and attention are often confused with malingering. Many assessments of effort may penalize people with ID for becoming frustrated. Frustration is common on testing that requires a person to continue answering beyond the point at which they are able (the revised *WAIS-IV* reduced the number of incorrect answers required before stopping, in part for this reason). In addition, testing that makes little sense to a person may lead the person to answer as quickly as possible to get finished. For instance, a person whose reading ability is lower than the *MMPI* requires, or just faced with the prospect of having to answer over 500 yes/no questions, may simply fill out the answer sheet to get done with the test, without reading, understanding, or caring about what the questions are asking. People with ID are particularly susceptible to this sort of frustration because of their cognitive impairment and adaptive deficits. The results, however, may present as lack of effort or lack of attention when in fact, the functionality associated with ID is directly causal of faulty answering patterns.

Fourth, a number of tests have a fundamental misconception about what a developmental disability is, how it manifests, and why it is different than an acquired illness or injury. The developmental course of ID means that, unlike with head injury research (where most malingering assessment protocols are generated), there is no "before" cognitive condition against which to compare the current functioning when considering malingering. Such approaches may fail to understand the trajectory of neurodevelopmental conditions and apply the wrong standards and expectations to testing.

This issue of neurodevelopmental trajectory points out the singular importance of historical data for determining a retrospective diagnosis of ID. Consistency is a critical concept for evaluating longitudinal data of a person's performance. Reviewing prior testing and the context of the administration of that testing, is critically important to developing a valid opinion as to a person's correct diagnosis. Accepting prior determinations of malingering or lack of effort without a review of the raw data and consideration of the methodological reliability of the test instruments is very inappropriate. Validity, consistency, patterns of deficit, competence of prior assessors, and the context of the prior testing should all be weighed in conducting an evaluation of malingering, especially in the context of a retrospective evaluation.

IQ and achievement testing are not the only areas in which people are thought to attempt to malinger ID. It has also been hypothesized that people may malinger adaptive functioning testing and questioning. Although there are no valid and reliable stand-alone test instruments for assessing malingered adaptive deficits (Salekin Doane, 2009), the comprehensive model of investigation which relies on a corroborated, multi-sourced reports of functioning at specific time points in a person's life history, is effective (Tassé, 2009).

Salekin and Doane (2009) reviewed methods of determining the existence of malingering and estimated the value of these methods that serves as an apt summary to this discussion. They concluded:

> [This] review of the research and assessment of malingered ID demonstrates that effort tests and indices of cognitive malingering are not working with this population, and that true cases can be misidentified as malingering. Some would say that the inclusion of multiple measures of malingering and the interpretation of all of the data together, rather than tests in isolation, provide control for diagnostic error. But to date, we have no data to suggest either of these techniques is protective and more importantly, we have no data on a juror or a judge might be impacted by even the slightest mention of malingering. Though untested, [we] posit that it is very unlikely a defense expert will succeed in supporting an *Atkins* claim if there is even a hint that malingering may have occurred. (p. 111)

Finally, there is one other scenario that may cause more difficulty in determining an accurate retrospective diagnosis that relates specifically to malingering. This situation can be puzzling for the clinician, particularly one lacking experience with those who have an intellectual disability. It is common for people who actually have ID to believe that they function significantly higher than they really do. This might simply be a defense mechanism against admitting one's personal deficits, or just another way to cloak the disability, but because many people who have ID in the upper ranges appear normal, it is possible that the denial of being disabled becomes their reality. Then, when asked to take an evaluation to show that they do, in fact, have ID, they may honestly believe that they function too well to be diagnosed with ID. Therefore, in an effort to avoid any question of qualifying for the diagnosis (thus avoiding the extreme punishment), the defendant may attempt to malinger, or deliberately perform worse, on tests of intelligence, academic achievement, or adaptive behavior, even though accurate performance would have qualified the defendant for the diagnosis.

In one case, the evaluator administered a Draw-A-Person test to the examinee, an inmate being tried for a double homicide for which the state was seeking death. The resulting stick figure was less than impressive, so the examinee was asked to repeat the test, again resulting in a stick figure. When the same examinee was given the Wide-Range Achievement Spelling Test, he missed all the words after the first three. Suspecting that the man was malingering, supplemental interviews were scheduled with the defendant's girlfriend, who was unaware that the defendant had performed so poorly in the examination. When asked if her boyfriend (the defendant) had ever written to her, or drawn pictures for her, she quickly supplied numerous examples of pictures he had drawn and letters he had written, in a flowery, cursive hand. Despite records that indicated the defendant had significant difficulty in learning during his limited education, he was still condemned (*Arizona v. Eric Boyston*, 2008).

Implications for Practice

The following considerations are important for practice as related to retrospective assessment and people with intellectual disability:

- Retrospective assessment becomes necessary when there is evidence that an individual may have had developmental delay that may previously have been overlooked or improperly diagnosed.
- Retrospective assessment requires a thorough examination based on multiple sources from the individual's past in order to determine whether there were adaptive behavior difficulties that may be associated with intellectual disability and that previously had been undiagnosed or misdiagnosed.
- Conducting a retrospective assessment will require a comprehensive, multi-generational social and family history. Documentation will need to be obtained from multiple sources, including interviews with family members, neighbors, associates, and former teachers. Input from former teachers as well as, for example, school psychologists, will have particular importance if these individuals had appropriate clinical training in ID. Further, information from professionals provides an important bases for corroboration (or noncorroboration) of data that may be obtained from family members.
- Prior formal assessments should be reviewed to determine the context of the referral and the evaluation of the individual, as well as the competence of the examiners performing the prior evaluations.

The following considerations are important for practice in terms of possible malingering in the assessment process:

- Professionals who are assessing possible malingering should have appropriate clinical experience in this area, as well as experience with people with ID and characteristic behaviors and traits.
- Tests of malingering often have insufficient reliability and validity, and these concerns are particularly problematic for their use in assessing possible malingering in people with ID..
- The consistency of test results over an extended period of time provide an important basis for protection against malingering within the assessment process. That is, if test results obtained from adults show congruence with assessments conducted at younger ages, it is probable that the contemporary performance on such assessment tools was not malingered. Therefore, if all measures of intellectual functioning, adaptive behavior, academic achievement, and other cognitive or language assessments are inconsistent in showing intellectual disability, then the likelihood of achieving standard scores within the range of intellectual disability as part of a contemporary assessment protocol would be highly unlikely.

References

Allen v. State, 749 N.E.2d 1158 (Ind. June 29, 2001).

Ali, A., Hassiotis, A., Strydom, A., & King, M. (2012). Self-stigma in people with intellectual disabilities and courtesy stigma in family carers: A systematic review. *Research in Develomental Disabililities, 33,* 2122–2140. doi: 10.1016/j.ridd.2012.06.013

An, K. Y.,. Zakzanis, K. K., &. Joordens, S. (2012). Conducting research with non-clinical healthy undergraduates: Does effort play a role in neuropsychological test performance? *Archives of Clinical Neuropsychology, 27,* 849–857. doi: 10.1093/arclin/acs085

American Psychiatric Association. (2013). *Diagnostic and statistical manual of mental disorders-V.* Washington, DC: Author.

Arizona v. Aurturo Canez, Arizona Supreme Court, CR-98-0488-AP (2003).

Arizona v. Eric Boyston, Arizona Supreme Court, CR-10-0052-AP (2008).

Arizona v. Kyle Allegria, (case pending trial), (2013).

Arizona v. Shawn Grell, AZ Supreme Court, CR-09-0199-AP (2011).

Armistead-Jehle, P. , & Buican, B. (2012). Evaluation context and symptom validity test performances in a U.S. military sample. *Archives of Clinical Neuropsychology, 27,* 828–839. doi: 10.1093/arclin/acs086

Arnold, M., & Lassmann, M. (2003). Overrepresentation of minority students in special education. *Education, 124,* 230–236.

Atkins v. Virginia, (00-8452) 536 U.S. 304 (2002).

Bigler, E. (2012). Symptom validity testing, effort, and neuropsychological assessment. *Journal of the International Neuropsychological Society, 18,* 632–642. doi: http://dx.doi.org/10.1017/S1355617712000252

Blume, J.H., Johnson, S.L., & Seeds, C.C. (2012). *Atkins:* State procedural choices and their effect on outcome in capital cases.

Butcher, J., Graham, J., Ben-Porath, Y., Tellegen, A., Dahlstrom, W., & Kaemmer, B. (2001). *Minnesota Multiphasic Personality Inventory-2.* Minneapolis, MN: University of Minnesota Press.

Chase v. State, 873 So.2d 1013 (Miss. 2004).

Cherry v. State, (02–2023) 959 U.S. 702 (2007).

Commonwealth of Kentucky v. Brian Crabtree (2011). Commonwealth of Kentucky, McClean Circuit Court, Civil Action No.12-CI-00144.

Conroy, M. A., & Kwartner, P. P. (2006). Malingering. *Applied Psychology in Criminal Justice, 2,* 29–51.

Doane, B. M., &. Salekin, K. L. (2009). Susceptibility of current adaptive behavior measures to feigned deficits. *Law and Human Behavior, 33,* 329–343.

Edgerton, R. B. (1967). *The cloak of competence: Stigma in the lives of the mentally retarded .* Berkeley, CA: University of California Press.

Edgerton, R., Bollinger, M., & Herr, B. (1984). The cloak of competence after two decades. *American Journal of Mental Deficiency, 88,* 345–351.

Everington, C., & Keyes, D. (1999). Diagnosing mental retardation in criminal proceedings: The critical importance of documenting adaptive behavior. *Forensic Examiner, 8*(7–8), 31–34.

Family Educational Rights and Privacy Act (FERPA) of 1974, 34 C.F.R Part 99 (1974).

Flynn, J. R. (2006). Tethering the elephant: Capital cases, IQ, and the Flynn effect. *Psychology, Public Policy, and Law, 12,* 170–189. doi: 10.1037/1076-8971.12.2.170

Flynn, J. R. , & Widaman, K. F. (2008). The Flynn effect and the shadow of the past: Mental retardation and the indefensible and indispensable role of IQ. *International Review of Research in Mental Retardation, 35,* 121–149.

Foster v. State, 848 So.2d 172 (Miss. 2003).

Frederick, R. I. (1997). *Validity Indicator Profile manual*. Minnetonka, MN: NCS Assessments.

Fuchs, D., & Fuchs, L. (2005). Responsiveness-to-intervention: A blueprint for practitioners, policymakers, and parents. *Teaching Exceptional Children, 38*(1), 57–61.

Graue, L. O., Berry, D. T. , Clark, J. A., Sollman, M. J., Cardi, M., Hopkins, J., & Werline, D. (2007). Identification of feigned mental retardation using the new generation of malingering detection instruments: Preliminary findings. *Clinical Neuropsychology, 21*, 929–942.

Hall v. Florida, (12–10882) 134 S. Ct. 1986 (2014).

Hayes v. State of Florida, (75-040) 581 U.S. 121 (1991).

Heward, W. (2013). *Exceptional children* (10th ed.). Boston, MA: Pearson.

Individuals with Disabilities Education Act. (20 USC at 1400, *et seq.*) (1991).

Jones v. State of Florida, (12-772) 966 U.S. 319 (2007).

Keyes, D. (1994). IQ and the death penalty: Verifying mental retardation. *Educational Resources Information Center* -ERIC Doc. # ED 374148.

Keyes, D. (1997). The expert witness: Issues of competence, criminal justice and mental retardation. *Impact, 10*(2), 14–15.

Keyes, D. (2004). Use of the Minnesota Multiphasic Personality Inventory (MMPI) to identify attempts at malingering mental retardation. *Mental Retardation, 42*, 151–153.

Keyes, D., & Edwards, W. (1995a). CAST-MR validly tests mentally retarded for competence. *Capital Report, 41*, 3–13 (non-continuous).

Keyes, D., & Edwards, W. (1996). Competence assessment: Questions and (some) answers. *Champion, 20*(4), 10–18 (non-continuous).

Kuentzel, J. G., Hetterscheidt, L. A., & Barnett, B. (2011). Testing intelligently includes double-checking Wechsler IQ scores. *Journal of Psychoeducational Assessment, 29*(1), 39–46. doi: 10.1177/0734282910362048

Larry P. v. Riles, (71-2270) 793 U.S. 343 (1972).

Lezak, M. D. (1995). *Neuropsychological assessment* (3rd ed.). New York, NY: Oxford University Press.

MacMillan, D., & Siperstein, G. (2002). *Learning disabilities as operationally defined by schools*. Retrieved from http://www.nrcld.org/resources/ldsummit/macmillan.html

MacMillan, D. L., & Reschly, D. J. (1998). Overrepresentation of minority students: The case for greater specificity or reconsideration of the variables examined. *Journal of Special Education, 32*(1), 15–24.

Macvaugh, G. S., Cunningham, M. D., & Tassé, M. J. (2014). Professional issues in *Atkins* assessments. In E. A. Polloway (Ed.), *Determining intellectual disability in the Courts: Focus on capital cases*. Washington, DC: AAIDD.

Mittenburg, W., Theroux, S., Aguila-Puentes, G., Bianchini, K., Greve, K., & Rayls, K. (2001). Identification of malingered head injury on the Wechsler Adult Intelligence Scale (3rd ed.). *The Clinical Neuropsychologist, 15*, 440–445.

Missouri v. Alis Ben Johns, Missouri SC81479 (2003).

Oklahoma v. Joshua Durcho, Oklahoma CF 2009-20 (2012).

Reschly, D. (1996). Identification and assessment of students with disabilities. *Special Education for Students with Disabilities, 6*(1), 40–53.

Rey, A. (1941). L'examen psychologie dans las cas d'encephalopathy traumatique. Archives de Psychologie, 23; (112), 286–340. Reported in: Lezak, M. D. (1995). *Neuropsychological assessment* (3rd ed.). New York, NY: Oxford University Press

Rey, A. (1964). L'examen clinique en psychologie. Paris: Presses, Universitaires de France. Reported in: Lezak, M. D. (1995). *Neuropsychological assessment* (3rd ed.). New York, NY: Oxford University Press

Salekin, K. M., & Doane, M. (2009). Malingering intellectual disability: The value of available measures and methods. *Applied Neuropsychology, 16*, 105–113.

Schalock, R. L., Buntinx, W. H. E., Borthwick-Duffy, S., Bradley, V., Craig, E. M., Coulter, D. L., Gomez, S. C., Lachapelle, Y., Luckasson, R. A., Reeve, A., Shogren, K. A., Snell, M. E., Spreat, S., Tassé, M. J., Thompson, J. R., Verdugo, M. A., Wehmeyer, M. L., & Yeager, M. H. (2010). *Intellectual disability: Definition, classification, and system of supports (11th ed.)*. Washington, DC: American Association on Intellectual and Developmental Disabilities.

Shandera, A. L., Berry, D. T., Clark, J. A., Schipper, L. J., Graue, L. O., & Harp, J. P. (2010). Detection of malingered mental retardation. *Psychological Assessment, 22*, 50–56.

Silver, J. M. (2012). Effort, exaggeration and malingering after concussion. *Journal of Neurology and Neurosurgery Psychiatry, 83*, 836–841. doi:10.1136/jnnp-2011-302078

South Carolina v. Robert Nance, South Carolina SC25814 (2012).

Tassé, M. J. (2009). Adaptive behavior assessment and the diagnosis of mental retardation in capital cases. *Applied Neuropsychology, 16*, 114–123. doi: 10.1080/09084280902864451

Tassé, M. J. (2014). Intellectual disability: A review of its definition and diagnosis criteria. In E. A. Polloway (Ed.), *Determining intellectual disability in the courts: Focus on capital cases*. Washington, DC: AAIDD.

Tombaugh, T. N. (1996). *Test of memory malingering*. North Tonawanda, NY: Multi-Health Systems.

U.S. v. Antun Lewis, USDC 1:08-CR-404 (2010).

Watson, D. (2014). Consideration in the selection and analysis of IQ tests. In E. A. Polloway (Ed.), *Determining intellectual disability in the courts: Focus on capital cases*. Washington, DC: AAIDD.

Weiss, R. A., Rosenfeld, B., & Farkas, M.R. (2011). The utility of the structured interview of reported symptoms in a sample of individuals with intellectual disabilities. *Assessment, 18*(3), 284–290. doi: 10.1177/1073191111408230

Woods, G. W., Freedman, D., &. Greenspan, S. (2012). Neurobehavioral assessment in forensic practice. *International Journal of Law and Psychiatry, 35*, 432–439. doi: 10.1016/j.ijlp.2012.09.014

19 | Intellectual Disability and Comorbid Disorders

George W. Woods
David Freedman
Timothy J. Derning

More than 40% of people with intellectual disability (ID) are also clinically diagnosed with another form of mental disorder. Co-occurring disorders present in synergy, typically displaying interactive symptomatology. This chapter discusses some of the mental disorders that most commonly co-occur with intellectual disability; however, co-occurring disorders span the complete range of clinical diagnoses (Cooper et al., 2007a, b; Einfeld, Ellis, & Emerson, 2011; Martorell et al., 2009). Individuals who have co-occurring mental disorders require greater support than those who do not, which makes the joint identification clinically and forensically critical (Martorell, Gutierrez-Recacha, Preda, & Ayuso-Mateos, 2008; Tasse & Wehmeyer, 2010).

It is impossible in this chapter to comprehensively explore the relationship between intellectual disability and the panoply of mental disorders. There are several mental disorders, however, that have particular relevance in forensic settings, including psychotic disorders, mood disorders, posttraumatic stress disorders, obsessive compulsive disorders, personality disorders, and dementia. A brief review of the research in each of these areas will be undertaken here.

Psychotic Disorders—Schizophrenia

Whereas most authorities report the incidence of schizophrenia worldwide at less than 1% (Jablensky, 2000; Kendler, Gallagher, Abelson & Kessler,1996; Saha, Chant, Welham, & McGrath, 2005), the incidence of schizophrenia in the population of people with ID has been estimated to be between 3% and 5.4% (Morgan, Leonard, Bourke, & Jablensky, 2008; Pitschel-Walz, Bauml, Froböse, Gsottschneider, & Jahn, 2009). These rates

appear to underestimate the prevalence of the degree of co-morbidity between intellectual disability and psychotic disorders, especially schizophrenia, which is thought
to be higher (Morgan et al., 2008). This underestimation is likely to be due primarily
to the separation of mental health services and intellectual disability services in many
agencies and in school contexts.

Morgan et al. (2008) used an Australian population-based registry to determine the
population prevalence of co-occurring ID and schizophrenia. The researchers linked
the Australian Intellectual Disability Registry with the Mental Health Information
System registry. The Australian Registry comprised 11,576 people who met the (then)
American Association of Mental Retardation criteria for ID. The Mental Health Information System registry, which included 236,973 people at the time of the linkage, contained information on those who had been identified as having mental illness. This
database captured both in-patient hospitalizations and out-patient services provided
by hospitals since 1966. The findings from this record linkage indicated that the prevalence of schizophrenia for those with ID in the 1950–1964 birth cohort was 5.2% and
in the 1965–1979 cohort it was 4.5%. This is compared to the population estimate for
schizophrenia of 1.4%. As noted previously, schizophrenia in those with ID is commonly underestimated (Morgan et al., 2008).

Many researchers believe there is no significant difference in the presentation of psychotic symptoms in the ID population that would warrant a more nuanced approach to
understanding the intellectual impairment (Johnstone et al., 2007). When attempting
to differentiate the psychotic symptoms associated with the ID population, the cognitive deficits of ID—particularly in receptive and expressive language, self-awareness,
insight, social isolation, and masking—may result in not only a lesser ability to express
experiences but also a less fully formed psychosis. For instance, delusions may be less
substantial and less complete, which makes recognition of them more difficult for clinicians. In those with more significant impairments, the concomitant language impairment can also make the assessment more difficult; however, no evidence currently supports the view that prevalence is decreased. In addition, there is current agreement that
the more subtle nuances in subset identification (e.g., the need to separate paranoid
schizophrenia from disorganized schizophrenia), is unwarranted. This is reflected in
the DSM-5's collapsing of many of these subsets into a broad schizophrenia category.

Diagnostic accuracy is paramount in determining psychotic illnesses, particularly
schizophrenia, among persons with ID. To achieve diagnostic accuracy, several factors
must be taken into consideration:

1. Diagnostic overshadowing is the assumption by clinicians that the presenting
    symptoms are secondary to organic, environmental, or social causes, rather
    than a psychotic illness. The overlay of nonspecific cognitive deficits may pro-
    vide challenges in differentiating symptoms that arise from psychotic processes
    from those that are better understood to be secondary to ID.

2. The delusions of people with intellectual disability may not be as rich in detail and may be more culturally naïve than those suffering from delusions who do not have ID. This lack of detail should not be mistaken for a lack of delusional strength or content; of importance are the pervasiveness and influence of the delusion, as well as the strength of the commitment to it.

3. People with ID may be less likely to hide perceptual disorders, such as hallucinations, delusions, or paranoid ideation; however, differentiation must be made between auditory hallucinations and other language-based disorders that may present or be described as "voices." For instance, "I hear my deceased mother's words," may be an auditory hallucination or a vivid recollection. It may be more difficult for a person with ID who is language-impaired to express the distinction.

4. Medications may affect the organic dysfunction of people with ID. They may present with mild delirium secondary to medication effects that may be incorrectly attributed to a psychotic illness (Fletcher, 2007). From a clinical standpoint, it appears that people with schizophrenia and borderline intellectual functioning obtain clear treatment benefit not only from antipsychotic medication, but also psychoeducational groups geared to their level of vocabulary and processing (Pitschel-Walz et al., 2009).

5. Neuropsychological testing during more florid periods of a psychotic disorder may be informative regarding the question of how behavior is affected by the co-morbid conditions, but may also be less stable and reliable compared to testing during remission or when the psychosis is better controlled.

Differentiation between the psychosis that can arise from neurological impairment, such as olfactory hallucinations in frontal lobe impairment or the schizophreniform presentation of temporal lobe impairment (Getz et al., 2002; Zeman, 2005), and true schizophrenia is critical for accurate diagnosis and analysis. In the forensic setting, the specific diagnostic determination for the psychosis may be less relevant than the quality, pervasiveness, and fluidity of the psychosis. Therefore, the ability to specify exact diagnostic categorization and sub-typing may be less important than understanding the way in which the psychosis affects life-course, experience and behavior. Once the scope and dimensions of the psychosis have been established, the next forensic step is to develop an understanding of the relationship between the psychosis and the behavior in question. This is accomplished through both careful clinical interviewing and reliance on a comprehensive family and social history that details the longitudinal course of the psychosis from the premorbid period through the prodromal phase and into mental illness.

The interaction between the psychosis and ID should be assessed, paying particular attention to the ways in which cognitive and adaptive functioning is impaired by ID. Such impairments may make "seeing" the behaviors of psychosis more difficult to separate. Critically assigning behaviors to one condition or the other is less important than understanding the relationship and interaction between these conditions.

Mood Disorders

Mood disorders also are often more difficult to diagnose accurately in people with ID (Cain et al., 2003). Once again, they are more prevalent when compared to the general population (Cooper et al., 2007a). Although depression and bipolar I disorder have been studied to some extent, rigorous studies of subsets such as bipolar II disorder, cyclothymia, and dysthymia in people with ID have not been undertaken (Gonzalez & Matson, 2006).

Much of the difficulty in accurately diagnosing mood disorders relates to the need to assess the person's inner life through language-based assessment of mood, which is limited in people with ID (Antonacci & Attiah, 2008; Davis, Judd, & Herman, 1997). Changes in sleep or appetite, irritation and aggression, increased isolation, and decreased communication skills may represent the onset of mood disorder in patients with ID. Quantifying symptoms—such as hopelessness and helplessness, as well as interpretation of changes in sleeping, eating, and activity, without medical records or a good historian—is extremely difficult because of language impairment. Increased physical illness may be one of the hallmark clues of depression in people with ID (Oeseburg, Jansen, Dijkstra, Groothoff, & Reijneveld, 2010). People with ID, particularly with moderate to severe impairment, may present somatic complaints, such as stomach ailments, apathy, and agitation, rather than common language-based symptoms of mood disorders.

Social and family history is the basis for determining any mood disorder. Understanding family history is critical when attempting to determine the presence of a mood disorder. As is true with mood disorders in the general population, people with ID who have primary and secondary family members suffering from depression and bipolar disorder are at significantly higher risk for mental illness (Gonzalez & Matson, 2006; Morgan et al., 2012).

Signs of depression may commonly be a manifestation of the stigma that people with ID live with, rather than a primary mood disorder. Differentiating these secondary, but extremely devastating, symptoms of secondary depression may be difficult. This is particularly true if the person has developed a "cloak of competence," a pattern of masking of nonadaptive behavior or maladaptive personal and community functioning (Edgerton, 1993).

The level of impairment of a person with ID may hinder recognition of signs of both depression and bipolar disorder. People with ID will often manifest symptoms that are more commonly seen in childhood presentations of both depression and bipolar disorders. These symptoms include agitation rather than melancholic withdrawal; insomnia instead of hypersomnia; and increased level of magical thinking, assault, disorders of conduct, and asocial behavior (Faust, Walker, & Sardo, 2006). People with ID have difficulty effectively expressing internal responses. They also may have impaired executive functioning that can limit the repertoire of behavioral responses in those people with ID who suffer from depression and bipolar disorder. Fletcher (2007) reported that successful intervention can focus on the behaviors that accompany symptoms of depression, such as assault, agitation, property destruction, and asocial conduct, particularly in those who are unable to adequately articulate emotional difficulties.

Major Depressive Disorder

Core symptoms of major depressive disorder in people with ID include sadness, hopelessness, irritable mood, anhedonia, and social withdrawal—symptoms that are more typically seen in children (Fletcher, 2007). Increased agitation, rather than withdrawal, may also be seen. Difficulty meeting full criteria for major depressive disorder is quite common, which often results in a diagnosis of major depressive disorder—not otherwise specified (NOS) (Mykletun et al., 2006).

Suicidal ideation may not be effectively expressed by persons with ID. Those with more significant ID may already manifest self-injurious behavior, including cutting and other self-harm behaviors, as well as agitation, creating challenges in separating suicidal ideation and actions. Depending on the severity of language impairment, some people with ID and suicidal ideation may have difficulty articulating suicidal thoughts despite experiencing strong feelings of wanting or planning to die.

The use of antidepressants and mood stabilizers in people with ID requires that undesirable cognitive side effects do not occur that would decrease the efficacy of treatment. In addition, people with ID may experience other cognitive deficits that may render them susceptible to other unusual side effects of the medications, including immunological, neurological, and cardiac vulnerabilities. Behavioral changes occurring after the initiation of medication treatment can be considered an effect of the treatment regimen, rather than an emotional response unless data indicate otherwise (Friedman, 1990). The differential diagnosis of mood disorders in people with ID must include physical illnesses first and foremost. As discussed here, cognitive impairment often shows up as altered mood, avolition, amotivation, and apathy syndromes, all of which can be misinterpreted as depression.

The relationship between trauma and depression, which are common co-morbid conditions in forensic populations, often makes the diagnosis of depression difficult to ascertain. The challenge is greater in the population of people with ID (Martorell & Tsakanikos, 2008). Atypical presentation of depressive symptoms, particularly agitation, may be incorrectly identified as conduct disorder or a simple behavioral dysregulation. People with ID are more likely to present with atypical depressive symptoms (Bakken et al., 2010; Davis et al., 1997).

Bipolar Disorder

Core symptoms of bipolar disorder in people with ID include mood, agitation, irritability, and changes in sleep (Fletcher, 2007). These symptoms are often misinterpreted in the forensic population, particularly when they occur close to the time of an offense. Substance abuse may also confound the picture, given the high co-morbidity between bipolar disorder and substance abuse. In people with ID, bipolar disorder may present with developmentally specific symptoms, such as aggression and psychosis, as well as externalized, rather than internalized, behavior symptoms consistent with childhood onset bipolar disorder (Gonzalez & Matson, 2006). Because irritability and aggression are often the presenting symptoms in people with ID who are also experiencing mood disorders, the DSM criteria often do not match. Obviously, irritability and aggression are common symptoms in forensic settings. The aggression seen in people with ID, particularly in higher functioning people, may appear no different in character than in people without ID. An incident involving a person with ID may include planning; however, one should look for gullibility and a lack of leadership that offsets culpability. The cause and motivation for the behaviors should be understood differently even if the narrow description of the behavior out of context may be identical. As with other symptoms presented by those with ID, these symptoms often may well mask significant manic behavior. Chemical dependency is generally also a strong co-morbid disorder in bipolar disorder; however, it may have a lower incidence in people diagnosed with ID.

Consequently, the differential diagnoses for mood disorders in people with ID must be broader than it is in other populations, given the high rate of medical problems, unusual responses to medications, atypical symptoms presentations, and unreliability of accuracy in self-reporting. People with ID and bipolar disorder will not only manifest the irritability, mood lability, and potential aggression seen in classic bipolar disorder, they will also manifest greater adaptive functioning impairments. Difficulties in activities of daily life, employment, and academic settings will be greater in the person with a comorbid diagnosis than a person with bipolar disorder alone (Cain et al., 2003). Increased interpersonal problems are found in people with ID (Sobsey, 1994) and bipolar disorder. Longitudinal histories are essential to any type of forensic evaluation, as are multiple interviews.

Post-traumatic Stress Disorder

Post-traumatic stress disorder (PTSD) in people with ID is also under-recognized (Turk, 2005). The few population-based trauma studies that have been conducted show a high prevalence of traumatic experiences in people with ID (Sobsey, 1994), with 75% reporting at least one traumatic event during their lifetime (Martorell et al., 2009). People with ID are more vulnerable to abuse and to exploitation. Further, experiences of abuse may impair the adaptive behaviors of someone with ID (Murphy, O'Callaghan, & Clare, 2007).

In people with ID, behavioral and emotional problems are more likely to reflect a history of family disruption, criminal justice proceedings, and deaths of loved ones, as well as frequent moves and the losses of homes and family care. People with ID who also experience behavioral and emotional problems more often reported instances of poor physical health, verbal abuse, sexual abuse, parents in prison, and the need of community services intervention (Doyle & Michell, 2003).

Exposure to trauma is complicated by the cognitive deficits seen in people with ID. Difficulties resulting from dysexecutive functioning, impairments of autobiographical memory, and poor social contextual understanding amplify the effect of, and subsequent response to, traumatic events in people with ID. They may lack the ability to weigh, deliberate, and take proactive and corrective steps necessary to process and overcome the trauma.

Trauma hits people with ID hardest in their areas of greatest weakness: new, novel, and stressful circumstances. Type I trauma, the single incident, disrupts cognitive symptoms already typically weak in ID, and action is a more common reaction than contemplation. Goal-directed behavior, or behavior with clear indications, may be mistaken for intentional behavior, which requires consideration and deliberation. Type II trauma, or developmental trauma, creates a panoply of behaviors for people with ID, including hypervigilance, emotional and physical dysregulation, chronic anger, hyperreactivity, substance abuse, and impaired relationships. These behaviors can lead to criminal behavior.

Perhaps the most concerning of all symptoms of trauma is emotional numbing. When augmented by the emotional flatness sometimes seen in ID, this can be perceived as noncaring coldness or glibness.

Lack of risk awareness is a primary impairment in an individual with ID. Instruments used to measure risk assessment lack the sensitivity to measure this impairment accurately. People with ID inadequately assess risk, which leads to gullibility. Gullibility is the tendency to accept or believe an idea, usually a highly questionable claim, despite evidence that it is not true or correct. It is seen as a core symptom in people with ID (Greenspan, 2009; 2011). Gullibility, coupled with the emotional numbing, must be differentiated from asocial behavior in higher functioning people with ID. This gullibility is often seen in people with ID who are identified as gang leaders, due to their violent behavior when, in fact, violence is the only service they are able to provide to the gang because of their academic and cognitive impairments. Consequently, these individuals are set up as enforcers by other gang members, who recognize their cognitive limitations.

The assessment of co-morbid childhood trauma and ID may raise some unique difficulties. Most importantly, the family and social history is likely to uncover symptom patterns that could be either trauma- or ID-related. These patterns also reflect the interaction of traumatic experiences with the limited cognitive capacity that supports resilience (Breslau, Lucia, & Alvarado, 2006). Moreover, people with ID are more likely to be targeted for abuse (Clark, Clark, & Adamec, 2007; Ryan, 1994). The social history is an integral component of making an accurate differential diagnosis, particularly in comorbid diagnoses. Parsing the behaviors that result may be of less significance than accurately documenting the interactions between ID, trauma, and the life-course consequences.

Obsessive Compulsive Disorders

Obsessive compulsive disorders have an incidence of approximately 3.5% among those with ID (Fletcher, 2007). Further, obsessions are also found in many genetic disorders that present with ID (Gothelf et al., 2004; Levitas & Reid, 1998). Obsessive compulsive disorders in people with ID may have fewer obsessive manifestations because the cognitive ability for abstract thought can be impaired, particularly in people with lower levels of functioning. The DSM-5 criteria have eliminated the need of being aware of one's obsessive thoughts as a criteria for obsessive compulsive disorder. Neuroleptics and some antidepressants may increase obsessive thinking. Consequently, understanding medication regimens is necessary when attempting to evaluate a person with ID who is either taking these medications for the treatment of obsessive compulsive disorder or when these medications are being used for other purposes.

Personality Disorders

Although all Axis I disorders and intellectual disability may have concomitant personality disorders, the diagnosis of personality disorders in people with ID is fraught with diagnostic challenges. People with ID may manifest a lack of empathy, asocial behavior, and impulsivity as a function of their cognitive impairments, rather than as a function of a personality disorder (Alexander & Sherva, 2003). As the DSM-IV-TR noted, the diagnosis of personality disorders should only be undertaken when other symptom complexes are under control.

Although ID may be associated with variant patterns, there are instances when functioning may deteriorate prematurely in cognitive, emotional, and motor domains. The DSM-5 maintains this position. Therefore, ID often amplifies personality traits. This may give the appearance of personality disorders, which can potentially stigmatize the person with ID by inappropriately transposing the symptom presentation of ID into a personality defect. The cultural context in which a person with ID has grown up must also be taken into consideration, because it is against that context that personality traits must be judged.

Depression, PTSD, bipolar disorder, and dysexecutive function may all present with asocial behavior, specifically aggression, assaultive behavior, conduct problems, and misunderstanding of social context and social understanding. Presentation of these diagnoses and symptoms is more prevalent in the person with ID as well (Anderson, Damasio, Tranel, & Damisio, 2000). However, it is inappropriate to assign these behaviors as personality disorders when they arise out of the functional impairment of a person with ID.

For instance, dependent personality disorder is commonly diagnosed in people with ID. The behavior that leads to this diagnosis develops from the limited adaptive functioning, social withdrawal, masking, and inability to be independent. This reflects a capacity deficit, not a psychological trait. Clinical differentiation between dependent personality disorder and intellectual disability has implications for services, supports, and forensic judgments.

The methodology used for determining personality disorders as identified under DSM-IV-TR has been criticized, as has been its presentation in DSM-5. The diagnosis of a personality disorder necessarily proceeds with caution, based on clinical assessment over multiple evaluations with supporting social history.

Dementia

People with intellectual disability are living longer, much like the general population. Consequently, the occurrence of dementia-related illnesses has become an increasing concern for people with ID. Although the incidence of dementia in Down syndrome remains extremely high, because of a genetic predisposition to Alzheimer's disease, dementiaform illness in people with ID is a complex matter. Previous beliefs that certain syndromes carry a 100% incidence of dementia have been reconsidered (Burt et al., 2005).

People with ID may have atypical presentation of, and differing criteria for, dementia (Strydom, Livingston, King, & Hassiotis, 2007). They may present with significant behavioral deterioration, rather than memory impairment. Changes in the complexity of life or executive dysfunction, which are more common in the early stages of dementia in people without ID, are not good markers for dementiaform illness in people with ID because their lives and cognitive functioning may already be limited.

Conclusion

Co-morbidities in the population of people with ID are the standard, rather than the exception. The presence of co-morbid disorders is common, but the diagnosis of such disorders requires more careful assessment. It is important to recognize that symptoms in people with ID may present in ways that differ from those in people without ID. The summative information presented here derives from the principles associated with the information provided within this chapter and provides implications for practice.

People with ID who come into contact with the criminal justice system may experience concomitant symptoms of comorbid mental disorders. As noted previously, an understanding of comorbid presentation is a requirement of appropriate practice and clinical judgment to ensure appropriate diagnosis.

Many specific principles are associated with the assessment of people who may have ID within the criminal justice system. First, as noted previously, the presentation of symptoms can be complex when a person presents with ID and comorbid illness; and a key consideration is analyzing the symptoms that shape behavior. ID, its underlying neural processes, the adaptive and maladaptive behavior that develop over life course, and the impaired social sophistication often result in exaggerated presentation of symptoms that may mask ID. Symptom identification, rather than diagnostic labeling during the clinical assessment, provides the strategy for considering what affects behavior and presentation, which is most important in the forensic assessment. Adequate time and reliance on a complete and accurate multigenerational social history serve as the basis for the application of clinical judgment to the interpretation of symptoms so that comorbid conditions are parsed and appropriately defined.

A second consideration that has been noted throughout the chapter is the importance of family social history as a cornerstone of a comprehensive neuropsychiatric evaluation, especially in the context of comorbid disorders (Woods, Freeman, & Greenspan, 2012). The diagnosis of ID is associated with consideration of collateral sources (e.g., family, teachers, social workers, and doctors, as well as medical, social service, employment, and school records) that provide a basis for determining adaptive functioning within the differential diagnosis process.

Thirdly, people with ID and comorbid illnesses may not manifest "classic" symptoms of either condition. Changes in baseline behaviors, gullible actions, and nonverbal behaviors, such as agitation and frustration, may signal increasing mental problems. Their ability to articulate their inner state may be more limited, due to language and executive deficits. The likelihood exists that the person may have also developed masking responses. As noted previously, these considerations make clinical judgment and a complete social and family history essential to the assessment process. The nonclassic presentation of symptoms requires assessment and presentation to fact finders because it is often not obvious understandable, without explanation, to those who do not specialize in ID without explanation.

A fourth consideration, which relates to effort and malingering, is not well researched in general, and particularly in those with ID (see Chapter 18 for full discussion of these considerations). The instruments used with populations of people with ID require rigorous study before reliance on them can be considered good practice (Bigler, 2012). The combination of cognitive deficits and psychiatric or neurologic symptoms can be confused and considered incorrectly to be malingering, especially given that the presentation of symptoms in ID is atypical and may not fit diagnostic criteria cleanly. In the context of comorbid ID, these test instruments and standard tools have not demonstrated validity and may not differentiate poor effort or malingering from unusual or atypical presentation (common in comorbid ID); therefore, their use does not constitute best practice for forensic assessment.

A fifth consideration relates to the assessment and presentation of symptoms and the behaviors that arise from comorbid ID. An important emphasis is on the assurance that the symptoms that result from ID, and a person's unique adaptation to living with

ID, be considered to avoid inaccurate labels that in turn can lead to lack of appropriate treatment, promote stigma, and have sentencing implications.

The final consideration is that clinical expertise, in combination with collateral evidence of the onset and course of symptoms, is most important when attempting to differentiate comorbid disorders in people with ID. Because *Atkins* evaluations are high-stake settings, the forensic questions can only be answered once the clinical formulation is fully established. Clinical judgment, preferably based on the extensive clinical experience working with people with ID, is required to understand the ways in which co-occurring conditions interact to shape behavior. Only then can the forensic determination as to whether a person meets the ID criteria recognized by *Atkins* be considered.

References

Alexander, R., & Sherva, C. (2003). Diagnosis of personality disorders in learning disability. *The British Journal of Psychiatry, 182,* 28–31. doi: 10.1192/bjp.182.44.s28

Anderson, S. W., Damasio, H., Tranel, D., & Damasio, A. R. (2000). Long-term sequelae of prefrontal cortex damage acquired in early childhood. *Developmental Neuropsychology, 18,* 281–296.

Antonacci, D. J., & Attiah, N. (2008). Diagnosis and treatment of mood disorders in adults with developmental disabilities. *Psychiatric Quarterly, 79,* 171–192.

Bakken, T. L., Helverschou, S. B., Eilertsen, D. E., Heggelund, T., Myrbakk, E., & Martinsen, H. (2010). Psychiatric disorders in adolescents and adults with autism and intellectual disability: A representative study in one county in Norway. *Research in Developmental Disabilities, 31,* 1669–1677.

Bigler, E. D. (2012). Symptom validity testing, effort, and neuropsychological assessment. *Journal of the International Neuropsychological Society, 18,* 632–640. DOI: http://dx.doi.org/10.1017/S1355617712000252

Breslau, N., Lucia, V. C., & Alvarado, G. F. (2006). Intelligence and other predisposing factors in exposure to trauma and posttraumatic stress disorder: A follow-up study at age 17 years. *Archives of General Psychiatry, 63,* 1238–1245.

Burt, D. B., Primeaux-Heart, S., Loveland, K., Cleveland, L., Lewis, K., Lesser, J., & Pearson, P. (2005). Aging in adults with intellectual disabilities. *American Journal on Mental Retardation, 110,* 268–284.

Cain, N. N., Davidson, P. W., Burhan, A. M., Andolsek, M. E., Baxter, J. T., Sullivan, L. . . . Deutsch, L. (2003). Identifying bipolar disorders in individuals with intellectual disability. *Journal of Intellectual Disability Research, 47*(Pt 1), 31–38.

Clark, R. E., Clark, J. F., & Adamec, C. A. (2007). *The encyclopedia of child abuse.* New York, NY: Facts on File.

Cooper, S. A., Smiley, E., Morrison, J., Allan, L., Williamson, A., Finlayson, J. . . . Mantry D. (2007a). Psychosis and adults with intellectual disabilities: Prevalence, incidence, and related factors. *Social Psychiatry and Psychiatric Epidemiology, 42,* 530–536.

Cooper, S. A., Smiley, E., Morrison, J., Williamson, A., & Allan, L. (2007b). An epidemiological investigation of affective disorders with a population-based cohort of 1023 adults with intellectual disabilities. *Psychological Medicine, 37,* 873–882. doi: http://dx.doi.org/10.1017/S0033291707009968

Davis, J. P., Judd, P. K., & Herrman, H. (1997). Depression in adults with intellectual disability. Part 1: A review. *Australian and New Zealand Journal of Psychiatry, 31,* 232–242.

Doyle, C., & Mitchell, D. (2003). Post traumatic stress disorder and people with learning disabilities. *Journal of Intellectual Disabilities, 7,* 23–33 doi: 10.1177/1469004703007001603

Edgerton, R. B. (1993). *The Cloak of Competence–Revised and Updated.* Berkeley, CA: University of California Press.

Einfeld, S. L., Ellis, L. A., & Emerson, E. (2011). Comorbidity of intellectual disability and mental disorder in children and adolescents: A systematic review. *Journal of Intellectual & Developmental Disability, 36,* 137–143. doi: 10.1080/13668250.2011.572548

Faust, D. S., Walker, D., & Sands, M. (2006). Diagnosis and management of childhood bipolar disorder in the primary care setting. *Clinical Pediatrics, 45,* 801–808. doi: 10.1177/0009922806295279

Fletcher, R. (2007). *Diagnostic manual–intellectual disability: A clinical guide for diagnosis of mental disorders in persons with intellectual disability.* Kingston, NY: NADD Press.

Friedman, D. (1990). Valproic acid for the treatment of children with mental retardation and mood symptomatology. *Pediatrics, 86,* 467–472.

Getz, K., Hermann, B., Seidenberg, M., Bell, B., Dow, C., Jones, J. . . . Magnotta, V. (2002). Negative symptoms in temporal lobe epilepsy. *The American Journal of Psychiatry, 159,* 644–651. doi: 10.1046/j.1535-7597.2002.00063.x

Gonzalez, M., & Matson, J. L. (2006). Mania and intellectual disability: The course of manic symptoms in persons with intellectual disability. *American Journal of Mental Retardation, 111,* 378–383.

Gothelf, D., Presburger, G., Zohar, A. H., Burg, M., Nahmani, A., Frydman, M. . . . Apter, A. (2004). Obsessive-compulsive disorder in patients with velocardiofacial (22q11 deletion) syndrome. *American Journal of Medical Genetics Part B: Neuropsychiatric Genetics,126B*(1), 99–105. doi: 10.1002/ajmg.b.20124

Greenspan, S. (2009). *Annals of gullibility:Why we get duped and how to avoid it.* Westport, CT: Greenwood Publishing,

Greenspan, S. (2011). Homicide defendants with intellectual disability: Issues in diagnosis in capital cases. *Exceptionality, 19,* 219–237. doi: 10.1080/09362835.2011.611086

Jablensky, A. (2000). Epidemiology of schizophrenia: The global burden of disease and disability. *European Archives of Psychiatry and Clinical Neuroscience, 250,* 274–285.

Johnstone, E. C., Owens, D. G. C., Hoare, P., Gaur, S., Spencer, M. D., Harris, J. . . . Muir, W. J. (2007). Schizotypal cognitions as a predictor of psychopathology in adolescents with mild intellectual impairment. *The British Journal of Psychiatry, 191,* 484–492.

Kendler, K. S., Gallagher, T. J., Abelson, J. M., & Kessler, R. C. (1996). Lifetime prevalence, demographic risk factors, and diagnostic validity of nonaffective psychosis as assessed in a U.S. community sample: The national comorbidity survey. *Archives of General Psychiatry, 53,* 1022–1031.

Levitas, A. S., & Reid, C. S. (1998). Rubinstein-Taybi syndrome and psychiatric disorders. *Journal of Intellectual Disability Research, 42*(Pt 4), 284–292.

Martorell, A., Gutierrez-Recacha, P., Pereda, A., & Ayuso-Mateos, J. L. (2008). Identification of personal factors that determine work outcome for adults with intellectual disability. *Journal of Intellectual Disability Research, 52,* 1091–1101. doi: 10.1111/j.1365-2788.2008.01098.x

Martorell, A.,& Tsakanikos, E. (2008). Traumatic experiences and life events in people with intellectual disability. *Current Opinion in Psychiatry, 21,* 445–448.

Martorell, A., Tsakanikos, E., Pereda, A., Gutierrez-Recacha, P., Bouras, N., & Ayuso-Mateos, J. L. (2009). Mental health in adults with mild and moderate intellectual disabilities: The role of recent life events and traumatic experiences across the life span. *Journal of Nervous and Mental Disease, 197,* 182–186. doi: 10.1097/NMD.0b013e3181923c8c

Morgan, V. A., Croft, M. L., Valuri, G. M., Zubrick, S. R., Bower, C., McNeil, T. F., & Jablensky, A. V. (2012). Intellectual disability and other neuropsychiatric outcomes in high-risk children of mothers with schizophrenia, bipolar disorder and unipolar major depression. *The British Journal of Psychiatry, 200,* 282–289.

Morgan, V. A., Leonard, H., Bourke, J., & Jablensky, A. (2008). Intellectual disability co-occurring with schizophrenia and other psychiatric illness: Population-based study. *The British Journal of Psychiatry, 193,* 364–372.

Murphy, G. H., O'Callaghan, A. C., & Clare, I. C. H. (2007). The impact of alleged abuse on behaviour in adults with severe intellectual disabilities. *Journal of Intellectual Disability Research, 51,* 741–749. doi: 10.1111/j.1365-2788.2007.00973.x

Mykletun, A., Overland, S., Dahl, A. A., Krokstad, S., Bjerkeset, O., Glozier, N. . . . Prince, M. (2006). A population-based cohort study of the effect of common mental disorders on disability pension awards. *The American Journal of Psychiatry, 163,* 1412–1418.

Oeseburg, B., Jansen, D. E., Dijkstra, G. J., Groothoff, J. W., & Reijneveld, S. A. (2010). Prevalence of chronic diseases in adolescents with intellectual disability. *Research in Developmental Disabilities, 31,* 698–704. doi:10.1016/j.ridd.2010.01.011

Pitschel-Walz, G., Bauml, J., Fröböse, T., Gsottschneider, A., & Jahn, T. (2009). Do individuals with schizophrenia and a borderline intellectual disability benefit from psychoeducational groups? *Journal of Intellectual Disabilities, 13*(305). doi: 10.1177/1744629509353237

Ryan, R. (1994). Posttraumatic-stress-disorder in persons with developmental-disabilities. *Community Mental Health Journal, 30,* 45–54.

Saha, S., Chant, D., Welham, J., & McGrath, J. (2005). A systematic review of the prevalence of schizophrenia. *PLOS Medicine, 2,* 413–433.

Sobsey, D. (1994). *Violence and abuse in the lives of people with disabilities: The end of the silent acceptance?* Baltimore, MD: Paul H. Brookes.

Strydom, A., Livingston, G., King, M., & Hassiotis, A. (2007). Prevalence of dementia in intellectual disability using different diagnostic criteria. *The British Journal Of Psychiatry, 191,*150–157. doi: 10.1192/bjp.bp.106.028845

Tasse, M. J., & Wehmeyer, M. L. (2010). Intensity of support needs in relation to co-occurring psychiatric disorders. *Exceptionality, 18,* 182–192. doi: 10.1080/09362835.2010.513922

Turk, J. (2005). Post-traumatic stress disorder in young people with intellectual disability. *Journal of Intellectual Disability Research, 49,* 872–875. doi: 10.1111/j.1365-2788.2005.00764.x

Woods, G. W., Freeman, D., & Greenspan, S. (2012). Neurobehavioral assessment in forensic practice. *International Journal of Law and Psychiatry, 35,* 432–439. doi:10.1016/j.ijlp.2012.09.014

Zeman, A. (2005). Tales from the temporal lobes. *The New England Journal of Medicine, 352,* 119–121.

20 | Educational Records

James R. Patton

Educational records, or school records, serve as a roadmap to what students have done and where they have been during their school years. At face value, school records seem to be straightforward. Understanding them, however, requires a certain level of sophistication and familiarity with what these records mean and include. Such reviews are an important part of assessments conducted in criminal justice proceedings when these records can reveal information concerning the possible diagnosis of intellectual disability (ID).

Although the focus of this chapter is on school records, other types of records are also important in legal cases. Employment, social security, and juvenile justice records provide information of value to understanding the life situation of an individual. Cautions need to be taken when interpreting these records as well (see also Chapter 13).

Under the Family Educational Rights and Privacy Act (FERPA) of 1974, a "record" is defined as "any information of data recorded in any medium (e.g., handwriting, print, tapes, film, microfilm, microfiche, any form of electronic data storage)." Under this law, an "educational record" is defined as "those records that are (1) directly related to a student; and (2) maintained by an educational agency or institution or by a party acting for the agency or institution" (FERPA, 1974).

Although the way educational information is organized in school records can vary across school systems and states, and although no standardized format for documenting educational information exists, the basic content provided in the records of a student is nevertheless fairly consistent. Typically the type of information that is found in a student's educational records will depend on whether a student is still in school or has recently been in school versus someone who has graduated or left school sometime in the past.

For a student who is still in school, a comprehensive set of data is usually available in the records. Most of this information, however, will be destroyed after a period of time. For a student who is no longer in school (more than 5 years), a more limited set of data, referred to as the "permanent record," will be available and usually includes the student's name, address, phone number, grades, attendance record, classes attended, grade level completed, and year completed. This permanent record can be maintained after a student leaves school without any time limitations. It is important to note that the type of educational information kept on a student may vary over time, as a result of various policy changes (as discussed in the next section).

School records serve many purposes. At a very basic level, school records provide an overall historical map of attendance and performance (Baroff, 2003). For school personnel, records are useful for determining how a student's "school life" has evolved. For parents, records can provide a source of information on their son or daughter that might be useful in a variety of contexts. For the student, school records contain information that will be used for future decisions, such as admission into college or for job-related purposes.

School records play an important role in legal cases, especially in cases where the determination of ID is being considered (Baroff, 2003; Macvaugh & Cunningham, 2009; Widaman & Siperstein, 2009). School records will be examined by experts, referred to in reports, and presented in testimony. School record information documents attendance and how a student has performed in school by way of grades given for courses the student has completed, as well as the results of group tests the student has taken. In capital cases, this information can be used to show an overall level of school behavior and can be an important component of the assessment of adaptive functioning (Everington & Olley, 2008; Tassé, 2009).

Types of Information Contained in School Records

The typical school record contains a range of information. Table 20.1 summarizes the nature of information contained in school records. Each of the sections presented in this table is discussed in this chapter.

The amount of information that may be included in the school records for an individual student will vary depending on that student's particular situation. A set of basic information, however, is typically available on all students. This information includes personal information, general school information, record of classes taken and grades received, attendance data, and other performance data (e.g., test scores). For some students, such as those students who qualify for special education, additional educational information may be available, depending on when the student was in school. The final two sections of Table 20.1 list special types of information.

Nature of the Problem

As mentioned previously, school records are more complicated than they may appear at initial consideration. To rely on the information contained in school records, a

TABLE 20.1. Types of Information in Student Records

Category	Specific Type of Information	
Directory Information	Name	Entry date
	Address	Exit date
	Date of birth	County of birth
	Home school	Country of birth
	Attending school	(Photo of student)
	Enrollment type	
Personal Identifiers	Personal ID number	Social security number
Demographic Information	Gender	Native language
	Race	Migrant status
	Ethnicity	Parent/guardian information
	LEP status	
General School Information	Attendance data	Last grade completed
Academic/Program Information	Courses and grades	Section 504 status
	(explanation of grades)	Bilingual/ESL program participation
	(indication of special courses)	Other specialized services/supports
	Last grade completed	Gifted/talented program, AP courses
	Standardized test scores	ACT/SAT scores
	Special education status	
Disciplinary Information	Withdrawal reason	Disciplinary reason
	(Coded reasons for withdrawal)	Number of absences
	Disciplinary action date	Number of suspensions
Economic Information	Free/reduced lunch	Homeless living setting
	Homeless status	
Health-Related Information	Insurance status	Immunization status
	Medicaid number	
Special Education Records	Referral form	Individualized education program (IEP)
(IF student determined eligible)	Assessment data	Special education and related services
	Eligibility determination form	Behavioral intervention plan
Section 504 Records	Referral information	Accommodation plan
	Eligibility determination materials	

reviewer must understand what the information means and be aware of various limitations inherent in the data provided. This section discusses the major cautions regarding school records.

Variations Across Schools

Although the information contained in Table 20.1 is typically available in the school records of students when they are still in school, it is possible for some of this information to be absent. For instance, the records of people who were in school many years ago may not have some of the information that is currently kept on students. Further, different school systems and different states do not use the same format for maintaining school records. So, one has to review a given school record closely to locate specific information.

The quality of the records in terms of the ease of deciphering the information also varies greatly (Everington & Olley, 2008). For example, the records of people who were in school many years ago may be difficult to read. As a result, it may be difficult to determine key information in the records, such as the actual course names, names of teachers who taught the courses, names of tests, and results of tests.

Schools systems also use differing coding systems in the educational records. This is an issue when trying to understand what course a student has taken or when interpreting grades and test scores, in particular. Letter grades need to be explained in terms of what they stand for—often provided in a grading key. Test scores must be clearly understood in terms of what a specific score is and how it was derived. Often, it may be necessary to go back and read a test administration manual to confirm what the scores actually mean. Some commonly used codes that are used when reporting scores are provided in Table 20.2.

Grades and Test Scores

One of the most important cautions in relation to school records is the interpretation of grades and test scores. For the most part, grades and test scores do provide an indication of how a student has done in school; however, this is not always true (Widaman & Siperstein, 2009).

Grades. Whereas grades in general are clearly a reflection of a person's performance in a particular class, the real meaning of a particular grade can be determined only if one is able to learn what the grade stands for and how that grade was obtained. In other words, without knowing what a grade means, as determined by a code provided in the records, and the criteria on which a grade is given, the real meaning of that grade may not be conclusively determined. For instance, a grade for a class might be equally divided across attendance, homework completion, and performance on various classroom tests. As a result, a student might obtain an acceptable, passing grade based on the fact that the student attends class regularly and turns in homework on time—and sometimes the homework might be a copy of the work of someone else (e.g., friend or relative) or completed in part by a parent or sibling.

Poor grades can result from many factors. Students might receive poor grades based on their inability to handle content, requirements, and other demands of a given class. Clearly one of the reasons for not being able to do well in some classes is academic difficulties associated with intellectual disability. Poor performance, however, may also result from other types of disabilities, such as learning disabilities, attention deficit hyperactivity disorder, or behavior disorders (Beirne-Smith, Patton & Kim, 2006). Low or failing grades can also result from attendance issues and lack of motivation to meet

TABLE 20.2. Codes Used in Educational Records

Code	What it Means
General Terms:	
CA	chronological age
DOB	date of birth
GED	General Educational Development
ELL	English language learner
ESL	English as a second language
LEP	limited English proficiency
PY	program year
Assessment Terms:	
AE	age equivalent
CI	confidence interval
FS/FSIQ	full scale/full scale IQ
GE	grade equivalent
GP	grade placement
Local	local percentile rank
National/NP	national percentile rank
NCE	normal curve equivalent
NS	not significant
PR	percentile rank
RS	raw score
SEM	standard error of measurement
S	stanine
SS	standard score
Special Education Terms:	
ABA	applied behavior analysis
AT	assistive technology
BIP/BP	behavior intervention plan/behavior plan
ECSE	early childhood special education
EI	early intervention
EYS	extended school year
FBA	functional behavior assessment
IEE	independent educational evaluation
IEP	individualize education program
MD/MDR	manifestation determination/manifestation determination review
MDT	multi-disciplinary team
OT	occupational therapy
PLAAFP	present level of academic achievement & functional performance
PT	physical therapy
RS	related services
RTI	response to intervention
SPED	special education
VR	vocational rehabilitation

(continued)

TABLE 20.2. Codes Used in Educational Records (*continued*)

Code	What it Means
Special Education Categories:	
ADHD	attention deficit hyperactivity disorder
ASD	autism spectrum disorder
AS	Asperger syndrome
DD	developmentally delayed
D/HH	deaf/hard of hearing
EBD/ED/SED	emotional-behavior disorder/emotional disorder/serious emotional disturbance
EMR	educable mentally retarded
ID	intellectual disability
LD/SLD	learning disability/specific learning disability
MR	mental retardation
TBI	traumatic brain injury
TMR	trainable mentally retarded

the performance demands of a class. Because students may receive poor grades for many reasons, a student's performance in a class must be understood in the context of that class. Relying on the face value of grades listed in the school records can lead to misinterpretation of the student's actual ability to perform in school (Macvaugh & Cunningham, 2009).

Standardized tests. Most school records will also contain data from various standardized tests that a student has taken. In recent years, these tests have been referred to as "high-stakes assessments." For people who were in school many years ago, these tests were typically administered once per year and were simply referred to as standardized tests. Tests such as the California Achievement Test, the Stanford Achievement Test, and the Iowa Tests of Basic Skills are examples of the tests that have been adopted by states to assess students in schools. In recent times, states developed standardized tests that were used with students across various grade levels and that were based on a particular state's content and performance standards. In the past few years, many states have started using standardized tests based on the Common Core Standards.

For the most part, standardized achievement test scores will provide a general indication of how well a student is doing in school. Some cautions regarding the interpretation of standardized test scores, however, are indicated. First, the meaning of various scores, especially standard scores, must be understood (see Table 20.2). Second, it is important to determine the environment in which a test was given. This environment may include whether there was sufficient space between students when they took the test, whether any major distractions were present that could interfere with performance, and whether adequate proctoring of the testing situation was provided. Third, it is important to interpret properly the results of a standardized test of a student who has repeated one or more grades in school because students who have repeated a grade level will be older than the other students taking the test—the students with whom the older students are being compared. Fourth, it is also important to determine whether any special accommodations were made when the testing was conducted. In many cases, students with disabilities have qualified for various accommodations when taking a test; this fact is noteworthy for interpretation purposes. Fifth, in the past and to some extent currently, certain students with disabilities, especially those students with ID, have been excluded from taking these group-administered standardized tests. This exemption is noteworthy in that taking such action suggests that a student displays significant learning-related issues that interfere with his/her ability to participate in the group testing.

Elimination of Special Education Records

A significant problem that exists in many cases is that certain records are no longer available. For most students, the permanent records, as discussed previously, should be available years after that student has completed school. For those students who were served in special education programs, however, schools are able legally to destroy these records. According to Wright and Wright (2007), "pursuant to the General Educational Provisions Act, schools must retain records for at least five years. The school may not destroy any educational records if there is an outstanding request to inspect or review the records under this section" (p. 308). As a result, educational information and data that may have been extremely useful may not be available for students in special education.

Special education records (see the next section) contain information that should elaborate on the specific challenges, issues, and needs of students who qualify for such services. These important records, as noted, may not be readily available; however, these records may still exist. Schools often had a second copy of key documents of students with disabilities. Parents or guardians have the right to request a copy of all pertinent special education documents. Although many parents do not make this request, nevertheless, in some cases, parents may have retained copies of these documents long after they have been destroyed by the school system.

Confidentiality

A key concern for schools is to maintain the confidentiality of school records. Under the Family Education Rights and Privacy Act (FERPA, 1974), schools are required to follow certain guidelines to ensure that the information in school records remains confidential. Murphy and Dishman (2010) indicated that FERPA has three primary purposes:

- To provide parents or eligible students with the right to inspect and review educational records;
- To permit parents or eligible students to amend educational records; and
- To ensure that personally identifiable information about students will not be disclosed from educational records except as permitted by law. (p. 2)

Although certain exemptions exist, such as accessing school records in legal proceedings, information contained in school records should not be shared with people who do not have authorization to view them.

Nature of the Information Contained in School Records

This section of the chapter describes each section listed in Table 20.1. In addition, the implications of the information for practice will be provided.

Directory Information

Information in this section provides basic information about a student and when the student was in a particular school. The value of this information is that it provides confirmation of date of birth, the dates when a student started attending a particular school, and when that student stopped attending a particular school. Dates of attendance are particularly useful when a student moves from one school to another. It is not uncommon for some students to have attended many different schools over the time they are in school.

Personal Identifiers

Typically, a school will assign a student ID number to each student in a school. This particular number has no real significance other than for internal administrative purposes. In the past, it was common to also find the social security number of a student. This school information is not particularly useful in legal proceedings unless the data assist in cross-referencing to other records.

Demographic Information

Demographic information is important for a variety of administrative purposes within a school. In other words, school administrators are required to keep track of the demographics of students in their school and report this information to the local school district and state educational agency.

The discovery that a student's native language is not English or that the student has been identified as having limited English proficiency (LEP) will be important information in terms of understanding a student's school performance. Knowing that a student lives in a family that is migratory may also contribute to a better understanding of a student's attendance record and school performance.

Academic Information

This section of a student's school record is likely to be the most often reviewed, cited, and relied on information within legal proceedings. Of all of the records that might exist on a particular student—with the exception of students who have special education records—academic records are the most requested records. Academic records provide an index of student performance (e.g., courses taken, grades, test scores). This section of student records also contains information related to programs, placements, and services that a student might have received while in school.

Whether or not the school records are complete, a listing of the grade level and year when the student was in a particular grade will be recorded and retained as part of the permanent record. There should also be a clear indication of the last grade that a student completed or the date when a student exited school. In addition to this information, the name of the teacher who taught a particular course may also be provided (in such cases, a teacher may consequently be interviewed to further assess a former student's adaptive behavior).

If the student were enrolled in a "special" class of any type—usually at the secondary level—this information is likely to be noted, as well. When this occurs, the course number is likely to have a code associated with it to indicate that it was a different course offering than the typical course at a particular grade level. At the secondary level, the school records will often also include documentation of the credits earned for each class; this information is important for meeting the requirements for graduation.

The school records should also indicate if the student received any special services such as special education/Section 504 services (see corresponding sections), Title I services, or other specialized interventions. The records would also indicate if a student were in a bilingual education or English-as-a-second-language (ESL) program. Detailed information, such as the nature of the services and the duration of the services, however, is less likely to be provided. What is important, from the perspective of legal proceedings, is that some indication exists that a student did receive special services of some type.

Some schools are designated as Title I schools, in which a substantial percentage of the school population qualifies as low income. The schools typically provide special programs in the areas of reading and math for students who are struggling in these areas, as determined through an internal assessment process. It should be noted, at least in the past, that some students with disabilities, including students with intellectual disability, who were receiving Title I services, may not have also been provided special education services in the early grades, even though they might otherwise have qualified for them. In some locations, students with special needs would be determined eligible for special education and begin receiving services when they no longer qualified for or were provided Title I assistance.

Disciplinary Information

Many students encounter disciplinary problems while they are in school. Some of these students also encounter the criminal justice system in some way. The school records should contain information related to the action that has been taken with regard to a student who violates the disciplinary policy of the school. This information will include dates when disciplinary action was taken and the reasons for the action. This information is helpful for obtaining an indication of behavioral problems that a student may have displayed while in school. It should be noted, however, that disciplinary decisions and action are applied in disproportional ways as a function of race and ethnicity (Skiba, Michael, Nardo, & Peterson, 2002).

Economic Information

This information relates to socioeconomic status. As indicated in the table, whether a student qualifies for free or reduced-price lunch is provided in the records. When it is determined that a student qualifies as homeless, various types of information related to this status might be indicated as well.

Health-related Information

Basic information related to immunizations and other health/medical coverage may be indicated. If a student has a Medicaid number, this finding may be an indication that the student has qualified as having a disability of some type.

Special Education Records

The fact that a student might have been in special education is typically provided as part of the academic part of the school records. The detailed information related to a student's disability, however, is part of the student's special education file. Such details include the reason for referral for special education, assessment data used for eligibility determination, program planning information (i.e., individualized education program—IEP), any related services (i.e., speech and language services), progress as a result of the special education services, and transition services (i.e., for high school students).

The major components of the special education file, mandated by the Individuals with Disabilities Education Act (IDEA) of 2004, are extremely useful for understanding a student's particular educational situation. The information provided in various special education documents should provide a comprehensive picture of the student's present levels of academic achievement and functional performance and an indication of the measurable goals that need to be addressed each year for the student to benefit from education.

States have used various terms to describe students with intellectual disability who qualify for special education. It is extremely important to identify the term that was used to describe intellectual disability at any given point in time and to review the criteria that were used for eligibility purposes. As has been noted elsewhere in this book, the term "mental retardation," or some variation of this term, was used widely throughout the United States to describe this population until recently. The term "intellectual disability" is now the professionally recognized term (Schalock, Luckasson, & Shogren, 2007) and used on the federal level for referring to this population. Most states have also changed their terminology to reflect the preferred term *intellectual disability*.

Section 504 Records

Some students who encounter difficulty in school may not have qualified for special education, as defined by IDEA disability categories. Nevertheless, these students display problems that are significant enough to inhibit their ability to be successful in school. Section 504 (of the Rehabilitation Act of 1973) ultimately provides accommodations that will assist students in addressing their area(s) of need. The services provided under Section 504 are not disability specific. In other words, a student is not identified as having a specific disability. Under Section 504, if a student demonstrates a "substantial limitation" in a "major life function" such as learning, attending, or some other school-related area, then the student will be provided with an accommodation plan that includes specific actions that are designed to benefit the student in various school situations.

Discussion

The purpose of this chapter is to emphasize the importance of school records and provide a context for understanding them. Given the importance that school records play in many legal proceedings, especially in death penalty cases, it is extremely important to understand and accurately interpret a range of topics related to school that are provided in records. Although this chapter has raised a number of cautions related to the use of school records, the documents that comprise school records are extremely valuable sources of information in acquiring a complete picture of a person's early years. Reviewing school records requires sophistication to truly obtain meaningful information about students, their school experiences, and the impact of these factors on functioning.

References

Baroff, G. S. (2003). Establishing mental retardation in capital cases: An update. *Mental Retardation, 41,* 198–202. doi: http://dx.doi.org/10.1352/0047-6765(2003)41<198:EMRICC>2.0.CO;2

Beirne-Smith, M., Patton, J. R., & Kim, S. H. (2006). *Mental retardation: An introduction to intellectual disabilities.* Upper Saddle River, NJ: Pearson.

Everington, C., & Olley, J. G. (2008). Implications of *Atkins v. Virginia:* Issues in defining and diagnosing mental retardation. *Journal of Forensic Psychology Practice, 8,* 1–23. doi: 10.1080/15228930801947278

Family Educational Rights and Privacy Act (FERPA) of 1974, 34 C.F.R Part 99.

Individuals with Disabilities Education Improvement Act of 2004, 20 U.S.C. § 1400 et seq. (2004)

Macvaugh III, G.S., & Cunningham, M. D. (2009). Atkins v. Virginia: Implications and recommendations for forensic practice. *Journal of Psychiatry & Law, 37,* 131–187.

Murphy, D. R., & Dishman, M. L. (2010). *Educational records: A practical guide for legal compliance.* Lantham, NY: Rowman & Littlefield Publishers.

Rehabilitation Act of 1973, 29 U.S.C. § 701 et seq. (1973)

Schalock, R. L., Luckasson, R. A., & Shogren, K. A. (2007). The renaming of *mental retardation:* Understanding the change to the term *intellectual disability. Intellectual and Developmental Disabilities, 45,* 116–124.

Skiba, R. J., Michael, R. S., Nardo, A. C., & Peterson, R. L. (2002). The color of discipline: Sources of racial and gender disproportionality in school punishment. *Urban Review, 34,* 317. doi: 10.1023/A:1021320817372

Tassé, M. J. (2009). Adaptive behavior assessment and the diagnosis of mental retardation in capital cases. *Applied Neuropsychology, (16),* 114–123. doi: 10.1080/09084280902864451

Widaman, K. F., & Siperstein, G. N. (2009). Assessing adaptive behavior of criminal defendants in capital cases: A reconsideration. *American Journal of Forensic Psychology, 27,* 5–13.

Wright, P. W. D., & Wright, P. D. (2007). *Wrightslaw: Special education law* (2nd ed.). Hartfield, VA: Harbor House Law Press.

21 | Relevance of Other Assessment Instruments

Karen L. Salekin
Gilbert S. Macvaugh III
Timothy J. Derning

In addition to the types of psychological tests that are routinely used to assess intellectual and adaptive functioning in *Atkins* evaluations, several other categories of assessment instruments are also used by examiners in capital cases. A comprehensive listing of the many different specific tests that examiners have been known to administer in *Atkins* cases is beyond the scope of this chapter. In view of the wide range of instruments available to examiners in general, as well as the variability with regard to relevance, we focus only on three categories of tests that are often used in assessments of intellectual disability in *Atkins* cases: (a) tests of achievement, (b) personality tests, and (c) neuropsychological tests. In doing so, we provide information regarding these tests and their overall relevance for the assessment of ID, and we discuss some of the strengths and limitations of these assessment instruments when used in the context of an *Atkins* evaluation.

Tests of Achievement

To begin, it is important to note that no direct relationship exists between scores on an achievement test and the diagnostic criteria for intellectual disability. Scores on achievement tests cannot be used as a surrogate for a measure of functional academics, nor are such scores necessary to the evaluation of intellectual disability. A potential benefit of using a scale of achievement, however, is to provide the examiner with a different lens from which to look at current abilities for people undergoing an evaluation. What will not come from such an assessment is how these abilities or deficits are used on a practical, day-to-day basis. As noted by Baroff and Olley (1999), it is not the scores on tests that matter, but the ability of the person to apply their knowledge and abilities to activities of daily living. Academic achievement scores supplement data obtained from prior school records (if available), information gathered from tests of adaptive behavior, and information provided by collateral sources. Most clinicians who conduct evaluations of ID would agree that functioning within the school environment is an important piece of information; scores on measures of achievement can be viewed as part of the information to be considered. Scores obtained from a measure of achievement are related to the conceptual domain of the American Association on Intellectual and Developmental Disabilities (AAIDD) definition (Schalock et al., 2010), as well as the functional academics area, as set forth in the current criteria by the American Psychiatric Association (2000).

In this section, we provide information on one screening measure of achievement and one comprehensive measure of achievement. These tests were chosen because they are commonly used and are familiar to many examiners; and they have been used previously in *Atkins* cases. In addition, these are two of the few tests that contain adult norms. The majority of achievement tests are normed to age 18 or 21 and are thus inappropriate for use with adults. This chapter provides examples of how these tests, and others like them, could be used in capital cases. Of note, these are not the only valid and reliable tests of academic achievement that could be administered within the context of an *Atkins* evaluation.

Wide Range Achievement Test, 4th Edition (WRAT-4)

According to a study by Hedge (unpublished thesis), the Wide Range Achievement Test, 4th Edition (WRAT-4; Wilkinson & Robertson, 2006) is one of a handful of achievement tests used by experts in *Atkins* cases, as well as in other types of forensic mental health evaluations. For example, the WRAT-4 has been described as an appropriate instrument for use in evaluations of defendants' competence to waive *Miranda* rights (Atkins & Weiss; 2011; DeClue, 2005; Heilbrun, Marczyk, & DeMatteo, 2002; Oberlander, Goldstein, & Goldstein, 2003). In a useful discussion of the role of testing in capital cases, Goldstein and Bursztajn (2011) cautioned against the use of abbreviated measures of intelligence and argued that "the savings in time and effort come at the sacrifice of potentially valuable data, a trade-off that is inappropriate when the defendant's life is at risk" (p. 161). Goldstein and Bursztajn (2011) noted that in capital cases, "tests that measure academically oriented abilities may be of value as well. These tests may include the Wide Range Achievement Test, 4th Edition" (p. 161). We submit that sole reliance on the WRAT-4 in *Atkins* cases may be misleading, and the potential for error leads one to question the cost-benefit ratio. We agree with Goldstein and Bursztajn's (2011) reasoned opinion to use only comprehensive IQ tests in capital cases, and we argue that such reasoning also should apply to the use of achievement tests within the context of adaptive behavior assessments in *Atkins* cases. The Educational Testing Service (2012), for example, also has cautioned against the exclusive use of the

WRAT-4 when diagnosing learning disabilities and do so because it "is not a comprehensive measure of achievement, and therefore, should not be used as the sole measure of achievement" (Appendix B–Tests of Achievement, para. 2).

Compared to comprehensive achievement tests, screening tests are generally faster to administer and to score, and can be useful in determining whether to administer a comprehensive test (Stetson, Stetson, & Sattler, 2001). According to Stetson et al. (2001), "to be classified as a comprehensive achievement test, a test should (a) assess three or more subject areas typically taught in schools, (b) include at least two different subtests for each subject area, and (c) assess both lower and higher levels of cognitive skills within each subject area" (p. 577).

The previous version of the WRAT-4, the Wide Range Achievement Test, Third Edition (WRAT-3; Wilkinson, 1993), was developed as a multiple-subject screening test and was designed to assess basic skills of reading, spelling, and arithmetic. Stetson et al. (2001) described the WRAT-3 as "an acceptable screening measure of lower level cognitive abilities, one aspect of achievement," but stated that an in-depth analysis of an examinee's skills can only arise from the administration of a comprehensive achievement test. These authors accurately noted that the WRAT-3 does not assess essential skills, such as reading comprehension, written expression, and math applications, all of which are valuable in the assessment of ID.

Similar to its predecessor, the WRAT-4 retained its focus on the assessment of the three basic academic codes of reading, writing, and arithmetic, but improved on the WRAT-3 by adding the Sentence Comprehension subtest and providing a Reading Composite score (Wilkinson & Robertson, 2006). Nonetheless, the WRAT-4 remains limited in terms of breadth of information it yields. According to the WRAT-4 professional manual (Wilkinson & Robertson, 2006), "the WRAT-4 is intended for use by those professionals who need a quick, simple, psychometrically sound assessment of important fundamental academic skills" (p. 3).

Heilbrun (1992) proposed that when selecting psychological tests to be used in forensic assessments, "reliability should be considered. The use of tests with a reliability coefficient of less than .80 is not advisable" (p. 265). The guiding principles of relevance and reliability also are described in the U. S. Supreme Court decision in *Daubert v. Merrell Dow Pharmaceuticals* (1993), which provided the standard that governs the admissibility of scientific evidence in federal court and in state courts in many death penalty jurisdictions. These standards should be kept in mind when conducting an evaluation of ID, even in cases that fall under the less stringent *Frye* standard (*Frye v. United States*, 1923) where the technique used is generally accepted as reliable in the relevant scientific community).

The manual of the WRAT-4 includes numerical values that provide clinicians with data from which they can determine whether they believe that the measure is suitable for the needs of the current case. Within the manual, it is found that the median coefficient alpha subtest internal consistency reliability coefficients range, by age, from .87

to .93 for the four WRAT-4 subtests. The median alpha reliabilities for the Reading Composite range from .95 to .96 for the two alternate (Blue and Green) forms, while the Combined Form has a median alpha coefficient of .98. The average alternate-form subtest reliability coefficient is .86, and the delayed-retest subtest reliability coefficient is .84 for all ages combined (Wilkinson & Robertson, 2006). Evidence of its validity was derived from correlations with cognitive ability tests (i.e., Wechsler Adult Intelligence Scale, Third Edition (WAIS-III; Wechsler, 1997), Stanford-Binet Intelligence Scales, Fifth Edition (SB5; Roid, 2003), in which a moderate relationship was shown between the WRAT-4 subtests and tests of cognitive ability; these values range from .57 for the Spelling subtest and .72 for the Reading Composite. Despite the WRAT-4's being better than the WRAT-3 in many respects, including having psychometric properties that are in line with the criteria proposed by Heilbrun (1992) and Melton, Petrila, Poythress and Slobogin (2007), the WRAT-4 continues to warrant classification as an academic achievement screening test, not a comprehensive test of achievement.

If the WRAT-4 is used within the context of *Atkins*-related litigation, the test's results are better used to determine if further assessment using a comprehensive measure might be beneficial. In this regard, no particular cut-score is recommended, and the findings obtained from the WRAT-4 should never be relied on as the only source of information related to an *Atkins* claimant's academic abilities or conceptual skills. Because the results of this screening test may be misinterpreted, the onus is on the expert to clearly describe, in both the written report and during testimony, the limitations of screening instruments and the weight given to the WRAT-4 results to increase the reliability of the expert's opinion.

Woodcock-Johnson III Tests of Achievement–Third Edition (WJ III ACH)

One of the most commonly used comprehensive measures of academic achievement is the Woodcock-Johnson III Tests of Achievement (WJ III ACH; Woodcock, McGrew, & Mather, 2001). The WJ III ACH is an individually administered, norm-referenced test for measuring academic achievement. The original WJ III ACH normative sample included 8,818 individuals who ranged in age from 24 months to 90+ years. This sample consisted of 1,143 preschool subjects, 4,784 kindergarten to 12th grade subjects, 1,165 college and university subjects, and 1,843 adult subjects. With the goal of representing the U.S. population, the sample was collected in more than 100 communities throughout the United States. The sampling design controlled for community, individual, and socioeconomic variables. The WJ III ACH is appropriate for use with people between 2 and 90+ years and provides grade equivalent scores from kindergarten to graduate school.

The WJ III ACH is available in two forms, with each containing 22 tests. There are three modes of administration for the WJ III ACH: (a) the Standard Battery; (b) the Extended Battery; and (c) client centered. The client-centered method provides the examiner with the opportunity to choose which tests to administer, based on what is needed in that case. The Standard Battery includes Tests 1 through 12, and the Extended

Battery includes Tests 13–22. The value of the latter is that it provides a thorough assessment of academic ability in multiple domains, as well as providing a method to evaluate an individual's strengths and weaknesses if more information is desired in assessing a particular area. There are many levels of interpretation for the WJ III ACH, including percentile rank, age and grade equivalent, W difference score, standard score, and relative proficiency index. Administration time is approximately 5 minutes per test, resulting in an estimated 1 hr and 50 minutes to administer both the WJ III ACH Standard and Extended Batteries.

Woodcock-Johnson III Normative Update

The Woodcock-Johnson III Normative Update (WJ III ACH NU; Woodcock, McGrew, Schrank, & Mather, 2001, 2007) does not replace the individual items found in the WJ III ACH batteries, but it does replace the normative comparisons. The WJ III ACH NU is a "recalculation of the normative data for the Woodcock-Johnson III (WJ III ACH) (Woodcock, McGrew, & Mather, 2001), based on the final 2000 U.S. Census statistics" (McGrew, Dailey, & Schrank, 2007, p. 1). "The WJ III ACH NU norms replace the original WJ III ACH norms, which were based on the U.S. Census Bureau's 2000 census projections issued in 1996" (McGrew, Dailey & Schrank, 2007, p. 1); these norms are reflected in the scoring and interpretation provided by the WJ III ACH Normative Update Compuscore® and Profiles Program (Compuscore; Schrank & Woodcock, 2007). Because the normative sample for the WJ III ACH NU is the same as that of the WJ III ACH, the NU norms do not account for population changes that may have occurred in the period between the end of the norming cycle and 2000.

Of great import in *Atkins* cases is the validity of the data put forth to the trier-of-fact. Examiners are required to use the best and most recently developed tests that are appropriate to the case. Questions regarding the norms of any test used usually occur during the course of testimony in an *Atkins* hearing. According to McGrew and colleagues (McGrew, Schrank, & Woodcock, 2007), the WJ III ACH NU recalculation of data and development of new norms provide a more precise estimate of a person's performance and allows for greater confidence in the accuracy of the scores.

Concordance between scores obtained by the WJ III ACH NU and those of the WJ III ACH is another question that may be of interest to the Court. The authors of the WJ III ACH NU reviewed the 2000 U.S. Census data and identified changes in the characteristics of the population that were sufficient in degree so that noticeable differences between the WJ III ACH and the WJ III ACH NU would be observed. As noted by McGrew, Schrank and Woodcock (2007), "Many (but not all) of the resulting WJ III ACH NU scores will be lower, particularly at the youngest and oldest age groups" (p. 242). This information is particularly useful in providing an explanation for discrepant findings in cases where both the WJ III ACH and the WJ III ACH NU exist.

Perhaps the most important issue regarding the use of achievement tests is whether these tests aid the trier-of-fact in making a determination with regard to the legal question. In the current discussion, the legal question is whether the claimant has an intellectual disability, and whether the WJ III ACH NU provides reliable and valid data that are valuable in making this determination. Data from achievement tests have probative value in that they provide another means to assess the abilities of an individual, supplementing other sources of data both qualitative and quantitative, to increase the reliability of expert opinions and legal findings.

An in-depth review of how to use this measure is outside the scope of this chapter, but a few important points are worth mentioning. First, examiners must look at both the cluster scores and the subtest scores for interpretive information. For example, it is safe to say that people with ID have difficulty with a number of tasks associated with learning. Though reading, mathematics, and writing are common areas of inquiry, an additional measure of oral language skills is also key; and most important, all these domains are assessed by the WJ III ACH and must be scored with the WJ III NU normative tables. The Court should be provided with detailed information regarding the claimant's abilities in each of these domains of academic achievement, and it is up to the expert to articulate how scores on these measures either support or refute the diagnosis of ID. In doing so, it is necessary to look to the constructs measured by the clusters and associated subtests. For example, one subtest on the reading cluster assesses reading comprehension, which is an area that would be expected to be a problem for people with ID. Listening ability and verbal comprehension fall within the oral language cluster, as do expressive vocabulary, reasoning, and semantic memory (see Chapter 3 for further information regarding the characteristics of people with ID in the upper ranges). Similar links can be made throughout the test, so familiarity with the WJ III ACH NU is critical for adequate assessment of functional academic skills related to ID.

If the choice is made to administer a comprehensive test of achievement, such as the WJ III ACH, there are at least two important caveats about appropriately interpreting the data. The first is that in an *Atkins* case, the administration of the achievement test produces scores that reflect a claimant's *current* status, and what is at issue is their prior status, whether that is a few years ago (e.g., someone who is 20 years old), or at the time of the alleged crime (which could be relatively recent or at some time in the past). For cases in which the alleged capital offense occurred decades prior, making a connection between the presence of current deficits on a standardized academic achievement measure and the person's functioning at some previous point in time can be challenging, but not insurmountable. Establishing the link may be less difficult for younger claimants because the time between participation in school and date of the alleged capital offense may be substantially shorter. In our view, the importance of considering the totality of information available is paramount because that is the only way to interpret scores obtained from tests of achievement.

To adequately discuss the findings of an achievement test, one must appreciate that the claimant will demonstrate strengths and weakness within and between the academic domains. Further, it also is important to understand that the science has not yet developed a defining profile of scores that reflects the level of achievement to be expected for an individual with mild intellectual disability. Similar to persons with ID, some variability should be expected both between tests of achievement and within a single test of achievement.

A third important consideration is the relationship between an *Atkins* claimant's IQ and achievement test scores. According to McGrew (2012a),

> Too many lay persons and, unfortunately many educators and psychologists, have fallen prey to the *IQ-achievement fallacy*, which is the non-science based assumption or belief that individuals can only achieve at or below their measured achievement. The appropriate scientific fact is that for any IQ score there is a symmetrical range of possible expected achievement scores which, whether reported in terms of standard scores or GE's [grade equivalents], can be large. Achievement scores that are above predicted levels based on measured IQ scores will occur with some degree of regularity for individuals with mild MR/ID. (p. 1).

McGrew (2012b) further has recommended that achievement test scores should neither be interpreted without consideration of the correlation between achievement and intelligence test scores, nor as "a knee-jerk indication" that an *Atkins* claimant does not have ID. This is of particular concern in cases in which an *Atkins* claimant's achievement test scores may appear higher than expected based on the claimant's IQ scores, particularly when credible data suggest that criteria for all three prongs have been met. The critical issue is the strength of the correlation between IQ scores and achievement tests and what these scores look like when converted to grade equivalents.

Using data from the Wechsler Adult Intelligence Scale–Fourth Edition (WAIS-IV) *Technical and Interpretive Manual* (Wechsler, 2008), Wechsler Individual Achievement Test–Second Edition (WIAT-II, Wechsler, 2001), and the Woodcock Johnson Battery–Third Edition–Normative Update (WJ III ACH NU; Woodcock, Schrank, Mather, & McGrew, 2007), McGrew (2012a) indicated positive correlations between the Full Scale /General Intellectual Ability scores on the intelligence tests and math, reading, and written language composite/cluster scores on the achievement tests. In deriving the best estimate of expected achievement, he calculated the *median* value of .75 for the six correlations. Using an example of an individual with a measured IQ of 70, and after accounting for the statistical phenomenon known as *regression to the mean,* McGrew (2012a, p. I, para. 6) concluded, "The best single point estimate of their expected achievement is a standard score of 78." Keeping in mind that error is inherent in any correlation-based prediction between psychological test scores, McGrew and Watson (2012) also calculated the Standard Error of Estimate (SEest) to account for this type of comparison between IQ and achievement tests. The SEest provides a metric for the amount of prediction error present when one test score is predicted from the other (see Chapter 5). The SEest provides a prediction confidence band from which to determine if a person's measured achievement scores are in line with the range of expected scores based on their measured IQ. Using the median SEest value for the six correlations, he obtained a SEest of approximately 9, which "means that for any specific IQ score there is an expected/predicted achievement test score that has a *68% confidence band of prediction* of + 9 points (from 9 points lower to 9 points higher than the expected/predicted score). The *95% prediction confidence band* is twice the 68% value—18 points." This means that when attempting to determine the relationship between an *Atkins* claimant's IQ and achievement test scores at the 95% confidence level—which is customary in forensic cases—one should be prepared to use a 36-point standard score span to account for the correct band of error associated with such a comparison (e.g., a score of 70 would have a confidence interval that ranged from 52 to 88).

Whereas interpretation of standard scores is the most precise method of evaluating scores, it is common to consider a second level interpretation based on grade equivalents (GEs). Despite their appeal, grade-based interpretations are deceiving and can be difficult to explain because of their nonlinear relationship to standard scores. The reasons for this nonlinear relationship are complex and beyond the scope of this chapter, but McGrew (2012b) has provided a glimpse into the basis for this relationship:

> The answer lies in the fact that (a) standard scores are equal interval metrics and GEs are *not*, (b) standard scores are partially derived from the standard deviation (*SD*) of the *W*-scores at each age within each achievement domain, and these values are *not* the same across achievement domains *nor* across ages, and (c) *W*-score growth score curves show differential rates of rapid growth during the early ages/ grades, then a plateau, and then a much slower rate of decline. (p. 1)

As previously noted, the best single point estimate of expected achievement for a person with an IQ of 70 is 78. Using a 95% confidence band, the standard scores for this person would range between 60 and 96. To convert standard scores to grade equivalents, the age of the person must be known. To provide insight into the standard score—grade equivalent conversion—McGrew (2012b) completed the conversion (based on the WJ III ACH NU normative tables) for a person who obtained an IQ of 70 and did so at three age points (i.e., 25, 35, and 45), as well as the three points that delimit the 95% confidence interval (i.e., 60, 78, and 96). Figure 21.1 depicts the values obtained for the Broad Reading Cluster from the WJ III ACH NU when using a measured IQ of 70 from the WJ III ACH COG GIA-Std. (Woodcock-Johnson III Tests of Achievement, Cognitive Abilities, General Intellectual Ability- Standard).

As evident from Figure 21.1, the expected range of grade equivalents for adults with an IQ of 70 varies greatly. In an *Atkins* case, such variability may result in a number of inaccurate interpretations and this would be true across the continuum. A grade equivalent of kindergarten on one or more subtests does not automatically mean that a person has ID; similarly, a score or two above the 10th grade level in particularly narrow tasks (e.g., memory for designs,) does not mean that ID can be ruled out (Scores for Written Language and Math are available at http://www.atkinsmrdeathpenalty. com/2012/11/ap-101-brief-18-misunderstanding-and.html.).

FIGURE 21.1. Values Obtained from the Broad Reading Cluster from the Woodcock-Johnson Tests of Achievement III Normative Updates (WJ III ACH NU)

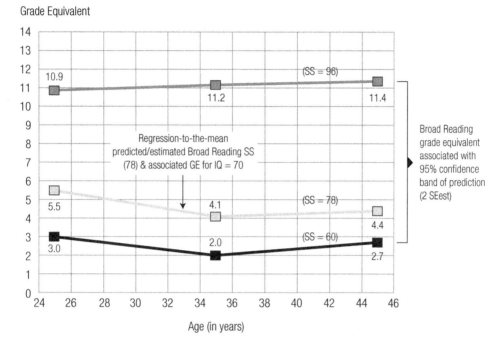

WJ III NU Broad Reading achievement grade equivalent (GE) and 95% confidence band GEs, associated with IQ score (Woodcock-Johnson III General Intellectual Ability–Standard) of 70 for adults from age 25 to 45

Source: McGrew, K. S. (2012b, November 20). AP 101 Brief #18: Misunderstanding and misuse of achievement test scores in Atkins MR/ID death penalty cases: Part 2—Range of expected grade equivalents. *Intellectual Competence and the Death Penalty.* Retrieved from http://www.atkinsmrdeathpenalty.com/2012/11/ap-101-brief-18-misunderstanding-and.html

Personality Tests

Though the purpose of personality testing varies depending on the goals of the assessment, personality testing is irrelevant to an evaluation of ID. Examples of appropriate uses of personality tests include developing plans for treatment, evaluating fit between personality traits and occupational goals, and assessing for psychopathology. These tests do not tap intellectual abilities and do not tap any skill area relevant to the assessment of adaptive behavior. As such, there is no psychometrically valid reason to use these measures in an *Atkins* evaluation. It is for this reason that one of the most prominent personality measures, the Minnesota Multiphasic Personality Inventory–Second Edition (MMPI-2; Butcher, Dahlstrom, Graham, Tellegen, & Kreammer, 1989), and others like it, are inappropriate for the purposes of evaluating intellectual disability. Although there are concerns specifically related to the use of the MMPI-2 in *Atkins* cases, similar concerns also exist regarding the use of any measure of personality within this type of context.

Minnesota Multiphasic Personality Inventories

The Minnesota Multiphasic Personality Inventory–Second Edition (MMPI-2) is regarded as the most widely used objective personality inventory in the world (Butcher et al., 1989). It is consistently ranked as the leading personality inventory and has been a leader in test reference for years. Its popularity results from its simplicity of scoring and administration, and its objective format, which lends itself to research designs and useful applications in many settings (Friedman, Lewak, Nichols, & Webb, 2001). As previously mentioned, however, the MMPI-2 is not designed to assess core factors related to the diagnosis of intellectual disability.

According to its manual for administration and scoring (Butcher et al., 1989), the MMPI-2 is "a broad-band test designed to assess a number of the major patterns of personality and emotional disorders" (p. 1). Despite voluminous research on the original MMPI (e.g., Dahlstrom, Welsh, & Dahlstrom, 1972; Hathaway & McKinley, 1942) and the MMPI-2 (Butcher et al., 1989, 2001), relatively little is known about the interpretation of MMPI-2 scores and profiles specific to people with ID. Numeric intelligence levels (IQ) were not isolated in MMPI-2 normative samples; only indirect measures of low intelligence, such as occupational level, educational level, and socioeconomic status, were used.

The original MMPI was first published in 1942 (Hathaway & McKinley, 1942), and the normative sample consisted of friends and relatives of patients being seen at the University of Minnesota Hospital outpatient department. Later, people who were administered the MMPI were compared to the responses of a "Minnesota normal adult" who was someone approximately 35 years old, of Caucasian/European descent, married, living in a small town or rural area, and had completed approximately 8 years of schooling (Friedman et al., 2001).

In 1989, the MMPI-2 (Butcher et al., 1989, 2001) was published. Among the many changes, one of the primary goals was to replace the outdated normative data of the MMPI. The new norms were developed from the responses of 2,600 adults who represented seven states across the United States. The ethnic diversity of the sample was improved and included African-Americans (12%), Hispanics (3%), Native Americans (3%), and Asian-Americans (1%, one man and six women) (Graham, 1993). Unfortunately, a review of the 1980 U.S. Census data indicates that minorities were still underrepresented in the MMPI-2 sample, and thus, the MMPI-2 normative sample remains weighted toward Caucasians (81% of the normative sample).

Importantly, with respect to people with ID, the greatest differences between the MMPI-2 re-standardization group and the 1980 census were found in the areas of education and socioeconomic status. As noted by Friedman and colleagues (2001),

> Well-educated participants are notably over-represented in the new sample at the expense of individuals with a high school education or less. For example, 27.2% of male participants were college graduates compared to 9.8% of the general population in 1980. (p. 14)

Similarly, with respect to females,

> [A total of] 26.7% of the female participants were college graduates compared with 7.5% of the general population in 1980. The average educational level in the new sample was close to 2.5 years of college. This level of education is not only higher than the 1980 census data, but it's vastly higher than the original norm group. (Friedman et al., 2001, p. 14)

With respect to occupational level, the MMPI-2 normative sample is much higher than levels attained by persons with ID. In the MMPI-2 sample, approximately 32% of the men and 21% of the women had professional or managerial positions; only 12% of the men and 5% of the women were laborers. In addition, marital status of the MMPI-2 sample is skewed toward those who are married: men, 61.6%, and women, 61.2% (Graham, 1993).

With respect to socioeconomic status, Stancliffe and Lakin (2007) noted that people with ID have a median income that "was 20% below the poverty threshold and about one-third of the median total income of the general population" (p. 437). For those who are able to live independently or with a roommate, it is typical for their level of income to be below the poverty level (Stancliffe & Lakin, 2007). When compared to adults without ID, however, those with ID have lower rates of living independently (Blackorby & Wagner, 1996; Luftig & Muthert, 2005) and may be partially or fully dependent on others for their monetary needs. Friedman et al. (2001) cautioned that, "when testing a low SES individual, the reader is advised to be aware that the positive skew in the MMPI-2 normative sample toward upper SES generates the impression of psychopathology" (p. 24).

In addition to concerns regarding the norming sample, reading ability and comprehension are two of the major concerns with using any of the three versions of the MMPI (i.e., the MMPI, the MMPI-2, or the more recent version, Minnesota Multiphasic Personality Inventory–2–Restructured Form (MMPI-2-RF; Tellegen et al., 2003) with people possibly having ID. For the original MMPI, the recommended reading level was the sixth grade (Dahlstrom et al., 1972), but subsequent studies indicated that the measure is written at the seventh- or eighth-grade level (Ward & Ward, 1980). According to Friedman et al., (2001), one study they cited (i.e., Blanchard, 1981) found some items of the original MMPI required 10th-grade reading skills.

To consider further the minimum reading level required for the MMPI-2 varies depending on the source. The recommended reading levels reported include the sixth grade (Butcher et al., 2001; and the eighth grade (Bow, Flens, Gould, & Greenhut, 2005; Hathaway & McKinley, 1989); further, according to the test publishers, the MMPI-2 has readability statistics of the fifth grade (Lexile average) and the 4.6 grade level (Flesch-Kincaid). According to the MMPI-2 manual for administration and scoring (Butcher et al., 1989), however, "an eighth-grade elementary-school level of reading comprehension is required" (p. 1). Bow, Flens, and Gould (2006) provided a concise overview of the studies that have looked at the readability of the MMPI-2 and attempt to demonstrate the reasons underlying the different perspectives.

A common and simplistic approach employed by some clinicians to determine whether a person has sufficient reading ability to complete the MMPI-2 is to rely on the subject's stated years of education. Dahlstrom et al., (1972) cautioned against this practice because it may be unreliable and misleading; people may overstate their education history or fail to report that their academic achievement was well below that of their peers. Greene (2000) echoed this sentiment and advised against using completed years of education to establish a person's reading comprehension level.

The Minnesota Multiphasic Personality Inventory–2-Restructured Format (MMPI-2-RF; Ben-Porath & Tellegen, 2008/2011; Tellegen & Ben-Porath, 2008/2011) is the latest version of the MMPI series and is a 338-item true/false self-report inventory, which is conceptually and empirically linked to contemporary models of personality and psychopathology. It was constructed to provide efficient and up-to-date measurement of the meaningful clinical substance in the MMPI-2, using scales that meet contemporary psychometric standards. The test uses the nongendered version of MMPI-2 normative sample (Ben-Porath & Forbey, 2003). The standard scales of the MMPI-2-RF include nine Validity scales, three Higher-Order (H-O) scales, nine Restructured Clinical (RC) scales, 23 Specific Problem (SP) scales, two Interest Scales, and five revised Personality Psychopathology Five (PSY-5) Scales. A majority of the scales of the MMPI-2-RF are organized in a hierarchical fashion with H-O scales at the top, RC scales in the middle, and SP scales at lowest level.

Like other measures of personality, the MMPI-2-RF was not developed to assess intellectual disability. The measure is useful in many forensic contexts, although its newness leaves questions of normative validity unanswered as of yet, but it has no probative value in Atkins assessments. For example, personality measures in general are helpful when the issue is related to the diagnosis of major mental illnesses (i.e., when there are no concerns that the person also has intellectual disability); and this is particularly important for issues such as criminal responsibility, mitigation, and risk assessment, to name a few. Within the department of corrections, these measures can be helpful in terms of classification and placement within the facility. In addition, there are many noted strengths to the use of personality measures outside of the forensic setting, and these can include general clinical assessment of psychiatric illness, treatment planning, career counseling, job selection, and others.

Given that Atkins claimants must be evaluated for ID, regardless of their grade or reading level, the MMPI-2 should not be administered for any purpose in Atkins cases. Because the purpose of the MMPI-2 is to assess for personality and emotional disorders, it has no relevance to an assessment for intellectual disability. Concerns regarding the inappropriate use of the MMPI-2, particularly in Atkins evaluations, have been addressed in the literature along with specific practice recommendations related to this (see Keyes, 2004; Macvaugh & Cunningham, 2009).

Neuropsychological Tests

According to Lezak, Howieson, Loring, Hannay, and Fischer (2004), clinical neuro-psychology is "an applied science concerned with the behavioral expression of brain dysfunction" (p. 3). An issue relevant to the use of these measures is whether they have ecological validity such that the results can be linked to observable limitations and strengths for people with ID. At the time of this writing, research specific to this population does not exist; however, studies on other populations who present with similar issues do. For example, studies have investigated the ability of people to per-form activities of daily living (Baird, Podell, Lovell, & McGinty, 2001; Cahn et al., 1998; Cahn-Weiner, Boyle, & Malloy, 2002), their psychosocial outcomes (Ross, Mills, & Rosenthal, 1997), and their functioning within the workplace (Ross et al., 1997). In an *Atkins* evaluation, links between brain and behavior are made when the results of neuropsychological testing are relevant to the assessment of the functional abilities. This section of the chapter focuses on the application of neuropsychological tests to the assessment of adaptive behavior.

As evident from the definition of clinical neuropsychology and research therein, it is clear that information resulting from these tests has probative value in an *Atkins* case. In fact, in arriving at their decision in *Atkins v. Virginia* (2002), the Justices considered how impairments related to intellectual disability lead to reduced moral culpability for offenders with ID, as well as the need for constitutional protection from the death penalty. For example, in the majority opinion, Justice Stevens wrote,

> Because of their impairments, however, by definition they have diminished capacities to understand and process information, to communicate, to abstract from mistakes and learn from experience, to engage in logical reasoning, to con-trol impulses, and to understand the reactions of others (Justice Stevens Deliv-ered the Opinion of the Court, para. 1).

The impairments listed by the Court are exactly those that are assessed through neuro-psychological tests.

To provide a real-life example, in the case of *Thomas v. Allen* (2009), clinical neu-ropsychologist Dr. Daniel Marson described to the Court how the results of neuro-psychological testing can assist the Court in making a determination regarding the level of impairment present in certain domains of adaptive behavior. As is delineated here (in the direct examination), Marson's testimony highlights the conceptual links between adaptive behavior deficits and test scores by providing concrete examples of how such scores on neuropsychological tests can translate into real-world deficits in adaptive behavior.

> Q: And what light can neuropsychology shed on adaptive behavior in connec-tion with[intellectual disability]?

A: Well, a neuropsychologist will conduct an evaluation where they will look at a wide range of specific or discreet cognitive functions, like, memory, attention, perceptual abilities, problem solving. And that can help the parties in a case, the Court, understand how these specific deficits translate into specific kinds of problems in adaptive functioning.

Q: So for example, if you heard testimony or an account of a person who had difficulty taking or understanding instructions, is there a concomitant test or testing that would shed light on that disability?

A: Yes. Understanding instructions might. It may also relate to problems in actually understanding the content of the instruction. So again, a neuropsychologist can look at sort of the component cognitive abilities and relate them to specific deficits in everyday functioning.

Q: And we'll get into them later, but are there tests that would confirm or support the problem in adaptive functioning, say, with respect to understanding and following instructions?

A: Yes. Indeed.

Q: Let's move to the next category of tests, then. They are tests regarding attention ability. And what's this category of tests do for us?

A: These are tests that provide information about an individual's auditory/verbal attention. Their ability to attend, say, to things that are spoken to them and their visual attention, their ability to attend to information in their--visual information in their environment.

Q: And what relationship do those tests have to adaptive ability, such as being able to work, follow instruction, and so forth?

A: Well, you essentially have to pay attention to your boss or team leader if you're receiving instruction. And sometimes, you're getting multiple instructions. So you have to pay attention to each component of it. In the workplace, you need to be attentive to new, say, developments in your workplace. If there's a new sign or there's a caution area sign that's been put up, you need to be aware of those things (*Thomas v. Allen*, 2009, Section 1287).

Though research has shown that neuropsychological testing has ecological validity, caution should be used when interpreting neuropsychological test data in the context of an *Atkins* evaluation, especially when considering demographically adjusted norms. McGrew and Watson (2012) observed that the use of demographically adjusted norms has been applied in neuropsychological assessment for many years to differentiate acquired neurological deficits from developmental deficiencies. Adjusted

neuropsychological norms are advantageous in assessments in which the neuropsychologist wishes to document a change from premorbid functioning. Demographically
adjusted norms assume the subject had normal or typical development, with mainstream educational opportunities, and no history of brain damage or disease (Heaton,
Ryan, & Grant, 2009).

Demographically adjusted norms do not compare a person against the general
population norms; rather they compare a person to a smaller, select group of people
that are similar to the subject. These norms typically are modified based on the demographic characteristics of age, gender, race, and level of education. As McGrew and
Watson (2012) illustrated, a professional (e.g., a lawyer) may have a high IQ (e.g., 130)
at the top 2% of the general population, but when compared only to other lawyers, the
relative standing of the 130 IQ may be found to be more average in comparison to this
specific group of professionals. This phenomenon is often seen in institutional settings
that serve only people with ID. Within that setting, some clients with ID may be seen
as bright or clever in comparison to other peers in that setting, whereas in the larger
population context they are not sophisticated.

As McGrew and Watson (2012) pointed out, the diagnosis of ID requires a comparison against nationally representative normative data and not a comparison to a
select demographically matched subgroup. This speaks against any practice that asserts
a person is normal or average only because within a narrowly selected subgroup, the
person's level of functioning appears to be common or typical. According to McGrew
and Watson (2012),

> *Norm-referenced testing* is at the heart of psychological assessment for the diag-
> nosis of ID (retrieved from http://www.atkinsmrdeathpenalty.com/2012/07/ap-
> 101-brief-14-demographically.html November 30, 2012). The diagnosis of ID
> requires comparison of a person's scores against *nationally representative norms*,
> not a comparison to others of the same age, gender, race and level of education.
> (McGrew & Watson, 2012, Demographically Adjusted Test Norm Interpretation
> is Inappropriate in the Diagnosis of Atkins MR/ID in Capital Cases para. 4).

According to the authors, demographically adjusted norms become a "sliding reference
point" of general intellectual functioning that would be inappropriately applied in ID
determinations because the level of intellectual functioning is not derived from a comparison to the general population.

As the preceding discussion suggests, neuropsychological tests can play an important role in the assessment of ID within the context of *Atkins* cases. Because neuropsychological tests are specifically designed to measure the presence or absence of certain
types of brain dysfunction, such instruments allow for norm-referenced assessments
of many of the same types of impairments that were identified in the Court's reasoning
underlying the *Atkins* decision. Not only do these types of assessments supplement findings from standardized measures of adaptive behavior by providing psychometrically

relevant data to pinpoint specific types of deficits, but these measures also can be particularly helpful in determining differential diagnoses in *Atkins* claimants (i.e., dementia and traumatic brain injury vs. ID), as well as identifying potential comorbid conditions that may coexist with ID. Although examiners are cautioned against relying on demographically adjusted norms when using neuropsychological tests in an *Atkins* context, proper use of these types of assessments using norm-referenced procedures can be beneficial in strengthening the validity of diagnostic conclusions related to deficits in adaptive behavior.

Conclusion

Several different types of psychological tests may be used by examiners who conduct evaluations of ID in capital cases. While certain types of tests are of course required to address the specific diagnostic criteria for the disability, including those instruments that have been developed for assessing both intellectual and adaptive functioning, other types of tests that may not necessarily be required in such cases are also often used to collect additional data relevant to the legal question at hand. In this chapter, we reviewed three specific categories of these other types of assessment instruments (i.e., achievement, personality, and neuropsychological tests) and described their relevance to *Atkins* evaluations.

Achievement tests should be administered primarily to supplement data derived from measures of adaptive behavior; however, one should not solely rely on screening tests of achievement. The benefits of using neuropsychological measures should be considered whenever possible in *Atkins* cases because these types of tests are considered to be useful in identifying specific types of brain-based impairments that are thought to underlie certain types of deficits in adaptive behavior. Finally, the use of personality assessment instruments is not recommended with *Atkins* claimants because these measures are not intended to measure ID, are not relevant to the overall assessment of ID in a capital context, and are not appropriate for people possibly having ID.

References

American Psychiatric Association. (2000). *Diagnostic and statistical manual of mental disorders* (4th ed. text rev.). Washington, DC: Author.

Atkins, E. L., & Weiss, K. (2011). Competency to waive *Miranda* rights. In E. Y. Drogin, F. M. Dattilo, R. L. Sadoff, & T. G. Gutheil (Eds.), *Handbook of forensic assessment: Psychological and psychiatric perspectives* (pp. 25–48). Hoboken, NJ: Wiley.

Atkins v. Virginia, 536 U.S. 304, 310 (2002).

Baird, A., Podell, K., Lovell, M. & McGinty, S.B. (2001). Complex real-world functioning and neuropsychological test performance in older adults. *The Clinical Neuropsychologist, 15,* 369–379.

Baroff, G., & Olley, J. G. (1999). *Mental retardation: Nature, cause, and management* (3rd ed.). New York, NY: Routledge.

Ben-Porath, Y. S., & Forbey, J. D. (2003). *Non-gendered norms for the MMPI-2.* Minneapolis, MN.: University of Minnesota Press.

Ben-Porath, Y. S., & Tellegen, A. (2008). *MMPI-2-RF (Minnesota Multiphasic Personality Inventory-2): Manual for administration, scoring, and interpretation.* Minneapolis, MN: University of Minnesota Press

Blackorby, J., & Wagner, M. (1996). Longitudinal postschool outcomes of youth with disabilities: Findings from the National Longitudinal Transition Study. *Exceptional Children, 62,* 399–413.

Bow, J. N., Flens, J. R., & Gould, J. W., (2006). Commentary: MMPI-2 readability. *Journal of Child Custody: Research, Issues, and Practices, 3,* 71–75. doi: 10.1300/J190v03n01_05

Bow, J. N., Flens, J. R., Gould, J. W., & Greenhut, D. (2005). An analysis of administration, scoring, and interpretation of the MMPI-2 and MCMI-II/III in child custody evaluations. *Journal of Child Custody, 2*(4), 1–22. doi: 10.1300/J190v02n04_01

Butcher, J. N., Dahlstrom, W. G., Graham, J. R., Tellegen, A., & Kaemmer, B. (1989). *Manual for the restandardized Minnesota Multiphasic Personality Inventory: MMPI—2. An administrative and interpretive guide.* Minneapolis, MN: University of Minnesota Press.

Butcher, J. N., Graham, J. R., Ben-Porath, Y. S., Tellegen, A., Dahlstrom, W. G., & Kaemmer, B. K. (2001). *Minnesota Multiphasic Personality Inventory-2: Manual for administration, scoring, and interpretation* (rev. ed.). Minneapolis, MN: University of Minnesota Press.

Cahn, D. A., Sullivan, E.V., Shear, P. K., Fama, R., Lim, K.O., Tinklenberg, J. R., Yesavage, J. A., Pfefferbaum, A. (1999). Structural correlates of clock drawing performance in Alzheimer's disease. *Journal of the International Neuropsychological Society, 5,* 502–509. doi: 10.1017/S1355617799566034

Cahn-Weiner, D. A., Boyle, P. A., & Malloy, P. F. (2002). Tests of executive function predict instrumental activities of daily living in community-dwelling older individuals. *Applied Neuropsychology, 9,* 187–191.

Dahlstrom, W. G., Welsh, G. S., & Dahlstrom, L. E. (1972). *An MMPI handbook: Vol. 1. Clinical interpretation* (2nd ed.). Minneapolis, MN: University of Minnesota Press.

Daubert v. Merrell Dow Pharmaceuticals, Inc., 509 U.S. 579 (1993).

DeClue, G. (2005). *Interrogations and disputed confessions: A manual for forensic psychological practice.* Sarasota, FL: Professional Resource Press

Educational Testing Service. (2012). Policy statement for documentation of a learning disability in adolescents and adults (2nd ed.). Retrieved from http://www.ets.org/disabilities/documentation/documenting_learning_disabilities#ach

Friedman, A., Lewak, R., Nichols, D., & Webb, J. (2001). *Psychological assessment with the MMPI-2.* Mahwah, NJ: Lawrence Erlbaum Associates.

Frye v. United States, 293 F. 1013 (D.C. Cir. 1923).

Goldstein, A. M., & Bursztajn, H. J. (2011). Capital litigation: Special considerations. In E. Y. Drogin, F. M. Dattilo, R. L. Sadoff, T. G. Gutheil (Ed.), *Handbook of forensic assessment: Psychological and psychiatric perspectives* (pp. 145–170). Hoboken, NJ: John Wiley & Sons, Inc.

Graham, J. R. (1993). *MMPI-2: Assessing personality and psychopathology* (2nd ed.). New York, NY: Oxford University Press.

Greene, R. L. (2000). *The MMPI-2: An interpretive manual.* Boston, MA: Allyn & Bacon.

Hathaway, S. R., & McKinley, J. C. (1942). *The Minnesota Multiphasic Personality Inventory manual.* New York, NY: Psychological Corporation.

Hathaway, S., & McKinley, J. C. (1989). *Minnesota Multiphasic Personality Inventory (MMPI-2).* Columbus, OH: Merrill/Prentice-Hall.

Heaton, R. K., Ryan, L., & Grant, I. (2009). Demographic influences and use of demographically corrected norms in neuropsychological assessment. In I. Grant & K. M. Adams (Eds.), *Neuropsychological assessment of neuropsychiatric and neuromedical disorders* (pp. 127–155). New York, NY: Oxford University Press.

Heilbrun, K. (1992). The role of psychological testing in forensic assessment. *Law and Human Behavior, 16,* 257–272.

Heilbrun, K., Marczyk, G., & DeMatteo, D. (2002). *Forensic mental health assessment: A casebook.* New York, NY: Oxford University Press.

Keyes, D. W. (2004). Use of the Minnesota Multiphasic Personality Inventory (MMPI) to identify malingering mental retardation. *Mental Retardation, 42,* 151–153. doi: 10.1352/0047-7765(2004)42<151:UOTMMP>2.0.CO;2

Lezak, M. D., Howieson, D. B., Loring, D. W., Hannay, H. J., & Fischer, J. S. (2004). *Neuropsychological assessment (4th edition).* New York: Oxford University Press.

Luftig, R. L., & Muthert, D. (2005). Patterns of employment and independent living of adult graduates with learning disabilities and mental retardation of an inclusionary high school vocational program. *Research in Developmental Disabilities: A Multidisciplinary Journal, 26,* 317–325. doi: 10.1016/j.ridd.2003.08.001

Macvaugh, G. S., & Cunningham, M. D. (2009). *Atkins v. Virginia*: Implications and recommendations for forensic practice. *Journal of Psychiatry & Law, 37,* 131–187.

Mather, N., & Woodcock, R. W. (2001). *Examiner's manual. Woodcock-Johnson III.* Rolling Meadows, IL: Riverside Publishing.

McGrew, K. S. (2012a, November 18). AP 101 Brief #17: Misunderstanding and misuse of achievement test scores in *Atkins* MR/ID death penalty cases: Part 1—Range of expected standard scores. *Intellectual Competence and the Death Penalty).* Retrieved from http://www.atkinsmrdeathpenalty.com/2012/11/ap-101-brief-15-and-misuse-of.html

McGrew, K. S. (2012b, November 20). AP 101 Brief #18: Misunderstanding and misuse of achievement test scores in *Atkins* MR/ID death penalty cases: Part 2—Range of expected grade equivalents. *Intellectual Competence and the Death Penalty.* Retrieved from http://www.atkinsmrdeathpenalty.com/2012/11/ap-101-brief-18-misunderstanding-and.html

McGrew, K. S., Dailey, D. E. H., & Schrank, F. A. (2007). *Woodcock-Johnson III®/Woodcock-Johnson III Normative Update score differences: What the user can expect and why.* (Woodcock-Johnson III Assessment Service Bulletin No. 9). Itasca, IL: Riverside.

McGrew, K. S., Schrank, F. A., & Woodcock, R. W. (2007). *Technical manual. Woodcock-Johnson III normative update.* Rolling Meadows, IL: Riverside Publishing.

McGrew, K. S., & Watson, D. (2012). AP 101 Brief #14. Demographically adjusted neuropsych (Heaton) norm-based scores inappropriate for ID dx. *Intellectual Competence and the Death Penalty.* Retrieved from http://www.atkinsmrdeathpenalty.com/2012/07/ap-101-brief-14-demographically.html

Melton, G. B., Petrila, J., Poythress, N.G., & Slobogin, C. (2007). *Psychological evaluations for the courts* (3rd ed.). New York, NY: Guilford Press.

Oberlander, L., Goldstein, N. E., & Goldstein, A. M. (2003). Competence to confess: Evaluating the validity of Miranda waivers and trustworthiness of confessions. In A. M. Goldstein (Ed.), *Handbook of psychology: Vol. 11, Forensic psychology* (pp. 335–357). Hoboken, NJ: Wiley.

Roid, G. H. (2003). *Stanford-Binet Intelligence Scales* (5th ed.). Itasca, IL: Riverside.

Ross, S. R., Mills, S. R., & Rosenthal, M. (1997). Neuropsychological prediction of psychosocial outcome after traumatic brain injury. *Applied Neuropsychology, 4,* 165–170.

Schalock, R. L., Buntinx, W. H. E., Borthwick-Duffy, S., Bradley, V., Craig, E. M., Coulter, D. L., Gomez, S. C., Lachapelle, Y., Luckasson, R. A., Reeve, A., Shogren, K. A., Snell, M. E., Spreat, S., Tassé, M. J., Thompson, J. R., Verdugo, M. A., Wehmeyer, M. L., & Yeager, M. H. (2010). *Intellectual disability: Definition, classification, and system of supports* (11th ed). Washington, DC: American Association on Intellectual and Developmental Disabilities.

Schrank, F. A., & Woodcock, R. W. (2007). *WJ III Compuscore and Profiles Program–Version 2.* Itasca, IL: Riverside.

Stancliffe, R. J., & Lakin, K. C. (2007). Independent living. In S. L. Odom, R. H. Horner, M. E. Snell, & J. Blacher (Eds.), *Handbook of developmental disabilities* (pp. 429–448). New York, NY: Guilford Press.

Stetson, R., Stetson, E. G., & Sattler, J. M. (2001). Assessment of academic achievement. In J. M. Sattler, *Assessment of children: Cognitive applications* (4th ed., pp. 576–609). La Mesa, CA: Jerome M. Sattler Publisher.

Tellegen, A., & Ben-Porath, Y. S. (2008/2011). *MMPI-2-RF (Minnesota Multiphasic Personality Inventory-2 Restructured Form): Technical manual.* Minneapolis, MN: University of Minnesota Press.

Tellegen, A., Ben-Porath, Y. S., McNulty, J. L., Arbisi, P. A.,Graham, J. R., & Kaemmer, B. (2003). *MMPI-2 Restructured Clinical (RC) Scales: Development, validation, and interpretation.* Minneapolis, MN: University of Minnesota Press.

Thomas v. Allen, 614 F. Supp.2d 1257 (N.D. Ala. 2009).

Ward, L. C., & Ward, J. W. (1980). MMPI readability reconsidered. *Journal of Personality Assessment, 44,* 387–389.

Wechsler, D. (2008). *Technical and interpretive manual for the Wechsler Adult Intelligence Scale–Fourth Edition.* San Antonio, TX: Pearson.

Wechsler, D. (1997). *Wechsler Adult Intelligence Scale* (3rd ed.). San Antonio, TX: Psychological Corporation.

Wechsler, D. (2008). *Wechsler Adult Intelligence Scale* (4th ed.). San Antonio, TX: Pearson.

Wechsler, D. (2001). *Wechsler Individual Achievement Test* (2nd ed.). San Antonio, TX: Psychological Corporation.

Wilkinson, G. S. (1993). *Wide Range Achievement Test–Revision 3.* Wilmington, DE: Jastak Associates.

Wilkinson, G. S., & Robertson, G. J. (2006). *Wide Range Achievement Test–4: Professional manual.* Lutz, FL: Professional Assessment Resources.

Woodcock, R. W., McGrew, K. S., & Mather, N. (2001). *The Woodcock-Johnson III.* Itasca, IL: Riverside.

Woodcock, R. W., McGrew, K. S., Schrank. F. A., & Mather, N. (2001, 2007). *Woodcock-Johnson III normative update.* Rolling Meadows, IL: Riverside Publishing.

Woodcock, R. W., Schrank, F. A., Mather, N., & McGrew, K. S. (2007). *Woodcock-Johnson III Tests of Achievement Form C/Brief Battery.* Rolling Meadows, IL: Riverside Publishing.

22 | Professional Issues in *Atkins* Assessments

Gilbert S. Macvaugh III
Mark D. Cunningham
Marc J. Tassé

As discussed throughout each chapter of this text, experts who participate in *Atkins* proceedings must be knowledgeable about the challenges and complexities involved with conducting assessments of intellectual disability (ID) in capital cases. Previous chapters primarily address the myriad issues related to the people being evaluated who are the primary focus of attention in these high-stakes cases. Equally important issues, however, affect the *evaluators*; and many of these issues stem from the ethical obligations arising out of professionals' involvement in such cases. Among these, the professional competence of the expert and the underlying training and qualifications of the expert are critical to the quality of these assessments. Additional issues related to inter-jurisdictional practices of experts, and the tension between best practices and jurisprudence are also a growing part of the *Atkins* (*Atkins v. Virginia*, 2002) landscape. The scope of this chapter, therefore, is to describe some of these ethical and professional issues and to offer recommendations for practice.

Ethical Considerations

Because of the complexities involved in determinations of ID in capital cases, a number of potential ethical dilemmas may arise for experts within the context of *Atkins* assessments. In one of the first published articles addressing these ethical concerns following the *Atkins* decision, Brodsky and Galloway (2003) noted:

> Five interrelated ethical and legal concerns arise when one considers these forensic-intellectual evaluations in populations of alleged and convicted murderers. First, how should assessors best attend to and deal with the entrepreneurial pull

engendered by the Court's recent decision? Second, and closely related, how should evaluators maintain objectivity and avoid getting caught in the pull to affiliation with attorneys? Third, does one take into account the base-rate low IQs of correctional populations? Fourth, how do professionals evaluate the adaptive functioning of people who have been institutionalized and controlled in prisons or other institutions for many years? Fifth, how should assessors screen for malingering of cognitive impairment in this population? (p. 4)

Other commentators also have described ethical challenges confronting evaluators in *Atkins* assessments, including the need for neutrality and objectivity versus an advocacy role, protection of raw test data and test protocols (Olley, Greenspan, & Switzky, 2006) (considerations that are not unique to ID evaluations), and the appropriate use of assessment instruments with this population (Duvall & Morris, 2006; Keyes, 2004; Macvaugh & Cunningham, 2009). Though now in the second decade of the post-*Atkins* era, these and other ethical and professional issues continue to significantly affect experts' involvement in these cases. Clarity in terms of available standards to assist practitioners in navigating such potential pitfalls is crucial to any discussion of best practice in the field.

As with any type of clinical assessment, psychologists who participate in *Atkins* assessments, at a minimum, should be familiar with the relevant ethical standards and practice guidelines, including the *Ethical Principles of Psychologists and Code of Conduct* (American Psychological Association, 2002); *Standards for Educational and Psychological Testing* (Joint Committee on Standards for Educational and Psychological Testing, 1999); *Specialty Guidelines for Forensic Psychology* (American Psychological Association, 2013), and the recommendations outlined by the American Association on Intellectual and Developmental Disabilities (AAIDD), in the *User's Guide to Intellectual Disability: Definition, Classification, and Systems of Supports* (Schalock et al., 2012). A comprehensive analysis of each of the specific ethical standards, guidelines, and recommendations promulgated by professional organizations that affect psychologists' (and others') clinical methods, judgments, and practices in *Atkins* assessments is beyond the scope of this chapter. That said, people involved in assessment should carefully attend to those American Psychological Association ethical standards that have particular relevance to *Atkins* assessments: (a) 2.01 Boundaries of Competence; (b) 2.03 Maintaining Competence; (c) 3.07 Third-Party Requests for Services; (d) 4.02 Discussing the Limits of Confidentiality; (e) 9.02 Use of Assessments; (f) 9.04 Release of Test Data; (g) 9.11 Maintaining Test Security; and (h) 9.08 Obsolete Tests and Outdated Test Results. Additional guidance in terms of how practitioners should best approach the different types of ethical issues confronting examiners in a legal context is provided in the most recent edition of the Specialty Guidelines for Forensic Psychology (American Psychological Association, 2013), most of which closely parallel those standards as set forth in psychologists' ethics code. For more extensive reviews, analysis, and discussion of the ethical contours of forensic mental health practice in general, practitioners should refer to Melton, Petrila, Poythress, and Slobogin (2007), as well as Weissman and DeBow (2003).

Competence, Expert Qualifications, and Training

As is the case with any type of mental health assessment, a critical requirement of experts is competence within the field. "Competence" is defined in *Black's Law Dictionary* (Garner, 1999) as "a basic or minimal ability to do something; qualification, esp. to testify" (p. 278). The ultimate gravity of an *Atkins* determination, however, calls for more than "basic or minimal ability" from the mental health professional. Rather, the experts' methods, conclusions, and opinions should rest on a sophisticated understanding of the presentation and course of mental disability (see American Psychological Association, Division 33, Mental Retardation and Developmental Disabilities, 1996), assessment methodologies in ID, and the psychometric literature in IQ assessments. This application of the best available science also comports with the standards governing the admissibility of scientific evidence as set forth by the U.S. Supreme Court in *Daubert v. Merrell Dow Pharmaceuticals, Inc.* (1993).

Such sophisticated understanding and the application of the best available science, however, cannot be assumed from simply holding a mental health credential (Olley et al., 2006). Olley (2009) observed that most forensic psychologists lack adequate training in the field of ID. But as Brodsky and Galloway (2003) point out, "nonforensic intellectual assessors" who serve as experts in *Atkins* cases may receive disapproval because they have conducted "few evaluations for the Court" (p. 4). Similarly, Ellis (2003) noted that "although some psychiatrists have experience in assessing people with mental retardation, most do not" (p. 10). For this reason, Ellis pointed out that the clinical assistance required in *Akins* cases will not always (nor even frequently) be from a psychiatrist. In a useful discussion pertaining to the qualifications of physicians in particular, Ellis and Luckasson (1985) observed that intellectual disability differs so much from other forms of mental disorders, that training in mental illness alone does not, "without more," qualify one as an expert on ID; nor does such training guarantee the necessary competence required to testify as an "expert" in this area for the purpose of a legal proceeding. Thus, psychiatrists and psychologists who have specialized knowledge, training, and experience in the field of forensic mental health assessment are unlikely, "without more," to have the necessary expertise to perform *Atkins* assessments or possess the required clinical judgment (Schalock & Luckasson, 2005). Moreover, this is a bidirectional problem. Because of the legal context of *Atkins* assessments, even the most skilled professional in the field of ID also may not, "without more," be sufficiently prepared to meet the ethical and professional demands as required by the nature of the forensic role associated with performing *Atkins* assessments.

Unfortunately, "something more" than general forensic expertise may not be normative among professionals conducting *Atkins* assessments—at least in some jurisdictions.

To illustrate, in an unpublished survey by Macvaugh and Grisso (2006) of forensic clinicians' professional practices in post-conviction *Atkins* cases: less than half of the doctoral level practitioners who were surveyed reported receiving formal training in ID; less than half reported formal training in forensic evaluation; and only one of the 20 clinicians reported having received formal training in both the fields of ID and forensic evaluation. Other research finds that the absence of such formal training results in significant gaps in the psychometric sophistication of mental health professionals providing *Atkins* assessments. In a survey of 20 professionals who had provided *Atkins* assessments in Texas, for example, 23% of psychologists and 70% of psychiatrists were unfamiliar with the Flynn effect by name or by its IQ score impact (Young, Boccaccini, Conroy, & Lawson, 2007).

What, then, constitutes appropriate training and experience for professionals who wish to engage in the practice of providing expert witness services in *Atkins* cases? Although it is of course a reasonable expectation that the mental health professional needs to possess sufficient training and expertise to provide professional services in such cases, what is less clear is the specific amount, duration, and types of training experiences that should be required to capture the breadth and depth of expertise needed to perform these types of assessments competently. Additional questions remain concerning what qualifications are needed for those who are charged with the task of providing such training, under what circumstances the training should occur, and what outcome measures are needed to ensure an adequate and effective training experience.

Some jurisdictions have addressed evaluator competence to perform *Atkins* evaluations. For example, Virginia requires that experts who are court appointed to conduct *Atkins* evaluations in that state must have a combination of specialized expertise in the assessment of mental retardation and specialized training in conducting forensic evaluations (Bonnie & Gustafson, 2007). More specifically, mental health experts providing assessments in Virginia *Atkins* cases must be

> (a) a psychiatrist, a clinical psychologist or an individual with a doctorate degree in clinical psychology, (b) skilled in the administration, scoring and interpretation of intelligence tests and measures of adaptive behavior and (c) qualified by experience and by specialized training, approved by the Commissioner of Mental Health, Mental Retardation and Substance Abuse Services, to perform forensic evaluations. (See Va. Code Ann. § 19.2-264.3:1.2(A) (Repl. Vol. 2004).

The Virginia model arguably represents the training, experience, and expertise most consistent with best practice in foundational aspects of forensic mental health assessment as defined by Heilbrun, Grisso, and Goldstein (2009). However, variability across death penalty jurisdictions in terms of the minimum qualifications of experts necessary for participation in *Atkins* proceedings limits uniformity in this regard. The distinction between the professional roles of an *evaluating* expert (who performs a forensic assessment of an *Atkins* claimant and offers a diagnostic and forensic opinion as to the issue before the court) and that of a *teaching* expert (who may be retained in *Atkins* cases to educate the court with regard to a specialized area) also can be confusing for the trier-of-fact in such cases, particularly when both types of experts are involved in the same case and have vastly different professional backgrounds and qualifications. Courts' ultimate determinations regarding how much weight to attach to the different types of expert opinions, however, are likely to be based on the degree to which experts have the necessary knowledge, education, training, and experience in the area most relevant to the legal issue.

Mental health professionals may benefit most by obtaining *supervised* training experiences in the form of predoctoral and postdoctoral training programs in clinical forensic psychology with an emphasis on populations with ID (for a review of issues related to specialized training in the field of forensic psychology, see Packer & Borum, 2003). Participation in continuing education workshops, such as those sponsored by the American Academy of Forensic Psychology (AAFP) and AAIDD, are especially encouraged. Olley (2009) recommended that psychologists who are interested in participating in *Atkins* proceedings maintain professional affiliations that may support remaining current in the field, including becoming members of two divisions of the American Psychological Association: Division 33 (Intellectual and Developmental Disabilities) and Division 41 (American Psychology-Law Society). Psychologists may also benefit from becoming members of AAIDD, and regularly consulting online resources, such as the *Intellectual Competence & the Death Penalty* blog (Available at: http://www.atkinsmrdeathpenalty.com), both of which can be particularly valuable in advancing one's knowledge about the relevant issues involved.

As the previous outline of resources reflects, historical training—however extensive—is insufficient to maintain *current* competence. Intellectual and adaptive functioning assessments are not simply "clerical" enterprises where scores can be uncritically applied. Rather, these are assessments resting on an advancing scientific foundation. It is thus necessary to conduct recurrent literature searches and demonstrate careful consideration of the most up-to-date scholarly perspectives and research, including, for example:

- issues related to the nature of intellectual disability (see Olley, 2009),
- the Flynn effect (see Chapter 10; Cunningham & Tassé, 2010; Kaufman, 2010),
- the limitations of measures of malingering with people with low IQ or ID (see Chapter 18; Dean, Victor, Boone, & Arnold, 2008; Salekin & Doane, 2009; Shandera et al., 2010), and
- the latest advances in the assessment of adaptive behavior (see Tassé, 2009).

Continuous, ongoing education is essential to competence in performing *Atkins* assessments.

Neutrality vs. Advocacy

Mental health professionals providing assessment in *Atkins* cases, as in any forensic evaluation, are subjected to forces that may consciously or unconsciously bias the assessment methodology and interpretation of the data. When this occurs, the essential role of the forensic evaluator is as an advocate for the data and the best science, *not* for a particular outcome independent of those data. Recognition of these forces may better equip the mental health professional to resist their influence. First and most overt among these forces is financial compensation (Brodsky & Galloway, 2003; Weissman & DeBow, 2003; see also Specialty Guidelines for Forensic Psychology, American Psychological Association, 2013). Because mental health experts are typically paid for their time in performing *Atkins* assessments, there are financial incentives to report findings that will result in additional work in the current case (e.g., hearing testimony) or retention by like referral sources (i.e., defense or prosecution) in future cases. Second, both the prosecution and the defense in capital cases involve teams of attorneys and investigators who are highly invested in advocating for their respective interests. This team approach may contribute to group pressures of affiliation and approval, resulting in the mental health professional's coming to identify with the goals and interests of the retaining party. Third, the criminal history, the common significant history of trauma and abuse of the defendant, and the invariably tragic violence of the offense may trigger pejorative attitudinal responses in the evaluator that are inconsistent with dispassionate clinical neutrality. Fourth, the advocacy context of the assessment may encourage the expert to view the determination as a game of finesse and persuasion, with winning and losing experts. Fifth, strong advocacy positions in favor of or opposed to the death penalty have the potential to influence the clinical judgment of the evaluator.

These potential sources of biasing influence on the methodology and opinions of *Atkins* evaluators call for vigilance and careful introspection by experts. This process may be facilitated by consideration of the following 10 self-examination questions:

1. Are financial or practice development pressures present?
2. Has the retaining party been referred to as "we" and/or has the affiliation with the "team" come to be rewarding?
3. Are attitudinal responses to the person being evaluated present—either disgust or protective benevolence?
4. Was there deviation from standardized testing procedures that would serve to maximize or minimize IQ scores?
5. Have literature searches regarding relevant psychometric considerations been neglected, or the associated scientific findings selectively reported?
6. Has the assessment of adaptive functioning been distorted by over-focusing on verbal behavior, criminal conduct, stereotypes of intellectual disability, and strengths, rather than more relevant factors?
7. In performing adaptive functioning interviews, were steps taken to ensure that respondents were selected based on the extent and quality of their observation of the evaluee in the community, and to ensure that the information obtained from them is reliable?

8. Have adaptive functioning interviews been "steered" by overly broad queries, leading questions, normalizing of deficits, topic changes, other techniques?
9. Have alternative perspectives regarding the assessment been neglected or unexpressed resulting in an imbalanced presentation of the data in the expert's report or testimony?
10. What steps did the evaluator take to de-bias him/herself, and how would the assessment methodology or findings have been different if the expert had been hired by the opposing party?

Inter-jurisdictional Practice

Another professional issue affecting experts in *Atkins* cases is whether they have obtained appropriate approval from the relevant licensing board when practicing in a state other than that in which they are licensed. Several articles have been published on the topic of interstate forensic consultations (see Drogin, 1999; Reid, 2000; Simon & Shuman, 1999; Shuman, Cunningham, Connell, & Reid, 2003; Tucillo, DeFilippis, Denney, & Dsurney, 2002). The behavior of experts in this regard may run the gamut; some practitioners go so far as to obtain multiple licenses in a number of different states, whereas others remain unaware of this issue altogether. Although forensic practitioners are likely to be familiar with the issues surrounding out-of-state practice, those who participate in *Atkins* proceedings who lack a background and training in forensic evaluation may be less familiar with these requirements and, as a result, could potentially find themselves in the unfortunate position of not being permitted to testify. Such an oversight may not only be damaging to the credibility and reputation of the expert, but also may include the possibility of criminal sanctions for violations of licensure board rules and regulations. Most importantly, a capital defendant may be deprived of critical expert testimony when life and death hang in the balance.

In at least one known instance in the authors' experience, two out-of-state psychologists who were retained by the defense to perform evaluations in a postconviction *Atkins* case failed to obtain approval to practice in the state in which the inmate was incarcerated. At the evidentiary hearing, both experts were questioned extensively by counsel opposite regarding this lack of approval. As a result, one of the two experts was admonished by the judge for violating state licensure laws. In fact, after both experts admitted that they had not obtained approval from the licensure board to practice in that state, the judge read one of the experts her *Miranda* rights while she was on the witness stand and explained to the expert that if she chose to further testify, she would be incriminating herself and could face prosecution for violating state law. Both of the experts subsequently requested counsel of their own before testifying further; and after a brief recess, each expert again took the stand, and upon the advice of counsel, immediately asserted their right to remain silent. The defense attorney who had retained both experts then requested that the judge order them to testify at the hearing. The judge did not order the defense experts to testify, but did give them an opportunity to obtain appropriate approval from the relevant licensing authority and continued the hearing for a later date. Although this series of events is likely a rare occurrence in such cases, practitioners who participate in *Atkins* proceedings in jurisdictions other than those in which they hold a license to practice should seek the appropriate approval from the relevant licensing authority before providing evaluation or expert witness services. Cunningham (2010) has provided recommendations in the form of eight steps experts should take when providing forensic services in capital cases in a jurisdiction in which the expert is not licensed. It also is important for practitioners to understand that it is the responsibility of the expert to become familiar with the laws governing the practice of their profession in whichever jurisdiction they provide professional expert services; it is not the responsibility of the attorney or court who retains the expert.

Best Practice vs. Statute

Atkins determinations represent a curious duality: a clinical diagnosis in a legal context. Of the many forensic nuances of this duality, three aspects call for discussion. First, although the *Atkins* issue in most jurisdictions is whether the capital evaluee is a person with ID, in Texas, appellate courts have opined that the issue is whether the evaluee is "retarded enough" (see *Ex parte Briseño*, 2004). As discussed in Chapter 15, the *Briseño* factors recommended by the Texas Court of Criminal Appeals in making this determination are characteristic of people in more impaired categories. Though mental health experts should be familiar with jurisdictionally specific *Atkins* standards, Macvaugh and Cunningham (2009) recommended that experts employ DSM and AAIDD criteria in making diagnoses of ID in *Atkins* cases, with jurisdictionally specific criteria representing an ancillary finding. This represents best clinical practices, the foundation of an accurate forensic finding.

Second, courts in some jurisdictions may request an assessment for ID in an omnibus order, to be conducted along with the more traditional forensic evaluation questions of adjudicative competence and mental state at the time of an alleged offense. Indeed, courts in Mississippi routinely issue omnibus orders to evaluate *all* of the potential referral questions in pretrial capital cases (i.e., competence to stand trial; mental state at the time of the alleged offense(s); competence to waive *Miranda* rights at the time of a statement to law enforcement; capital statutory mitigation, and *Atkins*), with reports distributed to the defense, the prosecution, and the Court. A discussion of the implications of such "bundled" evaluations within the context of a defendant's constitutional rights and in terms of what effect they have on the quality of the resulting assessments is beyond the scope of this chapter (for a broader discussion, see Cunningham, 2006; 2010). But to briefly explain the associated problems: (a) the psychological issues involved are sufficiently distinct that there may be little economy of scale from bundling the assessments, and (b) bundled referral questions encourage cursory assessment procedures and conclusory reports. In addition, the defendant's

Fifth Amendment right against self-incrimination may be breached when an assessment of his or her mental state at the time of the alleged index offense and *Atkins* eligibility are comingled. Moreover, the defendant's Sixth Amendment right to counsel is undermined when the results of the defense preliminary investigations are shared with the State and the Court. These implications call for detailed informed consent discussions (see Cunningham, 2006, 2010) with defense counsel before initiating the evaluation(s). Such informed consent discussions should address the parameters of the evaluation, whether there will be inquiry regarding the defendant's account of the charged offense, and how the findings will be disseminated. In cases where the expert has been retained by the State or the evaluation is court ordered, notice of the preceding features of the anticipated evaluation should be made to defense counsel. This notice respects the Constitutional rights of the defendant by providing the opportunity for these matters to be litigated in advance of the evaluation. Of course, defendants should not be evaluated for *Atkins* considerations or other forensic purposes until they are represented by counsel.

Third, statutes in some jurisdictions may require administration of a particular test (e.g., Minnesota Multiphasic Personality Inventory, Second Edition (MMPI-2) or type of test (e.g., measure of malingering) as part of an *Atkins* evaluation. However well-intentioned, such prescriptions may be inconsistent with whether that instrument or type of instrument will provide valid information regarding a person whose intellectual abilities are possibly deficient. This presents the mental health professional with a mismatch between science and statute. In these cases, professionals should bring this inconsistency to the attention of the Court, the retaining party, and the defense before initiating the evaluation. The scientific limitations of the required procedure should be clearly presented in any report or testimony.

Concluding Comments

Practitioners must remain cognizant of various ethical considerations when conducting assessments of ID in capital cases. Though we seek to inform the discussion of the development of standards regarding the training and basic competencies necessary to promote best practice in the field, this chapter (and this book in general) is not an exhaustive resource, nor is it intended to serve as a substitute for the types of more formal training and experience necessary to meet the professional demands of these high-stakes types of assessments.

It is recommended that to achieve the level of competence required for ethical participation in *Atkins* assessments, practitioners must become well versed in the fields of *both* intellectual disability *and* forensic mental health assessment. In the view of the authors of this chapter, expertise in only one of these fields is insufficient. Experts in *Atkins* cases should, ideally, have previous experience conducting forensic evaluations with people who may have ID, as well as prior experience providing expert testimony regarding ID in other types of noncapital cases. Generally speaking, a practitioner's first time to perform a forensic mental health assessment should not occur within the context of a capital case. Similarly, practitioners should be careful not to have *Atkins* cases serve as their inaugural experience as an evaluating and testifying mental health expert in a criminal proceeding. The heightened ethical responsibilities that come with practicing in a forensic role, especially in death penalty cases, require experts to maintain a highly specialized area of expertise that is generally not possessed simply by holding an advanced clinical degree and licensure to practice independently.

Ongoing efforts to increase high-quality training opportunities for evaluators should facilitate a clearer understanding of this highly specialized area and bridge the gap between the fields of intellectual disability and forensic mental health assessment. Practitioners from both of these fields must benefit from the expertise of each other to improve the quality of assessments in these life and death types of cases and to further inform the discussion of best practice in the field. The information presented in this book is intended in part to serve this purpose.

References

American Psychological Association. (2002). Ethical principles of psychologists and code of conduct. *American Psychologist, 57,* 1060–1073.

American Psychological Association. (2013). Specialty guidelines for forensic psychology. *American Psychologist, 68,* 7–18.

American Psychological Association, Division 33, Mental Retardation and Developmental Disabilities, Editorial Board. (1996). Definition of mental retardation. In J. W. Jacobson & J. A. Mulick (Eds.), *Manual of diagnosis and professional practice in mental retardation* (pp. 13–54). Washington, DC: American Psychological Association.

Atkins v. Virginia, 536 U.S. 304, 310, (2002).

Bonnie, R. J., & Gustafson, K. (2007). The challenges of implementing *Atkins v. Virginia:* How legislatures and courts can promote accurate assessments and adjudications of mental retardation in death penalty cases. *University of Richmond Law Review, 41,* 810–860.

Brodsky, S. L., & Galloway, V. A. (2003). Ethical and professional demands for forensic mental health professionals in the post-*Atkins* era. *Ethics & Behavior, 12*(1), 3–9.

Cunningham, M. D. (2006). Informed consent in capital sentencing evaluations: Targets and content. *Professional Psychology: Research and Practice, 37,* 452–459. doi:10.1037/0735-7028.37.5.452

Cunningham, M. D. (2010). Evaluation for capital sentencing. In A. Goldstein, T. Grisso, & K. Heilbrun (Eds.), *Oxford best practices in forensic mental health assessment series.* New York, NY: Oxford University Press.

Cunningham, M. D., & Tassé, M. (2010). Looking to science rather than convention in adjusting IQ scores when death is at issue. *Professional Psychology: Research and Practice, 41,* 413–419. doi:10.1037/a0020226

Daubert v. Merrell Dow Pharmaceuticals, Inc., 509 U.S. 579 (1993).

Dean, A. C., Victor, T. L., Boone, K. B., & Arnold (2008). The relationship of IQ to effort test performance. *The Clinical Neuropsychologist, 22,* 705–722. doi: 10.1080/13854040701440493

Drogin, E. Y. (1999). Prophets in another land: Utilizing psychological expertise from foreign jurisdictions. *Mental and Physical Disabilities Law Reporter, 23,* 767–770.

Duvall, J. C., & Morris, R. J. (2006). Assessing mental retardation in death penalty cases: Critical issues for psychology and psychological practice. *Professional Psychology: Research and Practice, 37,* 658–665. doi:10.1037/0735-7028.37.6.658

Ellis, J. W. (2003). Mental retardation and the death penalty: A guide to state legislative issues. *Mental and Physical Disability Law Reporter, 27*(1), 11–24.

Ellis, J. W., & Luckasson, R. A. (1985). Mentally retarded criminal defendants. *The George Washington Law Review, 53,* 414–493.

Ex parte Briseño, 135 S.W.3d 1 (2004).

Garner, B. A. (Ed.). (1999). *Black's law dictionary* (7th ed.). St. Paul, MN: West Group.

Heilbrun, K., Grisso, T., & Goldstein, A. (2009). Foundations of forensic mental health assessment. In A. Goldstein, T. Grisso, & K. Heilbrun (Eds.), *Oxford best practices in forensic mental health assessment series.* New York, NY: Oxford University Press.

Joint Committee on Standards for Educational and Psychological Testing. (1999). *Standards for educational and psychological testing.* Washington, DC: American Educational Research Association.

Kaufman, A. S. (2010). Looking through Flynn's rose-colored scientific spectacles. *Journal of Psychoeducational Assessment, 28,* 494–505. doi: 10.1177/0734282910373573

Keyes, D. W. (2004). Use of the Minnesota Multiphasic Personality Inventory (MMPI) to identify malingering mental retardation. *Mental Retardation, 42,* 151–153.

Macvaugh, G. S., & Cunningham, M. D. (2009). *Atkins v. Virginia*: Implications and recommendations for forensic practice. *Journal of Psychiatry and Law, 37,* 131–187.

Macvaugh, G. S., & Grisso, T. (2006, March). *Assessment of mental retardation in death row inmates: A survey of professional practices.* Paper presented at the conference of the American Psychology-Law Society, St. Petersburg, FL.

Melton, G., Petrila, J., Poythress, N., & Slobogin, C. (2007). *Psychological evaluations for the courts: A handbook for mental health professionals and lawyers* (3rd ed., pp. 69–100). New York, NY: Guilford.

Olley, J. G. (2009). Knowledge and experience required for experts in *Atkins* cases. *Applied Neuropsychology, 16,* 135–140. doi: 10.1080/09084280902864477

Olley, J. G., Greenspan, S., & Switzky, H. (2006). Division 33 ad hoc committee on mental retardation and the death penalty. *Psychology in Mental Retardation and Developmental Disabilities, 31,* 11–13.

Packer, I. K., & Borum, R. (2003). Forensic training and practice. In A. M. Goldstein (Ed.), *Handbook of psychology*, Vol. 11: *Forensic psychology* (pp. 21–32). Hoboken, NJ: Wiley.

Reid, W. H. (2000). Licensing requirements for out-of-state forensic examinations. *Journal of the American Academy of Psychiatry and Law, 28,* 433–437.

Salekin, K. L., & Doane, B. (2009). Malingering intellectual disability: The value of available measures and methods. *Applied Neuropsychology, 16,* 105–113. doi: 10.1080/09084280902864485

Schalock, R. L., & Luckasson, R. (2005). *Clinical judgment.* Washington, DC: American Association on Mental Retardation.

Schalock, R. L., Luckasson, R., Bradley, V., Buntinx, W. H. E., Lachapelle, Y., Shogren, K. A., Snell, M. E., Thompson, J. R., Tassé, M. J., Verdugo-Alonso, M. A., and Wehmeyer, M. L. (2012). *User's guide to intellectual disability: Definition, classification, and systems of supports.* Washington, DC: American Association on Intellectual and Developmental Disabilities.

Shandera, A. L., Berry, D. T. R., Clark, J. A., Schipper, L. J., Graue, L. O., & Harp, J. P. (2010). Detection of malingered mental retardation. *Psychological Assessment, 22*(1), 50–56. doi: 10.1037/a0016585

Shuman, D. W., Cunningham, M. D., Connell, M. A., & Reid, W. H. (2003). Interstate forensic psychology consultations: A call for reform and proposal of a model rule. *Professional Psychology: Research and practice, 34,* 233–239. doi: 10.1037/0735-7028.34.3.233

Simon, R. I., & Shuman, D. W. (1999). Conducting forensic examinations on the road: Are you practicing your profession without a license? *Journal of the American Academy of Psychiatry and Law, 27,* 75–82.

Tassé, M. J. (2009). Adaptive behavior assessment and the diagnosis of mental retardation in capital cases. *Applied Neuropsychology, 14,* 114–123. doi: 10.1080/09084280902864451

Tucillo, J. A., DeFilippis, N. A., Denney, R. L., & Dsurney, J. (2002). Licensure requirements for interjurisdictional forensic evaluations. *Professional Psychology: Research and Practice, 33,* 377–383. doi: 10.1037//0735-7028.33.4.377

Weissman, H. N., & DeBow, D. M. (2003). Ethical principles and professional competencies. In A. M. Goldstein (Ed.), *Handbook of psychology*, Vol. 11: Forensic psychology (pp. 33–54). Hoboken, NJ: Wiley.

Young, B., Boccacini, M. T., Conroy, M. A., & Lawson, K. (2007). Four practical and conceptual assessment issues that evaluators should address in capital case mental retardation evaluations. *Professional Psychology: Research and Practice, 38,* 169–178. doi: 10.1037/0735-7028.38.2.169

Index